The Unofficial Guide®

Dubai

Dar Al Masyaf hotel

1. Flood River at Wild Wadi
2. Spin Gear at SEGA Republic
3. & 5. Ski Dubai
4. Flow Rider at Wild Wadi
6. Bastakiya historical district
7. Dubai Drums
8. Desert safari

1. Hatta Heritage Village
2. Jumeirah Mosque
3. thejamjar painting workshop
4. 1x1 Art Gallery
5. Armani Privé
6. Jumeirah Bab Al Shams Desert Resort
7. Jumeirah Beach Hotel
8. & 9. Mina A'Salam hotel

1. Burj Khalifa, the world's tallest building
2. Al Badia Golf Course
3. Hole 17 at The Montgomerie Dubai
4. The Montgomerie Dubai golf course

1.

2.

3.

1. Raffles hotel
2. Al Qasr hotel with Burj Al Arab in the background
3. The Address Downtown Dubai
4. Dhow, a traditional boat

1.

1. Al Maha Desert Resort and Spa
2. XVA Art Hotel and Gallery
3. Royal Suite at Al Qasr
4. Full-moon yoga with Talise Spa

2.

3.

4.

1. The Grove at The Dubai Mall
2. Souk Madinat Jumeirah
3. Mall of the Emirates
4. Spice Souk
5. Talise Spa
6. Mandalay couple suite at SensAsia
7. The Spa at The Address Downtown
8. Relaxation area at SensAsia

1.

2.

1. Bahri Bar
2. Sheikh Zayed Road
3. Al Mahara at Burj Al Arab
4. Pierchic
5. The Agency
6. Madinat Theatre

Jumeirah Emirates Towers

THE
unofficial GUIDE®
to Dubai

1ST EDITION

THE *unofficial* GUIDE®
to Dubai

1ST EDITION

COLLETTE LYONS

UK Publisher: Sally Smith
Executive Project Editor: Daniel Mersey
Commissioning Editor: Fiona Quinn
Project Editor: Hannah Clement
Editorial and Production Manager (US): Molly B. Merkle
Project Editor (US): Amber Kaye Henderson
Copy-editor: Lynn Edwards
Proofreader: Lady Vowell Smith
Typesetter–Compositor: Annie Long
Cartographers: Andrew Murphy and Steve Jones
Photo Researcher: Amber Kaye Henderson
Colour Insert Designer: Travis Bryant
Cover Designer: Paul Dinovo
Interior Designer: Vertigo Design
Indexer: Ann Cassar
Pre-press Operations: Wiley Composition Services, Indianapolis, Indiana, USA
Printing and Binding: TJ International Ltd, Padstow, Cornwall, UK

Photography credits, colour insert: *Dubai Department of Tourism and Commerce Marketing*: Pages 2 (center right), 3 (top, center and bottom right), 4 (top right), 7 (top left), 9 (center right), 12 (center right) and 14 (bottom). *Dubai Drums*: Page 3 (bottom left). *The Dubai Mall:* Pages 2 (left) and 12 (left). *Emaar Hospitality Group*: Pages 4 (bottom right), 6, 7 (center and bottom), 9 (top left) and 13 (center). *The Emirates Group*: Page 10 (top). *Hamad Mejren/Dubai Department of Tourism and Commerce Marketing*: Pages 4 (top left) and 12 (bottom right). *The Jumeirah Group*: Pages 1, 2 (top right and bottom right), 5, 8 (bottom), 10 (bottom), 11, 13 (top left), 14 (top), 15 and 16. *Mall of the Emirates*: Page 12 (top right). *1x1 Art Gallery*: Page 4 (bottom left). *Raffles*: Page 8 (top). *SensAsia:* Page 13 (top right and bottom). *thejamjar*: Page 4 (center). *XVA Art Hotel & Gallery*: Page 10 (center).

British Library Cataloguing in Publication Data
A catalogue record for this book is available from the British Library.

ISBN 978-0-470-68866-3

5 4 3 2 1

CONTENTS

LIST *of* MAPS

ACKNOWLEDGMENTS

MANY THANKS TO DEBORAH SMITH, RICHARD DAVIES and Helen Spearman for being gracious hosts; Nadia Evans and Tanzeed Alam for help with drinking and eating my way around Dubai; and Matt Powell for his unparalleled map prowess.

Special mention to Dominic Wanders of ticket_dxb for his architectural knowledge, Nouf Al-Qassimi for her expertise on Emirati food, Minty Clinch for the section on golf, Hallie Campbell for her help with the history bit and Danielle Simpson for her wonderful work on hotels and attractions. Mention must go to the folks at Menasha Ridge, especially Bob Sehlinger and his unending patience.

Finally, this book is for my beaty friend Karolyn Fairs, who made Dubai brilliant.

– Collette Lyons

ABOUT *the* AUTHOR

COLLETTE LYONS'S WRITING CAREER has so far proved a rather wonderful excuse to disappear around the world for years at a time. The London-born, Cambridge-educated writer has been putting pen to paper for magazines and newspapers including *The Guardian*, *The Independent* and *The Sunday Times* in the United Kingdom, as well as Arabian titles such as *The National, Time Out Dubai* and *OK! Middle East* for almost 15 years. Most recently, three years in Dubai dining, drinking and dropping far too much money in the city's malls have left her well qualified to provide an exhaustive guide to the city's best.

INTRODUCTION

█ HELLO, DUBAI!

EVERYBODY KNOWS THAT DUBAI is the place to go for sun and sand within a seven-hour flight (in fact, in the summer – although we Brits don't seem to believe that this can ever be the case – there is a bit too much sun). And of course, it is entirely possible – and no doubt pleasurable – to spend your days sitting in a hotel sunlounger while being handed cold towels and watermelon, and to spend your evenings swigging a cocktail and sampling the standard meze in the same immediate vicinity. Believe it or not, though, there is an awful lot more to the most exciting city in the Middle East than this. Whether it's local flavour – and yes, you hecklers at the back, Dubai *does* have some – haute cuisine, international art galleries or world-class shopping you are after (seriously, if there were a consumer Olympics, Dubai would bring home gold in every event), you'll find it here. And knowing where to look for it is where we come in.

Of course, Dubai is world-famous for its opulence – the world's first seven-star hotel, topped with a helipad; the man-made, palm-shaped island that can be seen from space; the decade's most expensive private party to celebrate the launch of the Atlantis hotel; the world's tallest building. To understand what an achievement this is, you only need turn back to the early 1960s in the history books, when the city was still largely a low-rise trading port, or a hundred years before that, when most of its inhabitants were still Bedouin. Some may accuse Dubai of being vulgar, but even critics must admit that the sheer scale of the vision is mind-blowing.

Of course, this gold-plated lifestyle may put off visitors who are keen to watch their bank balance – but there are options for most budgets. For every Burj Al Arab, there is a shiny new four-star with eminently affordable room rates. For every Gary Rhodes or Gordon Ramsay, a first-generation Pakistani or Iranian chef is serving pitch-perfect curries or kebabs. For every full-service hotel beach, a free stretch of sand is filled with local families and their 4x4s, and if you can't stretch to a family trip to the top of the Burj Khalifa, you can always get your highs from the cable car that runs along Dubai Creek. The other bonus for the visitor is that the city is relatively small and split into pretty discrete areas – easy and fairly cheap to navigate by taxi. So whether you want to be prostrate on the sand, haggling in a souk or sipping Champagne on the 63rd floor, it's almost certain that you'll find it in Dubai.

ABOUT THIS GUIDE

WHY 'UNOFFICIAL'?

DUBAI TRAVEL GUIDES ARE TRICKY things to compile. Ask any long-term expat (we're talking 15-plus years here) and they will go misty-eyed telling you about the time when the only building on the Sheikh Zayed Road (the city's superhotel-lined main artery) was the now ancient-looking World Trade Centre, and the best dining experience was at Planet Hollywood. Now it is populated with futuristic glass towers and high-class sushi joints. Things here change so fast and so furiously that it's tempting to be lazy and just recommend the same old favourites in the same old tourist traps. That is not, you'll be pleased to hear, the *Unofficial* way.

We won't tell you to follow the usual tracks of the typical tourist, automatically sending everyone to the well-known sights without offering any information about how to do this painlessly, recommending restaurants and hotels indiscriminately, and failing to recognise the limits of human endurance in sightseeing (especially in the searing heat of the summer or the restrictions of Ramadan). This guide attempts to be different: we understand that in a city as different as Dubai, it is essential to discriminate, make plans and be flexible when taxi queues appear out of nowhere or the sandstorms hit.

We'll be honest about certain tourist traps, give you the real story on celebrity chefs' restaurants and world-famous hotels, show you options for going off the beaten track (and, more important, tell you how to get back) and advise you how to spend a little less money on some things so you can spend more on others. We'll complain about rip-offs, and we'll fill you in on bargains. We also hope to give you the kind of information that will help you get under the skin of one of the world's most fascinating emerging cities. We've tried in this book to anticipate the special needs of older people, families with young children, families with teenagers, solo female travellers and people with physical challenges.

We cover the hotels, restaurants and attractions in depth and minute detail because we want you to be able to make the most informed decisions possible about where to go and what to do. Please do remember that prices, admission hours, special offers and – worst of all – exchange rates change. We've listed the most up-to-date information we can get, but it never hurts to double-check before you head out the hotel door. Remember, this is a city that changes on an almost weekly basis, so in the case of a hot restaurant table, a sell-out sporting event or a mind-blowing mega-suite, be sure to make your reservations early and reconfirm.

ABOUT *UNOFFICIAL GUIDES*

READERS CARE ABOUT AUTHORS' OPINIONS. The authors, after all, are paid to know what they are talking about. This, coupled with the fact that the visitor wants quick answers, dictates that we are explicit, prescriptive and, above all, direct. The authors of the *Unofficial Guide* try to be just that. We don't beat around the bush. We spell out alternatives and recommend specific courses of action. We simplify complicated destinations and attractions to allow the visitor to feel in control in even the most unfamiliar environments – and, though Dubai is a truly global city, you will still have your share of 'What the?!' moments. Our objective is not to give the most information or all the information but the most accessible, useful information. Of course, in a city like Dubai, many hotels, restaurants and attractions are so well known that to omit them from this guide because we can't recommend them would be a disservice to our readers. Where this is the case, we have included them but given 100% honest opinions and experiences of them, in the hopes that you will approach (or avoid) these institutions armed with the necessary intelligence.

An *Unofficial Guide* is a critical reference work; we focus on a travel destination that appears to be especially complex. Our authors and researchers are completely independent from the attractions, restaurants and hotels we describe. *The Unofficial Guide to Dubai* is designed for individuals and families travelling for fun as well as for business, or even using Dubai as a stop-off on the way to a longer-haul destination. The guide is directed at value-conscious, consumer-oriented adults who seek a cost-effective but not overly spartan travel style.

SPECIAL FEATURES

- Vital information about travelling abroad
- Listings keyed to your interests and type of visit, so you can pick and choose what's right for you
- Advice to sightseers on how to get the best deals, as well as advice to business travellers on how to avoid traffic and excessive costs
- Recommendations for lesser-known sights that are off the well-beaten tourist path

- Maps that make it easy to find places you want to go – or avoid
- A hotel section that helps you narrow down your choices quickly, according to your needs and preferences
- A table of contents and detailed index to help you find things fast

WHAT YOU WON'T GET

- Long, useless lists in which everything looks the same
- Information that gets you to your destination at the worst possible time
- Information without advice on how to use it

HOW THIS GUIDE WAS RESEARCHED AND WRITTEN

IN PREPARING THIS WORK, we took nothing for granted. Each hotel, restaurant, shop and attraction was visited by trained observers who conducted detailed evaluations and rated each according to formal criteria.

Though our observers are independent and impartial, they are otherwise 'ordinary' travellers. Like you, they visited Dubai as tourists or business travellers, noting their satisfaction or dissatisfaction.

The primary difference between the average tourist and the trained evaluator is the latter's skills in organisation, preparation and observation. A trained evaluator is responsible for more than just observing and cataloguing. Observer teams use detailed checklists to analyse hotel rooms, restaurants, nightclubs and attractions. Finally, evaluator ratings and observations are integrated with tourist reactions and the opinions of patrons for a comprehensive quality profile of each feature and service.

In compiling this guide, we recognise that a tourist's age, background and interests will strongly influence his or her taste in Dubai's range of attractions and will account for a preference for one sight or museum over another. Our sole objective is to provide the reader with sufficient description, critical evaluation and pertinent data to help him or her make knowledgeable decisions according to individual tastes.

LETTERS, COMMENTS AND QUESTIONS FROM READERS

WE EXPECT TO LEARN FROM OUR MISTAKES, as well as from the input of our readers, and to improve with each new book and edition. Many of those who use the *Unofficial Guides* write to us asking questions, making comments or sharing their own discoveries and lessons learned in Dubai. We appreciate all such input, both positive and critical, and encourage our readers to continue writing. Readers' comments and observations will frequently be incorporated into revised editions of the *Unofficial Guide* and will contribute immeasurably to its improvement.

How to Write to the Author

Collette Lyons
The Unofficial Guide to Dubai
PO Box 43673
Birmingham, AL 35243
USA
unofficialguides@menasharidge.com

When you write, be sure to put your return address on your letter as well as on the envelope – sometimes envelopes and letters get separated. And remember that our work takes us out of the office for long periods of time, so forgive us if our response is delayed.

HOW INFORMATION IS ORGANISED

TO GIVE YOU FAST ACCESS TO INFORMATION about the best of Dubai, we've organised material in several formats.

Hotels

So many dramatically different hotels are in Dubai – ranging from the tatty around the edges to ridiculously large and opulent. Perhaps because Dubai is a destination that has built its reputation on luxury, the star rating is pretty fastidious at the top end of the scale. Rooms are always large and well appointed and facilities are generally good across the board – if you book into the Atlantis or any of the Jumeirah Group or Address hotels, you can be assured that you won't get stuck in a box room facing the car park – but only those opened in the last five or so years have really got a handle on modern interior design. Many also offer amazing added value, whether it's waterparks, camel rides or giant aquariums. We have profiled hotels in the three- and four-star categories extensively, as these are where you find the biggest discrepancy in quality – some are almost as good as five stars; some you'd be surprised if they scraped two. Boutique hotels don't really exist, bar a couple of hidden gems – the authorities, who believe big is beautiful, are notorious for capriciousness with their licensing. We have tried to focus on hotels that have a solid reputation, and we have attempted to summarise this somewhat unwieldy and problematic subject in ratings and rankings that quickly allow you to crystallise your choice. We concentrate on the specific variables that differentiate one hotel from another: location, size, room quality, services, amenities and cost.

Entertainment and Nightlife

Visitors will have very personal ideas of what constitutes a good night out on the town, depending on their age, background, bank account and bedtime. Some night owls will want to hit as many different clubs as possible during their stay, but they will probably prefer to party with like-minded people, or at least want to blend in a bit. Because nightspots so often have a very specific clientele and ambience, we believe that detailed descriptions are warranted, so that you don't end up in a lager-soaked theme pub when you're dressed for rosé and poolside recliners. Funnily enough for a city that is constantly on the move, nightclubs here actually seem to have some longevity – although bars go in and out of fashion like 'it' bags. So for these, we have made a point of selecting places that seem to have withstood the tests of time. If you do want to scout out new spots to sink a Cosmo (and they are opening all the time), then the best thing to do is to head to one of our recommended places and just ask around – as everybody travels in taxis, bar-hopping is de rigueur in Dubai. Sadly, it is very unlikely that the concierge in your hotel has ever been to any of these places, so this is one area where they can't give first-hand advice.

Restaurants

We provide plenty of detail when it comes to restaurants, and we wish we could promise you that they will be just as fresh as the daily catch by the time you have this book in your hands. But as with everything in the universe, the only constant is change. All we can do is try to focus on those things less likely to do a sudden about-face: location, reputation, clientele, service standards and calibre of chefs (although this is probably the most changeable aspect, sadly, as there is often quite a high turnover of staff). Given the high cost of eating in Dubai (unless you are prepared to go down the wipe-clean tables route), and the fact that you will probably eat at a dozen or more restaurants during your stay, you may benefit from discussing your choices with other visitors or acquaintances before you make your reservation, or consulting local guides such as *Time Out* or *What's On*. Of course, we know that you don't want a Michelin star at every meal, so we have also included a large selection of our favourite cheap eats and a few uniquely Dubai experiences, such as the all-you-can-eat brunch and Champagne afternoon tea. Try to vary your restaurant experiences according to cuisine, price and location – our dining profiles can get you started in that direction, and we hope the standards we observed at all these many tables have not slipped in the slightest by the time you put your napkin in your lap.

Dubai Neighbourhoods

Once you've decided where you're going, getting there becomes the issue. To help you do that, we refer consistently to eight Dubai neighbourhoods, described briefly below to give you a vague idea of what they're about. All profiles of hotels, restaurants, attractions, spas and nightspots include these neighbourhood references. Unfortunately, the lack of postcodes and even street names in most places make navigation a bit confusing initially, but Dubai is not that large a city, and most places you will visit to sightsee, eat or sunbathe are all signposted and well known by taxi drivers. The very few things that exist outside of the areas we cover here are on the way into the desert or out on the roads to other emirates – where this is the case, we have labelled it.

BUR DUBAI Lining the banks of Dubai Creek, facing Deira, this is one of the oldest areas of the city. It is from here that most of the dhows (sailing boats) depart on their scenic tours, where most of the international embassies are situated and where you can really get a feel for the bustling local culture. It is where the Dubai Museum is located, as is the historic Bastakiya district, with its reconstructed traditional Emirati houses, home to shops, art galleries and boutique hotels. It is probably not an area in which you will choose to stay, as most of the other lodging options are pretty down at heel, but it's a great place to grab a cheap bite to eat in one of the many Indian, Iranian, Pakistani and Lebanese eateries, and there are some fun nightclubs and bars too (although we'd suggest you stick to the places we've recommended, as this is also, unfortunately, the nexus of the city's prostitution). There is the odd shopping mall here, most notably BurJuman, but the best bargains are to be found in the old Textile Souk or in the Meena Bazaar, packed with fabric merchants and tailors. For the purposes of this guidebook, we have also included the small Satwa and Karama areas, slightly farther from Dubai Creek, under this heading.

DEIRA Along with Bur Dubai, this is an area to visit for local flavour. Unlike Bur Dubai, though, it does have a decent selection of hotels, including the beautiful Park Hyatt, probably due to its proximity to the airport. But most tourists are attracted here by the Gold Souk or the Spice Souk, or even just to walk along Dubai Creek to watch the old fishing boats that still ply their trade there. Some of the most interesting older skyscrapers are located here, including the National Bank of Dubai and the Dubai Chamber of Commerce. Again, there are some wonderful cheap eats, but there is also a raft of more expensive restaurants, including Gordon Ramsay's Verre. Golfers will appreciate the Dubai Creek Golf & Yacht Club and, if you are keen to sunbathe off the beaten track, Al Mamzar Beach Park is a hidden gem. We have also included the Garhoud area, which is slap bang next to the airport, under this banner, as well as nearby Festival City, with its mall, golf course and hotels.

JUMEIRAH We have actually used this as a catch-all for the beachside area that runs from the Dubai Marine Resort at one end to the Madinat Jumeirah at the other, although you will also hear people talk of Umm Suqeim and Al Wasl Road as distinct areas too. Although this has a high concentration of luxury beach hotels, including the Burj Al Arab and the Jumeirah Beach Hotel, it is also heavily populated with local Emirati families living in large, whitewashed villas. There are some great local cafes to stop in for a latte and a shisha and lots of small and

Dubai Neighbourhoods

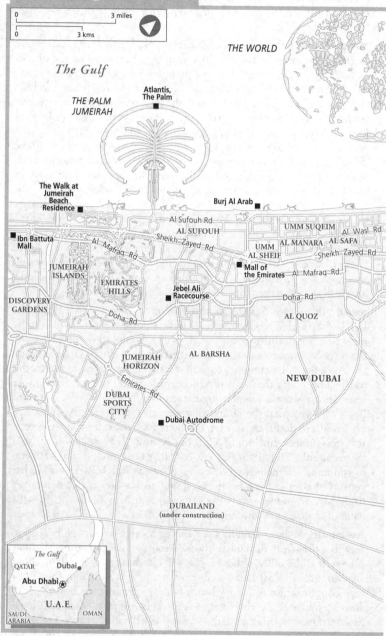

0 |———| 3 miles
0 |———| 3 kms

THE WORLD

The Gulf

THE PALM
JUMEIRAH

Atlantis,
The Palm

The Walk at
Jumeirah
Beach
Residence

Burj Al Arab

Al Sufouh Rd.

AL SUFOUH

UMM SUQEIM

Al Wasl Rd.

Ibn Battuta
Mall

Al Mafraq Rd.

Sheikh Zayed Rd.

UMM
AL SHEIF

AL MANARA

AL SAFA

JUMEIRAH
ISLANDS

EMIRATES
HILLS

Mall of
the Emirates

Sheikh Zayed Rd.

Al Mafraq Rd.

DISCOVERY
GARDENS

Jebel Ali
Racecourse

Doha Rd.

Doha Rd.

AL QUOZ

JUMEIRAH
HORIZON

AL BARSHA

NEW DUBAI

Emirates Rd.

DUBAI
SPORTS
CITY

Dubai Autodrome

DUBAILAND
(under construction)

The Gulf

QATAR   Dubai

Abu Dhabi ✪

U.A.E.

SAUDI
ARABIA   OMAN

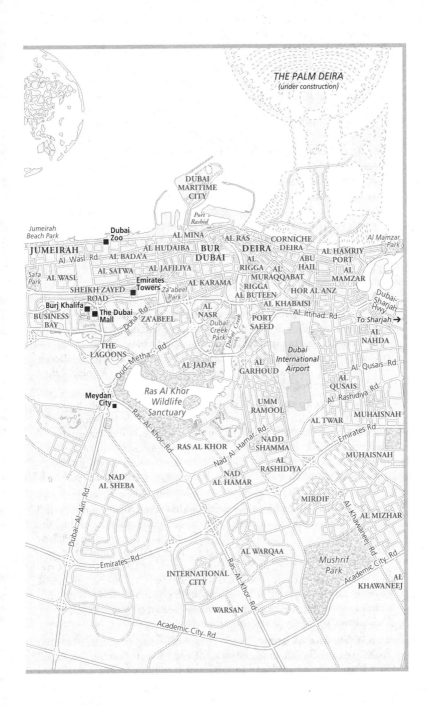

THE PALM DEIRA
(under construction)

DUBAI
MARITIME
CITY

*Port
Rashid*

*Jumeirah
Beach Park*

Dubai
Zoo

AL MINA

AL RAS

CORNICHE
DEIRA

*Al Mamzar
Park*

JUMEIRAH

AL HUDAIBA

BUR
DUBAI

DEIRA

AL HAMRIY
PORT

Al Wasl Rd.

AL BADA'A

AL
RIGGA

ABU
HAIL

AL WASL

AL SATWA

AL JAFILIYA

AL
MURAQQABAT

AL
MAMZAR

*Safa
Park*

Emirates
Towers

AL KARAMA

RIGGA

HOR AL ANZ

SHEIKH ZAYED
ROAD

*Za'abeel
Park*

AL BUTEEN

AL KHABAISI

*Dubai-
Sharjah
Hwy.*

Burj Khalifa

The Dubai
Mall

AL
NASR

Al Ittihad Rd.

To Sharjah →

BUSINESS
BAY

ZA'ABEEL

*Dubai
Creek
Park*

PORT
SAEED

AL
NAHDA

Doha Rd.

THE
LAGOONS

Dubai Creek

*Dubai
International
Airport*

AL Qusais Rd.

Oud-Metha Rd.

AL JADAF

AL
GARHOUD

AL
QUSAIS

Meydan
City

*Ras Al Khor
Wildlife
Sanctuary*

Al Rashidiya Rd.

UMM
RAMOOL

MUHAISNAH

Ras Al Khor Rd.

AL TWAR

Emirates Rd.

RAS AL KHOR

Nad Al Hamar Rd.

NADD
SHAMMA

MUHAISNAH

NAD
AL SHEBA

NAD
AL HAMAR

AL
RASHIDIYA

MIRDIF

Dubai-Al-Ain-Rd.

AL MIZHAR

Al Khawaneej Rd.

Emirates Rd.

AL WARQAA

*Mushrif
Park*

INTERNATIONAL
CITY

Ras-Al-Khor-Rd.

Academic City Rd.

AL
KHAWANEEJ

WARSAN

Academic City Rd.

mid-size malls for chi-chi fashion and gifts. This is also where most of the public beaches are to be found.

THE MARINA Again, we have slightly condensed this area – when we use this term, we are talking about anywhere along the coastline from after the Madinat Jumeirah right up to the end of Jumeirah Beach Residence and its public beach and just behind. This has a very heavy concentration of Western expat residents and day-tripping tourists, attracted by the cafes and shops of Jumeirah Beach Residence's The Walk, or the beach hotels including the new Sofitel, the old favourite The Ritz-Carlton and the business-friendly bolt-hole Grosvenor House. This is also where a lot of the party crowd head for the week-end, with perennial favourites Buddha Bar and Barasti consistently packing them in. We have also included the Media City area, which sits just behind the coastline, under this heading – it is a free zone where foreign companies are allowed to operate without a local part-ner, so it is primarily business-oriented, although there are a few great bars and restaurants too.

PALM JUMEIRAH Currently, the only place that you will visit on the Palm will probably be the Atlantis or a small handful of independent spas and restaurants. But this resort is so epic that it really does deserve its own separate category. The rest of the man-made island's trunk and fronds are dedicated to residential developments, from multi-storey apartment blocks to beachside villas. Soon, though – probably by the end of 2011 – there will be a huge number of hotels from which to choose, as they open one by one to flank the Atlantis on the ring around the palm tree.

SHEIKH ZAYED ROAD In this area, we have included all of the hotels and restaurants that line the Sheikh Zayed Road from the World Trade Centre up to the Mall of the Emirates and the Dubai International Financial District. This is where the largest concentration of business hotels and headquarters of global companies are located, although, due to the spending power of the clientele, their bars and restaurants are among the best (and most expensive) in the city.

DOWNTOWN This includes the Burj Khalifa, the Dubai Fountain and the epic Dubai Mall, as well as a handful of hotels including the original Address, The Palace and Al Manzil, all opened in 2008 or later. An area so good they named it three or four times, it is also called Downtown Burj Khalifa, Downtown Burj Dubai (by taxi driv-ers who haven't quite got used to the tower's last-minute name change) and Old Town. It has a very high concentration of bars and restaurants in the boutique mall Souk Al Bahar, frequented largely by Downtown's huge expat population.

AL BARSHA AND AL QUOZ To the casual observer, it may appear that these areas, tucked behind the Mall of the Emirates on Sheikh Zayed Road, are little more than sandpits and warehouses. But actually, Al

Quoz has made a name of itself as the artistic hub of the city, with some of Dubai's best-known and most exciting gallery spaces. The largest branches of some of Dubai's home-wares stalwarts, including Marina Home, are based here. Al Barsha is more residential – in fact, many local families moved here when the old villas around Jumeirah were earmarked for demolition (the recession unfortunately halted plans, and so now they sit empty). But some small hotels and apartments are also excellent value for the money and, of course, have close proximity to the aforementioned Dubai Mall and Ski Dubai. The largely residential areas of Emirates Hills, The Greens, The Springs, The Lakes and The Meadows also come under this heading, as do the Arabian Ranches, although as a tourist it is very unlikely you will visit these.

PART ONE

UNDERSTANDING DUBAI

EAT MY DUST:
A Brief History of Dubai

DUBAI HAS ALWAYS BEEN A BOOM AND BUST TOWN. Those who saw the recent crash as a portent of doom, imagining a great deserted cityscape gradually crumbling back into the sands from which it rose, just don't know Dubai and its amazing ability to reinvent itself. It's been like this ever since the Al Maktoum clan arrived to set up a trading outpost on a hot dusty day in 1833. They came out of Abu Dhabi in search of new territory and immediately grasped the potential for trading, thanks to Dubai's ideal location, perched between Dubai Creek and the Gulf. Dubai Creek was a natural harbour waterway, and Dubai soon became a magnet for the fishing, pearling and sea trades. By the turn of the century Dubai's port was thriving, and the Deira souk boasted more than 350 shops run by trading merchants from as far afield as India, Africa, Persia and throughout Arabia. This colourful cosmopolitan mix created the open, dynamic character that still defines Dubai today.

In 1894 Dubai's leaders offered tax exemption to traders, a masterstroke that catapulted Dubai far over the heads of its rivals. Trade in gold, silver, spices, textiles, dates and Dubai's famously lustrous pearls created a new class of wealthy merchant princes. The boom continued until 1929, when the double blow of the Great Depression and the invention of cheaper cultured Japanese pearls soon had Dubai fighting for its economic life. With trademark resilience, Dubai's Al Maktoum rulers diversified its trading base, but the shallow creek waterway wasn't deep enough to let in the massive container ships that could bring real profits. In a breathtakingly daring and risky move, Sheikh Rashid bin Saeed Al Maktoum mortgaged the entire emirate to finance dredging the creek – this first took place in 1961, although there have been successive programmes since. The gamble paid off and the big ships sailed in – and out again. Thus when, in 1966, oil was discovered in the offshore Fateh field, the infrastructure to export it already existed.

To understand the mercurial nature of Dubai, it helps to know about its remarkable royal family. The Al Maktoum dynasty must be one of the world's most successful, providing a unified vision that has powered Dubai into the 21st century. Dubai's dashing Al Maktoums make other world leaders look lacklustre. Their charisma is legendary. A typical anecdote recalls when a foreign diplomat was taken to the *Majlis* (audience chamber) to meet Sheikh Saeed, and he asked 'Your Highness, what about democracy?' The canny ruler replied, 'Did you need an appointment to see me? What can be more democratic than meeting the ruler without needing even so much as an appointment?'

Sheikh Saeed's son Sheikh Rashid worked closely with his father to create Dubai's infrastructure. He was an indefatigable vision-ary who had the common touch, always seeking a dialogue with his people and happy to promote anyone who served Dubai well. When his efforts paid off, rather than spending the money on shiny new palaces, he ploughed the profits back into Dubai. He loved the desert and hunting with his beloved falcons. He passed on his devo-tion to Bedouin culture and Dubai to his four extraordinary sons, Maktoum, Hamdan, Mohammed and Ahmed. The brothers were a dynamic team who helped forge modern Dubai, founding the Dubai Municipality, in charge of the day-to-day running of the emirate.

Sheikh Maktoum, who inherited the crown when his father passed away in 2006, had great diplomatic skills and was an essential driv-ing force in the formation of the United Arab Emirates. Although all the Maktoums are superb riders, earning awards in all aspects of horsemanship, it was Sheikh Maktoum who introduced Arabs to international horse racing, also founding the highly successful Godolphin stables in Dubai. A dapper and well-respected figure at race meets such as Royal Ascot, where he and Queen Elizabeth II often compared notes on the horses, he played a major role in raising the standard of international racing. When he died in 2006, much of Dubai's governance was already being handled by Crown Prince Mohammed, who then became ruler.

The current ruler, Sheikh Mo, as he is affectionately called, is a prince right out of a storybook: soldier, Cambridge-educated states-man, poet, a crack rider and thoroughbred racehorse breeder. He is also a leading philanthropist, having pledged a record £6.5 billion (US $10.2 billion) towards education in the Middle East. The sheikh is among the world's richest men, owning palatial homes in glamorous locations from Miami to London. His yacht is the world's biggest, and his trophy-winning racehorses travel the globe in a specially kitted-out 747. He is adored by Dubai residents, who love his flair,

Sheikh-spotting

MOST DUBAI RESIDENTS have, at one time or another, been in the presence of royalty. Their beloved Sheikh Mo is rather fond of the royal walk-about and is usually accompanied by a retinue of associates, all clad in the same pristine white *dishdashas*. We have seen him at the Bab Al Shams Desert Resort, enjoying lunch at Zuma and trotting around the Dubai International Financial Centre. He is said to be fairly approachable, although we wouldn't suggest you go and interrupt his sushi. You might find yourself driving behind a rather fancy-looking car with the number plate 1 – if so, Sheikh Mo is likely to be behind the wheel (just like many of his countrymen, he favours auto-mobiles the size of a small tank). In fact, if you spot any single-digit number plates, the chances are that a crowned head is in the driving seat – so best not to rev up and challenge him to a race at the traffic lights.

You may of course wonder how so many people recognise him – you'll stop wondering within half an hour of landing on Dubai soil. Sheikh Mohammed's laser-beam middle-distance stare can be seen boring down from the side of buildings, in supermarkets, on stickers covering the entire back windows of cars and on high kitsch wheel covers on the back of 4x4s. You will also see him in the lobby of every hotel in Dubai, usually flanked by the late Sheikh Zayed bin Sultan Al Nahyan – the principal architect of U.A.E., the ruler of Abu Dhabi and president of the U.A.E. from 1971 until his death in 2004 – and his son Sheikh Khalifa, the current president of the U.A.E. and emir of Abu Dhabi. You will also see images of Hollywood-hot Sheikh Hamdan everywhere – some particularly good airbrushed, Rayban-sporting billboards are on the Sheikh Zayed Road. Just try not to swoon and swerve.

his ability to embrace modernity without compromising traditional values and his belief that anything is possible.

He is married to senior wife Sheikha Hind bint Maktoum bin Juma Al Maktoum and more recently the glamorous Princess Haya, daughter of Jordan's King Hussein. Princess Haya is as dynamic as her husband and is also a top rider, Oxford graduate and a tireless champion of humanitarian projects throughout the Middle East. The sheikh's 19 recognised royal children guarantee the clan is well poised to keep Dubai in the limelight.

The British Special Air Service credo, 'He who dares, wins', could easily be the Al Maktoum family motto. Sheikh Mohammed's son Hamdan seems to be following in his father's footsteps. After graduating at the top of Britain's elite Sandhurst military college and studying at the London School of Economics, he has recently been appointed Crown Prince of Dubai and the heir apparent. He is also one of the world's most eligible bachelors. When he isn't zipping around town in a hot Ferrari or wowing the girls with his sultry good looks and romantic poetry (he publishes poems under the name Fazza), Prince Hamdan is busy roping in the best financial brains to boost Dubai's fortunes. One thing is for sure: Dubai's rags-to-riches sagas are never dull.

Dubai's rulers aren't perfect. There are issues with the treatment of foreign labourers, overdevelopment and the environment that need to be addressed. But rather than stick its head in all that sand, the government is facing up to its responsibilities and gradually tackling problems. OK, it isn't a democracy. There are no political parties, no general elections and no chance of a commoner getting the top job. That said, no one seems too unhappy about it – least of all the Emiratis themselves, who have one of the world's richest per capita lifestyles, all tax-free. Dubai is often compared to a corporation, a Dubai Inc, with Sheikh Mo as its unstoppable CEO. Dubai's goal is to be the hub of what Sheikh Mohammed calls the 'Central World', not east or west, but the ideal mover and shaker in between. With such clear-thinking, committed leadership, Dubai is well on its way to making its dreams come true, give or take a few more booms and busts.

The **GULF COOPERATION COUNCIL** *and the* **UNITED ARAB EMIRATES**

THE EMERGENCE OF DUBAI AS THE BUSINESS and tourism hub of the Middle East is, of course, strongly tied into the fact that it is seen as a haven of stability in what, it has to be said, is a pretty unstable region. A case in point is the fact that in the five years after 1990, when Iraq invaded Kuwait, bringing about the first Gulf War, Dubai's population almost doubled in size. Nor did growth slow down during U.S. President George W. Bush's more recent ill-fated war on terror. This has a lot to do with the fact that it sits in the only federal and unified state in the Arab world, the United Arab Emirates. Established on 2 December 1971 by Sheikh Zayed bin Sultan Al Nahyan, the ruler of Abu Dhabi, the federation of seven emirates (Sharjah, Dubai, Abu Dhabi, Umm Al-Quwain, Ras Al-Khaimah, Fujairah and Ajman) was previously known as the Trucial States, in reference to a 19th-century truce between the United Kingdom and several families of Arab sheikhs. Sheikh Khalifa bin Zayed bin Sultan Al Nahyan of Abu Dhabi is the current president of the U.A.E., with Dubai's Sheikh Mohammed serving as the U.A.E.'s prime minister and vice president. Each other emirate also has its own ruling family. The U.A.E. in turn is part of the Gulf Cooperation Council (GCC), a political and economic union of the six states of the Gulf – fellow members are Bahrain, Kuwait, Qatar, Saudi Arabia and Oman.

The **LANGUAGE**: *Arabic*

WE'LL BE HONEST – there is almost certainly going to be no call for you to speak or understand Arabic here. Obviously, Emiratis will communicate with each other in their mother tongue, but – perhaps quite sadly – you will have little cause to interact with them in the normal course of things. And, if you do, they probably speak better English than you do. With more than 200 nationalities living side by side here, the 'other' official language of Dubai is, luckily for us, English. Road signs are in English, shop staff speak English, waiters speak English and officials speak English. In fact, you are more likely to be able to use Urdu, Hindi, Russian or Filipino Tagalog than Gulf Arabic.

Expats do pepper their English with choice Arabic words and phrases though. The most oft-used are *yalla*, which means 'Get a move on!' or 'Let's go!'; *khalas* (pronounced halas), which means 'finished' or 'done'; and the dreaded *Insha'Allah*, literally translated as 'God willing', which is the answer to everything from 'Can you come over for dinner tomorrow?' to 'Will you be able to fix my toilet this week?' In practice, the reality is that it means anything from 'Not a chance, mate' to 'I've got no idea'. The same can be said of the term *mafi mushkila,* meaning 'no problem'. If someone says this to you, it's safe to assume that there is a big problem.

Other words you will hear thrown into everyday English are *habibi* (if addressing a man) and *habibti* (if addressing a woman), which means 'darling' – men use this with each other all the time. An Arab speaking English will also pepper his or her sentences with *yanni*, which basically means 'erm' or 'you know'. And one word that quite literally has a lot of clout is *wasta* – this is hard to translate, but in essence, someone with *wasta* has power, influence and a lot of friends in the right places, Godfather-style.

There are as many Arabic accents and argots as there are countries that speak the language. Levantine Arabic (especially as it's spoken in Lebanon and Syria) is quite sing-song, Egyptian Arabic

Hello or Welcome *Marhaba, Ahlan*	Thank you *Shukran*
Greetings *As-salam alaykum* (reply) *Walaykum as-salam*	Don't mention it *Hafwan*
	Congratulations *Mabruk*!
Good morning *Sabah al-khayr* (reply) *Sabah an-nur*	Yes *Naam* or *aiwa*
	No *La*
Good evening *Misa al-khayr* (reply) *Wa inta min ahlu*	Thanks be to God *Al hamdu li-la*
	Forbidden *Haram*
Goodbye *Maa Salama*	
How are you *Kayf halak* (to a man) *Kayf halik* (to a woman)	

is slang-filled, and Gulf Arabic is markedly more guttural. See the chart on the previous page for a few words and phrases that you might hear when you are in the U.A.E. (We have not included the Arabic script spelling as it's extremely unlikely that you will see these written, and if you did, you would need a high degree of proficiency in the language to read them.)

BUILDING CASTLES
in the SAND

UNDERWATER HOTELS, REVOLVING SKYSCRAPERS and upside-down towers – had the global credit crisis not felled the cranes in Dubai, it's anyone's guess what the city might have looked like come 2020. Certainly, several outlandish projects were completed before the crash – you only have to drive down the trunk of the Palm Jumeirah to get an idea of the scope of the city's vision. But for every Atlantis, there is a Trump Tower (which is still, according to developers, in the pipeline – although for the time being on hold); for every Burj Khalifa, there is a Universal Studios (get your camera out if you take a trip to the Dubai Outlet Mall – the gate to the theme park sits right next to it, in the middle of the desert with a lone JCB behind it). When it became clear how hard Dubai's developers had been hit by the crash, the Land Department announced all projects that broke ground would be finished – but it's not hard to see from the concrete shells that dot the Dubai landscape that this was rather wishful thinking.

We would love to be able to give you a rundown of the projects that have been shelved and those that are still going ahead. Unfortunately, this is nigh on impossible as there is a rather cloak-and-dagger approach to this state of financial emergency. State-run developer Dubai World – which has billions of pounds of liabilities – is obviously in trouble, but subsidiary Nakheel is still showing its promotional video that promises the man-made World Islands, which sit just off the coast, will be a billionaire's haven of Maldives-style resorts, super yachts and palaces. Fly over them and it's pretty plain that they are just piles of sand – and are likely to stay that way for the foreseeable future. The extant Palm Jumeirah was originally intended to be flanked by two sister palms. The Palm Jebel Ali, which is all but completed, is 50% larger than the original and has 70 kilometres (about 43.5 miles) of coastline that was intended to include villas, hotels and Sea World and Aquatica theme parks. Currently, very few of these projects have even broken ground. Despite appearing on many official maps, the dredging of the Palm Deira has ceased. The Universe, the planned man-made archipelago in the shape of the solar system that was to sit next to the World Islands, has been quietly shelved.

Property in Dubai: The 'Flip' Side

To UNDERSTAND QUITE HOW THE PROPERTY MARKET in Dubai bottomed out so quickly and so comprehensively, bringing much of the city's finances with it, it is necessary to understand two things. First, you need to understand the right of ownership in the city. The permitting of foreign ownership in designated areas – which include the Marina, Downtown and the Palm Jumeirah – kick-started the Dubai property boom. Outside of these designated areas in Dubai, you can only own land as a GCC national.

Second, you must also understand the process of flipping that was so common during the boom years. The way that developers financed their developments in these designated foreign-ownership areas was by selling their residential units off-plan. Usually a purchaser would pay a 10% deposit and then would be liable to make various instalment payments during the construction process. In theory this meant that a buyer's exposure was reasonably limited until the unit was finished, at which point the balance of the purchase price would become due. But as prices inflated – by several hundred percent in some cases – these title owners sold their unfinished properties. The new buyer would then be liable to make the remaining instalment payments, with the seller pocketing the profit made to date. Speculators were able to do this on a massive scale from 2005 to mid-2008 and made a fortune in doing so.

A property could be flipped a number of times before it was finished – so the prices kept rising and rising – but, crucially, the bulk of the profit was being made by the sellers along the way, not the original developers, who in many cases did not have enough money to finish – or maybe even start – the project. Unfortunately for many people who now own buildings that are not yet complete (or, in some cases, haven't even been started), if a project is cancelled, they are only entitled to the original sum that the first buyer paid – in some cases just a quarter of what they paid. Even worse, many people own apartments in projects that are on hold, meaning first, that no one has yet acknowledged that the project has failed, and second, they are in limbo. Thus, the people who got in and out of the market at breakneck speed made a fortune – and others have been left ruined and made a run for it to escape debtor's prison, as evidenced by the number of dust-covered cars dumped at the airport.

It is perhaps surprising that, given the number of buildings that have gone up in Dubai in the past ten years, almost <u>none</u> were designed by the world's most famous architects. Unfortunately for the city's aesthetic, the few that were commissioned from these maestros have also been put on hold. The Business Bay development, which it is hoped will be the new financial heart of the city, had the largest concentration of these. Originally more than 230 skyscrapers were planned, the most ambitious of these being the 510-metre (or 1,673-foot) Burj Al Alam, designed to resemble a crystal flower, and the three Signature Towers (formerly known as Dancing Towers) unveiled by architect Zaha Hadid at the Guggenheim Museum in New York in 2006. One iconic building that has gone full steam ahead is the Norman Foster–designed Index Tower, the residential skyscraper that is part of the Dubai International Financial District. It's not all doom and gloom though – the Palazzo Versace hotel is still very much in the pipeline, and the cheese-grater-style O14 tower is currently awaiting its tenants. There is of course also the Burj Khalifa, although its very name (Sheikh Khalifa is the ruler of oil and thus of cash-rich Abu Dhabi) is a reminder to the city of quite how much isn't in the city's coffers – the tower was hastily renamed after Abu Dhabi bailed out Dubai to the tune of billions.

Some think that Dubai has benefited from a slowdown in growth, and some areas have breathed a sigh of relief. In 2008 a programme was announced that would redevelop most of Satwa and Jumeirah 1, two of the most vibrant, if slightly down-at-heel, areas of the city. The process of taking over residences began with tenants being offered new villas in Al Barsha. Then the crunch hit and the project stalled, meaning vast swathes of Jumeirah 1 are now empty, dusty and full of uninhabited villas; but Satwa, or Little Manila as it is affectionately known, remains untouched.

The other mega-project in peril is Dubailand. Again, it is very hard to get an official line out of the developers, Tatweer, but it looks likely much of the planned 278 square kilometres (approximately 107 square miles) of theme parks and malls, which was to be twice the size of Walt Disney World Resort, has been canned. Some small projects have been finished – the Dubai Autodrome and the decidedly retro Global Village are already open to the public. But they are very much in the minority. The developers of Legoland, which was slated to open in 2011, have gone on record as saying that their project will go ahead but have given no time line. The developers of other planned parks, including Dreamworks, Six Flags, Universal Studios and Marvel Superheroes, have remained tight-lipped. Sadly, the Dubai Snowdome – an indoor ski slope with its own iceberg-shaped hotel – is also, ahem, on ice.

RELIGION *in* DUBAI

ISLAM IS THE OFFICIAL RELIGION of the U.A.E., with the majority of the population being Sunni. Dubai is as open and tolerant a society as you will find in the Gulf, but you will notice some things as a tourist in a Muslim country. Followers of Islam do not eat pork or drink alcohol, although both are available to non-Muslims in Dubai. The most glaring difference is the holy day, which is Friday. This means that the weekend here falls on Friday and Saturday, but in practice this will affect you very little – malls, shops and restaurants are open as usual, as are most tourist attractions. The holy month of Ramadan, which we discuss in detail on page 27, is an entirely different matter. As a visitor, you will be expected to adhere to the same rules as the locals – that is, no public consumption of food or drink during daylight hours, and a much more modest approach to dressing than is usually required.

Depending on which area you decide to stay in, you may also hear the call to prayer that emanates from mosques throughout the city five times a day. This can range from soft and tuneful to ear-splitting and gruff, alerting worshippers to the fact that it is time to prostrate themselves towards Mecca. This prayer is not limited to mosques – you will hear it on the radio and in malls (all of which have prayer rooms), and you will almost certainly see people kneeling by their car at the side of the road at these times.

Another thing which visitors may find surprising – although the chances of you actually noticing are slim – is that it is not an uncommon practice for a man to have multiple wives. A man is in fact allowed to marry up to four women, as long as he is able to treat them equally, both financially and emotionally. Another fairly unique thing in Emirati culture is the dowry, which is paid to the woman and her family in money or jewellery – these remain the property of the bride throughout the marriage and are seen as her fall-back in case of divorce. Under sharia law, a man is allowed to marry a non-Muslim woman, which happens increasingly often in Dubai, but it is unacceptable the other way around.

The basis of the legal system of the U.A.E. is sharia and Islamic courts working alongside the civil and criminal courts in the U.A.E. The sharia (or Qur'anic) court in the U.A.E. is primarily responsible for civil matters between Muslims, though, so it rarely affects foreigners.

Although Islam is the official religion, other faiths are very much tolerated here – a list of the largest churches and Hindu temples in the city are on the Dubai Explorer Web site (**liveworkexplore.com/dubai**).

CUSTOMS, COURTESIES, NORMS *and* NO-NOS

DUBAI IS BY NOW SO USED TO FOREIGN VISITORS that you won't be pilloried for accidental uncouth behaviour – in most instances at least. These indiscretions will at most cause a mild tut-tut (rather than a prison term or deportation), especially given the fact that you'll encounter very few Emiratis in the normal course of things. First and foremost, chill out. Things tend to get done here at their own pace – if you're rude or try to hurry things along, the only person you'll upset is yourself. In fact, this is a good rule of thumb in general – rudeness and aggressiveness are not tolerated from tourists here. Do not shout, swear or make offensive hand gestures to anyone, anywhere, but especially not to locals. Basically, if your mum would be ashamed of your behaviour, the Dubai police are unlikely to take too kindly to it either.

Another thing to watch out for is taking too much of an interest in the locals, especially women. Don't point your camera randomly at people in national dress – you will almost certainly see local women in the malls, although never in bars and rarely in restaurants – as this is seen as a huge invasion of privacy. Don't point your finger at people either – although the hands are used a lot to gesticulate while speaking, pointing directly at people is a no-no. If sitting among locals (again unlikely, but you never know), do not point the soles of your feet towards them. You should, however, remove your shoes before entering the house of a local. Also, do accept any hospitality offered – often this will come in the form of coffee and dates – as you may cause offence if you don't.

If you are introduced to an Emirati man, it is acceptable to shake hands with him. If he is with a local woman (most probably his wife or a family member), you may not even be introduced to her – and if you are, do not offer her your hand or, even worse, attempt the Continental-style kiss on both cheeks. You may be surprised to see groups of local men sitting on their own in bars, restaurants or cafes – it is the norm here to socialise in single-sex groups. Even weddings are segregated. One more thing – if in doubt, don't mention Israel; it is an incredibly emotive topic here and best avoided entirely.

Lastly, and probably most important – apologies for going on about this at length, both here and later in the book, but it cannot be overemphasised – is that public displays of affection are not acceptable anywhere. On the street, in clubs, in bars and in taxis – if you are feeling amorous, believe us, it is far better to take it inside. Again, the mum analogy works pretty well here – although on the safe side, maybe it would be better not to do anything of which your granny wouldn't approve in public with a member of the opposite sex, especially if you are unmarried. The only exception you will see is men with their arms around each other or holding hands (the latter is most frequently seen among workers from the Indian subcontinent). This brotherly sign of affection is perfectly acceptable.

NATIONAL DRESS

THE LOCAL DRESS OF THE U.A.E., which virtually every Emirati wears, is a rather breathtakingly elegant thing. The first time you will likely encounter the men's pristine white *dishdasha* will be at the airport, where a row of neat young men sit waiting to stamp your passport. You won't be able to see them, but underneath the counter is a pair of perfectly pedicured feet in leather sandals. On their heads sit the national headdress (usually either white or red-and-white), possibly held in place by a thick black rope (*iqal*). An Emirati man will usually have around 30–50 of these *dishdashas*, with at least 10 in the laundry at any one point (it is not unusual for them to change several times in one day). They are tailored to fit and sometimes made in other colours – you may see men in black or grey *dishdashas* in the winter, or a caramel colour in summer. On formal occasions, men may also wear a black overgarment edged in metallic thread.

Women cover their bodies in the flowing black *abaya*, which is usually worn over normal clothes. If you could see what was underneath them, you may well be astonished by the designer label count – the preponderance of Chanel bags and Gucci shoes poking out from underneath the flowing sleeves and hemlines might give you a good idea, though. Most women also wear a headscarf (*sheyla*) to cover their hair, although the current fashion for more relaxed youths is to not entirely cover the hairline. You may also notice how high these headscarves sit – many women have either elaborate hairstyles or hairpieces underneath them. Often both the *sheyla* and the *abaya* will be heavily decorated in crystals or embroidery. As great care is taken with what can be seen outside of the house, many women have perfect and striking make-up, often with heavily kohled eyes and bright-painted mouths.

You won't see it very often, but some of the older female generation in Dubai still wear the traditional burqa. This is a 'mask' with thin strips running across the forehead and under the eyes, joined by another strip that runs down the nose. Although the gold colour makes it look like metal, it is actually leather or painted, stiffened cotton. If you see a woman fully covered in a *niqab* (the black cloth that either covers the face entirely or everything apart from the eyes) and with black gloves to cover her hands, it is most likely that she is not originally from the U.A.E. – this form of covering is most common in Saudi Arabia.

PERSONAL HEALTH
and SECURITY

ALTHOUGH DUBAI MIGHT BE A BIT OF A CULTURE SHOCK for the first-time visitor to the Middle East, there is one thing you really don't need to worry about – your personal health and safety. In terms of illness, you don't need to take malaria pills, although do take mosquito repellent if they are a problem for you, as they can be vicious. It is also a good idea to keep your windows and balcony doors closed in case they invade your room. Snakes and spiders are not a problem

– you may see the odd harmless, tiny lizard hanging around, though. Similarly, there are very few stray dogs, and the few stray cats you see won't come near you. Jellyfish can be an issue in the height of summer and can give you a nasty sting, so do ask the lifeguard at the beach or your hotel concierge or check the local press for warnings. Medical care is of a high level, but it is worth investing in travel insurance, as you will almost certainly want to use the private hospitals and doctors if you fall ill.

The crime rate is low, and security in hotels is very good, although it is still worth locking your passports and valuables in your in-room or reception safe. Street crime is also not a problem, probably largely due to there being no pavements. On the very rare occasion of personal attacks, the victim is usually female and often intoxicated, and the perpetrator is rarely Emirati. If you are with friends, try not to get separated from them, and exercise the same precautions to ensure your safety as you would back home – don't get in an unlicensed taxi, don't leave with a stranger, and don't leave your drink unattended, as there are occasional reports of drink-spiking. Pickpocketing is extremely rare – if you find that you have lost your passport, wallet, phone or other valuables, do report it to the police or security at the last place you saw it. Whether that is the mall or the back of a taxi, nine times out of ten, it will turn up. The emergency service numbers are as follows:

- Ambulance ☎ 998 or 999
- Fire ☎ 997
- Police ☎ 999

PART TWO

PLANNING YOUR VISIT

WHEN *to* GO

THE WEATHER DURING PEAK SEASON makes Dubai the ideal holiday destination. November–April, the sun shines constantly and the temperature hovers around 25–30°C (77–86°F). It does get cooler at night, but it is unlikely that you will ever need more than a sweater or very light jacket, unless you decide to go to the cinema – for some reason, screens citywide chill their auditoriums to almost arctic conditions. The shoulder months of October and May are also bearable – just – although temperatures do hit the high 30s (high 90s). Rain is rare in the emirate, but there can be a bit of a deluge around January and February. When the rains do happen, the city gets gridlocked. It's not unknown for sodden roads to become car parks in minutes, so if it's really pelting down, it might be best to abort any planned day trips. Sandstorms are uncommon but can happen year-round and are actually an interesting phenomenon for visitors – the wind whips up the sand, which can cause a citywide white-out that drastically reduces visibility. But these really shouldn't be a consideration, as the instance of either per year can usually be counted on one hand. Because of the wonderful weather, November–April is when most outdoor events – from food festivals to racing carnivals and concerts – happen. During this period, you'll want to spend most of your time outside, although the post-Christmas sales (known as the **Dubai Shopping Festival**) are also a big draw indoors. If you are keen to get some sunshine over the festive season, hotels here do lay on luxurious Christmas feasts, and practically every bar, nightclub and restaurant has a no-expense-spared New Year's Eve extravaganza. Despite the fact that this is a Muslim country, malls also abound with Christmas carols, trees and confused-looking shop assistants in Santa and elf outfits.

HOT, HOT, HOT!

THE FACT THAT EXPATS OFTEN LEAVE the emirate for summer might give you a sense of quite how hot it can get; this is a desert, after all. Of course, prices for package holidays (and also flight prices and hotel room rates if you want to create your own package) go down dramatically as the mercury rises, and so hotels and beaches do still run at a respectable occupancy, and some real deals can be had during the very hottest months of June, July, August and September. If you think you can manage with high humidity and searing heat, you will find some amazing bargains. Having lived through it more than a few times, here is our advice on coping with the heat.

If you do take the plunge and book during this time, try to take advantage of the slashed prices and stay in a hotel where the facilities mean you don't have to travel far to stay occupied – even the trip from air-conditioned lobby to taxi will leave you dripping with sweat and with sunglasses fogged up so badly you won't be able to see. Temperatures can regularly reach 40°C, or 104°F (50°C, or 122°F, is not a rare occurrence), and the humidity rises to 90% – doctors here often see seasonal vitamin D deficiency in patients as, despite the sun shining constantly, it is too unpleasant to be outside to soak up its rays. Hotels do their best to keep you comfortable, chilling their pools and making sure plenty of waiters have cold towels on hand. They do tend to shut down outdoor terraces and bars, though, as there is simply no call for them after the middle of May, although some do have outdoor air-conditioning units or fans that spray water to keep you cool. If you do decide to go during this period, it's best to manage your time like a seasoned expat – get up early when the sun is lower and the temperatures more bearable and retire indoors 10 a.m.– 4 p.m. The malls provide some respite and have the added bonus of brilliant discounts at the **Dubai Summer Surprises** (also known as the sales) in June, July and August. Many spas also offer discount packages or two-for-ones. In addition, every summer, Emirates Airlines also spearheads the Kids Go Free promotion, which sees more than 100 hotels, malls and tourist attractions across the city link up to offer great summer value for families. From mid-May to the end of September, as long as they are accompanied by two adults, up to two children under age 16 get free accommodation, meals, rides on the Dubai Metro, airport transfers and entrance to numerous attractions including Wild Wadi and Aquaventure at the Atlantis.

unofficial **TIP**
Weekends in the U.A.E. are Friday (the Muslim holy day) and Saturday. If you want to make the most of the city's nightlife, it is worth trying to stay a Thursday and Friday night.

RAMADAN RESTRICTIONS:
Read Me!

EVEN IF YOU ARE HARDY ENOUGH for a Dubai summer, you will almost certainly want to avoid the holy month of Ramadan, which commemorates the revelation of the Holy Qur'an. As the ninth month of the Islamic calendar, which is lunar, the dates change each year, although it will start in June, July or August until the middle of this decade. The festival begins when the new moon is sighted, so until this happens, any dates given are informed estimates, accurate give or take a few days. The night before Ramadan begins is dry (that is, no alcohol) across the emirate. During Ramadan, Muslims fast between sunrise and sunset, eating and drinking only during the hours of darkness. Most will try to fit in three meals during this time, getting up before sunrise for a hearty breakfast and a lot of water.

This affects tourists much more than you might think, as you too will be expected to abstain from eating, drinking and smoking in public during those hours, as a mark of respect. Just to reiterate – unless you are behind closed doors, you must consume *nothing* – that includes bottles of water and chewing gum – during daylight hours. This includes in cars and on buses (it is irrelevant on the Dubai Metro, as eating and drinking in carriages isn't ever allowed). Even if the police don't catch you, a local is more than likely to ask you to desist, and in no uncertain terms. You may also see a rise in people spitting on the street during this period – as those most strictly observing fast will not even swallow their own saliva.

In hotels, you will still be able to dine, but only if the restaurants have been screened off. In malls, some cafes will have curtains, allowing them to continue serving, but open food courts will be all but closed. The few outlets that are still open will happily sell you food, but don't expect to eat it until you get home. (We have occasionally seen starving shoppers duck into mall toilets to sit in a stall and eat a sandwich. Not pleasant.) As live or loud music is not allowed even in the evening, nightclubs shut completely for the entire month. Cinemas remain open for the most part, but very few will release new films. Radio stations are expected to play soothing music rather than chart hits. It will be up to the discretion of your hotel whether you can eat or have drinks by the pool or on the beach – do phone first to check the rules. You are, however, still allowed to consume alcohol in hotel bars and restaurants, but only after dark. If you do come during this month, there are some plus points. Hotels, cafes and restaurants all serve some sort of *Iftar* feast (the meal that is served after sunset to break fast) that is delicious and a great way to get in touch with local customs. Many also have shisha lounges where you can sit smoking and sipping Arabic coffee until the wee hours. Malls are open until at least midnight every day.

During the month, many Muslims work Ramadan hours – starting later in the morning and finishing earlier in the afternoon. This means that rush-hour times change – see Part 5, Getting Around, for details.

Approximate dates for Ramadan in Dubai are 1–30 August 2011; 20 July–19 August 2012; and 9 July–8 August 2013. However, because the dates are based on the actual sighting of the new moon, they are subject to change.

We are just going to hammer home our point one more time: **Failure to comply with these rules could mean a reprimand from locals and the authorities alike, and at the worst a jail term.**

GATHERING INFORMATION

ONE OF THE BEST WEB SITES to help you get a handle on restaurants, bars, nightclubs and concerts comes courtesy of listings guide *Time Out* (**timeoutdubai.com**). Usefully, it also has an events sales section on the site, where you can purchase tickets for everything from rock concerts to go-karting days online. Dubai Explorer has a similarly useful site (**liveworkexplore.com/dubai**) that is slightly more geared towards residents (although helpful for practical things such as dentists and hospitals). *The National* newspaper, although based in Abu Dhabi, is probably the best source of local (and international) news here. Hard copies of the paper can be picked up from most outlets, and an online version is available at **thenational.ae.** A locally-printed international edition of U.K. newspaper *The Times* is also available. For a more sensationalist slant, it is also worth grabbing a copy of the popular free sheet *7Days,* or if you want to mug up before arriving, you can visit **7days.ae.** For the first-time visitor the Dubai Government Department of Tourism Web site (**dubaitourism.ae**) is very useful, with up-to-date information on visas, laws and regulations and interactive maps. The official government Web site, **uaeinteract.com,** sponsored by the National Media Council, also has up-to-date news from all over the U.A.E. For probably the most useful information on U.A.E. law as it pertains to visitors, your embassy is the best place to start. For Brits, the British Embassy has a list of dos and don'ts available at **ukinuae.fco. gov.uk.** Americans can obtain information from **dubai.usconsulate.gov** and Australians should take a look at **uae.embassy.gov.au.** Canadians should visit **tinyurl.com/3xy6uw9.** The Dubai government has also promised that an iPhone application will be available from 2011 onwards with comprehensive coverage of local laws that affect tourists – check on **elaws.gov.ae.** In addition, two local television stations, Dubai One and City7, will almost certainly be playing in your hotel room.

ENTRY REQUIREMENTS

FOR MOST TRAVELLERS, all you will need to travel to the U.A.E. is a passport valid for at least six months from the date of arrival. Citizens of the Gulf Cooperation Council (GCC) and the following countries do not require prearranged visas: Andorra, Australia, Austria, Belgium, Brunei, Canada, Denmark, Finland, France, Germany, Greece, Holland, Hong Kong, Iceland, Ireland, Italy, Japan, Liechtenstein, Luxembourg, Malaysia, Monaco, New Zealand, Norway, Portugal, San Marino, Singapore, South Korea, Spain, Sweden, Switzerland, United Kingdom, United States of America and the Vatican. Do check with the official tourism Web site (**dubaitourism.ae**) for updated advice on visitor visas for the U.A.E., as rules can change with little warning. You will be allowed to stay in the country for 30 days, non-renewable – it is not worth overstaying your welcome as fines or a jail term may be incurred. You can enter and exit through any part of the U.A.E. If you are not a citizen of the countries listed above, you are required to have a sponsor for your visit. This will be arranged by the hotel or travel agent, so enquire when booking. Non-U.K. nationals who book flights through Emirates Airlines can also obtain their visas online at the same time. A 30-day visa will cost AED 100 (£17.30 or US $27.25), not including service fees. Passengers can continually track the status of these applications, and they should be delivered via e-mail within four international working days. As always, these rules are subject to change, so it is worth checking with the U.A.E. embassy or visiting **government.ae**.

WHOM TO GO WITH

THIS IS A COMPLEX QUESTION, which you should give some real thought to before you book your ticket. Technically, under the sharia law by which the U.A.E. abides, it is illegal to share a room with a person of the opposite sex to whom you are not married. In practice, hotels turn a blind eye – in fact, our straw poll proved that most will tell you it's completely fine and will only ask for one passport on arrival (even if they do ask for both, Arab women in the U.A.E. keep their surnames when they marry, so there would be no reason for them to suspect). This is entirely at your own risk though, and should you for any reason have a run-in with the police during your stay, there may be consequences. Homosexuality is not illegal per se in Dubai, but homosexual acts are (although conversely it is much more acceptable to hold the hand of a person of the same sex as a sign of friendship than it is with someone of the opposite sex). It is, however, not illegal to share a hotel room with a person of the same sex, so again this is a judgement call that individual visitors must make for themselves.

Gay, straight, married or cohabiting, you will need to keep a very tight rein on public displays of affection while in the emirate. However innocuous you believe them to be, they are a total no-no. We really mean it. So that's no lewd behaviour and no kissing, even if you are in the back of a taxi and think you are safe from prying eyes. Such behaviour could easily lead to at least a night in a police cell, or much, much worse. Even a peck on the lips is pushing it if you are in a public area. So lovebirds – especially if unmarried – might want to hold off on a visit to Dubai until they've got a little bit bored with each other.

WHAT TO PACK

DUBAI HAS AS OPEN AND WELCOMING a culture as you will find in the Middle East, so the only time women will be expected to cover their heads as non-Muslims will be if they are visiting a mosque. As soon as you step off the aeroplane at Dubai International Airport, you will undoubtedly see men in the traditional long-sleeved, ankle-length *kandura* or *dishdasha* with a red-and-white *ghutra* or the black *iqal* band headdress, with women wearing *sheyla* headcoverings and elegant black *abaya*. You will not, at any point, be required to wear these – and it is extremely infrequently that you will ever see a non-Arab in traditional garb. If you do fancy a photo opportunity, most desert safari companies have a stock for men and women at the camp they will take you to after your dune bashing. Otherwise, leave it to the locals or you may cause offence.

When packing for everyday wear, do bear in mind that you are in a Muslim country. Bikinis are perfectly acceptable for the beach – although topless sunbathing most definitely is not, under any circumstances – but, unless you are in a hotel complex, do cover up the second you get off the sand. Shorts are completely acceptable for women and men; sleeveless tops will not cause offence. Cropped tops for women are not a great idea for daywear, and excessive cleavage will get you stared at, especially in the malls, where you may even get stopped by the authorities and told to cover up. Of course, the sun's strength also means that covering up is a good idea if you don't want to be burned to a crisp anyway. However, on an evening out, pretty much anything goes – just make sure that you don't end up wandering around outside the club or bar in very skimpy clothing, especially if you have been drinking heavily or are in Old Dubai (that is, the area around Dubai Creek), as you may cause offence. Venture outside of Dubai and rules are stricter – if you travel to Sharjah, you will need to cover your shoulders and legs, and it is best to dress more modestly in the nation's capital, Abu Dhabi, too. During Ramadan, you will also be expected to show more sensitivity – if in doubt, carry a light scarf so you can cover up at a moment's notice should you need to.

Dubai is such a new city that, even in the flashiest restaurants and bars, you won't be asked to don a tie or a jacket before entering. If you want to visit the chicest nightspots, though, you will have to impress the man with the magic clipboard, who usually awards entry to the highest heels, shortest skirt and largest cleavage on display. Dressing up in your best bling and loudest labels here is, quite simply, de rigueur of an evening. As everyone hails taxis to bar-hop as a matter of course, high heels are very much the order of the day. Men should be warned that most upmarket bars and nightclubs will refuse entry if you are wearing open-toed shoes or flip-flops, even if they do come from Gucci. In general, as Dubai is not really a walking city, there's really no need to go big on the sensible shoes. One pair of sneakers should suffice – over and above that, sandals and open-toed shoes will be your best friends.

The weather varies from warm to very hot, so it is extremely unlikely that you will need the sort of coat that would help you cope with a European winter. In the cooler months here (December–February) it is wise to take a light jacket, a cardigan or a wrap. Even in the summer months you will find them useful, as air conditioning can be quite fierce.

Although there are no reliable official figures, anybody here will tell you that the street crime rate is almost nonexistent. So the zip-up handbags and concealed money belts that the unversed might think useful in the Middle East are actually completely pointless. It's not worth testing the theory, but you could pretty much leave your wallet in the middle of the street and come back three hours later to find it still in the same spot.

DRUGS AND MEDICATION

AS MANY VISITORS WILL BE AWARE due to international press coverage, there is an absolutely zero-tolerance policy for narcotics in Dubai. You must also be extremely careful about travelling into the U.A.E. with any sort of prescribed or over-the-counter medication. If in doubt about your specific prescription, please speak to the U.A.E. embassy in your country before travelling, and carry your prescription with you when travelling. Restricted medicines include many commonly prescribed outside of the country, including Prozac, Ritalin, Roaccutane, Zyban and Valium. Unfortunately, even some medication that is available over the counter in many Western countries is banned, including some common cold and flu medicines such as Actifed and Tixylix. Take a look at the government Web site, **dubai.ae,** for a comprehensive list of restricted substances. Contravening these rules could mean four years in prison and/or deportation. It goes without saying that smuggling narcotics through customs is illegal and stupid – there have been several widely-reported cases of harsh jail terms for even microscopic amounts found on passengers or in their luggage. Poppy seeds are also banned, so refrain from that bagel on departure from your home country just in case you're a messy eater. In 2009 1,483 people were arrested in drug-related cases. Other things you should avoid carrying in your case are any sex aids and pornography. There is also a ban on goods of Israeli origin or bearing Israeli trademarks or logos.

FINDING AIRFARE DEALS *and* MAKING RESERVATIONS

THE U.A.E. HAS THREE NATIONAL AIRLINES: **Emirates,** based in Dubai, which also has a budget airline subsidiary, **flydubai; Etihad,** based in Abu Dhabi; and **Air Arabia,** based in Sharjah (although its reach doesn't stretch much beyond the Middle East, Africa and India). If you are very keen to travel from the U.K. on a tight budget and don't mind a two-centre holiday or a long connection, both Air Arabia (**airarabia.com**) and flydubai (**flydubai.com**) will get you as far as Istanbul from Dubai for around £155 return, and London–Istanbul flights from **easyJet** sell from £58 return. This can really only be recommended as an option if you are on a shoestring.

As far as direct flights are concerned, they take six or seven hours from the U.K. **Emirates** (**emirates.com**) is rarely the cheapest, but in terms of service and the quality of the fleet, it is one of the best. It also has the greatest number of daily flights and serves several British regional destinations – Glasgow, Manchester, Newcastle and Birmingham – as well as London Heathrow and London Gatwick. Emirates is also your best bet for flights from Australia, the U.S., Canada or South Africa. Those who travel the route frequently try to ensure that they are flying on the newest planes in the fleet, the A380s. There is more legroom in economy, and the ICE entertainment system lets you select from more than 1,000 films, TV programmes and music channels at your leisure. Even better, if you are really willing to push the boat out, private suites with a fully flat bed and 23-inch TV screen are being introduced, but standard first class is still pretty incredible, and the A380 has shower suites too. Business-class passengers might want to check whether they are paying the elevated fare for a flat bed or a seat, as this is not yet standardised across all aircraft.

Etihad (**etihadairways.com**) often has seat sales and is a great option if you are willing to fly into Abu Dhabi and take one of the Mercedes-Benz transfer buses that leave regularly and take just under two hours to Dubai (or, of course, a taxi, which should cost around AED 300 one way). On the return leg you can check in at the departure point located near the Crowne Plaza Hotel on Sheikh Zayed Road in the centre of Dubai. **Virgin Atlantic** offers one flight a day that leaves from London Heathrow in the evening and returns in the middle of the morning from Dubai (**virgin-atlantic.com**). **British Airways** (**britishairways.com**) and **Royal Brunei** (**bruneiair.com**) also have direct flights from the U.K.

If you are flying from the U.S., fares from **American Airlines** (**aa.com**) can sometimes undercut Emirates. Virgin Atlantic flies from several U.S. cities, but all stop in London en route. **Delta Airlines** offers regular services, connecting in Atlanta (**delta.com**), as does **Continental** (**continental.com**), flying through Washington, D.C. Do bear in mind when booking, though, that this is a long and disorientating flight – if you are planning a stop-off, you may be better to stay overnight, or you could be looking at a travel time of up to 24 hours.

If you don't mind a stop en route, you have a few choices. **KLM** (**klm.com**) connects in Amsterdam; **Qatar Airways** (**qatarairways. com**) connects in Doha; **Gulf Air** (**gulfair.com**) connects in Manama, Bahrain; **Air France** (**airfrance.com**) connects in Paris; **Lufthansa** (**lufthansa.com**) connects in Frankfurt; **Swissair** (**swissair.com**) connects in Zurich; **Oman Air** (**omanair.com**) connects in Muscat; and **Turkish Airlines** (**thy.com**) connects in Istanbul. All of these are bookable online, and without exception you will get a better deal by doing so.

For a quick and easy price comparison, Expedia (**expedia.com**) and Kayak (**kayak.com**) will give you an idea of the cheapest flights available and often have their own exclusive special offers. U.A.E.-based agency DNATA (**dnatatravel.com**) will also offer a selection of flights from different airlines, although you will have to convert the price of the flights back from dirhams.

PACKAGE DEALS

DUBAI CAN BE PACKAGE TOURIST HEAVEN, especially if you are looking for a bargain and are happy to book close to your departure date. Last-minute deals, especially during the summer, often make it more economical to book through an agent or operator, as the hotel and flight bundles offered can be extremely attractive. Even if the total price isn't necessarily cheaper than if you'd combined the elements yourself, often tour operators will have negotiated added value – for example free transfers or half board.

However, it pays to do your homework. We would first advise you to take a look at our Part Three, Hotels (from page 39) and decide where you want to stay. Many hotels – including the Jumeirah Group hotels, The Address hotels and the One&Only Royal Mirage – promise that their best available rates are on offer through their Web sites, so tap in your dates and see what comes up. Then make a search, either on Expedia, as described above, or individual airlines' sites, to work out the cost of your flights. You'll have a rough idea after this whether what you are getting from package tour operators is a bargain or a rip-off. Please bear in mind that budget operators will push hotels that we would not necessarily recommend due to location or room quality, or hotels in neighbouring emirates: Ras Al-Khaimah, Ajman or Fujairah. This is not necessarily a bad thing, but you are not buying a holiday in Dubai, so don't be fooled. You are looking at a minimum two-hour drive from the airport to any of these places, so although transfers will usually be included, you are not going to be able to nip to Dubai for a night out. Of course, there are many considerations above and beyond the price – booking a whole package, especially if you are a family group or honeymooners, can make your life a lot easier and includes flight transfers and even sometimes meals.

Straight from the Agent's Mouth

WE ASKED A DUBAI-BASED PACKAGE TOUR OPERATOR how she manages to get the best deals.

Tour operator packages, purchased directly through the operator or through travel agents, are often cheaper than doing it yourself. The reasons are quite simple. In order to fill their rooms, hotels prefer to sell through an operator who promises not to divulge the rate they get by adding a flight to the package. Therefore any Dubai beach hotel that may charge AED 1,000 per night if you call it directly is able to sell the same room at a rate of AED 300 through a hidden package rate to an operator without damaging the exclusivity of its brand. It's the same with the airlines – the airlines are able to offer operators a hidden fare (called an IT fare), which, when sold with a hotel room, means it doesn't damage the regular market rate the airline offers directly. In Europe, low-cost airlines have meant a change in this model; however, as Dubai is still a long-haul destination, it hasn't been affected by this scenario. Traditional high street tour operators are generally able to buy more beds in Dubai as they have the largest number of clients and so can buy rooms in the city at better rates. In addition, summer rates in Dubai are much cheaper due to the heat. As summer is also a key travel period, it fits nicely that cheaper hotel rooms are available at a time when most people can travel. There should be some excellent offers into Dubai over the next few years, with so many new hotel beds available and the necessity that these beds be filled at a time when the regional travel market traditionally avoids the heat and humidity of the U.A.E.

The holiday arms of the airlines that fly direct to Dubai are where you should look first. Virgin Holidays (**virginholidays.co.uk;** ☎ 0844-557-5825) and British Airways (**britishairways.com**) will let you bundle a hotel and a flight. Emirates Holidays (**emirates-holidays. com**) partners with the largest selection of hotels, from holiday apartments to the Burj Al Arab. Well-priced packages are also available from Travelbag (**travelbag.co.uk**), Opodo (**opodo.co.uk**) and Thomas Cook (**thomascook.com**).

Luxury tour operators also offer many packages in this region. **Seasons in Style** (**seasonsinstyle.com;** ☎ 01244-202002) have exclusive deals for the Armani Hotel, including flights and accommodation, as well as packages for the Desert Palm and The Address Downtown. **Abercrombie & Kent** (**abercrombiekent.com**) will tailor-make private tours for visitors – which can include guided tours of the souks, a stay at the Burj Al Arab and romantic trips out to the desert. **Cox & Kings** (**coxandkings.co.uk**) does a similar thing, with several packages that allow you to explore multiple emirates with your own private guide, staying in five-star luxury. All of the travel agencies and tour operators mentioned above are bonded by the Association of British Travel Agents, offering you security and peace of mind.

DUBAI CALENDAR *of* EVENTS

WHAT FOLLOWS IS A LIST OF ALL OF THE REGULAR EVENTS that appear on the Dubai social calendar, listed month by month. You'll notice a concentration during the winter months (October–April), as many of these events take place outside. For one-off events – concerts, sporting matches and exhibitions – do check on the Web sites listed earlier in this chapter before your visit, as these are many, and they tend to be announced quite close to the actual date. In terms of ticketing, things rarely sell out here, but to get the best prices and decent seats, it's worth booking in advance. The *Time Out* tickets Web site (**timeouttickets.com**) is the best source.

January

DUBAI INTERNATIONAL RACING CARNIVAL Racing events are held every Thursday and Friday until the beginning of March at the state-of-the-art Meydan Racecourse. Admission is free, but unless you want to be in the bear pit or hungry all night, we'd suggest spending the AED 50 on a seat or making an evening of it and dining in one of the hotel's buffet restaurants, from AED 600 per head. Visit **dubai racingclub.com** for details.

DUBAI MARATHON You might not make it round the track faster than three-time winner Haile Gebrselassie, but the course, which takes you around Beach Road and Media City, is a great one, for runners and spectators. There is also a 10-kilometre run and 3-kilometre fun run. To register, visit **dubaimarathon.org.**

DUBAI SHOPPING FESTIVAL Otherwise known as the January sales, the DSF is homage to all things capitalist in a city that was born to shop. It runs from around the middle of January for six weeks, and most malls host special events, grand raffles, concerts by international stars, funfairs and even outdoor desert camps for families. For more information, visit **mydsf.com.**

February

THE DUBAI DESERT CLASSIC Some of the world's top golfers slog it out on the Majlis Course at Emirates Golf Club in this European PGA Tour golf tournament. Go to **dubaidesertclassic.com.**

DUBAI INTERNATIONAL JAZZ FESTIVAL Held in Dubai Media City, this jazz fest usually manages to punch way above its weight in terms of the talent it attracts, with major international names performing in the open air over seven days. There is also a free programme of concerts from up-and-coming stars. Visit **dubaijazzfest.com** for more details.

DUBAI PET SHOW Despite – or perhaps because of – being a distinctly pet-unfriendly city, Dubai hosts an annual Dubai Pet Show at Festival City, which is a big draw for families. OK, it's not exactly Crufts, but who can resist a dog in clothes? Not us. For more information, visit **dubaipetshow.com**.

DUBAI TENNIS CHAMPIONSHIPS Tucked behind Dubai's largest theme pub – the Irish Village – the Dubai Tennis Stadium hosts two weeks of world-class tennis every year in February. This is one event that does sell out, so book your tickets on **barclaysdubaitennischampionships. com** in advance.

March

ART DUBAI One of the biggest international art fairs in the Middle East brings together art from all over the world for a week-long programme of talks, exhibitions and events. Collectors, artists and the general public converge at the Madinat Jumeirah, where more than 70 galleries show work, but viewings and exhibitions are all over the city. Check out **artdubai.ae**.

BASTAKIYA ART FAIR Held alongside Art Dubai, Bastakiya Art Fair features works from up-and-coming local artists, exhibited in the historic Bastakiya district. The doors of all the houses are thrown open, and every spare space is filled with the art of the Arab world. **www.bastakiyaartfair.com**

CARTIER POLO VIP tickets for this gorgeous event at the Dubai Desert Palm hotel are like gold dust, so all but the most determined are likely to go without. However, for the past few years, the hotel has run a parallel event on the other side of the pitch – it's not quite Cartier jewels and A-listers, but for a fixed price you get to watch the matches, chow down on a barbecue and prop up the bar in the sunshine all day. Check **desertpalm.peraquum.com** for the date and more details.

DUBAI FOOTBALL SEVENS International teams compete at this three-day event, a relative newcomer with a carnival atmosphere. **dubaifootball7s.com**

DUBAI WORLD CUP The world's richest horse race is the king of spectacles in a city that is not short of such things. People fly from all over the world to sit trackside at the Meydan Racecourse in their finery (do not even consider dressing down), sip Champagne in the Bubble Lounge and – if we're honest – all but ignore the horses. This giant trackside party is topped off with a concert from a big-name star. Visit **dubaiworldcup.com** for tickets and hospitality packages.

EMIRATES LITERARY FESTIVAL A stellar line-up of more than 80 authors is always at this world-class literary event. The packed four-day programme includes panel discussions, readings, workshops, children's events and storytelling workshops. There is also a Fringe Festival with a programme of free events. Visit **eaifl.com** to see the programme and book tickets.

PERRIER CHILL OUT FESTIVAL This annual event is prone to changing venue but attracts great international bands and DJs with a chilled-out vibe over a weekend. Check *Time Out* for details (**timeoutdubai.com**).

TASTE OF DUBAI The Media City amphitheatre hosts this foodie event, which runs over four days. Dubai's best restaurants and bars set up stalls around relaxed outdoor seating and cook samplers of their signature dishes for a knock-down price.

April

GULF FILM FESTIVAL This festival celebrates Arabic and international films – even better, the programme of screenings and events is open to the public. It's especially interesting if you're keen to see Emirati-made films. **gulffilmfest.com**

May

DHOW RACING The Dubai International Marine Club hosts a series of traditional dhow boat races just off the coast. **dimc.ae**

June

DUBAI SUMMER SURPRISES Otherwise known as the summer sales, it usually starts around the first week of June and ends mid-August. All of the malls put on a special programme of events and giveaways, and Modesh – the very odd, yellow, springlike cartoon character that is the event's official mascot – pops up around the city. The last week or so of the sale, prices are usually slashed, sometimes dropping to 20% of the original ticket price. Visit **mydsf.ae**.

August

HOPFEST The Irish Village pub hosts an annual beer festival for three days in August in a large, air-conditioned marquee on the lawn, with cask ales, live music and food every night. **irishvillage.ae**

October

GITEX The Middle East's premier technology show takes over the Dubai International Exhibition and Convention Centre. **gitex.com**

November

DUBAI RUGBY SEVENS It feels as if the whole city descends on this stadium for three days to cheer on the country's team – festivities go on well past the end of play, with bands, beer tents and dancing. **dubairugby7s.com**

December

DUBAI INTERNATIONAL FILM FESTIVAL Such is the growing reputation of this festival that it has attracted A-listers such as Christina Ricci and Gerard Butler. The general public are able to buy tickets for many of the screenings. **dubaifilmfest.com**

U.A.E. NATIONAL DAY Take a seat at any cafe on Jumeirah Beach Road on 2 December and watch the procession of proud Emiratis with pimped-up cars fly the flag – one giant Hummer makes an appearance every year, entirely covered in Swarovski crystals in the U.A.E. colours.

PART THREE

HOTELS

THIS CITY IS DEFINITELY NOT SHORT OF HOTELS. In typical Dubai style, it is impossible to give you an accurate count of the number of rooms on offer across the emirate, as hotels open at the rate of one monolith a month. But to give you some idea of the scale, there were 47,000 hotel rooms in 2008, with plans to triple that to 141,000 rooms by 2015. In 2010 alone, more than 20,000 additional rooms, ranging from iconic to airport, five-star to frills-free, were expected to throw open their doors.

Despite the global recession, many major hotels have ploughed on with their plans, so 2010–2012 will be bumper years for new launches. The ring around the Palm Jumeirah will see the opening of the **Rixos, Essque Hotel & Spa, The Royal Amwaj, The Fairmont, The Oceana** and **The Taj Exotica.** The Dubai International Financial Centre (DIFC) will be home to a brand-new **Ritz-Carlton,** only the second hotel to open in the middle of this business district. Because Dubai is already a haven for label lovers, top catwalk designers were quick to spot the potential of having their brands attached to hotels. The **Armani Hotel & Residences,** where everything from the carpets to the candles was designed by the maestro, opened at the bottom of the Burj Khalifa in 2010. The Gucci group has announced that it has plans to open an 87-suite hotel in Dubai's Media City in 2011, which should provide some fairly stiff competition for the **Palazzo Versace,** which is already under construction.

Sadly, news of the refurbishment of the **QE2,** which was to be a luxurious floating hotel just off the Palm Jumeirah, is hard to come by. Although the assumption is that, after spending £65 million (about US $102.4 million) buying the behemoth and sailing it to Dubai, the owners will eventually start work, it currently sits unoccupied in Port Rashid. There has also been little news of the **W Hotel** that was to open in Festival City, the hoardings quietly taken down when nobody was looking. New budget hotels are not thin on the ground either, with **easyHotel** and **Courtyard by Marriott** opening new ventures. At press time, no fixed dates were available for any of these, but the canny traveller can keep an eye on announcements in the trade magazine *Hotelier Middle East* (**hoteliermiddleeast.com**). This runs up-to-date news on soft launches, when huge discounts on rack rates are often available, as long as you are willing to put up with a few teething troubles.

Of course, the cynical might doubt whether there will be enough people to fill all these four-posters, but ye of little faith just need to look at the current occupancy rates. During the first four months of 2010, Dubai witnessed occupancy of 77.4% across the board. The most popular tourist hotels were fully booked. Even the summer, with its scorching temperatures, still attracts visitors in droves, with discount hotel rates and packages.

TYPES *of* LODGING

THERE REALLY IS SOMETHING FOR EVERY TASTE, pocket and lifestyle in Dubai – but we would characterise the below as the principal types of accommodation. In this chapter, we have only included hotels in which we would actually want to stay – believe us, we have seen some bedbug-infested, prostitute-ridden fleapits. None of those appears here – if you do decide to go off-piste, we would strongly suggest that you take the hotel's own descriptions with a pinch (or maybe even an entire cellar) of salt.

DUBAI ICONS

BIG, BRASH AND BLOODY EXPENSIVE are probably the four words that best describe Dubai's superhotels. Dubai doesn't do museums, opera houses, art galleries or theatres – the drive to attract tourism is, perhaps sensibly, focused around the places that a visitor sees the most: their lodgings. Of course, any hotel that takes pride of place on a city's car number plates, as the **Burj Al Arab** used to, is in a class of its own. This 'seven-star' (the classification was self-awarded) sail-shaped hotel is still the most expensive across the board (although suites elsewhere in the city top its highest room rate) and functions as a tourist attraction in its own right. But since it opened, there has been an arms race to go one better. Hence the **Kempinski Hotel Mall of the Emirates** is attached to a real-snow indoor ski slope; the **Atlantis** has its own shark-filled mega-aquarium and more celebrity chefs than you could shake a Michelin star at; the **Jumeirah Beach Hotel** offers free access to Wild Wadi waterpark; and the hotels of the **Madinat Jumeirah** have their own souk and complex of waterways. And, of course, we can't forget the Armani Hotel & Residences, which opened on the bottom floors of the Burj Khalifa in April 2010. If you want a true Dubai experience, and you are willing to pay for it, then these should be your first choice.

THE BEACH HOTEL

YEAR-ROUND SUN AND WARM WATER mean that the beaches here are a massive draw, and if that's what you are after, then proximity to them should be top of your list. These places have private stretches of sand, umbrellas, loungers, towels and waiters on hand to serve you drinks, food and chilled hand towels. They also offer a kids' club, a water sports centre and a diving centre. Of course, the raft of new hotels opening on the Palm Jumeirah in 2010–2012 will almost double the number of beach hotels in Dubai, but currently the only ones accepting guests there are the Atlantis, Kempinski and One&Only. The rest are situated along Jumeirah, starting with **Dubai Marine Resort,** then running to the **Jumeirah Beach Hotel, Madinat Jumeirah, One&Only Royal Mirage, The Westin, Grosvenor House, Le Royal Méridien Beach Resort & Spa, Ritz-Carlton** and **Mövenpick.** If you are unwilling or unable to pay the premium for the seaside location, many of these hotels offer a day rate to use their facilities. Others that don't have their own beach access make their swimming pools and outdoor areas as appealing as possible – from **The Address Downtown**'s three-tier infinity pool to the **Park Hyatt**'s palm-shaded, whirlpool-filled dream.

THE NOUVEAU FIVE-STAR

BRIGHT COLOURS AND BLING are overused in accommodations here, but a new breed of low-key luxury hotels has sprung up in Dubai in the past few years. Instead of the gold, chandeliers and marble, you can now find leather walls, modern art and muted soft furnishings. Spearheading this trend is **The Address Hotels + Resorts** group, with its 63-floor hotel in Downtown, attached to the Dubai Mall, and **The Palace,** designed in a new-Arabia style. **The Address Dubai Marina** has a similarly chic aesthetic. The low-rise, whitewashed Park Hyatt is a very feminine version of minimalist.

THE BUSINESS HOTEL

THIS IS REALLY DEPENDENT on what sort of business you will be doing in Dubai. For some, proximity to the airport is a major bonus, in which case many hotels are nearby, including the Park Hyatt, **Hilton Dubai Creek, Novotel Deira City Centre, InterContinental** and **Crowne Plaza Festival City.** If your business is media-related, plenty of hotels are situated in Media City – our favourite is the **Media One,** which is as close as Dubai gets to trendy London Soho styling. But as Dubai Marina is also very close by, you have your pick of places to lay your head too. Other than that, the biggest concentration of hotels aimed at business travellers is at the Dubai Creek end of the Sheikh Zayed Road, predictably near the Dubai International Financial Centre. These are the **Dusit Thani, The Fairmont, The Monarch, The Shangri-La** and the **Jumeirah Emirates Towers.** In addition to these, most of the larger hotels, especially the five- and four-stars, have extensive conference facilities – ranging from the Atlantis's epic ballrooms to the Armani Hotel & Residences' stand-alone structure. These amenities are listed under each individual hotel. A business centre is also standard in most hotels three-star and above, offering mobile phone rental, fax and scanning facilities, secretarial services, small libraries and offices and meeting rooms. These are usually charged for by usage. In addition, many also have executive clubs (where this is available, we have listed it under the individual hotel) that offer larger rooms on designated floors, and many have a communal lounge with a quiet space to work, as well as free food, soft drinks and cocktails and free local calls. If you are planning on holding meetings in your suite, do check that it is possible to block off the living room from the bedroom – the Park Hyatt and Jumeirah Emirates Towers are both particularly good for this. One last thing to check is whether free Internet or Wi-Fi is offered. Although we are of the opinion that every hotel should provide this free of charge, many hotels in Dubai don't (especially the more tourist-oriented places), levying a fairly hefty rate for 24 hours of Internet.

THREE- AND FOUR-STAR

THE STANDARD WE FOUND in four-star hotels is good across the board – sometimes even indistinguishable from five-stars. If there is a difference, it is that the locations tend not to be quite as good – for example, to get to the Dubai Mall or the Burj Khalifa from **Al Manzil** and the **Qamardeen Hotel,** both of which are brand-new, beautiful and have great facilities, you have to cross the road. Rooms may also be slightly smaller. There are often swimming pools, spas, kids' clubs and business centres, and staff are often well trained. In terms of three-stars, there is a much bigger variance – the best tend to be the international chains such as **Traders** and the **Golden Tulip.**

BOUTIQUE HOTELS AND BED-AND-BREAKFASTS

SMALL DOES NOT OFTEN MEAN BEAUTIFUL when talking about Dubai bolt-holes, but a very few do boutique well. The most luxurious of these is the **Desert Palm,** with its individual pool villas and rooms with views over the neighbouring private polo field. This is the only licensed boutique hotel. Bastakiya, the art and culture district, is home to the two most characterful bed-and-breakfasts of the lot – the **Orient Guest House** and the **XVA Art Hotel.**

THE (VERY) BUDGET HOTEL

CHOOSING SUPER-CHEAP ACCOMMODATIONS in Dubai is a very different ball game to doing the same thing in Europe. Indeed, you'll find a wide selection of places at the lower end of the price range, but very few that are charming, quirky or authentic. The truth is that if you want to pay lower prices, you will have to settle for a much, much lower quality. And by that we don't just mean the neighbourhood is less salubrious. You risk dirty rooms stinking of cigarettes, the presence of prostitutes, music playing until the wee hours in nearby nightclubs and drunk and disorderly guests. We've explored the two-star hotels around Dubai and found that if you are going low, it's much better to stick with chains such as **Ibis** than independents.

The **ANATOMY** of a **DUBAI HOTEL**

THE ROOMS

UNLIKE THOSE IN MANY MAJOR CITIES, even the smallest Dubai hotel room is remarkably large. OK, well that's not quite true – some are very small even by London or New York standards, such as the two-star Ibis's 19 square metres (204.5 square feet) or **Gold Swiss-Belhotel**'s 20. But as a rule, a standard room hovers around the roomy 35–45 square metre (376.7–484.4 square feet) mark. Many, especially those aimed at families, have two decent-size double beds definitely large enough to accommodate two adults and two children, or three adults. Very few have their own kitchens – the **Beach Hotel Apartment** and the Kempinski Hotel Mall of the Emirates are the notable exceptions to this – although most have a minibar (sometimes alcohol-free). Almost all of the five-stars we saw have walk-in showers, a large bath and a double sink, but at the lower price points, this can vary. Many have adopted the sliding bathroom panel, which means you can open up the bathroom to the main bedroom area to watch TV. All rooms we saw do have a TV, and most have a hairdryer and kettle. At the higher end, there is a trend towards installing upmarket coffee makers so that you can make your own espresso in the morning.

Whether your room has a balcony or not is pot luck – some very expensive hotels don't have them; some cheaper ones do – and some properties only have them attached to a small percentage of the rooms. If it is important to you, ask. Bear in mind, though, that during the summer, they will be all but useless for everything apart from drying your bikini. The same applies to views – even some of the beach hotels have not been designed with your ocular pleasure in mind, with some of their rooms looking out over the main road or a scrubby car park instead of the ocean. Again, if it is important to you, make it known. Noise pollution has become less of a problem as the rate of construction has slowed in Dubai – many workers used to be on-site all night, with cranes whirring and delivery lorries beeping well into the wee hours. Now they keep far more civilized hours.

There is also another sort of accommodation proposition entirely. Just as the city excels in showpiece hotels, so it also prides itself on its singular suites. All of the luxury hotels, and even some of the cheaper ones, have one- and two-bed suites, and often a royal or presidential one too. These can run well into the hundreds of square metres. But a few truly breathtaking mega-suites are also dotted around. The Monarch has one that boasts its own roof terrace, cinema and pool; the Armani Hotel & Residences' best suite, where the designer stays himself when he is in town, has a full-service bar and a library, not to mention stunning views of the World Islands. The amazing 'underwater' suites are actually not the most expensive at the Atlantis – that honour goes to the Bridge Suite, which is in fact the most expensive in the world. Stay at one of the Kempinski Hotel Mall of the Emirates' alpine-influenced ski chalets and you have direct views out over the real-snow slopes of Ski Dubai.

AMENITIES

THESE VARY WILDLY FROM HOTEL TO HOTEL. Most, but not all, have at least one indoor or outdoor swimming pool and a gym. Some also have beach access, with water sports or diving centres. Many of the four- and five-stars have some sort of children's club, or at the least a baby listening or nanny service. Pampering is such a common pastime here that even some of the cheaper hotels have their own day spas, where you can get a bargain massage or manicure. This goes all the way up the scale to the Madinat Jumeirah's Talise Spa, which is housed in its own separate building, with gym, whirlpool and swimming pool. One of the most unexpected, but infinitely useful, perks that lots of the hotels offer is a complimentary shuttle bus to beaches, malls and attractions. Where this is available, we have listed the destinations.

FOOD AND DRINK

NEARLY ALL OF THE HOTELS WE HAVE INCLUDED have their own coffee shop, or at the very least room service so you can eat in your room, should you wish. Where there is only one restaurant, it will usually serve an international mix, from Arabic to Indian to Italian, by way of bog standard sandwiches and burgers. Bars are also in most of the hotels we have covered, but at the lower end of the scale, they might not be somewhere you'd be happy to sip a pint. Most of these are open until 3 a.m. Of course, some hotels have far more on offer – with dining options running well into double figures – and they are, due to the alcohol licensing laws, where you will find the best upscale cooking in the city, some of it by Michelin-starred chefs. We have quoted the rack rates for each of our chosen hotels, most of which do not include any extras, but this is a very rough guide, as deals and specials are always going on – many hotels will throw in breakfast or even half board. This will usually give you the right to eat in the buffet restaurants in the morning and evening and will include soft drinks but not alcohol. We were told by one disgruntled food and beverage manager of a large hotel that half-board guests were taking advantage of the breakfast spread to avoid pricey lunches to such an extent that they had to start cutting up the apples, bananas and oranges, as so many were being sneaked into beach bags.

SERVICE

WHAT CAN WE SAY? This is as unpredictable as a British summer. Despite being one of the Middle East's most popular tourist destinations, Dubai still hasn't quite got this right across the board. As you might expect, expensive hotels such as the Armani are most likely to get it correct – in fact, they offer each guest their own lifestyle concierge, who will contact you before arrival and be on hand throughout your stay. The Jumeirah Group also has a high standard of service. As for the rest, well, sometimes it will be amazing, and sometimes you will be left exasperated. The usual travel rule of thumb – that smaller hotels give better service – doesn't really apply, as often the staff are under-trained and have only a basic grasp of English. All we can say is that if you are unhappy, do make your feelings known. We have found the best tactic – whether you are unhappy with the cleanliness or facilities in your room or the attitude of the staff – is to go directly to management. At the lower level, you may well be shrugged off or simply ignored.

CLUB CLASS

ONE FEATURE THAT WE CAME ACROSS REPEATEDLY on visiting Dubai's hotels is the presence of a special club, which, for a higher rate, offers guests extra amenities. Whether this is worth paying extra will take some calculation on your part. Club rooms are usually aimed at business travellers, although they do exist for holidaymakers too, most notably at the Jumeirah Group hotels and the Atlantis. What is on offer ranges from place to place, but most give a larger room, free snacks (which actually resemble full meals a lot of the time – with sandwiches, a cheese board and often hot food too) and soft drinks throughout the day, often with a cocktail hour in the evening. There is also usually a private lounge. Some also offer late checkout and complimentary airport transfers. Where these exist, they have been listed.

RATES, RULES *and* RECOMMENDATIONS

WE HAVE DISCUSSED AIRFARE AND HOTEL PACKAGES in detail on page 33, but bear in mind a few things if you are going it alone and booking rooms separately. The rack rates quoted here are the top end of what you will pay – at any one time, every hotel in Dubai will have some sort of offer, whether that is one free night when you buy a bundle, discounted half board or a complimentary upgrade. We have

NOTABLE DUBAI LODGING

Best for Breakfast

The Fairmont Dubai
The Park Hyatt

Best for Restaurants

Atlantis
Jumeirah Emirates Towers
Mina A'Salam
The Monarch
One&Only Royal Mirage
Al Qasr Hotel

Executive Clubs

The Address Downtown Dubai
Atlantis
Burj Al Arab
Dusit Thani Dubai
Jumeirah Beach Hotel
Jumeirah Emirates Towers
Mina A'Salam
Al Qasr Hotel
Traders Hotel Deira

Great for Beaches

Atlantis
Burj Al Arab
Dar Al Masyaf
Jumeirah Beach Hotel
Mina A'Salam
One&Only Royal Mirage
Al Qasr Hotel

Great for Business

Dusit Thani Dubai
The Fairmont Dubai
Jumeirah Emirates Towers
Media One
Qamardeen Hotel

Great for Character

Orient Guest House
XVA Art Hotel

Great for Families

Atlantis
Mina A'Salam
One&Only Royal Mirage
The Palace
Al Qasr Hotel

Great for Groups

Dar Al Masyaf

Great for Romance

Burj Al Arab
Jumeirah Bab Al Shams Desert
    Resort
One&Only Royal Mirage
The Park Hyatt

Trendy Bars and Lounges

The Address Downtown Dubai
Grosvenor House
The Monarch

been told by representatives of the large hotel chains that by far the best rate – if you are not planning to book a package – is to be found online. Rates vary hugely, from around AED 350 per night to more than AED 10,000, but all are slapped with a 20% tax and municipality charges. Do ascertain whether this is included in the given rate, as it can significantly bump up the total. Other rules of thumb are to book as far in advance as possible and always book online – hotels will usually have special Internet-only rates. If you are a family of four, you can save by all staying in one room – this is possible in many places that either have two double beds or can put extras in the rooms. With Dubai being such a tourist destination, prices obviously shoot up during Christmas holidays. Many hotels have adopted a bookings system that pushes prices up as more rooms get booked up – and during peak season, many hotels are close to fully booked.

By far the cheapest rates you will find advertised are for the summer months, where prices can be slashed by up to 75% and you may be offered extras including spa treatments and food.

HOTEL PROFILES

STAR RATING The star rating here refers to the Dubai Department of Tourism and Commerce rating. For a more comprehensive overview of our thoughts on the hotel, we recommend that you read the full review. All of the hotels we have included here get our recommendation – if we wouldn't stay in it, we wouldn't tell you to.

COST We have given the quoted rack rate for a standard room, not including the 20% taxes and municipality charges. The amount listed is for the room only, unless otherwise noted.

The Address Downtown Dubai ★ ★ ★ ★ ★
**Emaar Boulevard, Downtown, PO Box 123234; ☎ 04-436-8888;
{vfl 04-436-8888; theaddress.com**

Cost AED 1,199 **Location** Downtown **Number of rooms** 171 rooms, plus 26 suites **Room sq m** 55–200 **Conference facilities** Yes **Pool/sauna** Yes **Beach access** No **Exercise facilities** Yes **Spa** Yes **Parking/valet** Yes **Licensed bar** Yes **On-site dining** Chinese, International, coffee shop, shisha terrace **Extra amenities** Hairdryer, Wi-Fi, iPod dock, free local calls **Business amenities** Executive Club lounge, 24-hour business centre, full-size desk in all rooms **Shuttle buses** None **Wheelchair facilities** Yes

IT IS A TESTAMENT TO THE INSANE HEIGHT of the Burj Khalifa that its 63-floor, neon-lit neighbour looks positively stumpy in comparison; but if you want a killer view of the world's tallest building, this is the right hotel (just make sure you specify that's what you want when booking). It's right next to the Dubai Mall with its aquarium, cinema and ice rink, and Souk Al Bahar, which is packed with bars and restaurants, so if you aren't bothered about the beach, you could happily spend an entire short break here.

Opened in late 2008, it is split into hotel rooms and residences, with the former only occupying the 7th–12th floors. This means two things: first, a constant stock of resident bachelors will be prowling Neos, the top-floor Champagne bar, willing to show you their in-room amenities (if you know what we mean), and second, that the enormous five-tiered infinity pool that overlooks the Dubai Fountain can get quite packed at the weekend. This is in part made up for by the uniformed staff, who are always hovering by your elbow to offer you a cold towel and a slice of watermelon. Non-residents are welcome too, for a day rate of AED 300.

continued on page 51

Where to Stay in Deira & Bur Dubai

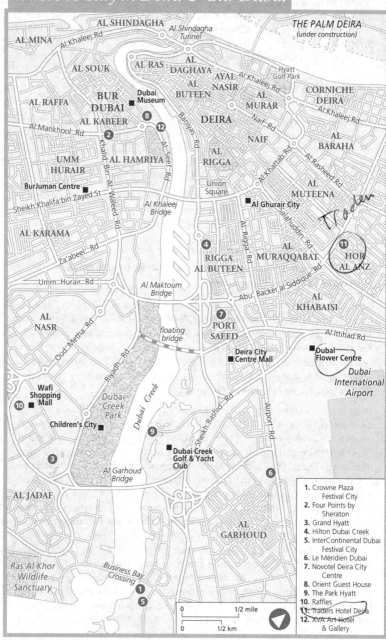

1. Crowne Plaza
   Festival City
2. Four Points by
   Sheraton
3. Grand Hyatt
4. Hilton Dubai Creek
5. InterContinental Dubai
   Festival City
6. Le Méridien Dubai
7. Novotel Deira City
   Centre
8. Orient Guest House
9. The Park Hyatt
10. Raffles
11. Traders Hotel Deira
12. XVA Art Hotel
    & Gallery

| 0 | 1/2 mile |
| 0 | 1/2 km |

Where to Stay in Jumeirah

1. The Address Dubai Marina
2. The Address Montgomerie
3. Atlantis, The Palm
4. Beach Hotel Apartment
5. Burj Al Arab
6. Dar Al Masyaf
7. Dubai Marine Beach Resort & Spa
8. Golden Tulip Suites
9. Gold Swiss-Belhotel
10. Grandeur Hotel
11. Grosvenor House
12. Ibis Mall of the Emirates
13. Jumeirah Beach Hotel
14. Kempinski Hotel Mall of the Emirates
15. Kempinski Hotel & Residences Palm Jumeirah
16. Al Manzil Hotel
17. Media One
18. Mina A'Salam
19. Mövenpick Jumeirah Beach
20. One&Only The Palm
21. One&Only Royal Mirage
22. Qamardeen Hotel
23. Al Qasr Hotel
24. Le Royal Méridien Beach Resort & Spa
25. Sofitel Jumeirah Beach Residence
26. Suite Novotel Mall of the Emirates
27. Villa Rotana
28. The Westin Mina Seyahi

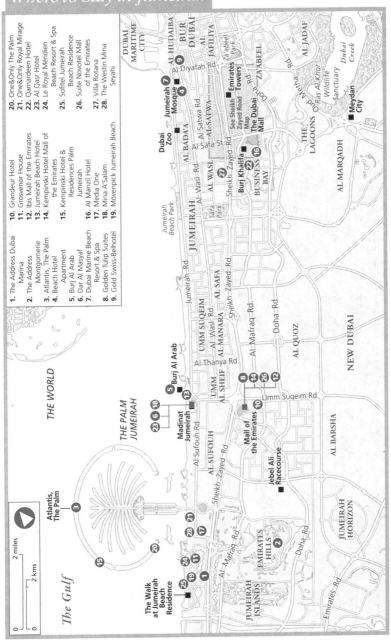

Where to Stay on Sheikh Zayed Road

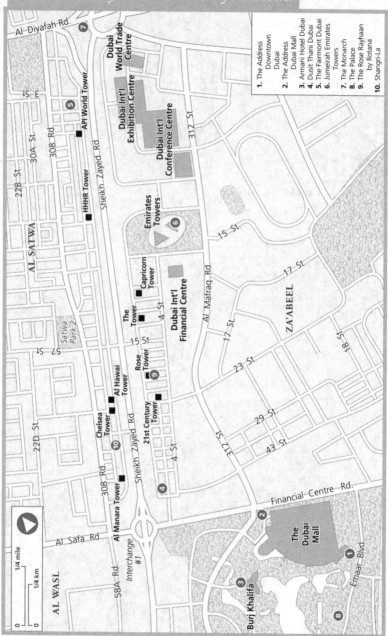

1. The Address Downtown Dubai
2. The Address Dubai Mall
3. Armani Hotel Dubai
4. Dusit Thani Dubai
5. The Fairmont Dubai
6. Jumeirah Emirates Towers
7. The Monarch
8. The Palace
9. The Rose Rayhaan by Rotana
10. Shangri-La

continued from page 47

Apart from Neos, all of the restaurants and bars radiate out from the vast lobby. Hukama consistently wins awards for its modern Chinese cuisine; Fazaris gives good breakfast and handles most cuisines more than competently at lunch and dinner (they do a different all-you-can-eat buffet, from sushi to Indian, most nights). The poolside watering hole Calabar is a buzzing nightspot, but the staff can be a bit snotty – they have a habit of kicking you off empty tables 'in case a VIP comes' – and the drinks are a tad overpriced.

Each room and suite is individually decorated in the brand's signature Arabic chic, with cutwork screens, richly-coloured furnishings and flashy flat-panel TVs. If you really want to splash out, the four spa suites on the 12th floor are almost laughably huge, with – you guessed it – a whirlpool tub and assorted loungers and daybeds on the terrace overlooking the Burj Khalifa.

Upgrade to an Executive Club room and you will get a VIP welcome service when you step off the plane, private limousine airport transfers, a complete 24-hour stay whatever time you check in and access to a private lounge with its own terrace.

The Address Dubai Mall ★ ★ ★ ★ ★

Dubai Mall, Downtown, PO Box 31166; ☎ 04-438-8888;
{vfl 04-436-8880; theaddress.com

Cost AED 950 **Location** Downtown **Number of rooms** 192 rooms, plus 53 suites **Room sq m** 38–331 **Conference facilities** Yes **Pool/sauna** Yes **Beach access** No **Exercise facilities** Yes **Spa** Yes **Parking/valet** Yes **Licensed bar** Yes **On-site dining** Arabic, International, fine dining, tea room, poolside grill, patisserie **Extra amenities** iPod docking station, tea/coffee facilities, Wi-Fi **Business amenities** Business centre, library **Shuttle buses** None **Wheelchair facilities** Yes

THE CLIENTELE IS NOTICEABLY Gulf Cooperation Council–heavy, especially in summer when many families stop off on their way to Europe. There is also quite a large besuited contingent, as the hotel has very impressive state-of-the-art conference facilities and a huge business centre on the first floor.

An entrance leads directly into the perfume department of Bloomingdale's, which means that it's not only a shopper's paradise but also that it has access to the literally hundreds of cafes, restaurants and bars in The Dubai Mall and also just across the bridge in Souk Al Bahar. This is probably just as well, as only a few dining options are here – Ember, an expensive fine dining restaurant; Cabana, the poolside grill and pizza joint; and Na3Na3, the Arabic all-day dining restaurant where breakfast is served (those with a sweet tooth will approve the selection – there is always a groaning table full of pre-midday cake).

The rooms are well appointed and large, many have floor-to-ceiling windows next to the bath and all have balconies. The infinity pool is large and benefits from being surrounded by cabanas, but sun worshippers

How the Hotels Compare in Dubai

HOTEL	OVERALL RATING	COST RATING	VALUE
Burj Al Arab	★★★★★★★	AED 10,000	½
Sofitel Jumeirah Beach Residence	★★★★★	AED 750	★★★
The Address Dubai Marina	★★★★★	AED 799	★★★
Hilton Dubai Creek	★★★★★	AED 850	★★★
Mövenpick Jumeirah Beach	★★★★★	AED 900	★★★
Le Royal Méridien Beach Resort & Spa	★★★★★	AED 900	★★★
The Address Dubai Mall	★★★★★	AED 950	★★½
Crowne Plaza Festival City	★★★★★	AED 950	★★½
Grosvenor House	★★★★★	AED 950	★★½
InterContinental Dubai Festival City	★★★★★	AED 950	★★½
The Palace	★★★★★	AED 1,000	★★½
Grand Hyatt	★★★★★	AED 1,050	★★½
The Address Downtown Dubai	★★★★★	AED 1,199	★★
The Fairmont Dubai	★★★★★	AED 1,199	★★
Kempinski Hotel Mall of the Emirates	★★★★★	AED 1,200	★★
Shangri-La	★★★★★	AED 1,200	★★
Jumeirah Emirates Towers	★★★★★	AED 1,300	★★
Dubai Marine Beach Resort & Spa	★★★★★	AED 1,380	★★
Raffles	★★★★★	AED 1,500	★★
Le Méridien Dubai	★★★★★	AED 1,600	★½
The Westin Mina Seyahi	★★★★★	AED 1,600	★½
The Park Hyatt	★★★★★	AED 1,675	★½
Armani Hotel Dubai	★★★★★	AED 1,700	★½
The Address Montgomerie Dubai	★★★★★	AED 1,750	★½
One&Only Royal Mirage	★★★★★	AED 1,800	★½
Dusit Thani Dubai	★★★★★	AED 2,000	★
Desert Palm	★★★★★	AED 2,450	★

HOTEL	OVERALL RATING	COST RATING	
Jumeirah Bab Al Shams Desert Resort	★★★★★	AED 2,520	
The Monarch	★★★★★	AED 2,899	
Atlantis, The Palm	★★★★★	AED 3,100	★
Al Maha Desert Resort and Spa	★★★★★	AED 3,200	★
Jumeirah Beach Hotel	★★★★★	AED 3,200	★
One&Only The Palm	★★★★★	AED 3,490	★
Mina A'Salam	★★★★★	AED 3,500	★
Al Qasr Hotel	★★★★★	AED 3,700	★
Dar Al Masyaf	★★★★★	AED 3,900	½
Kempinski Hotel & Residences Palm Jumeirah	★★★★★	AED 4,500	½
The Hatta Fort Hotel	★★★★	AED 595	★★★
Novotel Deira City Centre	★★★★	AED 665	★★½
Golden Tulip Suites	★★★★	AED 1,350	★
Gold Swiss-Belhotel	★★★★	AED 1,450	★
Villa Rotana	★★★★	AED 1,450	★
The Rose Rayhaan by Rotana	★★★★	AED 1,600	★
Media One	★★★★	AED 1,750	★
Four Points by Sheraton	★★★★	AED 1,800	★
Traders Hotel Deira	★★★★	AED 1,940	★
Qamardeen Hotel	★★★★	AED 2,150	★
Al Manzil Hotel	★★★★	AED 2,150	★
Suite Novotel Mall of the Emirates	★★★	AED 450	★★
Orient Guest House	★★★	AED 500	★★
Grandeur Hotel	★★★	AED 850	★
XVA Art Hotel & Gallery	★★★	AED 900	★
Beach Hotel Apartment	★★★	AED 960	★
Ibis Mall of the Emirates	★★	AED 320	★

Handwritten annotations near "Traders Hotel Deira": 272.2 / 544.5 (circled)

...be a bit miffed that the sun disappears behind the hotel from 2 p.m. ...wards. The gym is large and runs group classes, and the spa, which has a *rasul* room and ice cave, is a wonderfully-tranquil space with very well-trained therapists (see page 266).

It's pretty reasonably priced for what you get too, especially as you receive a 25% discount on the rack rate when you book more than 14 days in advance, common with all the Address hotels.

The Address Dubai Marina ★★★★★

Dubai Marina, PO Box 32923; ☎ 04-436-7777; {∨fl 04-436-7788; theaddress.com

---

Cost AED 799 **Location** The Marina **Number of rooms** 142 rooms, plus 58 suites **Room sq m** 42–271 **Conference facilities** Yes **Pool/sauna** Yes **Beach access** No **Exercise facilities** Yes **Spa** Yes **Parking/valet** Yes **Licensed bar** Yes **On-site dining** French, International, coffee shop **Extra amenities** Pillow menu, iPod docking station, Wi-Fi, tea/coffee facilities **Business amenities** Desk in all rooms, business centre **Shuttle buses** To Dubai Mall **Wheelchair facilities** Yes

WE CAN'T HELP BUT FEEL THAT THE LOCATION of this hotel misses the point of being in the Dubai Marina. Sure, you get great views of the yachts below, but you are a good 15-minute walk from the sea, although the large, infinity-edge pool on the fourth floor goes some way to make up for it. If you don't mind a stroll, though, you have the open beach at Jumeirah Beach Residence and the cafes and shops of The Walk quite nearby.

The hotel is also attached to the Marina Mall, which is a more manageable size than most of Dubai's mega-temples to consumerism and has an edited selection of fashion and lifestyle stores and a small selection of cafes. The hotel itself has an upscale French restaurant, Rive Gauche, which has received consistently good reviews; Mazina, which has live cooking stations where you can eat your way around the world; a poolside cafe that turns into a DJ bar at night; and Blends – a moodily-lit bar with a cigar room.

The guest rooms are the cream and cappuccino colours that the group has made its trademark, with floor-to-ceiling feature windows. The hotel has very good conference facilities, with a ballroom that can accommodate 1,000 people, and 15 meeting rooms.

The Address Montgomerie Dubai ★★★★★

Emirates Hills, PO Box 36700; ☎ 04-390-5600; {∨fl 04-360-8981; theaddress.com

---

Cost AED 1,750 **Location** Emirates Hills **Number of rooms** 18 rooms, plus 3 suites **Room sq m** 44–125 **Conference facilities** Yes **Pool/sauna** Yes **Beach access** No **Exercise facilities** Yes **Spa** Yes **Parking/valet** Yes **Licensed bar** Yes **On-site dining** Pub/restaurant, fine dining and grill, cigar bar **Extra amenities** Personalised butler service, coffee machine, minibar, 24-hour room service, in-house movie and music library, safe boxes, tea/coffee facilities, hairdryer, iron/ ironing board, airport transfers, same-day dry-cleaning, pressing and laundry services, 18-hole champion golf course **Business amenities** Business centre, complimentary high-speed Internet **Shuttle buses** To Mall of the Emirates, Ibn Battuta Mall, Jumeirah Beach **Wheelchair facilities** Yes

VISITING THE ADDRESS MONTGOMERIE DUBAI is like entering a parallel universe. It is set in the middle of Emirates Hills, a scarily Stepford Wives 'living' community, sort of in the middle of nowhere. You drive and you drive through non-signposted avenues of massive villas in various stages of construction until you reach large, unmarked gates. And then you realise you are there.

The hotel looks lovely from the outside, but the lobby is dull and unwelcoming, and the staff have an indifference we haven't noticed in other hotels. The Angsana Spa is lovely in a peaceful, Zen-like way, with treatments and massages to suit even the most stressed-out guest.

Bedrooms are extremely comfortable, with dark brown being the dominant colour throughout, accented with splashes of red and an abundance of leather. There are masculine, and practical, king-size beds, as well as plenty of pillows, large flat-panel TVs, comfortable leather chairs, large bathrooms with a bathtub and walk-in shower and an abundance of toiletries. The rooms either overlook the courtyard or the golf course, for which you pay more. There are also three suites.

Three restaurants are located in the hotel: The Academy, a sports-themed eatery and lounge area, serving pub grub and showing all major international sporting events; Bunkers Restaurant, which is accessible directly off the golf course overlooking the 18th hole; and the main restaurant in the hotel, Nineteen, a fine-dining venue with an open kitchen, a grill menu, live music and a wine list with 250-plus vintages.

Monty Cristo's Cigar Lounge is a throwback to an era when men got up from the table after dinner to enjoy a drink and a cigar with the boys and left the little ladies to sit and talk. There is a lovely pool, a decent gym and of course a stunning golf course – AED 595 for guests, AED 795 for non-guests. If you are coming to Dubai to play golf, this is a great hotel.

Armani Hotel Dubai ★ ★ ★ ★ ★

Burj Khalifa, Downtown, PO Box 888333; ☎ 04-888-3888;
{vfl **04-888-3777; dubai.armanihotels.com**

Cost AED 1,700 **Location** Downtown **Number of rooms** 108 rooms, plus 52 suites **Room sq m** 45–390 **Conference facilities** Yes **Pool/sauna** Yes **Beach access** No **Exercise facilities** Yes **Spa** Yes **Parking/valet** Yes **Licensed bar** Yes **On-site dining** Mediterranean, Indian, Japanese, deli, cafe **Extra amenities** Wi-Fi, full-size Armani toiletries, complimentary non-alcoholic minibar **Business amenities** Desk in all rooms, business centre, Armani-branded stationery **Shuttle buses** None **Wheelchair facilities** Yes

HOUSED IN THE FIRST 39 FLOORS of the *other* Burj, the first hotel from the king of greige couldn't be further removed from the rainbow-coloured opulence of the original sail-shaped seven-star. In keeping with its nearly-namesake, the Armani Hotel doesn't accept walk-ins – to get within its hallowed, satin-covered walls (which, interestingly, carry not one single piece of art), you have to make a booking at one of its eight restaurants and cafes. Unlike the Burj Al Arab, though, if all you wanted was a nose around, you could happily come for a croissant and a coffee in the lounge or lobby cafes for around AED 50.

Of course, there are also pricier options – Mediterraneo is as chic a buffet as we've ever seen – and at AED 150 for lunch and AED 190 for dinner, it has a great selection of cold starters, salads, grills, pizza and pasta, as well as cheese and a huge range of desserts. Mr Armani imported his favourite Milanese deli, Peck, which not only offers relaxed all-day dining but also sells products to take away, from cheese to pasta sauce, vinegar to patisserie (although you still won't get in if you're sporting shorts and flip-flops).

At the other end of the scale is the Italian fine-dining Ristorante, with an adjoining cigar lounge, which serves heavy but beautifully-executed Tuscan fare. Amal is the evening-only Indian offering, with live musicians daily, and Hashi serves up modern Japanese food and a huge selection of sake. All of these overlook the Dubai Fountain so are especially pleasant at night.

At uber-cool nightclub Armani Privé, the moneyed go to eye up each other's handbags. The Armani-clad staff in all of these joints – in fact the whole hotel – look as if they have just stepped off the catwalk. As the decor reflects the tastes of the great man himself, there is a unity of design here that is often lacking in larger chain hotels – but you'd better like beige if you're booking in, as it's all you're going to get, apart from the occasional splashes of red and aqua. The residential corridors feel a bit spaceship-like, with black tatami matting on the floor and dark wood walls and doors with no obvious handles.

Once inside your room, you are encouraged to 'discover' the space – the curved walls slide back to reveal bathrooms, workspaces and dressing rooms; lift the leaves on what appears to be a black lacquer box on legs, and you'll find a fully-equipped desk (we defy you not to pocket the Armani-branded pencil-sharpener). Mr Armani himself stays in the Armani Dubai Suite on the 39th floor (if you check in, take a look at the language setting of the remote, which controls everything from the air conditioner to the curtains – if it's in Italian, Giorgio might have been the last person to sleep in your king-size bed). The unobstructed views from this suite out over the World Islands are breathtaking.

Everything, everywhere, is Armani-branded, from the sugar cubes to the satin cushions, and your dedicated lifestyle concierge will be more than happy to help you procure them from the selection of Armani shops in the neighbouring Dubai Mall, which can be reached via a special indoor walkway from the hotel. If you'd rather not shop with the great unwashed, they can also set up an in-store appointment outside of opening hours.

You also get fast-track access to At The Top, the 124th-floor observation deck of the Burj Khalifa. At the luxurious black-and-cream spa, you book time instead of treatments (the minimum is 90 minutes), and a programme is tailored around your needs. The sauna, steam and ice rooms, which fan out around a completely black marble room with central fountain, are stunning but small, but the tiny pool, which is in shade for most of the day, is a real disappointment – we'd wager it's not where Mr Armani gets his mahogany hue.

Atlantis, The Palm ★ ★ ★ ★ ★
Crescent Road, Palm Jumeirah; PO Box 211222;
☎ **04-426-0000; atlantisthepalm.com**

Cost AED 3,100 **Location** The Palm Jumeirah **Number of rooms** 1,373 rooms, plus 166 suites **Room sq m** 45–924 **Conference facilities** Yes **Pool/sauna** Yes **Beach access** Yes **Exercise facilities** Yes **Spa** Yes **Parking/valet** Yes **Licensed bar** Yes **On-site dining** Italian, French, Japanese, International, Arabic, seafood, steakhouse, coffee shop, ice cream parlour **Extra amenities** Wi-Fi, kettle, hairdryer, iPod dock, complimentary bottled water **Business amenities** Business centre, secretarial services, mobile phone rental **Shuttle buses** To Mall of the Emirates, Dubai Mall, Dubai Outlet Mall **Wheelchair facilities** Yes

THIS HOTEL IS IMPOSSIBLE TO DESCRIBE without resorting to superlatives. It has 17 restaurants and 65,000 fish, and it cost £1 billion (US $1.6 billion) to build. Richard Branson called the £15 million (US $23.6 million) opening party, held on 20 November 1998, the 'last great party of the decade'. Guests Lindsay Lohan, Charlize Theron and Kylie Minogue agreed, although Bollywood superstar Shahrukh Khan was probably the happiest with his lot as he stayed in the Bridge Suite, which spans the top of the hotel's giant Moorish dome; at AED 92,000 (approximately £16,000 or US $25,000) a night, it's the world's most expensive.

Unlike the Burj Al Arab, the other must-visit hotel in Dubai, the Atlantis has absolutely zero architectural merit. Located in the centre of the crescent around the Palm Jumeirah's fronds, it rises out of the sea like a Pepto Bismol–pink Poseidon. Fanning out from a central atrium, a vast domed space decorated with rather remedial murals and a ten-metre-tall (almost 33-feet-tall) blown-glass sculpture by Dale Chihuly (we overheard one perplexed guest describe it as 'looking like they let a drunk loose on 5,000 modelling balloons'), it really is a gargantuan resort. You have to admire it for the sheer audacity of the offering, even if it does feel like a slice of Vegas airlifted into the Gulf.

Talk about taking a theme and running with it – from the columns to the carpets, doorknobs to dado rails, pretty much everything in the public areas has an aquatic bent. So far, so over the top – so it comes as a bit of a surprise that the rooms are actually quite low-key and chic (apart from the swirly carpets, that is). Decorated in cream and beige, all have balconies and sea views; even the smallest can accommodate two adults and two children (or three adults) in the two double beds. The large, spacious bathrooms with sliding screens allow you to watch your plasma-screen TV from the bath.

Of course, if you are willing to pay a premium, try one of the seven Super Suites – the famed Bridge might be the most expensive, but it's the Neptune and Poseidon that are the most impressive. Set over three floors, with their own separate lifts, the bathrooms and bedrooms in these suites have huge windows with views directly onto the Ambassador Lagoon, the 11-million-litre (2.9-million-gallon) aquarium. Again, these are surprisingly tasteful and even feature their own private *Majlis* room, where you can lie back against your red satin padded walls and smoke a shisha.

Teenagers are remarkably well catered for in the resort, with their own 'bar' serving mocktails until midnight, an Internet cafe and an entertainment zone with games consoles and a sound system. For children ages 4–12, an enormous kids' club has a climbing wall, a creation zone and a screening room with special viewing bubbles leading into the giant aquarium. There are also cooking classes, specially-organised back-of-house tours where they can watch the fish being fed, organised trips to Dolphin Bay and even special summer camps where youngsters can spend the week pretending to be rock stars. Unless you are paying extra for an Imperial Club room, all of these activities will be charged per session, which can add up. For the Premium Club price, adults will also get complimentary afternoon tea, soft drinks and snacks, as well as cocktails and canapés 6–8 p.m. You'll also have free in-room Internet access and use of the steam room, sauna and whirlpool in the 27-room spa.

Aquaventure, the resort's mammoth waterpark complete with flumes that take you through a shark tank, is as popular with adults as it is with children – especially during the summer months when, every Thursday, it is open until midnight, as is Dolphin Bay, where you can watch the porpoises perform or even swim with them. If you'd rather not get wet, the Lost Chambers, an Atlantis-themed attraction, takes you deep into the heart of the 'lost city' (suspension of disbelief imperative), past tanks of jellyfish, lobsters, moray eels and sea horses. Guests of the hotel get free entry to all of these attractions for the duration of their stay (although you must pay extra to interact with the dolphins). Try the brand-new dive centre if you'd like to get more involved.

The dining options range from Starbucks to Nobu, beluga caviar to burgers. The four celebrity restaurants include the aforementioned Nobu; Ossiano, presided over by Santi Santamaria, holder of three Michelin stars; Giorgio Locatelli's upscale pizza and pasta joint, Ronda Locatelli; and the all-day-dining bistro Rostang, by Michel Rostang. There are also standard buffet joints, a cavernous Arabic restaurant with a shisha terrace and nightly belly dancer, and Nassimi Beach, where you can drink and snack with the sand between your toes.

If you want a holiday without ever having to leave the resort and its 1.4 kilometres (almost a mile) of private beach (apart from maybe the odd trip to the mall by complimentary shuttle bus), this is the place for you.

Beach Hotel Apartment ★ ★ ★

Jumeirah Road, Jumeirah, PO Box 111496;
☎ **04-345-2444;** {∨fl **04-345-3111; beachhotelapartment.ae**

Cost AED 960 **Location** Jumeirah **Number of rooms** 30 one-bedroom and 6 two-bedroom **Room sq m** 40 (1 bedroom) **Conference facilities** No **Pool/sauna** Yes **Beach access** Yes (the private beach at the resort across the road at extra cost, or the free beach adjacent to it) **Exercise facilities** Yes **Spa** No **Parking/valet** Yes **Licensed bar** No **On-site dining** Seafood **Extra amenities** 24-hour room service, apartment serviced daily, laundry and housekeeping, bathrobes, slippers, tea/coffee facilities, room service using outsourced restaurants, iron/ironing board, hairdryer, safe box, car rental, airport pickup **Business amenities** Wi-Fi, high-speed Internet access **Shuttle buses** None **Wheelchair facilities** Yes

THESE LUXURY HOTEL APARTMENTS are in an excellent location – next to the Jumeirah Mosque, across the road from glorious beaches and in the same strip as the excellent Lime Tree Café and Spinney's supermarket (very useful if you're self-catering). They do not have an official star rating, and we have only allotted three stars to them, as they do not have a restaurant. However, the apartments and the facilities are more like four-star in terms of quality. What's more, they are in a low-rise hotel, not a massive tower block – you can walk to great boutiques, cafes and shops, and this neighbourhood has a real summer holiday feel to it. Plus, the apartments are lovely, and the staff are extremely nice.

Apartments are either one or two bedrooms, very contemporary, extremely comfortable and very well equipped. All have very modern kitchens with oven, hob, microwave, fridge, cutlery, crockery and everything else you would need for a self-catering holiday, as well as a washing machine and dryer. If you don't want to cook, you can order room service or staff will advise you of local restaurants offering very good delivery services. Apartments are decorated in soothing earth tones, and bedrooms have either a king bed or twins, and a flat-panel TV. Living rooms have funky brown sofas, abstract-design rugs, low glass coffee tables, cable TV and a DVD player. Towels and sheets are changed and the apartment cleaned daily. A glass dining table has seating for either four or six people depending on the apartment size.

A pleasant rooftop pool and a small gym are other amenities. If you want to go to the beach, you have two choices: a huge free beach across the road (two-minute walk), or pay to use the smallish, sometimes quite crowded, private beach belonging to the Dubai Marine Beach Resort & Spa.

Burj Al Arab ★★★★★★★
Jumeirah, PO Box 74147; ☎ 04-301-7777;
{vfl **04-301-7000; jumeirah.com**

Cost AED 10,000 **Location** Jumeirah **Number of rooms** 202 suites **Room sq m** 170–780 **Conference facilities** Yes **Pool/sauna** Yes **Beach access** Yes **Exercise facilities** Yes **Spa** Yes **Parking/valet** Yes **Licensed bar** Yes **On-site dining** European, Arabic, Asian, Mediterranean, seafood, coffee shop **Extra amenities** Personal entryphone, Wi-Fi, 24-hour butler, full-size Hermès bath products, pre-loaded DVD players **Business amenities** Laptop, printer, scanner, fax **Shuttle buses** To Madinat Jumeirah, Jumeirah Beach Hotel, Jumeirah Bab Al Shams **Wheelchair facilities** Yes

THERE AREN'T MANY HOTELS IN THE WORLD about which apocryphal stories abound, but such is the Burj's status that we could fill this book with them. Heard the one about former U.S. President Bill Clinton sneaking in through the kitchens? Or the man who sent a diver into the giant aquarium with an engagement ring and a sign saying 'marry me'? Do we really buy that it was built on its own island because it was originally intended to be an offshore super-casino? Whatever you choose to believe, one thing is definitely true – this seven-star superstar is the building that single-handedly put Dubai on the map.

Whether you love it or loathe it, many holiday albums feature at least one photo of it since it opened in 1999 (our favourite is the Burj-as-natty-headgear shot). The structure, which sits 280 metres (918.6 feet) offshore and is accessed via its own bridge, was designed by architect Tom Wright to be an icon; his philosophy was that a landmark structure should have only three or four simple lines to make it easy for people to remember. He sure succeeded – more than any other structure, this is the symbol of modern Dubai. A double-skinned Teflon-coated sail covers the outside of the building, and it was the first time such technology had been used vertically and to such an extent anywhere in the world. At 321 metres (about 1,053 feet) the hotel is still the tallest all-suite hotel in the world.

The interior, by Khuan Chew of KCA International, is perhaps responsible for the love-it-or-loathe-it aspect of the Burj – it is certainly over the top for Western tastes. What you see from the outside gives scant impression of the ocular assault that awaits you inside. If we were being kind, we'd call the tallest atrium in the world a 'wow' experience. There's no reception as such, just a couple of discreet desks (well, what passes for discreet in a place embellished with 1,590 square metres, or almost 17,115 square feet, of 24-carat gold leaf). This is because each floor boasts its own reception.

Two lifts flanking a central dancing fountain take you past the enormous aquariums to the first floor, where another fountain periodically issues jets of water four storeys up into the air. The underside of each floor fans out and is painted a different colour, not unlike a massive Pantone chart. Carpets are migraine-inducing, every single fixture and fitting gleams gold and the furniture is primary-coloured pleather. Understated it is not, but we defy you not to warm to the all-out bling of it all. Of course, the hotel is aware of what a tourist attraction this all is, so if you want to experience any of it, you'll need a reservation for one of the restaurants (they recently installed a man with a phone at the gate so that people turning up on spec can book right there and then). The staff are all incredibly polite, aware and ever present – as they should be, with a ratio of eight to every one guest.

The suites, all of which are duplex, continue the almost comedy-opulent theme. The living room, with guest bathroom, is downstairs, and boasts an enormous flat-panel TV along with a desk on which sits your own fully-loaded laptop and Bond-villain–style touch screen nerve centre, from which you can open the curtains, turn on the music, order a martini or plot global domination (probably). The views, either over to the World Islands or the Palm, are incredible and unobstructed. Upstairs, the beds face the floor-to-ceiling windows, and the televisions that sit in front of them can be raised and lowered at the touch of a button. For a more risqué form of entertainment, mirrors above the mattresses come as standard, although these can be covered up on request. The bathrooms all come complete with full-size Hermès products and a high-camp mural of Dubai's sights above the whirlpool bath, which your butler will fill with scented oils, fragrant herbs or even caviar on demand.

If this isn't enough pampering, a whole floor of the hotel is devoted to separate male and female spas, and there's a private beach and a swimming pool (if guests have one gripe, it's that this is a bit small and doesn't catch the sun until after midday). Obviously, all of this luxury comes at a price, and you'll probably feel this the most at mealtimes. Many people choose to eat in-room – after all, anyone can book dinner at the Burj, but only a handful will ever be able to afford supper in their suite. Thus, the room-service menu is phone-directory thick, and you are encouraged to go off-piste with it – they are happy to send a chef up to cook in your private kitchen and serve you at your own dining table.

The flagship restaurant is Al Mahara, the 'underwater' eatery (which is actually on the ground floor but has a huge aquarium in the middle), which can be accessed via a 'submarine' (that is, a big lift with seat belts). The newish all-white Asian restaurant cooks up competent buffet fare, and the Arabic place gets great reviews, but it sure is an expensive *shawarma* (a sandwich-like wrap with grilled, shaved meat). If you are spending more than a few nights there, you are right next door to the Madinat Jumeirah (accessed by golf buggy) and its multitude of cheaper dining options.

The location is also perfect for the Mall of the Emirates and is ten minutes away from the shops and cafes of Jumeirah Beach Residence. But let's be realistic – if you're spending AED 10,000 a night, you're probably going to want to get your money's worth and stay in the hotel the whole time.

Crowne Plaza Festival City ★ ★ ★ ★ ★
**Dubai Festival City, PO Box 45777; ☎ 04-701-2222;
{vfl 04-232-9097; ichotelsgroup.com**

Cost AED 950 **Location** Deira **Number of rooms** 298 rooms, plus 18 suites **Room sq m** 34–124 **Conference facilities** Yes **Pool/sauna** Yes **Beach access** No **Exercise facilities** Yes **Spa** In the adjoining InterContinental hotel **Parking/valet** Yes **Licensed bar** Yes **On-site dining** Arabic/International, Belgian, coffee shop **Extra amenities** Self-service laundry facilities, iron/ironing board, scales, coffee machine, kettle **Business amenities** Desks, secretarial services, 24-hour business centre, laptops and mobile phones for hire **Shuttle buses** To Dubai International Airport, Al Badia Golf Club, Jumeirah Beach Park, Mall of the Emirates **Wheelchair facilities** Yes

THIS FIVE-STAR IS POPULAR WITH PEOPLE spending only one or two nights in Dubai – it is literally five minutes from the airport and right next to the Festival Centre (and a giant Ikea, although obviously the flat-pack merchant is less of a tourist draw). The parent company also recently took over what was formerly the Four Seasons golf club, renaming it Al Badia, so an 18-hole championship course is just three minutes away. The hotel is attached via a connecting walkway to the neighbouring, more upmarket, InterContinental hotel, so it also benefits from access to the dining outlets and spa.

The standard rooms are smaller than at most five-star Dubai hotels, and they are fairly masculine, with dark wood, faux leather headboards and cream carpets. The beds are large and comfortable, though, and the bathrooms have the ubiquitous slide-back screen so you can watch your flat-panel TV from the bath. There is an outdoor baby splash pool but no kids' club, although the mall's cinema, bowling alley, arcade, *abra* rides and, during the more temperate months, outdoor funfair should keep little ones happy.

The dining options are limited here to a large Belgian-themed pub and a rather workaday Arabic/International restaurant. It's worth specifying that you would like a Dubai Creek view from your room so you don't get an eyeful of a roundabout every time you open your curtains. You can avoid paying the AED 140 per day for an Internet connection by shelling out around 50% extra for a larger Executive Club room – this will also get you breakfast, access to the Club Lounge, free drinks 6–8 p.m. and transfers from the airport.

Dar Al Masyaf ★ ★ ★ ★ ★

Madinat Jumeirah, PO Box 75157; ☎ 04-366-8888; {vfl 04-366-7788; jumeirah.com

Cost AED 3,900 **Location** Jumeirah **Number of rooms** 254 rooms, plus 29 suites **Room sq m** 60–130 **Conference facilities** Yes **Pool/sauna** Yes **Beach access** Yes **Exercise facilities** Yes **Spa** Yes **Parking/valet** Yes **Licensed bar** Yes **On-site dining** International **Extra amenities** Internet; private butler; drinks 6–8 p.m. daily in private courtyard; tea/coffee facilities; dates, fruit and chocolate in rooms **Business amenities** Business centre in Al Qasr and Mina A'Salam **Shuttle buses** To Jumeirah Beach Hotel, Mall of the Emirates, Jumeirah Bab Al Shams **Wheelchair facilities** Yes

SITUATED IN THE MIDDLE OF THE MADINAT JUMEIRAH'S waterways, rooms in these villas, set around their own leafy central courtyards, can be booked individually or, if you have a large group, you can take over the whole two-storey house yourself. Built in the same old Arabia style as the rest of the resort, these are chic and discreet and popular with large families from the Gulf who would rather stay away from prying eyes. Each has its own butler, who is on hand in the communal lounge area should you need any assistance (or 6–8 p.m. daily, should you need a complimentary gin and tonic poured). The rooms are larger and grander than at neighbouring hotels Mina A'Salam and Al Qasr – with a minimum of 60 square metres (almost 646 square feet), each one has at least one large terrace (some which lead directly out onto the lawns, others which have sea or waterway views) and can sleep a family of four comfortably. The facilities are the same as outlined for Al Qasr but are closer to the sea and also share their own exclusive pools.

Desert Palm ★ ★ ★ ★

Al Awir Road, PO Box 119171; ☎ 04-323-8888;
{vfl **04-323-8053; desertpalm.ae**

Cost AED 2,450, including breakfast **Location** Al Awir Road **Number of rooms** 26 suites **Room sq m** 45–585 **Conference facilities** Yes **Pool/sauna** Yes **Beach access** No **Exercise facilities** Yes **Spa** Yes **Parking/valet** Yes **Licensed bar** Yes **On-site dining** International, steakhouse **Extra amenities** Tea/coffee facilities, loaded iPod, Wi-Fi, private in-room bar **Business amenities** International direct-dial telephones **Shuttle buses** None **Wheelchair facilities** Yes

To give you an idea of the calibre of the accommodation on offer here, the Desert Palm annually hosts the most VIP-packed event of the season, the Cartier Polo. It's certainly a fitting venue – the hotel is designed to offer the best possible views of the neighbouring polo field from all the public spaces and a good proportion of the rooms. Even the spa has windows directly out onto the grass.

It is a boutique hotel in the true sense of the word – designed in Arabian avant-garde style, which roughly translates as lots of cool neutrals and dark wood, with the occasional splash of aqua and some equine-themed art – and it has only 26 guest suites. Light streams through the huge windows of those that overlook the pitch. Each of the one-bedroom Palm Villas, two-bedroom Pool Villas and enormous two-bedroom Villa Layali, with its own courtyard garden and roof terrace, has its own private swimming pool. Many guests still choose to use the main pool, though, with its infinity edge overlooking the manicured lawns and giant floating beanbags where, every Wednesday night during the summer, movies are played al fresco.

Because the hotel is so small, there is a limited selection of dining options – Epicure is cafe-style and open throughout the day, serving sandwiches, burgers and pizza, and Rare is an evening-only fine-dining steakhouse with a wood-fired oven. A cosy bar with a wrap-around terrace and huge sofas has live music at the weekends.

If we had to level any complaints, it would firstly be the location – it is on Al Awir Road, a 30-minute drive from the centre of Dubai, surrounded by not very much at all – and secondly, presumably because of the proximity to the stables, the plague of flies, which in the summer can reach biblical proportions.

Dubai Marine Beach Resort & Spa ★ ★ ★ ★ ★

Jumeirah Road, PO Box 5182; ☎ 04-346-1111;
{vfl **04-346-0234; dxbmarine.com**

Cost AED 1,380 **Location** Jumeirah **Number of rooms** 195 rooms, plus 95 suites **Room sq m** 25 **Conference facilities** Yes **Pool/sauna** Yes **Beach access** Yes **Exercise facilities** Yes **Spa** Yes **Parking/valet** Yes **Licensed bar** Yes **On-site dining** Lebanese, French, Italian, Cuban, Mediterranean, Tex-Mex, Thai, Greek, Japanese fusion, Arabic fusion, seafood, Arabic juices and shisha, lounge bar **Extra amenities** Boutique, florist shop, hair salon, gift shop, minibar, 24-hour room service, hairdryer, iron/ironing board on request **Business amenities** Wi-Fi, business centre, high-speed Internet **Shuttle buses** To Dubai Mall, Mall of the Emirates **Wheelchair facilities** Yes

YOU MIGHT WELL ENJOY THIS BEACH RESORT if you're a bit of a hippy at heart and you love beaches and good food, but you don't want commercialism and bling and can sacrifice the luxury a little. It's a little less polished, a little more rough and ready, but it is in a really nice part of Jumeirah, within walking distance of a fabulous range of cafes and shops. And if you don't want to leave the resort, you also have 13 restaurants on-site from which to choose.

On the downside, we don't think this hotel deserves to have five stars, and it is overpriced for what it does offer compared with the beach resorts at the other end of Jumeirah Road, which are ultraluxurious in comparison. It doesn't have basics such as tea- and coffee-making facilities, or mineral water in the bedrooms, the standard rooms are small for Dubai sizes and none of the bathrooms in the hotel has a walk-in shower. The beach here isn't vast, but it is pretty. Apart from the beach, the resort has two large swimming pools, a children's pool, a decent gym, tennis courts and a spa offering a wide range of treatments.

Bedrooms come in a selection of sizes: standard, standard with balcony, junior suite, family room and executive suite. Furnished in creams, contemporary but not in-your-face modern, with white bed linens, beige throws, off-white seating, rugs and plants, it all makes for a safe, comfortable ambience.

An International buffet breakfast is served in Taverna overlooking the beach – it's actually open 24 hours a day and serves cuisines culled from around the world. Other restaurants include Al Khayma, a cafe serving Arabic specialties, juices and shisha; Capanna Nouva, serving Italian standard fare; El Malecon, cooking up Cuban cuisine; Flooka for Mediterranean seafood; and Yia Yia for traditional Greek.

You'd have wondered why we hadn't included it if you'd stumbled across it, but at these prices we'd probably recommend staying somewhere else if you're after five-star beach resort luxury with all the trimmings.

Dusit Thani Dubai ★★★★★

133, Sheikh Zayed Road, PO Box 23335; ☎ **04-343-3333;**
{vf] **04-343-4222; dubai.dusit.com**

Cost AED 2,000 **Location** Sheikh Zayed Road **Number of rooms** 321 rooms, plus 148 suites **Room sq m** 39–135 **Conference facilities** Yes **Pool/sauna** Yes **Beach access** No **Exercise facilities** Yes **Spa** Yes **Parking/valet** Yes **Licensed bar** Yes **On-site dining** International, Thai, Italian, deli **Extra amenities** 24-hour room service, bathroom vanity sets, dressing gown, tea/coffee facilities, safe box, hairdryer, minibar, beauty salon, gift and souvenir shop, florist, airport transfer, laundry and dry-cleaning service, car rental, nurse and doctor on call, babysitting, outside catering **Business amenities** Wi-Fi, high-speed Internet, business centre, business lounge **Shuttle buses** To Dubai Mall, Mall of the Emirates, Jumeirah Beach Park **Wheelchair facilities** Yes

SITUATED ON THE SHEIKH ZAYED ROAD in the heart of Dubai's business district, a few minutes from the World Trade Centre, the Convention Centre and the Dubai International Financial Centre, as well as Burj Khalifa and Dubai Mall, this is an excellently located business hotel with great amenities, convenient for work and pleasure. It combines luxury with traditional Thai hospitality.

It is a well-oiled, well-run hotel that understands the needs of its business travellers. Staff remember frequently-returning guests, business facilities are excellent, the restaurants are consistently good and even the smallest bedrooms are some of the largest in Dubai. The decor is Thai in style, and the lobby is a vast glass atrium. When booking, do make sure you are not given one of the older apartment rooms, which have not been refurbished and are old and worn.

Bedrooms in the main hotel have an old Colonial feel about them – contemporary but not ultramodern. Dark wood louvred blinds and accents of ochre, earth and sand colours in the cushions, bed throws and rugs punctuate the cool creams of the walls and white of the bed linens. You can look out into the bedrooms from the bathroom if you raise the blind, which gives a nice feeling of light and space, and all bathrooms have walk-in showers and bathtubs.

Deluxe king, queen and twin bedrooms are located on the 26th–32nd floors, whilst Club king, queen and twin rooms – the Executive Rooms – are located on the top three floors, providing panoramic views over the city and offering a wide range of extra benefits to the Deluxe Room benefits.

A cordless work desk phone and Gaggia espresso machines are included in the Deluxe Rooms, and guests are entitled to use the Dusit Club facilities, which include private express check-in and checkout at the Dusit Club, located on the 34th floor; complimentary return to and from the Dubai International Airport; complimentary high-speed Internet access in your room and the Dusit Club; complimentary local telephone calls; complimentary laundry and pressing services, to the value of AED 35 per day; private meeting room access for a maximum of two hours per stay; butler and shoeshine service upon request; assistance with packing and unpacking of your luggage; Executive Breakfast at PAX on the 24th floor or Continental business breakfast at Dusit Club on the 34th floor; complimentary tea, coffee, juices and soft drinks throughout the day; and afternoon tea and snacks followed by a happy hour with cocktails and canapés in the evening.

The Presidential Suite, on the 34th floor, is palatial at 135 square metres (about 1,453 square feet) and comes with panoramic views. The bedroom has magnificent walk-in wardrobes and an ultraluxurious bathroom, complete with whirlpool tub.

Food is good, with a range of cuisines, led by the hotel's signature restaurant, the Benjarong, with blue and gold walls, intricate carvings and Thai music. Buffet breakfasts and lunches are served in the Californian Restaurant, and an Asian-themed buffet is served in the evening. PAX (the hotel's Italian restaurant) and the Dusit Delicatessen provide all-day dining. MyBar, an Asian-inspired piano bar, is worth visiting to hear Johnny, the jazz and soul singer. The Splash Pool Bar – high up on the 36th floor next to the pool – is the place for cocktails, fresh juices and snacks.

The pool itself is mostly shaded, so not ideal for sunbathing, but when it's 40°C (104°F) out there, that's not a bad thing. There is also a reasonable gym and a hot tub.

The Fairmont Dubai ★★★★★

Sheikh Zayed Road, PO Box 97555; ☎ 04-332-5555;
{vfl **04-332-4555; fairmont.com/dubai**

Cost AED 1,199 **Location** Sheikh Zayed Road **Number of rooms** 204 rooms, plus 86 suites **Room sq m** 40–550 **Conference facilities** Yes **Pool/sauna** Yes **Beach access** No **Exercise facilities** Yes **Spa** Yes **Parking/valet** Yes **Licensed bar** Yes **On-site dining** International, Arabic, Italian, Japanese, steak, juice bar, coffee shop **Extra amenities** CD alarm clocks, hairdryer, iron/ironing board, international adaptor, Internet **Business amenities** Business centre, laptop rental, secretarial services **Shuttle buses** To Dubai Mall, Mirdif City Centre **Wheelchair facilities** Yes

LOCATED MINUTES FROM THE DUBAI INTERNATIONAL Financial Centre and the World Trade Centre, this Dubai stalwart is predictably primarily a business hotel. This is reflected in the decor, which is pretty straightforward but expensive-looking. Don't be put off by the lobby, which is an odd combo of *Majlis* seating, mismatched chairs, glass and steel.

The rooms are large, with Miller Harris toiletries and a surround-sound system that pumps music into the bathroom. The bedrooms are decorated in dark, masculine neutrals with high, padded headboards, and all have a seating area and desk. They don't all have balconies, though, which is probably just as well, as most only have a view of the Sheikh Zayed Road or the maze of old, low-rise buildings behind.

For a hotel that clearly hasn't put much store in the designer flourishes of its more recently-opened neighbours, it actually does rather well on the fashionable food and drink front. The year 2009 saw the opening of the world's first Cavalli Club – the king of bling's cavernous and wildly-expensive nightlife offering (think black marble, faux fur, Swarovski-draped ceilings and gold-leaf sushi). The crowd here are predictably overdressed and underweight, and come the 2 a.m. closing time, they all head down to The Fairmont's basement club, 400, where they dance on tables and order super-size bottles of premium vodka served on velvet cushions with sparklers.

Less ostentatious is Spectrum on One, an International restaurant that manages the impossible by tackling each cuisine brilliantly – the Friday brunch is particularly lauded. There's also the much-garlanded Exchange Grill, and the quite frankly odd Japanese joint called Kitsune, that wows diners with its Clockwork Orange–meets–Narnia decor and dry ice instead of its cooking. Cin-Cin is a pretty wine bar but a bit of a pickup joint, and cripplingly expensive. There is also a sandwich joint and a conveyer-belt sushi cafe.

The pool is pretty small and overlooks Sheikh Zayed Road, so really more for business types than sun worshippers, but the Willow Stream spa, decorated in a faux Roman style, is large and well appointed (it is particularly hot on half- or whole-day packages).

Four Points by Sheraton ★ ★ ★ ★

Mankhool Road, Bur Dubai, PO Box 116162; ☎ 04-354-3333;
{vfl **04-354-3111; fourpointsdowntowndubai.com**

Cost AED 1,800 **Location** Bur Dubai **Number of rooms** 250 rooms, plus 28 suites **Room sq m** 40 **Conference facilities** Yes **Pool/sauna** Yes **Beach access** No **Exercise facilities** Yes **Spa** No **Parking/valet** Yes **Licensed bar** Yes **On-site dining** International, Italian, bar food **Extra amenities** Airport pickup, sauna, family room in lobby, magazines, 24-hour room service, hairdryer, iron, kettle, safe and scales in all bedrooms, dressing gown and slippers in Preferred Rooms and Suites, flat-panel TV in every room, Internet in every room **Business amenities** Complimentary Wi-Fi in public areas, business centre **Shuttle buses** To Jumeirah Beach Park, Dubai Mall, Mall of the Emirates, BurJuman Centre **Wheelchair facilities** No

THIS HOTEL IS SITUATED IN A LOCATION THAT, whilst ugly in its own right, is only 12 minutes away from Dubai International Airport. And you can enjoy the best of all worlds, as the hotel is a few minutes away from Dubai World Trade Centre, Jumeirah Beach Park, the major shopping malls, Dubai Museum and Dubai Creek Park.

First impressions as you enter the hotel are of a modern, upbeat, welcoming, lively hotel. It is contemporary, pristine and attractive, and its exterior does not reflect how nice it is inside. The staff are helpful and friendly, and they speak excellent English.

The bedrooms are spacious and extremely comfortable, with either king-size or twin beds, with four comfortable pillows and a cosy duvet. High-speed Internet is available in the bedrooms, and the interactive 32-inch TVs show more than 60 international channels.

A variety of restaurants provide 24-hour dining facilities. The Eatery, an easy-going family restaurant, serves International cuisine; Centro Citta is an Italian restaurant serving familiar pasta and pizzas, with a buffet set up as well. Yesterday Restaurant and Pub pays homage to the Beatles (hence the name) and plays music mainly from the '60s to the '80s.

This is a good hotel if you have children. A pleasant pool and kiddies' pool are on the roof, and the sixth and seventh floors have interconnecting rooms more than able to accommodate a large group or family with several children.

Although you are in an older part of Dubai, you are in the centre of everything, and a free shuttle bus travels three times a day to the excellent Jumeirah Beach Park. This hotel is an excellent all-rounder for business and leisure travellers.

Golden Tulip Suites ★ ★ ★ ★

2A Street, Al Barsha, PO Box 282464; ☎ 04-341-7474;
{vfl **04-341-7475; goldentulipsuitesdubai.com**

Cost AED 1,350 (Club Studio) **Location** Al Barsha and Al Quoz **Number of rooms** 90 apartments, 60 studios, 18 one-bedrooms, 12 two-bedrooms **Room sq m** 34–43 (studio) **Conference facilities** Yes **Pool/sauna** Yes **Beach access** No **Exercise facilities** Yes **Spa** Yes **Parking/valet** Yes/no **Licensed bar** No **On-site dining** International **Extra amenities** Airport pickup, car rentals, complimentary tea, coffee, interactive TV systems, babysitting, laundry service, full-size fridge, stove, microwave, toaster, espresso machine, washer and dryer, iron/ironing board, electronic safe **Business amenities** Laptop in each bedroom, high-speed Internet and Wi-Fi throughout the hotel, secretarial service **Shuttle buses** To Jumeirah Open Beach at Jumeirah Beach Residence **Wheelchair facilities** No

OPPOSITE THE IBIS AND SUITE NOVOTEL, the Golden Tulip Suites stands imposing with an all-glass facade. Within spitting distance of Mall of the Emirates, and a block back from Sheikh Zayed Road, we think that, if you're after an apartment with hotel facilities at medium prices, you've found a winner.

Golden Tulip Suites markets itself as ideal for business travellers, and with three conference rooms and executive business packages, not to mention location and accessibility to either the financial district (15 minutes) or Media/Internet City (15 minutes), it is ideal. However, it would also suit the family who wants the comfort of a hotel but the space and flexibility of an apartment. And as you are opposite two hotels and neighbouring another, all with several restaurants, and Mall of the Emirates has the vast Carrefour if you wish to self-cater, you are spoilt for choice when it comes to eating in or out.

The apartments are spacious, well designed, modern and very comfortable. There are four types: Standard Studio, Club Studio, one-bedroom suites and two-bedroom suites. All have fully-equipped kitchens with the amenities outlined above. The studios are one room – a living area separated by a wooden partition from the sleeping area with a king-size bed. There is a separate bathroom. Standard has a shower; Club has a bath.

The one-bedroom apartment has a separate living room and dining area, a kitchen and a large bedroom with a king-size bed. The two-bedroom apartment has a living room and dining area, a kitchen, one bedroom with king-size bed and one with two single beds. The bedrooms in the two-bed apartment both have en suite bathrooms, and there is a guest toilet as well. All the bedrooms in all the apartments have their own flat-panel TVs and desk areas, as well as plenty of seating, and tables are in the living areas. All can have an extra bed added if required.

The health club on the seventh floor has a decent gym and two calming, candle-lit massage rooms. The swimming pool on the roof, with good views over Dubai, is lovely – not huge, but decorated with trees and plants, and with comfortable dark-wood, cream-cushion sunloungers. A funky rooftop bar – Garden Roof Cafe – with big black wicker chairs, a red bar area, lots of black marble and a fountain, serves soft drinks and food, as well as shisha, 4 p.m.–2 a.m. The restaurant La Mode offers 24-hour dining, serving International and local cuisine.

Gold Swiss-Belhotel ★ ★ ★ ★
**Al Mina Road, Bur Dubai, PO Box 66431; ☎ 04-345-9992;
{vfl 04-345-9994; dubai.swiss-belhotel.com**

Cost AED 1,450 **Location** Bur Dubai **Number of rooms** 184 rooms, plus 16 suites **Room sq m** 22–55 **Conference facilities** Two meeting rooms **Pool/ sauna** Yes **Beach access** No **Exercise facilities** Yes **Spa** No **Parking/valet** Yes **Licensed bar** Yes **On-site dining** International, speciality kebabs from around the world, bar, tapas-style snacks **Extra amenities** Tea/coffee facilities, minibar, satellite TV, safe box, iron/ironing board on request, gift shop, airport transfers **Business amenities** Business centre, high-speed Internet, Wi-Fi **Shuttle buses** To Jumeirah Beach Park, Dubai Mall, Mall of the Emirates **Wheelchair facilities** Yes

GOLD SWISS-BELHOTEL, which opened at the end of 2009, is well situated for the business traveller, as it is just a few minutes from the World Trade Centre and within easy access of the airport. Additionally, it is close to Jumeirah and the Beach Park, as well as Dubai Mall and the historical parts of Dubai, and it is situated in a relatively quiet part of Al Mina Road. It is lacking in any particular style but is contemporary, if rather dull in design. It ticks the functional box.

Bedrooms have a uniform look – neutral with cream walls and carpets, white bed linens with orange bed runners, bright red easy chairs, very dark wood furniture and doors and other chairs with beige upholstery. It's all a bit of a mishmash that doesn't really come together. Everything you need is there, and it's modern, clean and comfortable; it's just not particularly elegant.

There are five categories of room. Classic (22 square metres, or about 237 square feet) is for individual travellers – who hopefully will be out most of the time, as their rooms are quite cosy, with single beds. Deluxe (30 square metres, or 323 square feet) and Superior (35 square metres, or 376.7 square feet) rooms offer king-size or twin beds. Premier (37 square metres, or 398 square feet) rooms have a king-size bed, and Executive suites (55 square metres, or 592 square feet) offer a separate living room with guest water closet, whilst the bedroom has a separate dressing room. All bathrooms have cream marble, black granite and tiled flooring, a full-size bath and glass-encased rain forest–style shower.

Check when you are booking your room that you are on one of the higher floors, as the ground floor bar has a live band that can be heard from the lower levels. The hotel has a rooftop pool, which is very small, and there are about four sunloungers for the entire hotel. The gym is adequate, and there are steam rooms.

Food-wise, the hotel has a 24-hour International restaurant called Senses featuring a live cooking station, and at breakfast the chef prepares fresh pancakes and omelettes. Lunch is also buffet style, while dinner is à la carte. The Kebab Connection is a meat-lover's paradise, with the focus being on more than 150 varieties of kebabs from all over the world. The Liquid Lounge is open from midday, with the Golden Duo Jazz Band performing live every evening.

We probably wouldn't recommend this hotel for holidaymakers, but it's OK for business travellers looking for a convenient location.

Grandeur Hotel ★★★

Al Barsha 1, PO Box 282429; ☎ 04-341-8777;
{vfl 04-323-4722; grandeurhotel.com

Cost AED 850 **Location** Al Barsha and Al Quoz **Number of rooms** 100 rooms, plus 25 suites **Room sq m** 35 **Conference facilities** Yes **Pool/sauna** Yes **Beach access** No **Exercise facilities** Yes **Spa** No **Parking/valet** Yes **Licensed bar** Yes **On-site dining** International, Indian **Extra amenities** Hairdryer, iron/ironing board on request, minibar, safe box, flat-panel TV, 24-hour room service, airport pickup **Business amenities** Business centre, laptop rentals, Wi-Fi, high-speed Internet **Shuttle buses** To Jumeirah Open Beach **Wheelchair facilities** No

THIS IS A BIT OF A WILD CARD OF A HOTEL. It is in a less exciting area – Al Barsha, notable for Mall of the Emirates, and pretty much a construction site for a lot of new hotels that are springing up – but it is a really elegant cheaper hotel, and in a very convenient location for sightseeing, shopping and going to the beach. The lobby is delightful, with a beautiful glass-bauble light feature, and the staff are extremely friendly.

The hotel's signature restaurant, d'fusion, serves a fusion of Indian cuisine from the north and south, combined with flavours from around the globe. Café La Rez is a 24/7 cafe serving an International buffet breakfast 6–10 a.m. for AED 40. Spirals Sports Bar is a proper, smoky bar with big screens, a DJ at weekends and a pool table.

Bedrooms in the hotel are surprisingly good: contemporary decor, modern fittings, king-size beds, work desks and lovely bathrooms with walk-in showers, baths and basins. The rooms are cream and brown, fairly safe in terms of style, but recently renovated and contemporary in feel. The suites have living rooms with workspaces and flat-panel TVs. Beds have crisp white linens with chocolate-brown throws. They are elegant and comfortable.

So if you're looking for inexpensive but comfortable accommodations and love Indian food, or want a hotel with a good bar and a bit of a party feel on weekends, we'd recommend the Grandeur.

Grand Hyatt ★★★★★

Oud Metha, Bur Dubai, PO Box 7978; ☎ 04-317-1234;
{vfl 04-317-1235; dubai.grand.hyatt.com

Cost AED 1,050 **Location** Bur Dubai **Number of rooms** 632 rooms, plus 42 suites **Room sq m** 42–295 **Conference facilities** Yes **Pool/sauna** Yes **Beach access** No **Exercise facilities** Yes **Spa** Yes **Parking/valet** Yes **Licensed bar** Yes

On-site dining Arabic, International, Singaporean, Japanese, Indian, Southeast Asian, steak **Extra amenities** Wi-Fi, hairdryer **Business amenities** Dedicated conference concierge, business centre **Shuttle buses** To Wafi Mall, Mercato Mall, Mirdif City Centre, Jumeirah Beach Park **Wheelchair facilities** Yes

ALTHOUGH THE GRAND HYATT IS ACTUALLY on the same road as the newer and more expensive Raffles hotel, because of the hotel's epic size and extensive garden, you feel a lot less like you're perched next to a motorway here. The number of rooms lends itself to large group travel, so it's used by quite a few airlines to house cabin crew, and it's also a popular place for conferences. But don't overlook it as a holiday destination, as although it's some distance from the beach, it has a raft of facilities and a huge selection of restaurants and bars.

Peppercrab, one of the city's few Singaporean restaurants, is noteworthy – although the bibs they present you with on arrival mean that it's not the world's most romantic evening out. The moodily-lit Manhattan Grill rates better for that, serving some of the best steaks in Dubai. Italian joint Andiamo! and the Southeast Asian canteen Wox are great for dining en famille.

It also has its own spa (its chocolate body treatments are unique to the Hyatt), a 450-metre (about 1,476-foot) outdoor running track set in its 15 hectares (37 acres) of gardens, a vast complex of three outdoor pools including baby and toddler areas, a 20-metre (65.6-foot) indoor lap pool, floodlit tennis courts and a 24-hour gym. An on-site kids' club is useful if you are planning to play at Al Badia or Dubai Creek golf courses five minutes away.

The hotel is a short drive from the souks and *abra* rides of Deira and Bur Dubai, and Festival Centre, Wafi Mall and BurJuman Centre are on the doorstep. A huge cinema is also right next door. The Grand Hyatt is unlikely to win any interior design awards, but it is a lot of fun – massive dhow hulls are suspended from the ceiling in the lobby, and an indoor tropical garden spans two floors. The rooms verge on the bland but are decked out in inoffensive cream, and all have large desks and huge windows.

Grosvenor House ★ ★ ★ ★ ★

Dubai Marina, PO Box 118500; ☎ 04-399-8888;
{∨fl **04-399-8444; grosvenorhouse-dubai.com**

Cost AED 950 **Location** The Marina **Number of rooms** 217 rooms, plus 205 apartments **Room sq m** 35–268 **Conference facilities** Yes **Pool/sauna** Yes **Beach access** Courtesy buses to Le Royal Méridien Beach Resort & Spa **Exercise facilities** Yes **Spa** Yes **Parking/valet** Yes **Licensed bar** Yes **On-site dining** British, Arabic, Turkish, International, Pan-Asian, Indian, deli, coffee shop **Extra amenities** Free Wi-Fi, tea/coffee facilities, fresh flowers **Business amenities** Business centre **Shuttle buses** To Dubai Mall, Mall of the Emirates **Wheelchair facilities** Yes

SITUATED AT THE MOUTH OF DUBAI MARINA, this 422-room hotel is probably more famous for its selection of bars and restaurants than its rooms. The top floor Bar 44 has brilliant views out over the neon lights of its neighbours, and, in a city that values novelty above all else, the ground-floor Buddha Bar has miraculously managed to hang onto its status as one of the coolest late-night watering holes in town for more than a week (staying at the hotel will ensure you entry, which might otherwise be tricky if you are hoping to secure a table for dinner or even standing room by the bar at weekends). Brit celebrity chef Gary Rhodes oversees fine-dining restaurant Mezzanine, and there is also an Indian restaurant from fellow Michelin star-holder Vineet Bhatia, as well as a Turkish restaurant and a deli-cafe.

Aimed more at business travellers, the rooms, suites and one-, two- and three-bedroom apartments all have desks and are decorated in inoffensive, standard-issue cream and brown, with brilliant blackout curtains. Many have balconies, but due to the incessant surrounding construction (the powers that be are particularly keen on repeatedly digging up the roads outside for no apparent reason), you probably won't want to spend much time on them. Unfortunately, this noise from neighbouring building sites tends to start early and finish late, so on the lower floors this may bother light (or late) sleepers.

The hotel does have its own hair salon, nail bar, two spas (one just for men) and a large pool, but shuttle buses also leave every 15 minutes to Le Royal Méridien, which has beach access, swimming pools and a kids' club.

The Hatta Fort Hotel ★ ★ ★ ★
PO Box 9277, Hatta; ☎ 04-809-9333;
{vfl **04-852-3561; jebelali-international.com**

Cost AED 595, half board **Location** Hatta **Number of rooms** 50 rooms, plus 2 suites **Room sq m** 45 **Conference facilities** Yes **Pool/sauna** Yes **Beach access** No **Exercise facilities** Yes **Spa** Yes **Parking/valet** Yes/no **Licensed bar** Yes **On-site dining** International, bar snacks **Extra amenities** Minibar, safe boxes, bathrobes, slippers, hairdryer, tea/coffee facilities, DVD player, DVDs for hire **Business amenities** High-speed Internet, business centre **Shuttle buses** None **Wheelchair facilities** Yes

THE HATTA FORT HOTEL IS NESTLED IN THE FOOTHILLS of the Hajar Mountains, about an hour from the Dubai airport, in 32.4 hectares (80 acres) of gardens. It has very pleasant, spacious rooms, with chaletlike wooden ceilings, decorated in warm, earthy tones – ochre, sienna, teak, coral and bronze – with pretty rugs, lovely dark wooden furniture, clean modern bathrooms with walk-in showers and wonderful mountain views.

The Deluxe Chalets have a private terrace and can accommodate two adults and two children under age 12; the suites also have a spacious lounge, an extra bathroom and two terraces, and also sleep two adults and two children under age 12, or they can interconnect for larger groups. Villas accommodate the whole family, contain a hot tub, have a master bedroom en suite and include a second bedroom with a guest bathroom, a private garden, a kitchen and a lounge and dining area.

And if you're feeling really alternative, you can rent a Winnebago: it is 11.6 metres (38 feet) long by 2.6 metres (8.5 feet) wide and features a master bedroom, kitchen with microwave, toilet and shower, TV and sun-shade canopy. It is fully equipped, fully furnished and air conditioned, and the Winnebago gives you complete freedom to take off and travel in the mountains independently.

The hotel's half-decent restaurant – Jeema – has an International à la carte menu and live music each evening, and the pretty, glass-enclosed Cafe Gazebo, with an open terrace that overlooks one of the swimming pools, serves a buffet breakfast, lunch and snacks. The Roumoul Cocktail Bar has vintage leather seating and wooden panelling (more wood), and at the Sunset Terrace, you can enjoy drinks ordered from Roumoul's and – guess what – watch the sunset. You can also enjoy a drink at the Gazebo Pool Bar.

The two lovely swimming pools – Gazebo Pool and the garden rock pool – are both temperature-controlled, with sunloungers, parasols and beautiful views, as well as a children's pool. Alternative facilities include a golf driving range, mini-golf and an archery, and the hotel organises four-wheel excursions into the Hajar Mountains and through the wadis, as well as a variety of road trips within the region. This is also a great hotel for families with children, as various organised activity programmes are available for different age ranges. The gym is well equipped, and a health club offers a wide range of treatments.

Hilton Dubai Creek ★ ★ ★ ★ ★

Beniyas Road, Deira, PO Box 33398; ☎ 04-227-1111;
{vfl **04-227-1131; hilton.com**

Cost AED 850, including breakfast **Location** Deira **Number of rooms** 150 rooms, plus 4 suites **Room sq m** 37–69 **Conference facilities** Yes **Pool/sauna** Yes **Beach access** No **Exercise facilities** Yes **Spa** No **Parking/valet** Yes **Licensed bar** Yes **On-site dining** Mediterranean brasserie, fine dining, bar and lounge, pool bar **Extra amenities** Airport pickup, executive chauffeur service, iron/ironing board, hairdryer, scales, hair salon, gift shop, tea/coffee facilities, espresso maker (executive floors), flat-panel TV, music system (executive floors), minibar, walk-in shower, bathrobe, safe box, babysitting, laundry and dry-cleaning, car rental **Business amenities** Business centre, executive lounge, wireless Internet in all public areas, high-speed Internet in bedrooms, boardroom, meeting room **Shuttle buses** To Jumeirah Beach Park **Wheelchair facilities** Yes

---

A VERY SMART, MODERN IMPOSING BLACK MARBLE BUILDING, Hilton Dubai Creek has the most incredible views over Dubai Creek, with floor-to-ceiling windows (we'd stay here for the views alone, so be sure to ask for rooms with a view of Dubai Creek), and Gordon Ramsay's restaurant Verre. With excellent facilities, a range of room sizes and delightful staff, there is very little to fault. The majority of guests staying here are on business – the airport is a ten-minute drive away, as are the business districts – but so are all the really interesting touristy areas – the souks, Heritage Village and the historical part of Dubai. The beach is 15 minutes away, and Mall of the Emirates is 20 minutes away. The lobby is light and spacious, with sparkly lights on the stairs, black leather seating and black, silver and wood fittings.

It's all very efficient and masculine, and that is the style of the bedrooms too. All have crisp, modern, smooth lines and neutral colours, and the rooms are spacious with lots of light but err on the side of functional rather than luxurious. Deluxe and Executive rooms on the top floor have access to the Executive Lounge, free Continental breakfast and refreshments, and a choice of king or queen beds, and the rooms sleep two adults and one child. Suites – which offer spacious family-size accommodation with living room, kitchenette, balcony and king-size bed in the bedroom – can sleep two adults and two children and have complimentary access to the Executive Lounge, complimentary airport transfers and free breakfast and refreshments.

Restaurants include the Glasshouse Brasserie, offering European cuisine, and Verre by Gordon Ramsay – fine dining with fine prices to match. Issimo Bar is a bit like being on a ship – chrome and curvy. The Pool Bar on the roof is casual and relaxed, and it offers lunch and dinner.

The rooftop pool has fantastic views but low glass barriers all the way round, so watch your children. The health club has a gym and a massage room, with a range of massages on offer. This is an excellent city hotel that takes itself very seriously.

Ibis Mall of the Emirates ★★

(linked to Suite Novotel; see page 99)

2A Street, PO Box 283825, Al Barsha; ☎ **04-382-3000;** ' z"z' › ∨«~ƒ¥"
☎ **04-702-8000;** {∨fl **04-382-3001; ibishotel.com; accorhotels.com**

Cost AED 320 **Location** Al Barsha and Al Quoz **Number of rooms** 204 **Room sq m** 19 **Conference facilities** No **Pool/sauna** No, but you can use the pool at adjoining sister hotel Suite Novotel for AED 30/day **Beach access** No **Exercise facilities** No, but you can use Suite Novotel's gym for AED 30/day **Spa** No **Parking/valet** Yes/no **Licensed bar** Yes **On-site dining** Italian, International snack food, bar food **Extra amenities** Flat-panel TV, special-needs rooms with wheelchair access, e-corner with games in lobby, 24-hour snack service, laundry and dry-cleaning, airport pickup **Business amenities** High-speed Internet, Wi-Fi enabled in lobby areas **Shuttle buses** To Jumeirah Open Beach, Jumeirah Beach Residence **Wheelchair facilities** Yes

IBIS HAS COME UP TRUMPS WITH THIS AMAZING two-star hotel, providing outstanding facilities at budget prices. Rooms are larger than their European counterparts, are simply but thoughtfully furnished and are comfortable and stylish. The foyer of this hotel is enormous, 1970s-retro in design, with fantastic doughnut-shaped orange and cream leather seats. The staff are friendly and helpful and speak excellent English.

Location-wise, this is a great up-and-coming area, with plenty of cafes, a stone's throw from Mall of the Emirates and Ski Dubai, 10 minutes from the beautiful open beaches at Jumeirah Beach Residence and no more than 20 minutes from Downtown. Ibis is attached to **Suite Novotel**, an equally-attractive three-star hotel, and you are able to use all the facilities here as well for a small fee.

Bedrooms are well thought out, with queen-size or twin beds, flat-panel TVs and en suite bathrooms with shower, toilet and basins. All fittings are sparkling and modern. If you are a larger family, interconnecting rooms are available.

Whilst there is no room service or tea-making facilities, vending machines with juice and water for sale are on each floor, or if you prefer, you can order from the restaurant at Suite Novotel by phone, and they will bring your food to your room at Ibis. Both hotels have several very affordable restaurants – Amici, which serves Italian cuisine, a daily buffet breakfast, lunch and dinner; Ezaz, a lounge bar that serves cocktails and bar food; and Deli Boutique at Suite Novotel, which serves sweet and savoury treats 24 hours a day. The Ibis is connected to Suite Novotel on every floor. This is a great example of how style and service don't need to be compromised for cost.

InterContinental Dubai Festival City ★ ★ ★ ★
Dubai Festival City, PO Box 45777; ☎ 04-701-1111;
{vfl **04-232-9098; ichotelsgroup.com**

Cost AED 950 **Location** Deira **Number of rooms** 377 rooms, plus 121 suites **Room sq m** 43–246 **Conference facilities** Yes **Pool/sauna** Yes **Beach access** No **Exercise facilities** Yes **Spa** Yes **Parking/valet** Yes **Licensed bar** Yes **On-site dining** Lebanese, French, International, fine dining **Extra amenities** Complimentary newspaper, DVD player, tea/coffee facilities, trouser press, iron/ironing board **Business amenities** Desk in all rooms, business centre, PCs and mobile phones for rent **Shuttle buses** To Al Badia golf course **Wheelchair facilities** Yes

LIKE ITS SISTER HOTEL THE CROWNE PLAZA, the InterContinental is a ten-minute drive from the airport, directly connected to the large Festival Centre and overlooks a 600-berth marina on Dubai Creek. Only opened in 2008, it is still sparklingly new, although the gleaming cream marble and the vast windows in the lobby make it feel a little bit soulless. Just off said lobby is Anise, the all-day dining restaurant that has lots of live cooking stations. Downstairs are Al Sultan Brahim, the only Dubai outpost of one of Beirut's most celebrated fish restaurants, and Bistro Madeleine, a French diner that wouldn't look out of place in the Marais area of Paris. Reflets par Pierre Gagnaire is the wildly-expensive conceptual dining experience from the three-Michelin-star winner.

The rooms are significantly larger than those at the Crowne Plaza, and the aubergine and buttercup decor makes a bit of a welcome relief from the inoffensive creams found in many other five-stars. The 'wet rooms' are particularly noteworthy – both the shower and bath are enclosed in the same glass cubicle, the tub fills from a jet in the ceiling, and many are right next to the window so have a great night-time vista.

Surprisingly for what is primarily a business hotel, there's a large pool, with a vertigo-inducing Perspex bottom hanging out over the marina below. There are large umbrellas, plenty of loungers and, somewhat unexpectedly given that it is on the fourth floor, a plethora of palm trees that offer lots of shade. On the same level are a 24-hour gym and a large spa that uses products from Dubai-based brand Shiffa, and sauna and steam rooms are in the male and female changing rooms.

Pay extra for an Executive Club room and you will have access to the huge and well-appointed 26th-floor Club InterContinental Lounge, with its own boardroom, complimentary breakfast, afternoon tea and evening drinks and also free local calls and high-speed Wi-Fi.

Jumeirah Bab Al Shams Desert Resort ★ ★ ★ ★ ★

Near Dubai Endurance City, PO Box 8168; ☎ 04-809-6100; {vfl 04-832-6698; jumeirah.com

Cost AED 2,520 **Location** Near Endurance City **Number of rooms** 103 rooms, plus 8 suites **Room sq m** 47–68 **Conference facilities** Yes **Pool/sauna** Yes **Beach access** No **Exercise facilities** Yes **Spa** Yes **Parking/valet** Yes **Licensed bar** Yes **On-site dining** Arabic, Italian, Indian, International **Extra amenities** Dates and fruit on arrival, Wi-Fi **Business amenities** Five meeting rooms, full conference facilities at neighbouring Endurance City **Shuttle buses** To Madinat Jumeirah, Jumeirah Beach Hotel **Wheelchair facilities** Yes

FOR NEW COUPLES IN DUBAI, there is pretty much a set progression. Sure, you might start off with a couple of drinks, then a few dinner dates. But it is pretty much a given that if your new amour hasn't whisked you off to Bab Al Shams within the month, you might as well stockpile the chick flicks, Kleenex and ice cream and put your best friend on speed dial. Because, apart from the prohibitively expensive Al Maha resort, this is as romantic as the desert gets.

As a tourist, the easiest way to get here is by taxi, which should come in at around AED 200 and take 45 minutes, although the hotel can arrange transfers, and there is also a shuttle bus from the Jumeirah Beach Hotel. Until mid-2009, the road out here was lined with massive hoardings promising theme parks and hotels galore. These were quietly taken down overnight, and now it's just sand, sand and more sand, with the occasional half-finished building dotting the landscape for light relief. Although all this is not great news for the economy, Bab Al Shams has benefited from the halt of encroaching developments, as you really do feel as if you are out in the middle of nowhere.

Just like the Madinat Jumeirah, the architecture here draws from the same traditional Emirati houses you will find in the historic Bastakiya district. Low rise, ochre coloured and built around a series of courtyards, they manage to fit pretty seamlessly into the surroundings. This means that there are no breathtaking indoor spaces – but it's all warm and homely, with Persian rugs, wall hangings and *Majlis*-style low, cushioned seating. The rooms are the same – most have a corner seating area; some have a small, grassy outdoor terrace. The bathrooms are also themed, with a rustic round tub that would easily fit two.

The swimming pools here are a real star attraction; one has an infinity edge that overlooks the desert, and another has an in-pool rain shower and a swim-up bar, as well as several children's areas. Non-residents of the hotel can use the facilities for AED 350 per day (AED 500 on Fridays), including lunch buffet. The whole place is very child-friendly, with a kids' club for tots ages 2–12, but unless you are desperate for peace and quiet, you may well not use it – most of the organised activities on offer, including falconry displays, archery, camel rides and 4x4 tours, are suitable for the whole family.

One thing you must experience here is the spectacle of Al Hadheerah, the enormous Arabic buffet restaurant that has a nightly themed show. See page 240 for a longer description, but suffice to say it includes goats, camels, a whirling dervish of dubious gender and some swordsmen on horseback. The food's pretty good too, and it's one of the only places you will experience real Emirati cuisine. There are also Italian, Indian and Arabic restaurants, and a rooftop shisha bar that's great for sundowners. Our tip is to spend a maximum of two nights here as part of a two-centre holiday, as the desert is definitely worth experiencing, but there are only so many dunes you need to see in your life.

Jumeirah Beach Hotel ★ ★ ★ ★
Jumeirah Road, Jumeirah, PO Box 11416; ☎ 04-348-0000;
{vfl **04-301-6800; jumeirah.com**

Cost AED 3,200 **Location** Jumeirah **Number of rooms** 550 rooms, plus 48 suites **Room sq m** 50–216 **Conference facilities** Yes **Pool/sauna** Yes **Beach access** Yes **Exercise facilities** Yes **Spa** Yes **Parking/valet** Yes **Licensed bar** Yes **On-site dining** Argentinian, Lebanese, Italian, Mediterranean, International, pan-Asian, German, Tex-Mex, English pub, seafood, health food, coffee shop **Extra amenities** Free entry to Wild Wadi waterpark, hairdryer, iron/ironing board **Business amenities** Private fax/photocopier, business centre, voice mail **Shuttle buses** To Jumeirah Bab Al Shams, Jumeirah Emirates Towers, Mall of the Emirates **Wheelchair facilities** Yes

---

THIS WAVE-SHAPED BUILDING RISES FROM THE BEACH just behind the Burj Al Arab's gargantuan sail, and the interiors are from exactly the same drawing board. Opened in 1997, it was one of the city's first mega-hotels, with nearly 600 rooms and suites. Unfortunately, it has begun to show its age – the rooms are dated and the decor a bit naff, with provincial placemat-style art, swirly carpets and your granny's bed throws. You may well be willing to overlook this if you have a family, though, as they all are spacious, sleeping two adults and two children, and every single one has a sea view.

More tasteful are the 19 one- and two-bed Beit Al Bahar villas, each of which has its own private garden and plunge pool. This resort-within-a-resort has its own reception, restaurant, pool and sun deck and is just opposite the Executive Pool and private beach. Guests paying a premium for Executive Club or Premium Leisure Club rooms in the main hotel are also allowed entrance here, and other complimentary facilities include tea, soft drinks and coffee all day, and pre-dinner canapés and cocktails in the private lounge.

Even standard rooms come with complimentary access to the adjoining Wild Wadi waterpark (which for a family of four represents quite a saving) and use of the fully-supervised Sinbad's Kids club (for children ages 2–12 8 a.m.–8 p.m.), which has its own shaded pool and air-conditioned play centre housed in a giant pirate's ship. Adults can occupy themselves at the Professional Association of Diving Instructors dive centre, squash and tennis courts or water sports centre, or take it easy at the spa.

The family bias is also apparent in the dining options – kids' menus and high chairs are available at most of the restaurants, although the cowboy-themed Go West and the beachside pizza joint La Veranda are the most popular. Latitude, the all-day buffet restaurant, has a designated kids' area where small hands can help themselves.

If you want to take advantage of the babysitting services, nightspots here include 360°, Uptown Bar and The Apartment, and grown-up dining includes the award-winning Argentinian La Parilla. The hotel is also minutes away on foot or golf buggy from the Madinat Jumeirah and its almost endless dining options. So vast is this place (it has five pools and 17 restaurants) that it will take you a while to get oriented – our top tip is to rent a Segway at AED 150 per half hour.

Jumeirah Emirates Towers ★★★★★

Dubai International Financial Centre, PO Box 72127; ☎ 04-330-0000; {vfl 04-330-3030; jumeirah.com

Cost AED 1,300 **Location** Sheikh Zayed Road **Number of rooms** 360 rooms, plus 40 suites **Room sq m** 44–312 **Conference facilities** Yes **Pool/sauna** Yes **Beach access** Not on-site, but free access to Jumeirah Beach Hotel and Wild Wadi **Exercise facilities** Yes **Spa** Yes **Parking/valet** Yes **Licensed bar** Yes **On-site dining** Lebanese, International, Tex-Mex, French, sushi, coffee shop **Extra amenities** Wi-Fi, hairdryer, jogging map and sweatband **Business amenities** Large desk in rooms, 24-hour business centre, on-call secretaries **Shuttle buses** To Madinat Jumeirah, Jumeirah Beach Hotel **Wheelchair facilities** Yes

BEFORE THE BURJ KHALIFA WAS BUILT and the Palm was but a twinkle in Sheikh Mohammed's eye, Jumeirah Emirates Towers were two of the city's few iconic buildings. The twin towers, one of which is devoted to office space, still cut a pretty impressive swagger on the Sheikh Zayed Road. Located in the financial district, next to the convention centre, this is first and foremost a business hotel. That means the H2O spa is men only (although women can have treatments in the sports club), the gym is weight-machine heavy and the sunbathing area around the ground-floor 25-metre (82-foot) swimming pool is a bit lacklustre. Oh, and a lot of, erm, single ladies hang out at the top-floor Champagne bar.

The restaurants have a similarly male bent – the Rib Room is serious steak-based dining, and Vu's is heavy French. Mosaico has a buffet-style range of International cuisine, and the attached Boulevard Mall offers sushi, noodles, Lebanese and Tex-Mex. With no major refurb since it opened in 2000, the decor of the rooms is dated and a touch Playskool – think primary-coloured sofas, checked cushions and Ikea-esque art. In the suites on higher floors, you can look out over the DIFC's Gate Village from the bath (although we've no idea why you would want to). The views are stonking whichever way you look – whether it's at the Burj Khalifa, out towards the World Islands or over Sheikh Mohammed's racehorse stables. You are also within a 15-minute cab radius of The Dubai Mall, the historical Bastakiya district and the Jumeirah Open Beach, and a Metro stop is right out front.

There are some female- and family-friendly touches here and there – a baby pool and a ladies-only floor, staffed entirely by the fairer sex and stocked with Chopard beauty products, pink towels, yoga mats, DVDs and a low-calorie menu. There are special rates at the weekend for leisure travellers, packages with twin-centre trips to Jumeirah Bab Al Shams Desert Resort and a free shuttle bus that travels to Jumeirah Beach Hotel, where guests enjoy free entrance to the beach and Wild Wadi waterpark. Pay a slightly higher rate for an Executive Club room or suite and you will be picked up by a limousine at the airport and have your suit pressed on arrival. You'll also have access to the Club Lounge, where you can graze on free food, soft drinks and house alcohol from breakfast onwards, and indulge in martinis 6:30–8 p.m.

Kempinski Hotel & Residences Palm Jumeirah ★ ★ ★ ★ ★

The Crescent West, Palm Jumeirah, PO Box 213208; ☎ 04-444-2000; {vfl 04-444-2777; kempinski.com/palmjumeirah

Cost AED 4,500 **Location** The Palm Jumeirah **Number of rooms** 52 one-bedroom suites, 109 two-bedroom suites, 32 three-bedroom suites, 1 two-bedroom penthouse, 6 three-bedroom penthouses, 30 four-bedroom penthouses, 2 five-bedroom penthouses, 12 five-bedroom villas **Room sq m** 98–893 **Conference facilities** Yes **Pool/sauna** Yes **Beach access** Yes **Exercise facilities** Yes **Spa** Yes **Parking/valet** Yes **Licensed bar** Yes **On-site dining** Mediterranean, seafood, lounge, in-room dining **Extra amenities** Hairdryer, bathrobe, slippers, coffee machine, private safe, fruit on arrival, daily mineral water, laundry, dry-cleaning and ironing, babysitting, car rental, DVD rentals, car wash, on-call medical assistance, pet or plant care **Business amenities** Wireless Internet in rooms, international direct-dial telephones with voice mail, business centre, Internet corner, foreign exchange **Shuttle buses** To Dubai Mall, Mall of the Emirates **Wheelchair facilities** Yes

ANOTHER LATE 2010 ADDITION to the row of Palm Jumeirah accommodations, Kempinski Hotel & Residences Palm Jumeirah promises to uphold the level of service expected from the group. Marble floors, columns and a dome grace the entrance of the hotel, and the European gold-and-cream interiors are grand. A myriad of outlets within the hotel create a shopper's paradise.

Enjoy a brunch on Fridays at the hotel's palatial Mediterranean restaurant, or try some fresh fish beachside. Lounge music and cigars accompany cocktails in the lounge, or for a little privacy, take dinner in your room.

The large penthouses and villas are ideal for families, and a kids' club and playground help keep the children entertained. A separate children's pool offers protection from the sun. A beach club and an abundance of water sports and shops keep the grown-ups amused.

A hairdresser, shoeshine service and tailor keep guests looking their best, and a spa and fitness centre make sure they feel their best too. Pampering and indulgence are the buzzwords here. Take a yoga class on the beach, or work with a personal trainer.

A living room, dining area and kitchen come standard with each unit, and the master bathrooms include both a separate shower and tub. A high-definition LCD TV and DVD player provide entertainment in each bedroom and living room, and some rooms include Bose sound systems and iPod docking stations. All units benefit from a private terrace and incredible vistas.

Kempinski Hotel Mall of the Emirates ★★★★★
Sheikh Zayed Road, Al Barsha, PO Box 120679; ☎ 04-341-0000; {vfl 04-341-4500; kempinski.com/dubai

Cost AED 1,200 **Location** Al Barsha and Al Quoz **Number of rooms** 336 rooms, plus 33 suites **Room sq m** 34–300 **Conference facilities** Yes **Pool/sauna** Yes **Beach access** Yes **Exercise facilities** Yes **Spa** Yes **Parking/valet** Yes **Licensed bar** Yes **On-site dining** International **Extra amenities** Wi-Fi, tea/coffee facilities **Business amenities** Business centre, desk in all rooms **Shuttle buses** None **Wheelchair facilities** Yes

IN MOST CITIES, YOU'D HAVE TO BE A PRETTY DEDICATED shopper to think that staying in a mall was a good idea. Not so in Dubai. In fact, this hotel has many more things going for it than its proximity to the shops. Although in many senses the Dubai Mall has stolen the Mall of the Emirates' thunder, it still has a trump card up its sleeve – a real-snow ski slope. The Kempinski certainly uses this to its best advantage – its 15 ski chalets, some of the most expensive rooms in the city, look directly out over the piste. If you book into one of these, complimentary entry to Ski Dubai is included in your suite price, with all other guests enjoying a 20% discount.

Every room has a pantry and dining table, which is especially handy for families with fussy eaters or those on a budget – literally hundreds of delis and sandwich shops, as well as a Carrefour hypermarket, are in the Mall of the Emirates. Apart from Sezzam, a food court–like restaurant where you can eat your way around the world, the dining options in the hotel itself are a bit sub-par; but with so many places to grab a bite at the mall, that's not really a problem. The smallish pool area tries its hand at Ibiza-style chic and is strewn with beanbags and pretty people smoking shisha at night, but it still overlooks a main road so won't be to everyone's taste. There is also a tennis court, gym and spa, although again, if you find it a little pricey, you can choose from ample pampering day spas in the mall.

The location is pretty much slap bang in the middle of the Sheikh Zayed Road – 5 minutes from the Madinat Jumeirah, 15 minutes from

Jumeirah Beach Residence and 15 minutes from Downtown. It also benefits from being right next to the Mall of the Emirates Metro stop, and literally hundreds of cabs are always outside. It's unlikely that you'd choose this as a business hotel, but we would warn against it if you were considering it – it's a fair distance from the financial district, and traffic can get gridlocked at rush hour.

Al Maha Desert Resort and Spa ★ ★ ★ ★ ★

Dubai Desert Conservation Reserve, PO Box 7632; ☎ **04-832-9900;** {vfl **04-832-9211; emirateshotelsresorts.com**

Cost AED 3,200, inclusive of meals and activities **Location** Dubai Desert Conservation Reserve **Number of rooms** 42 suites **Room sq m** 75–530 **Conference facilities** Yes **Pool/sauna** Yes **Beach access** No **Exercise facilities** Yes **Spa** Yes **Parking/valet** Yes **Licensed bar** Yes **On-site dining** Fine dining **Extra amenities** Tea/coffee facilities, hairdryer **Business amenities** Business centre **Shuttle buses** None **Wheelchair facilities** Yes

THIS PLACE IS A POKE IN THE EYE for all the people who think that Dubai only does eco-unfriendly excess. A 30-minute drive from the centre of Dubai (it really would be better to book a transfer through the hotel for the trip – it's very easy to miss the turning if you are in a taxi or self-drive, and the driveway could only very loosely be termed a road), it is remarkably low-key, rising out of the desert like an upscale Bedouin camp. The all-villa resort really is one for couples – children under age 12 are not even allowed.

Each villa has its own secluded private pool (heated or cooled as the season demands), so the only prying eyes you might see will belong to the odd endangered Arabian oryx. Al Maha actually has a whole 225 square kilometres (86.9 square miles) of designated desert nature reserve to itself and never feels crowded, as no outside guests are allowed to use the facilities.

There is only one restaurant, and to be honest, the breakfast and lunch buffets aren't particularly inspiring. It does up its game in the evening, though, with a five-course menu packed with foie gras and Wagyu. You can also take dinner on your own private deck, or be driven into the desert, where you will be served your meal and left to lounge on cushions under the stars, with a phone to call for a jeep when you're done.

The specials the hotel runs over the summer season are often a significant reduction on rack rate, and the desert is surprisingly bearable in the heat, given you have your own pool, a shaded courtyard and spacious air-conditioned room to duck into. A large spa with treatment rooms overlooks the dunes, and loungers surround a large communal pool. An impressive collection of architecture and antiques from the Gulf features in the rooms and public areas, and also, for those of an artistic bent, a chaise longue, an easel and a set of pastels are provided in each suite. The bathrooms, all of which have double sinks, large corner spa baths and a walk-in shower, are huge, as are the specially-built jumbo king-size beds.

This is the very top end of all-inclusive, with all meals (although not alcohol) and two complimentary activities per day thrown in – there is a full programme, from nature walks to four-wheel-drive desert safaris and falconry displays. Many of these take place early morning or late afternoon to avoid the midday sun.

Equine fans will be especially keen on riding the Arabian horses from the stables of Sheikh Mohammed, but be warned: no fibbing, for if you are not a very competent rider, you will be summarily dispatched back to the hotel. Even the sunset camel rides here are superior – it might just be us, but the camels here seem slightly better looking than the spitting dromedaries on which you are usually expected to sit.

Al Manzil Hotel ★ ★ ★ ★
Emaar Boulevard, The Old Town, Downtown; ☎ 04-428-5888; {vfl 04-428-5999; southernsunme.com/almanzil

---

Cost AED 2,150 **Location** Downtown **Number of rooms** 197 rooms, plus 8 suites **Room sq m** 33.4 **Conference facilities** Yes **Pool/sauna** Yes **Beach access** No **Exercise facilities** Yes **Spa** No **Parking/valet** Yes **Licensed bar** Yes **On-site dining** International, Arabic cuisine and shisha, South African and Australian pub, cafe snacks **Extra amenities** Minibar, 24-hour room service, mineral water, tea/coffee facilities, bathrobe, slippers, hairdryer, iron on request, newspapers **Business amenities** Business centre, business lounge, complimentary Internet, Wi-Fi in public areas **Shuttle buses** To Dubai Mall, Jumeirah Beach Park **Wheelchair facilities** Yes

AL MANZIL IS AN OUTSTANDING FOUR-STAR DELUXE HOTEL without fanfare or ostentation. It's refreshingly contemporary – modern Arabic in style – in a lively, vibrant location, and exquisite attention has been paid to detail. The staff are kind and helpful, and the moment you walk in you are aware of a really easy, laid-back, gentle charm. It is linked by an underground souk, which has a supermarket and various decent shops, to its sister hotel Qamardeen, equally as fabulous, but maybe more business oriented. The good thing is that you can use the facilities of both hotels and cross-charge.

Al Manzil Hotel considers itself primarily a business hotel too, but we think it would make an ideal family hotel, as it is a five-minute walk to The Dubai Mall, Souk Al Bahar and the Burj Khalifa, and has a great pool, lovely restaurants and a free shuttle bus to the best beach park in Dubai. The temperature-controlled swimming pool on the first floor is delightful, with stylish sunloungers, tables and parasols. The gym, while not huge, is spacious and airy.

Bedrooms have just the right mix of elegance, comfort and functionality – king-size beds with funky, stripy covers, cool yellow walls and chic white armchairs. The bathroom is open plan – enclosed in glass, so not much privacy when performing your ablutions. The flat-panel TV swivels, so you can watch it from anywhere in the room. The Burj-view rooms have (obviously) superb views of the Burj Khalifa, while pool-view rooms look over the inner courtyard pool. The suites have big oval baths and a walk-in shower with huge rain forest showerhead, and the toilet has a floor-to-ceiling window, so you definitely get a room with a view.

Breakfast (Continental, AED 85; full, AED 95) can be eaten in the Conservatory Restaurant or the Courtyard. The restaurants are elegant and sophisticated, and the bar, with four screens on the walls and ten screens around the central bar area, is the sports lover's dream come true.

Media One ★ ★ ★ ★
Media City, PO Box 121818; ☎ 04-427-1000;
{vfl **04-427-1001; mediaonehotel.com**

Cost AED 1,750 **Location** New Dubai **Number of rooms** 260 rooms, plus 10 suites **Room sq m** 28 **Conference facilities** Yes **Pool/sauna** Yes **Beach access** No **Exercise facilities** Yes **Spa** No **Parking/valet** Yes **Licensed bar** Yes **On-site dining** Mediterranean/International, cafe snacks, bar food, poolside grill and bar **Extra amenities** Flower shop, hair salon, gift shop, 24-hour room service, tea/coffee facilities, minibar, hairdryer, safe box, iron/ironing board **Business amenities** Business centre, high-speed Internet, Wi-Fi in public areas **Shuttle buses** None **Wheelchair facilities** Yes

FUNKY, URBAN AND EDGY. The staff have attitude – a good attitude. They are confident and friendly without being too servile, and the uniforms are oh-so-urban – lime-green shirts for the reception staff, and jeans and jackets for the restaurant staff. The lobby sets the tone: a big silver curve of a reception desk, lime-green chaises longues, cream sofas and brown rugs, cream cubes and a central glass bit with glowing colour-changing lights that houses the lifts.

There are six types of bedroom: Hip, Hip Urban, Hip VIP, Cool, Calm Suite and Chill Out Suite. The bedrooms have modern furnishings – queen or king beds, glass-enclosed bathrooms with huge rain showers, walk-in showers in the larger rooms and a big bath or a shower over the bath in the smaller ones. These are no-nonsense, comfortable rooms, with all modern conveniences. The Cool room has a separate bathroom, not glass enclosed; the Calm Suite is a studio suite with living room area; and the Chill Out Suite has a living room, separate bedroom, glass walk-in bathroom and a guest bathroom.

The hotel has a health club with steam rooms and saunas, a well-equipped cardio and weight gym with personal trainers if required and a really fantastic infinity pool, with lots of white leather seating, sunloungers, parasols and a Chill Out lounge, grill and bar. Every Thursday and Friday night a DJ party is held at the pool. Eateries include CafeM for coffees and snacks; The Z:ONE Bar and Lounge for light meals and evening drinks; and The MED, a Mediterranean restaurant offering a breakfast buffet (AED 85, 6:30–10:30 a.m.), lunch buffet and à la carte dinner. This is a great inexpensive hotel for business travellers and couples who are looking for somewhere to stay with loads of energy and buzz.

Le Méridien Dubai ★ ★ ★ ★ ★

Airport Road, PO Box 10001; ☎ 04-217-0000;
{vfl **04-282-1650; starwoodhotels.com/lemeridien**

Cost AED 1,600 **Location** Deira **Number of rooms** 383 rooms, plus 19 suites **Room sq m** 35 **Conference facilities** 9 meeting rooms, 3 function rooms **Pool/ sauna** Yes **Beach access** No **Exercise facilities** Yes **Spa** Yes **Parking/valet** Yes **Licensed bar** Yes **On-site dining** 18 restaurants, including Australian, French, Chinese, Japanese, Lebanese, Thai, Italian, Mexican, Irish pub, steakhouse, seafood, vodka bar and patisserie **Extra amenities** DVD player, minibar, daily newspaper, tea/coffee facilities, bathrobe, slippers, hairdryer, iron/ironing board, safe box, 24-hour room service, beauty/hair salon, barber shop, florist, car rental **Business amenities** Wi-Fi, high-speed Internet, business centre **Shuttle buses** To Deira City Centre Mall, Gold Souk, Jumeirah Beach Park **Wheelchair facilities** Yes

LE MÉRIDIEN IS LOCATED AT DUBAI AIRPORT and is typical of an airport hotel: it is functional and convenient. Taxis arrive day and night; the lobby is full of suitcases and businessmen snatching a quick meeting. If you're a tourist, there's a danger that you'll feel as if you're intruding on a private business function. Rooms are contemporary and also functional, clean and convenient. If you have business near the airport or an early flight and want to catch a valuable extra hour's sleep, then we'd recommend this hotel. It is worth noting, though, that recently this hotel has started to look a little worn and grubby around the edges, especially in the smaller, cheaper rooms.

Food-wise, Le Méridien really does have something for everyone. Yalumba features modern Australian cuisine; Café Chic serves French; Long Yin offers Cantonese and Szechuan; Kiku cooks Japanese; Seafood Market is where you can shop for fresh seafood and vegetables and have them prepared to your liking. Méridien Village Terrace offers themed cuisine evenings and live entertainment; Al Mijana is Lebanese cuisine with an oud player and belly dancer; Sukhothai offers pretty appalling Thai cuisine; Casa Mia is an Italian restaurant; Jules Bar & Bistro features Mexican food and live music. Warehouse includes a European-style cafe bar and garden, a wine bar on the ground floor, a vodka bar and fusion restaurant on the upper level and a resident DJ and dance floor. The Dubliner's Traditional Irish Pub does what it says on the tin; Gourmandises is a patisserie and deli; L'Atelier des Chefs offers cookery classes.

Once you've tried all these eateries, you might waddle over to Natural Elements Spa & Fitness, a 2,000-square-metre (21,528-square-foot) wellness facility that offers distinct areas providing body and wellness treatments; a state-of-the-art fitness centre with gym, power plate studio, aerobics studio and racquet sports courts; spa areas; four lovely outdoor swimming pools, surrounded by trees and 15 hectares (38 acres) of landscaped gardens; and personal trainers on hand to offer advice and consultations.

Bedrooms at Le Méridien come in a variety of sizes and colours: Classic, Superior Deluxe, Royal Club and Art & Tech rooms, along with the Presidential and Royal suites. The Royal Club is an exclusive wing of the hotel with a private entrance and check-in facilities; 24-hour butler service; private lounge serving complimentary Continental breakfast, cocktails and beverages; complimentary limousine airport transfers; and a dedicated business centre and boardroom. Art & Tech rooms have been completely renovated and feature an espresso maker as well as a dedicated work area, which includes a specially-designed desk with plug-in data port and wireless Internet. These rooms also offer a power shower with separate rain shower and movement sensors for bedroom and bathroom light activation. All of the Art & Tech rooms feature a scenic view of the gardens and swimming pools. Complimentary breakfast is also offered. Stay in the suites, and you'll get extremely nice decor with a slightly Colonial feel, walk-in rain showers, baths and lots of amenities. If you stay in the Classic rooms, be prepared for a bit of wear and tear, with dark wood, patterned carpets and white bed linens – pleasant but unoriginal and dull, and not the largest bathrooms in the world.

Mina A'Salam ★★★★★

Madinat Jumeirah, PO Box 75157; ☎ 04-366-8888;
{vfl **04-366-7788; jumeirah.com**

Cost AED 3,500 **Location** Jumeirah **Number of rooms** 280 rooms, plus 12 suites **Room sq m** 50–268 **Conference facilities** Yes **Pool/sauna** Yes **Beach access** Yes **Exercise facilities** Yes **Spa** Yes **Parking/valet** Yes **Licensed bar** Yes **On-site dining** International, Arabic, Chinese, British **Extra amenities** Wi-Fi, complimentary entry to Wild Wadi waterpark **Business amenities** Business centre **Shuttle buses** To Jumeirah Bab Al Shams, Jumeirah Beach Hotel **Wheelchair facilities** Yes

SET IN THE MASSIVE MADINAT JUMEIRAH COMPLEX of shops, hotels, restaurants and waterways, Mina A'Salam was designed to be the cosier, more homely twin to its imposing neighbour, Al Qasr Hotel. So instead of lofty, chandelier-bedecked ceilings, it has Moroccan lamps, antique-looking murals, rose-petal-filled fountains and more throw cushions than an average-size Ikea. It shares the same facilities as Al Qasr – beach access, free *abra* rides on the waterways, passes to Wild Wadi waterpark and use of the extensive Quay health club and the gorgeous Talise Spa. The complimentary Sinbad's Kids club is located at Al Qasr.

Rooms are slightly smaller than at Al Qasr but decorated in a similar Arabic style. All have a balcony, and all can sleep two adults and two children under age 12. All of the eateries at the Madinat Jumeirah are at your disposal, but specifically on-site is the award-winning Chinese restaurant Zheng He's and British-style gastro-pub The Wharf, which serves the best fish-and-chips in the city. For evening drinks, Bahri Bar has a large terrace overlooking the Burj Al Arab – a great spot for the ubiquitous 'I've been to Dubai' photo.

Probably the most unusual feature of the Mina A'Salam, though, is the small on-site turtle sanctuary, which rehabilitates sick native Arabian hawks-bills and releases them back into the wild. As with all Jumeirah properties, pay extra for a Premium Leisure or Executive Club room and you will receive complimentary breakfast; airport transfer; all-day tea, coffee and soft drinks; afternoon tea; and canapés and cocktails 6–8 p.m. daily.

The Monarch ★ ★ ★ ★ ★

Sheikh Zayed Road, PO Box 125511; ☎ 04-501-8888;
{vfl **04-501-8899; themonarchdubai.com**

Cost AED 2,899 **Location** Sheikh Zayed Road **Number of rooms** 194 rooms, plus 42 suites **Room sq m** 50–1,130 **Conference facilities** Yes **Pool/sauna** Yes **Beach access** No **Exercise facilities** Yes **Spa** Yes **Parking/valet** Yes **Licensed bar** Yes **On-site dining** Japanese, Arabic, International, steakhouse, cafe **Extra amenities** Wi-Fi, Egyptian cotton sheets, TV in bathrooms **Business amenities** Business centre, full-size desk and touch-screen telephone in rooms **Shuttle buses** None **Wheelchair facilities** Yes

TOTALLY GEARED TOWARDS BUSINESS TRAVELLERS, this is not a hotel to book if you are in Dubai for sun and sand, or if you have a family in tow. But it is located right at the top of the Sheikh Zayed Road, opposite the Dubai World Trade Centre, 5 minutes from the DIFC and 15 minutes from the airport. The restaurant options are expensive and grown-up – hipster hangout Okku serves superior cocktails and dispenses modern sushi in its dark, sexy interior, and American chain Ruth's Chris operates a steakhouse just next door. Both are brilliant, but neither comes cheap. Steer clear of the dreadful basement club Gold though – despite charging men a cool AED 1,000 for entry, it looks like a regional branch of The Gadget Shop.

Although the slightly claustrophobic design of the spa leaves a lot to be desired, the treatments – especially the Mandara massage, performed by two therapists – are sublime. Some hilariously over-the-top suites are on offer – the duplex Monarch suite, on the 32nd and 33rd floors, has its own gym, movie theatre, sauna and pool on the terrace. The standard rooms are fairly well appointed too, with large leather desks, lounge areas and state-of-the-art music systems. The ones higher up have pretty killer views of the Sheikh Zayed Road's neon strip too. There is a small fourth-floor pool with a few sunloungers and a ladies-only gym, as well as a mixed gym.

Mövenpick Jumeirah Beach ★ ★ ★ ★ ★

Jumeirah Beach, PO Box 282825; ☎ 04-449-8888;
{vfl **04-449-8889; moevenpick-hotels.com**

Cost AED 900 **Location** The Marina **Number of rooms** 294 rooms, plus 16 suites **Room sq m** 35 **Conference facilities** Yes **Pool/sauna** Yes **Beach access** Yes, but not a private beach **Exercise facilities** Yes **Spa** Yes **Parking/valet** Yes **Licensed bar** Yes **On-site dining** International bar food, healthy juices, organic snacks **Extra amenities** Hairdryer, bathrobe, slippers, tea/coffee facilities, 24-hour room service, turndown service, minibar, cable TV, balconies, airport pickup **Business amenities** Wi-Fi, business centre, high-speed Internet **Shuttle buses** To Mall of the Emirates, BurJuman Centre **Wheelchair facilities** Yes

LOCATED IN ONE OF DUBAI'S newest neighbourhoods, with its cafes and restaurants, cobbled streets and a weekend street market, Mövenpick Jumeirah Beach is ideally located across the road from the lovely Jumeirah Beach, with a range of small boutiques and interior design shops close by. This feels like a real seaside resort, and the hotel has maximised on its location. The entrance is so unassuming that you could miss it, but once you enter, the hotel seems to open up.

Decor is simple, contemporary and unfussy. Staff are friendly and greet guests with fresh juice and cold flannels. The pool on the first floor is delightful with a grassy terrace and a bar area. Our only criticism is that there are not enough sunloungers for the number of guests in the hotel, and unless you get up early and reserve your seat with a towel, you are unlikely to get one later. The pool terrace leads through to the hotel's main restaurant – The Talk – an all-day food emporium with pizza oven, pasta station, tandoori oven, live cooking station and sushi bar. Glass walls look out onto the pool terrace, and you can eat inside or out. If you take the hotel's half-board option, you will certainly save money and not go hungry. West Beach Bistro is an informal gastro bar serving modern International cuisine, and the Falls, open 24 hours and situated in the lobby, serves healthy fresh juices, organic snacks, pastries and coffee.

A decent health club overlooks the pool, with a small, well-equipped gym, steam room and sauna, and a spa with a comprehensive range of treatments. Bedrooms are light, spacious and very comfortable. Decor is not particularly cutting-edge, but it is contemporary nevertheless. The bathroom opens out into the bedroom through folding wooden doors, which enhances the feeling of space. Furniture is simple, with a good-size desk and a comfortable sofa on which to relax. Three types of bedroom – Superior, Deluxe and Executive – have either king beds or twin beds. Executive rooms have access to the executive lounge and a happy hour. All the bedrooms have balconies overlooking the sea.

Novotel Deira City Centre ★★★★

Eighth Street, Port Saeed District, Front of Deira City Centre Mall, PO Box 1853100; ☎ 04-292-5200; {vfl 04-292-5201; novotel.com

Cost AED 665 Location Deira **Number of rooms** 188 rooms, plus 1 suite **Room sq m** 30 **Conference facilities** 3 meeting rooms **Pool/sauna** Yes **Beach access** No **Exercise facilities** Yes **Spa** No **Parking/valet** Yes **Licensed bar** Yes **On-site dining** International, light snack food, French cuisine in Ibis next door **Extra amenities** Sofa bed in each room, work desk, iPod docking station, hairdryer, minibar, tea/coffee facilities, bathrobes, 24-hour room service, solarium, shoeshine machine, dry-cleaning/ironing, babysitting on request **Business amenities** Wi-Fi, high-speed Internet, business facilities (printing, faxing, photocopying), secretarial services **Shuttle buses** To Jumeirah Beach Park **Wheelchair facilities** Yes

IF YOU'RE FEELING MORE ADVENTUROUS or you're here on business, then staying in Deira City Centre will give you insight into another side of

Dubai. You are close to the souks, Dubai Creek, historic Dubai and Dubai Creek Park, and the Novotel is an unpretentious, reasonably priced hotel. It's not luxurious, and it's not near the beach, but the facilities are fine, and the hotel is light, bright and modern. And it is certainly superior to many Novotels in Europe. It is linked to Ibis Deira City Centre (which we don't review in this guide because it's not that good) and is situated directly opposite Deira City Centre Mall, which has loads of great shops. And you're within walking distance of the Metro, which is very convenient.

The lobby is airy and spacious, with an Oriental feel. All facilities are on the ground level and first floor, where the meeting rooms, swimming pool and gym facilities are located. Bedrooms err on the side of functional, but they are great for families with children, as they all have a king bed, a sofa bed and an en suite bathroom with bath and separate walk-in shower. Rooms are decorated in a modern, contemporary style, with cream walls and grey-green carpets. The bathrooms are modern and spotless; the towels are not the most luxurious we've seen but are fine. Some rooms face the mosque, so bear in mind that, while the call to prayer does become white noise after a while, it starts at 5 a.m. and occurs five times a day, and in some rooms we've been told that you can hear loud music from a nightclub – worth checking where that is in comparison to your room.

Tala Cafe serves snacks and hot and cold beverages, and Tala Restaurant offers all-day buffet dining. Domino Bistro in Ibis Deira City Centre, which is linked to Novotel on the ground floor, offers half-decent French cuisine. Vertigo, a cocktail bar, offers a pleasant venue for an evening drink, with Asian and Mexican snacks. A pool is on the first floor in an open courtyard, with a large outdoor seating area and wooden sunloungers and parasols; however it is in the shade until later in the day. The gym is tiny, with only a small selection of equipment. Don't expect luxury, but it is modern, clean and comfortable.

One&Only Royal Mirage ★★★★★
**Al Sufouh Road, PO Box 37252; ☎ 04-399-9999;
{vfl 04-399-9998; oneandonlyresorts.com**

Cost AED 1,800, including breakfast **Location** The Marina **Number of rooms** 393 rooms, plus 58 suites **Room sq m** 45–3,498 **Conference facilities** Yes **Pool/sauna** Yes **Beach access** Yes **Exercise facilities** Yes **Spa** Yes **Parking/valet** Yes **Licensed bar** Yes **On-site dining** Arabic, International, Moroccan, European, Indian, seafood, shisha lounge **Extra amenities** Coffee machine, fruit on arrival **Business amenities** Internet in rooms, business centre **Shuttle buses** To Mall of the Emirates, Dubai Mall **Wheelchair facilities** Yes

OF ALL THE HOTELS IN DUBAI that suffered from the construction of the Palm Jumeirah, the One&Only Royal Mirage must be at the top of the list. Where there was once a relatively unspoilt view out to sea from its palm-fringed private beach, you now have a vista of an eight-lane highway and endless construction (not that you'd know it from the brochure shots, which remain rather cynically unchanged). The owner, South African magnate Sol Kerzner, can't have been too bitter though, for he also owns the Atlantis and One&Only The Palm. If you can't beat 'em, as they say . . .

The design is inspired by Arabian courtyard architecture – in truth, it looks more like a series of Moroccan or Syrian riads than the Madinat-style Emirati buildings. It's a low-key sort of luxury – lots of marble, tasteful chandeliers and rose-petal-filled fountains. It's also huge and split into three distinct areas – The Palace, Arabian Court and Residence & Spa. This makes booking slightly more complicated than it needs to be, but basically, the Residence is super high-end and has its own facilities to which guests in other parts of the hotel aren't allowed access (although Residence guests are free to use the facilities anywhere in the complex).

The Residence sits in the middle of the resort and has one garden villa, 16 suites and 28 rooms in total. Although children are welcome, the real core customers here are couples, often honeymooners. It has the highest staff-to-guest ratio, a dedicated swimming pool and one restaurant, where the selection changes daily but guests are encouraged to order off-menu. Also, they serve a very British afternoon tea every day. The buildings here are low-rise; all have a sea view and are surrounded by mature gardens. It's also a short enough distance to the spa that you could easily shuffle there in your bathrobe and slippers – we have gone into more detail on page 265, but this is as good a pampering experience as you'll have anywhere in Dubai, especially if you book yourself in for a Royal Hammam treatment.

Next up is the Arabian Court, where all of the rooms and suites still have a sea view and are decked out with a similar signature Arabia-like palette of cream, brown and ochre shades, with wrought-iron tables, stained-glass lamps, dark wood beds and patterned carpets. All of the hotel's rooms underwent a programme of refurbishment in 2009–2010, so they're still box-fresh. The pool here, like all of the others in the resort, is chilled in summer and heated in winter and has direct access to the beach just in front. This part of the hotel is most suitable for families with older children – those with tots would do best to request a room or suite in the Palace section of the hotel, which has a lively pool area (although there's an adult-only quiet garden too). Non-guests are welcome to use the pool and beach facilities at a cost of AED 250 if you book 24 hours in advance, or AED 300 for walk-ins.

The Palace section has the smallest standard rooms in the resort, and not all of them are facing the beach, but the whole resort is set well back from Al Sufouh Road, so even if you can't see the sea, you won't have a traffic view.

As you might expect from a resort of this size, plenty of activities are on offer – a complimentary daily programme includes runs on the beach, aqua-aerobics and tennis for older children and adults, as well as a KidsOnly club, which runs a full schedule 10 a.m.–10 p.m. daily. A water sports centre on the beach also offers banana boats, waterskiing and windsurfing.

The restaurants manage to cover pretty much every cuisine and atmosphere you might fancy – EauZone, set in the middle of a swimming pool, offers pan-Asian food in a romantic setting; Beach Bar & Grill is a laid-back seafood spot during the day, which becomes all candle-lit and smoochy at night. Breakfast, lunch and dinner are served at several buffet restaurants, and the complex also offers a Moroccan eatery, a rooftop bar that is excellent for sundowners, a cushion-strewn shisha-and-meze courtyard and Kasbar, a nightclub for those over the age of 25. In essence, this is the sort of place you could happily come for a week and never leave, especially if you have kids.

But if you do feel the urge to escape, the Mall of the Emirates, the Walk at Jumeirah Beach Residence, The Atlantis and the Madinat Jumeirah are right on your doorstep. We wouldn't recommend it for business travellers, unless you're bringing family too – the business centre isn't very well designed, and connecting to the Internet in your room (there is no Wi-Fi) will cost you AED 121 per 24 hours.

One&Only The Palm ★ ★ ★ ★ ★
The Crescent West, Palm Jumeirah, PO Box 114843; ☎ 04-440-1010; {vfl 04-440-1011; oneandonlythepalm.com

Cost AED 3,490, including breakfast (AED 27,550 for the Grand Villa) **Location** The Palm Jumeirah **Number of rooms** 64 rooms, 26 suites, 3 two-bedroom villas, 1 three-bedroom Grand Villa **Room sq m** 65–425 **Conference facilities** Yes **Pool/sauna** Yes **Beach access** Yes **Exercise facilities** Yes **Spa** Yes **Parking/valet** Yes **Licensed bar** Yes **On-site dining** Oriental, Middle Eastern, Mediterranean, seafood **Extra amenities** Toaster, coffee machine, mini bar **Business amenities** Multifunctional reception area, wireless Internet **Shuttle buses** To shopping malls **Wheelchair facilities** Yes

ONE OF THE NEWEST ADDITIONS to the Dubai hotel scene, One&Only The Palm opened in late 2010. Surrounded by palm trees and lush gardens, the Moorish- and Andalucian-inspired buildings face the beaches of Palm Jumeirah. Inside, the rooms showcase modern style accented by cream, turquoise and purple fabrics. Each of the rooms features a private balcony or garden patio, and private pools accompany the suites and villas. In addition, the villas come with their own kitchenettes, en suite bathrooms, parking spaces and a personal butler. All of the oversize bathrooms include a walk-in rain shower and free-standing bathtub.

Multiple activities are offered on-site. Play a round of tennis, have a manicure and pedicure, enjoy a spa treatment or try out the state-of-the-art fitness equipment. The hotel's private harbour and proximity to the beach mean that guests can participate in water sports, such as wind-surfing, sailing, fishing, kayaking or waterskiing. Sunseekers may relax on oversize daybeds, and those who shun the sun can unwind underneath an air-conditioned poolside cabana, which is comprised of a lounge area with a flat-panel TV and minibar.

At Zest, be entertained as cooks prepare Oriental and Middle Eastern cuisine before your eyes. Guests can dine al fresco, or they can simply enjoy the view from inside through the floor-to-ceiling windows. The conservatory-style restaurant overlooks the pool and Moorish gardens.

Partake in a fine-dining experience at Stay by Yannick Alléno, who is a Michelin-starred chef. Vaulted ceilings, rich colours and black crystal chandeliers set the mood. Socialise with other guests at the Conversation Table, design your own dessert at the Pastry Library or dine at the Sharing Table, which offers a private menu and dedicated host for parties of 12. At 101, gaze out at the marina, recline on a daybed or listen to a DJ play music, all while dining on light Mediterranean fare.

Orient Guest House ★ ★ ★

Al Fahidi Street, Bur Dubai, PO Box 46500; ☎ 04-351-9111; {vfl 04-351-7744; orientguesthouse.com

Cost AED 500, including breakfast **Location** Bur Dubai **Number of rooms** 10 **Room sq m** 25 **Conference facilities** No **Pool/sauna** No/yes **Beach access** No **Exercise facilities** No **Spa** No **Parking/valet** No **Licensed bar** No, but guests can consume their own alcohol in their rooms **On-site dining** English/ Arabic breakfast made to order every morning, light snacks and soft beverages available all day **Extra amenities** Airport transfers; 24-hour butler service; hairdryer; range of toiletries; complimentary mineral water; complimentary access to Arabian Courtyard Hotel & Spa (200 metres, or 600 feet, away) and its health club, outdoor swimming pool, gymnasium, sauna, steam room and hot tub **Business amenities** Wi-Fi, Internet **Shuttle buses** To Jumeirah Beach Park **Wheelchair facilities** No

Situated in the heart of Bastakiya Heritage District, this is a completely different sort of hotel to most you will find in Dubai. It is a beautifully-restored traditional two-storey villa and offers ten Arabian-style decorated rooms and a *Majlis* (lounge) in which to relax. The guesthouse is within walking distance of Dubai Museum, the souks and Dubai Creek, and it is only 6 kilometres, or 3.7 miles, from the airport. The roof terrace and two courtyards provide tranquil spots in which to relax and enjoy the peaceful surroundings. It has a covered courtyard, with black wrought-iron and marble tables and chairs. Breakfast is served 7–10 a.m., and the Courtyard Cafe incorporates a small Starbucks.

The bedrooms are lovely, all are en suite and all have king-size beds made of dark wood with ornate carvings of flowers. There are two types of rooms – Heritage and Mumtaz. Some rooms have windows, and others don't. Deep red and gold velvet throws cover the beds, and each room has a satellite TV and a telephone. Bathrooms have a shower and a bath and are modern and charming. It would only suit couples or families with older teenagers, as the rooms all have separate entrances onto the courtyard. This is a delightful hotel – more of a bed-and-breakfast that oozes charm and atmosphere. The nearby Arabian Courtyard Hotel, whilst not a hotel we have recommended in the guide, has a selection of reasonable restaurants and a pub, and the health club facilities are free of charge to Orient Guest House guests.

The Palace – The Old Town ★ ★ ★ ★ ★

Emaar Boulevard, The Old Town, Downtown, PO Box 9770; ☎ 04-428-7888; {vfl 04-428-7999; theaddress.com

Cost AED 1,000 **Location** Downtown **Number of rooms** 161 rooms, plus 81 suites **Room sq m** 55 **Conference facilities** Yes **Pool/sauna** Yes **Beach access**

No **Exercise facilities** Yes **Spa** Yes **Parking/valet** Yes **Licensed bar** Yes **On-site dining** Thai, Argentinian, Arabic, International, cafe **Extra amenities** Free Wi-Fi, tea/coffee facilities **Business amenities** Desk in all rooms, business centre, library **Shuttle buses** None **Wheelchair facilities** Yes

RIGHT IN THE MIDDLE of what developers Emaar would have you believe is the 'world's most prestigious square kilometre', the Palace is a beautiful anomaly. It sits right next to the big, brash and incredibly noisy Dubai Fountain and the glass-and-steel Burj Khalifa but is itself a wonderfully low-key, low-rise destination, decked out in modern Arabian style. The driveway takes you past a large gleaming blue pool and under Moorish arches, into a cosy lobby with a rose-filled fountain and cushion-strewn lounge bar. Rooms are more of the same – lots of pretty latticework screens and tasteful cream-and-brown furnishings. The suites have original Arabian antiques and artwork and come with a selection of fruit of which Carmen Miranda would be proud. All rooms look out over water, whether it's the Dubai Fountain (which can sound a bit like a succession of water cannons, although it gets switched off at midnight) or the more placid Burj Lake. The well-equipped gym looks out over the lake, while the large outdoor pool overlooks the fountain.

Dining options include Ewaan, the Arabic-International restaurant that has cosy raised seating for large groups in recesses around the outside of the lofty space and a delicious *Iftar* buffet during Ramadan. Asado, the Argentinian steakhouse, is consistently packed and is especially nice during summer, as there is a large outdoor seating area. The Thai restaurant, Thiptara, is perched romantically out over the water and is surrounded by large fire torches. At night, the *Majlis* tents around the pool are a wonderful place to smoke shisha in privacy. During the day, you have the Dubai Mall on your doorstep, and the hotel is directly connected to Souk Al Bahar, with its tens of bars and restaurants.

The Park Hyatt ★★★★★

Dubai Creek Golf & Yacht Club, Deira, PO Box 2822; ☎ **04-602-1234;** {vfl **04-602-1235; dubai.park.hyatt.com**

Cost AED 1,675 **Location** Deira **Number of rooms** 190 rooms, plus 35 suites **Room sq m** 52–220 **Conference facilities** Yes **Pool/sauna** Yes **Beach access** No **Exercise facilities** Yes **Spa** Yes **Parking/valet** Yes **Licensed bar** Yes **On-site dining** Arabic, French, International, seafood, tea room **Extra amenities** Daily fruit and mineral water, three phone lines, DVD player **Business amenities** Business centre, high-speed and wireless Internet, extensive conference facilities, suites suitable for meetings, phone and fax in rooms **Shuttle buses** To Wafi Mall, Dubai Mall, Festival Centre, Deira City Centre Mall **Wheelchair facilities** Yes

THIS IS HANDS DOWN THE PRETTIEST LOCATION in all of Dubai. Don't be nervous as you approach from the airport, which is only five minutes away. The driveway might be just off a main road, but the hotel itself is set in acres of mature gardens, right next to a stretch of Dubai Creek and just opposite a park. It resembles nothing so much as a Greek island resort, with low-rise white, domed buildings, blue roofs and tiled floors. Huge windows overlook date palms, and a glass-walled corridor leads you from the airy reception through leafy courtyards and into the chic Arabic-themed tea room.

Down a sweeping staircase is the fine-dining French restaurant set over two levels with its walls of wine, parquet floors and open-show kitchens. On Fridays, it does one of the best all-you-can-eat brunches in the city, with free-flowing Dom Pérignon all day. The Thai Kitchen, right next to Dubai Creek, is also famous for its weekend à la carte brunch. Café Arabesque is an all-day dining Arabic restaurant where breakfast is served, and which later in the day produces piping-hot breads and grills; and there is the squishy-sofa–packed outdoor Terrace bar.

The rooms, all of which feature water views and balconies, have a decidedly feminine edge, decorated in cream and white, and each room has a free-standing marble bath and walk-in shower. The bath products are all scented with a perfume specially created for the hotel. Should you take a particular shine to the artwork – the pictures are all black-and-white shots of Dubai's maritime history – they are available to buy. Standard rooms all sleep two adults and one child, and larger suites have screens that separate living and sleeping areas so business meetings can be held in-room.

A large conference centre on-site is a favourite with local fashion shows and charity events for ladies who lunch. As well as the proximity to affiliated Dubai Creek Golf & Yacht Club, where the hotel can arrange tee times, yachts are available to hire from the marina. The jewel in the crown of the resort, though, is the multiple-award-winning Amara Spa. Each spa suite, including two designed specially for couples, has its own leafy outdoor courtyard with rain shower for post-treatment tea and dates. Spend a minimum of AED 450 on a treatment, and you will also get full-day access to the palm-shaded pool, with its four whirlpool tubs and soft white padded loungers. Golf widows will also be pleased to hear that the hotel is minutes away from Bur Dubai's souks and the Wafi Mall and Festival Centre.

Qamardeen Hotel ★ ★ ★ ★

Emaar Boulevard, The Old Town, Downtown, PO Box 114822;
☎ **04-428-6888;** {vfl **04-428-6999; southernsunme.com/qamardeen**

Cost AED 2,150 **Location** Downtown **Number of rooms** 186 rooms, plus 13 suites **Room sq m** 32 **Conference facilities** Yes **Pool/sauna** Yes **Beach access** No **Exercise facilities** Yes **Spa** No **Parking/valet** Yes **Licensed bar** Yes **On-site dining** Italian, cafe **Extra amenities** Minibar, 24-hour room service, mineral water, tea/coffee facilities, hairdryer, iron on request, airport pickup **Business amenities** 24-hour business centre, complimentary Internet, Wi-Fi in public areas **Shuttle buses** To shopping malls, Jumeirah Beach Park, key business locations on Sheikh Zayed Road **Wheelchair facilities** Yes

SISTER HOTEL TO AL MANZIL and linked by Dukkan Qamardeen Souk, with about 30 shops and boutiques, Qamardeen is also a fabulous four-star hotel. Guests staying here can dine at Al Manzil's restaurants and cross-charge. Apart from its lobby, which is a bombardment of sumptuous jewel-coloured curtains, funky tall lamps and red velvet sofas, it is a simpler, plainer proposition than Al Manzil. It is contemporary but captures the Arabian heritage instantly.

The decor is clean and unfussy, but the rooms do not sacrifice comfort – bed linens are snow white, with accents of colour in the ruby red cushions. The standard bedrooms feature queen beds or twin beds and glass-enclosed open-plan bathrooms with bath and walk-in shower and separate toilet. Some have access to the pool or the garden. Ten executive suites with king beds have separate bathrooms with bath and shower, a lounge with guest toilet and a study area. They also have balconies overlooking the pool. King suites offer a fully-equipped desk and workspace, a butler's kitchen, a dining area with guest toilet, a lounge and a patio area overlooking the pool. Sliding screens close to separate the areas if desired.

The gym is small but modern and has a good range of equipment; the pool is beautiful, in the centre of a romantic central courtyard. Three eateries are in the hotel – the Mediterranean Esca, which provides a breakfast and lunch buffet and dinner with buffet hors d'oeuvres and à la carte main courses; a Lobby Lounge; and the Pool Café, providing drinks and snacks poolside.

Al Qasr Hotel ★★★★★

Madinat Jumeirah, PO Box 75157; ☎ 04-366-8888; {vfl 04-366-7788; jumeirah.com

Cost AED 3,700 **Location** Jumeirah **Number of rooms** 260 rooms, plus 18 suites **Room sq m** 55–550 **Conference facilities** Yes **Pool/sauna** Yes **Beach access** Yes **Exercise facilities** Yes **Spa** Yes **Parking/valet** Yes **Licensed bar** Yes **On-site dining** Arabic, Spanish, International, Thai, vegetarian, seafood, steak, cafe **Extra amenities** *Abra* tours, high-speed Internet, tea/coffee facilities, free access to Wild Wadi waterpark **Business amenities** Business centre **Shuttle buses** To Jumeirah Beach Hotel, Jumeirah Bab Al Shams **Wheelchair facilities** Yes

APPROACHED VIA A BROAD DRIVEWAY lined with life-size bucking gold stallions, Al Qasr (or 'the palace' translated from Arabic) does everything it can to live up to its lofty name. Part of the huge Madinat Jumeirah complex, with its network of waterways, it benefits from being just a boat ride away from the shops, bars, nightclubs and restaurants of the neighbouring souk. There is also direct beach access and free passes to the Wild Wadi waterpark, just five minutes away, for the duration of your stay.

The design of Al Qasr itself, which is located just a few doors down from the raft of royal palaces that line the beach between Jumeirah and the Marina, is based on the conceit of a sheikh's summer palace. Hence, the entrance hall has gargantuan crystal chandeliers, marble floors and legions of staff on hand to meet and greet you.

Downstairs is the all-day International dining restaurant, Arboretum, which on Fridays joins up with neighbouring Spanish eateries Alhabra and MJs Steakhouse to put on the best brunch in Dubai. For AED 495, guests get free-flowing bubbly and an almost obscene amount of food from the overflowing buffet. Also on-site are Pai Thai, a romantic Southeast Asian restaurant reached by *abra* on the Madinat's waterways, and Magnolia, a vegetarian restaurant where many of the ingredients have been grown on-site. At Pierchic restaurant, the ambience is so romantic that during high season, marriage proposals can reach double figures in a day.

Mercifully, as the waterways are filled with salt water, there isn't a massive mosquito problem – which means the balconies attached to all of the rooms are very pleasant in the evening. The heavenly Talise, which caters for the whole resort, is a step beyond the standard spa, with its own pool, multiple relaxation rooms, on-site complimentary therapists and even a psychologist. Despite its servicing the whole Madinat complex, the size of the Quay health club means that the gym never gets packed, and it includes a 25-metre (82-foot) indoor lap pool and a full timetable of complimentary classes, including boxing, Pilates, jogging and circuits. The club also has one of the largest outdoor swimming pools in the Middle East, no shortage of loungers or shade and a kids' club that will keep children ages 4–12 occupied 8 a.m.–7 p.m. (children under age 4 must be accompanied). Boat charters and water sports are available at the sister Jumeirah Beach Hotel, reached on foot or by golf buggy.

Even the smallest rooms come in at a whopping 55 square metres (592 square feet) and can accommodate two adults and two children, and all are decorated in the inoffensive creams, browns and dark wood that is a signature of the region's upscale hotels. As with all Jumeirah properties in Dubai, pay a supplement for Club Executive or Premium Leisure Club rooms and you will get free airport transfers, daily afternoon tea and complimentary happy hour drinks 6–8 p.m., as well as a late checkout. One more thing we must say – Dubai can often feel like the land of the 'No, ma'am!', but staff here are trained never to offer this as a first response – instead, they always offer solutions to guest gripes and requests.

Raffles ★ ★ ★ ★ ★

Sheikh Rashid Road, Bur Dubai, PO Box 121800; ☎ 04-324-8888; {vfl 04-324-6000; raffles.com

Cost AED 1,500 **Location** Bur Dubai **Number of rooms** 192 rooms, plus 56 suites **Room sq m** 70–650 **Conference facilities** Yes **Pool/sauna** Yes **Beach access** No **Exercise facilities** Yes **Spa** Yes **Parking/valet** Yes **Licensed bar** Yes **On-site dining** Asian, International, steakhouse, coffee shop **Extra amenities** Coffee machine, hairdryer, iPod docking station **Business amenities** Library and business centre, full-size desk in all rooms **Shuttle buses** None, but neighbouring Wafi Mall is the start of the Big Bus Tour route **Wheelchair facilities** Yes

WHAT MIGHT AT FIRST SEEM LIKE QUITE AN ODD LOCATION – right next to a main road, overlooking an apartment block – is actually a pretty sensible one, especially for the business traveller or the golfer. It's ten minutes from the airport and Al Badia and Dubai Creek golf courses and a ten-minute drive from the DIFC. Leisure travellers too may like being right next to the faux-Egyptian—themed Wafi Mall and its various rooftop bars and restaurants, the Grand cinema and only five minutes from Dubai's main artery, the Sheikh Zayed Road.

Raffles must have been aware, though, that with an absence of any view to speak of (which is a shame, as most rooms have balconies) and no beach access, it really needed to make the building, interiors and service first rate, which it has managed. The faux-Egyptian posturing of the attached mall and the hotel's glass pyramid design may seem a bit gimmicky from the outside, but that is a false impression – the decor inside is slick and chic, from the quadruple-height ceilings of the lobby, with its water features and glittering grey marble, to the cavernous spa and the rooftop botanical gardens. The rooms are enormous, with even the smallest coming in at 70 square metres (753 square feet) – all have a large living area with sofa and desk. The business centre and library are huge and extremely well appointed, with lots of small meeting areas, squishy sofas and more than 1,000 books. The pool area is slightly marred by the fact that it overlooks the road, but you would have to crane your neck over the side to see that.

We have heard occasional complaints that the area can get a little shabby, and the waterfalls and hot tub have been out of action on a couple of our visits. The Noble House, the haute cuisine Chinese restaurant at the top of the glass pyramid, has won a raft of awards, but be prepared to pay through the nose for it. Fire & Ice is a great steakhouse, the Crossroads bar is a pleasant but pricey place for a shisha, and the breakfast at Azur, the all-day International dining buffet, is, for our money, by far the best in Dubai. The Ferraris parked out front at the weekend attest to the fact that China Moon, the hotel's Champagne bar cum club, is a favourite with the Cristal-buying set.

We have heard on the grapevine that the occupancy rates are quite low, which is probably the reason that upgrades from rooms to suites seem quite a regular occurrence. If you pay extra for a Raffles Inc room, you will enjoy a complimentary breakfast, all-day soft drinks and finger food and afternoon tea 2–7 p.m., all served in the private lounge on the tenth floor.

The Rose Rayhaan by Rotana ★ ★ ★ ★
**Sheikh Zayed Road, PO Box 126452; ☎ 04-323-0111;
{vfl 04-323-0222; rotana.com**

Cost AED 1,600 **Location** Sheikh Zayed Road **Number of rooms** 482 rooms, plus 42 suites **Room sq m** 33 **Conference facilities** Yes **Pool/sauna** Yes **Beach access** No **Exercise facilities** Yes **Spa** No **Parking/valet** Yes **Licensed bar** No **On-site dining** International, lobby lounge, cafe **Extra amenities** Laundry and dry-cleaning facilities, babysitting on request, car and limo rental, complimentary tea/coffee facilities, complimentary daily newspapers, satellite TV, mini fridge, safe box, hairdryer, pillow menu, 24-hour room service **Business amenities** Wi-Fi, high-speed Internet, business centre **Shuttle buses** To Dubai Mall, Mall of the Emirates **Wheelchair facilities** Yes

THE ROSE RAYHAAN IS THE WORLD'S TALLEST HOTEL, soaring 333 metres (1,092.5 feet) and 72 storeys. According to the marketing blurb, it's 'the flagship of the alcohol-free brand Rayhaan Hotels & Resorts' and that says it all. It is owned by a Saudi group and very much targeted towards the Saudi market, and whilst as a hotel it's absolutely adequate (very dull, very plain, very staid), it just isn't an exciting place to stay in for either the Western tourist or businessperson. It's situated on Sheikh Zayed Road, convenient to Dubai International Financial Centre and Dubai Mall. The hotel is busy with families from the Gulf and Russian holidaymakers.

The main restaurant – Petals, on the first floor – is open for food 24 hours a day. It serves a buffet breakfast (AED 89), buffet lunch and dinner. Considering that The Rose Rayhaan is the world's tallest hotel, it's unfortunate that there are no restaurants or lounges on the upper floors to take advantage of the fabulous views. And in the evening, the restaurant has no atmosphere at all.

The swimming pool on the fourth floor is fine but overlooks a construction site – so lots of ogling workmen. Bodylines Health and Fitness Centre offers a fully-equipped gym, cardio and weight training, fitness classes, massage rooms, sauna, hot tub and steam room. Bedrooms are comfortable but unremarkable – petal-patterned carpets and bland wooden furniture – but do feature a fully-equipped kitchenette with microwave oven, which is useful if you are travelling with children. Bathrooms have either a rain forest walk-in shower, a bath with overhead shower or both. There are three types of room – Twin Classic with twin beds, King Deluxe and King Premium. And the Classic Suite has a living room area as well.

Le Royal Méridien Beach Resort & Spa ★ ★ ★ ★ ★
Dubai Marina, PO Box 24970; ☎ 04-399-5555;
{vfl **04-399-5999; leroyalmeridien-dubai.com**

Cost AED 900 **Location** The Marina **Number of rooms** 348 rooms, plus 152 suites **Room sq m** 35–83 **Conference facilities** Yes **Pool/sauna** Yes **Beach access** Yes **Exercise facilities** Yes **Spa** Yes **Parking/valet** Yes **Licensed bar** Yes **On-site dining** Arabic, Italian, Mexican, Mediterranean, International, Southeast Asian, cafe, pizzeria **Extra amenities** 42-inch LCD TV, DVD player, tea/coffee facilities, Wi-Fi, fruit basket **Business amenities** Desk in all rooms, business centre **Shuttle buses** To Mall of the Emirates, Dubai Mall **Wheelchair facilities** Yes

ONE OF THE OLDER HOTELS IN THE MARINA, Le Royal Méridien is a long-time favourite for weddings because of its beachside setting and pretty landscaped gardens. As the Marina has grown up around it, the location has become a slightly odd one – it is tucked behind other buildings and isn't visible from the main road – but it has the rare distinction of not being bombarded on all sides by construction noise. The lobby feels a bit like a massive conference venue, oddly cavernous and a bit '80s-looking, with some weird *Majlis* tent–type efforts, but staff are friendly and helpful. The hotel is so large that it's actually best to navigate the outdoor parts by golf buggy, of which there are many zipping about.

The outdoor pools have ample space to sit around and plenty of shade, and the wide beach is well stocked with loungers, with staff on hand with cold towels for when you overheat. A water sports centre offers banana boat rides, kayaking, windsurfing and sailing, and there's also a beach volleyball court. Parents are banned from Club Penguin, which has a full programme of activities held both outside and in the indoor air-conditioned play centre (it runs 9 a.m.–6 p.m. every day for children ages 4–12).

A Greco-Roman–themed spa has five whirlpools for adults, as well as a gym, sauna and steam room. There are 14 restaurants and bars, the nicest of which are haute cuisine Mexican eatery Maya, which also does great bar snacks and cocktails on its roof terrace, and Ossigeno, a fine-dining Italian restaurant. A pizzeria and an Arabic grill are more geared towards families.

Shangri-La ★ ★ ★ ★ ★

Sheikh Zayed Road, PO Box 75880; ☎ 04-343-8888;
{vfl **04-343-8886; shangri-la.com**

Cost AED 1,200 **Location** Sheikh Zayed Road **Number of rooms** 302 rooms, plus 29 suites **Room sq m** 45–435 **Conference facilities** Yes **Pool/sauna** Yes **Beach access** No **Exercise facilities** Yes **Spa** Yes **Parking/valet** Yes **Licensed bar** Yes **On-site dining** International, Arabic, Moroccan, Chinese, seafood **Extra amenities** Tea/coffee facilities, hairdryer, Wi-Fi **Business amenities** Full-size writing desk, business centre **Shuttle buses** To Jebel Ali Beach Resort & Spa, Dubai Mall, Wafi Mall, Mall of the Emirates **Wheelchair facilities** Yes

---

THE SHANGRI-LA IS ANOTHER SOLID BUSINESS HOTEL on Sheikh Zayed Road, although it suffers slightly by being at the wrong end – to make it to the DIFC, you have to do a bit of a complicated loop back round on yourself, often encountering quite heavy traffic. As the crow flies, it should be a short journey to the Downtown area too, but again it involves going round the houses a bit because of the counterintuitive road system. Having said that, the stop for the DIFC Metro can be accessed via a covered walkway across Sheikh Zayed Road and is a five-minute walk away, although you'd be mad to tackle this in a suit during summer.

The lobby is grand and the restaurants decent, although some are awkwardly located on balconies jutting out over the lobby. Hoi An is one of the only Vietnamese joints in town, but often its pretty, low-lit room is totally empty. There is also a Moroccan restaurant, Marrakech, and Shang Palace, which serves among the best dim sum in the city (and the crispy beef is to die for). The small fourth-floor swimming pool underlines the fact that it's not really geared up for leisure tourism, but it does come into its own at night when the DJ cranks the music up at the outdoor I-Kandy cocktail and shisha lounge. Luckily, the double glazing is hefty enough to keep the noise out of the rooms above.

As the large gym accepts outside members and also services the hotel's long-term rental apartments, it can get a bit busy at peak times. A spa is also on the same floor. The rooms are gentleman's-clubby, with a large desk, and there is a separate bath and shower. Pay a premium for a Horizon Club room on floors 40–41 and you get your own check-in desk, free suit pressing, health club with infinity pool, gym and sun deck, complimentary breakfast, soft beverages all day and alcoholic drinks during happy hour.

Sofitel Jumeirah Beach Residence ★★★★★

The Walk, Jumeirah Beach Residence, PO Box 87075;
☎ **04-448-4848;** {∨fl **04-432-8456; sofitel.com**

Cost AED 750 **Location** The Marina **Number of rooms** 398 rooms, plus 40 suites **Room sq m** 36–72 **Conference facilities** Yes **Pool/sauna** Yes **Beach access** Yes **Exercise facilities** Yes **Spa** Yes **Parking/valet** Yes **Licensed bar** Yes **On-site dining** Italian, Irish, British, International, cafe **Extra amenities** Tea/coffee facilities **Business amenities** Secretarial service, laptop hire, business centre **Shuttle buses** To Mall of the Emirates, Dubai Mall, Mercato Mall, Dubai Outlet Mall, BurJuman Centre **Wheelchair facilities** Yes

OPENED IN 2010, THIS IS THE FIRST OUTPOST of the French Sofitel chain in Dubai. Although it's situated on Jumeirah Beach Residence's The Walk, with its huge selection of shops and cafes, you actually have to cross the road to get to the public beach, although all the rooms do benefit from sea views. It is well located for Dubai Media City and the Jebel Ali Free Zone, though, and Ibn Battuta and Dubai Marina malls are nearby. Because the area is so popular with local families, alcohol is not allowed on the sea-facing terraces, which is a shame, as the jewel in the dining crown, Italian restaurant Rococo, would really benefit from useable outside tables. A poolside bar is next to the sea-facing infinity pool, and there is also an Irish pub and a French brasserie.

The decor here is more ambitious than at many of Dubai's new hotels – they have gone to town on the jewel colours, velvet and flock, but what you'll probably notice most are the beds. As with all Sofitel hotels, they are huge and bouncy and come with an extensive pillow menu. There is a very small on-site spa with a sauna and steam room, along with a well-equipped gym with loaded iPods on request.

Suite Novotel Mall of the Emirates ★★★

(linked to Ibis Mall of the Emirates; see page 74)
2A Street, PO Box 283825; ☎ **04-382-3200;** ' z"z' › ∨«~f¥" **04-702-8000;** {∨fl **04-382-3201; suitehotel.com**

Cost AED 450 **Location** Al Barsha and Al Quoz **Number of rooms** 180 suites **Room sq m** 34 **Conference facilities** No **Pool/sauna** Yes **Beach access** No **Exercise facilities** Yes **Spa** No **Parking/valet** Yes/no **Licensed bar** Yes **On-site dining** Italian, International, bar food **Extra amenities** Free shoulder massage for every guest each Thursday, flat-panel TV, e-corner in lobby with PlayStation 3s and games, library, shoeshine machine on each floor, 24-hour snack service, laundry and dry-cleaning, airport transfer **Business amenities** High-speed Internet, Wi-Fi in lobby areas, business corner **Shuttle buses** To Jumeirah Open Beach at Jumeirah Beach Residence **Wheelchair facilities** Yes

SUITE NOVOTEL IS LINKED TO THE IBIS MALL OF THE EMIRATES in Al Barsha, within a stone's throw of Mall of the Emirates, set back from the Sheikh Zayed Road. Whilst a lot of construction is going on in this area, it is not without its charm, and for convenience you can't go wrong. It is ten minutes from beautiful beaches, Madinat Jumeirah and Burj Al Arab, and no more than 20 minutes from Dubai centre.

Suite Novotel is designed with flexible living in mind. The idea is that the space can be used to suit you. The rooms, which are larger than your average hotel room, can be divided up into separate sleeping and living areas with pull-across curtain partitions. The design is fresh and modern, with splashes of colour amongst more subdued creams and beiges. In the largest suites, a rotating TV is at each end, so you can watch it from wherever you are sitting. Curtains separate the beds. Rooms may contain a queen-size bed, a sofa bed and a single bed. This is ideal for families with several children, and what we like is that style has not been compromised in any way. Bathrooms are modern and stylish.

The restaurants are shared with the Ibis – the Italian restaurant, Amici, is contemporary and chic, but don't expect gastronomic delights. Breakfast is a buffet, and there is a wide range of food to suit all tastes. If you prefer, you can have it in your room at no extra cost. The Deli Boutique is a trendy little cafe. Ezaz, the lounge bar, is a laid-back place to unwind during the day or evening.

The gym on the roof, whilst small, is light and airy, and a nice pool area is surrounded by foliage. As it is linked to the Ibis hotel on every floor, guests from both hotels are free to wander between the two and make use of the facilities in each. However, Ibis guests are not able to use Suite Novotel's e-corner and have to pay to use its pool and gym.

Traders Hotel Deira ★ ★ ★ ★

Corner of Abu Backer Al Siddique and Salah Al Din Road, PO Box 81877; ☎ 04-265-9888; {vfl 04-265-9777; shangri-la.com/en/property/dubai/traders

Cost AED 1,080–2,800 **Location** Deira **Number of rooms** 250 rooms, plus 12 suites **Room sq m** 28–145 **Conference facilities** Yes **Pool/sauna** Yes **Beach access** No **Exercise facilities** Yes **Spa** No **Parking/valet** Yes **Licensed bar** Yes **On-site dining** International, lounge, bar food **Extra amenities** Airport pickup, tea/coffee facilities, minibar, iron/ironing board, hairdryer, fax and printer in suites, safe box, ice dispenser on each floor, cross-signing facilities at the Shangri-La hotel, limousine and car rental, hotel shop **Business amenities** Complimentary Wi-Fi and high-speed Internet, business centre, Traders Club **Shuttle buses** To Jumeirah Beach Park, Deira City Centre Mall **Wheelchair facilities** Yes

ALTHOUGH NOT SITUATED IN THE MOST PICTURESQUE LOCATION, the hotel nevertheless looks smart and imposing and is ideally suited to the business traveller, as it is close to the airport and the business districts, with excellent business facilities. It is also conveniently placed for Deira, Dubai Creek and the historical part of Dubai. Used by Singapore Airlines' aircrew, Traders is part of the Shangri-La hotel group. It is in a very busy and buzzy area, very lively in the evenings.

There is a variety of bedroom types with smoking and non-smoking rooms. Decor throughout is smart, unoriginal, but contemporary, using earth tones and dark wood. Bedrooms are carpeted. All bedrooms have complimentary broadband access, satellite TV (TVs are changing to plasma TVs throughout the hotel) and desks. Bathrooms are clean and very contemporary. On the fifth floor is the Traders Club for frequent travellers. Membership includes club floor check-in and checkout, deluxe bedrooms, lounge facilities, complimentary buffet breakfast, newspaper, fresh fruits, free suit pressing and shoeshine, concierge service and complimentary beverages. Traders Club bedrooms include entry to the club. The suites also include entry to Traders Club and are laid out with separate sitting rooms and marble bathrooms. The Presidential Suite, often used by visiting sheikhs, includes a sitting room, kitchenette, dining area, master bedroom, spacious bathroom and a separate guest toilet.

The main restaurant in the hotel, The Junction, offers buffet-style International dining. A Filipino band plays nightly at the Chameleon Bar, and there is also a Lobby Lounge. The indoor swimming pool is small and rather dingy, but the health club offers a decent gym, hot tub, sauna and steam room facilities and a menu of massages. The Juice Bar is located at the health club.

Villa Rotana ★ ★ ★ ★
Sheikh Zayed Road (near Safestway), PO Box 118737;
☎ **04-321-6111; {vfl 04-321-5333; rotana.com**

Cost AED 1,450 **Location** Sheikh Zayed Road **Number of rooms** 118 apartments, 62 suites, 56 studios **Room sq m** 32 **Conference facilities** Yes **Pool/sauna** Yes **Beach access** No **Exercise facilities** Yes **Spa** No **Parking/valet** Yes **Licensed bar** No **On-site dining** International **Extra amenities** Car and limousine rental, complimentary tea/coffee facilities, flat-panel TV, local newspaper, babysitting service, daily turndown service, 24-hour in-room dining, laundry and dry-cleaning facilities, washing machine and dryer, safe box, iron/ironing board, hairdryer, fully-equipped kitchens, airport pickup **Business amenities** Business centre with secretarial support, Wi-Fi in the lobby areas, high-speed Internet in the apartments **Shuttle buses** To Dubai Mall, Jumeirah Beach Park **Wheelchair facilities** Yes

IT'S SITUATED IN AN EXCELLENT LOCATION, on the Sheikh Zayed Road, for getting to all parts of Dubai by car or taxi. However, as an area in which to stay, there are no attractions of any sort within walking distance. Villa Rotana is a collection of serviced apartments with a hotel ambience. The heart of the building is a big empty square space – five storeys built around a covered courtyard, which features a rather soulless International restaurant on the ground floor. Breakfast is a buffet, lunch is a buffet and dinner is à la carte. The apartments themselves are great, and the views over the Sheikh Zayed Road, while obviously not bucolic, are actually mesmerising. The Classic Studio has either a king bed or twin beds and is decorated in a sleek East-meets-West style, with kitchenette, dining area, living area and bedroom. The Premium suite – with red shaggy rugs, funky modern easy chairs, cool white leather sofas, large flat-panel TVs, a dining table, well-equipped kitchen and spacious bathrooms – is extremely pleasant.

There is a health and fitness centre, Bodylines, free for guests, but with outside membership as well. The gym is large and impressive, and there are steam rooms, saunas, a hot tub and showers. The outdoor rooftop swimming pool would be nice if it weren't currently overlooked by a massive building site – and lots of ogling workmen – but the views from here are fabulous, and a small cafe on the roof serves drinks and snacks.

The Westin Mina Seyahi ★★★★★

Al Sufouh Road, Jumeirah Beach, PO Box 24883; ☎ 04-399-4141;
{vfl **04-399-9144; westinminaseyahi.com**

Cost AED 1,600 **Location** Jumeirah **Number of rooms** 211 rooms, plus 29 suites **Room sq m** 34–79 **Conference facilities** Yes **Pool/sauna** Yes **Beach access** Yes **Exercise facilities** Yes **Spa** Yes **Parking/valet** Yes **Licensed bar** Yes **On-site dining** Southeast Asian, Italian, International, steakhouse, cafe **Extra amenities** Wi-Fi, video on demand **Business amenities** Business centre **Shuttle buses** To Mall of the Emirates, Wafi Mall, Dubai Mall **Wheelchair facilities** Yes

OPENED IN 1998, this hotel has not yet had time to show its age, although there have been several problems to iron out. The all-day dining restaurant, Blue Orange, had almost comically bad reviews when it opened, although it has improved since – slightly. The Spice Emporium restaurant came up with the novel idea of serving half the menu in glass jars – it's remarkable how much foie gras looks like it should be in a science lab when it comes encased in glass – but now, rather more sensibly, sticks to standard Thai. Oeno, the wine and cheese bar, managed to get it right from the start, although service can be a little slow. The jewel in the foodie crown, however, is Bussola, an Italian joint that has actually been on the same site for years (it was previously reached by golf buggy from the neighbouring hotel Le Méridien). Upstairs is a standard pizza joint, permanently packed with expats desperate for some pork; downstairs is a more grown-up, expensive affair.

The hotel's Heavenly spa is large and has some innovative treatments, which are changed regularly. It also has a lovely large whirlpool bath in the changing rooms, and a gym on the same level. The hotel opens directly out on a private beach, and a water sports centre offers kayaking, sailing and waterskiing.

If you're not keen on the sand beneath your toes (and in your hair and handbag), visit the huge outdoor pool and landscaped grounds with shady palm trees and lots of loungers. Rooms overlook either the sea or the 'city' (read: the large road behind) and most have balconies. Decor is neutral verging on dull, but the rooms do have an abundance of large mirrors, which makes them feel very spacious. Because of the complex of meeting rooms and the ballroom, the hotel is popular for large events and conferences. But a word of warning, especially for the summer: the terrace suffers from overlooking an open sewage plant, which isn't the best-ever view (or smell).

XVA Art Hotel & Gallery ★★★

Bastakiya, Bur Dubai, PO Box 37304; ☎ 04-353-5383;
{vfl 04-353-5988; xvagallery.com

Cost AED 900, including breakfast **Location** Bur Dubai **Number of rooms** 7 **Room sq m** 25 **Conference facilities** No **Pool/sauna** No **Beach access** No **Exercise facilities** No **Spa** No **Parking/valet** No **Licensed bar** No, but guests can consume their own alcohol in their rooms **On-site dining** International cafe **Extra amenities** Minibar, hairdryer, toiletries in bathrooms, iron/ironing board on request, TV in each room **Business amenities** Wi-Fi **Shuttle buses** None **Wheelchair facilities** No

A STYLISH AND PEACEFUL BOUTIQUE HOTEL in the heart of Bastakiya, XVA occupies a renovated *Majlis*-style residence, retaining the original architectural motifs, wind towers and three open courtyards. It is also home to one of Dubai's most respected art galleries, showcasing Middle Eastern and international contemporary art. This is a stunning small hotel, with seven original and quirky bedrooms designed by well-established artists from the region. All have air conditioning. There are single, double and deluxe bedrooms – all en suite with baths and showers. Walls are white stone with big mirrors. One room has a completely kitsch feel to it, another is pop-arty, one has a silver and purple gothic theme going on and yet another is modern and simple. The rooms are not huge, but what they lack in space, they more than make up for in originality. Upstairs on the rooftop there are rocking chairs from which you can enjoy the view over other rooftops – especially pretty at night.

The XVA's cafe serves award-winning Lebanese-Arabic vegetarian cuisine. A snug little library has old kilims on the floor, and art is displayed throughout the hotel. An in-house tailor will turn your fabric bought from the nearby Textile Souk into your outfit of choice, and S*uce Boutique has a small fashion and gift store here too. XVA has its own dhow on Dubai Creek and organises gourmet vegetarian dinner cruises on the dhow for hotel guests. It can also organise themed day tours.

PART FOUR

ARRIVING, DEPARTING *and* THINGS LOCALS ALREADY KNOW

ARRIVING: *Day One*

MANY VISITORS SHOULD BREEZE THROUGH IMMIGRATION at Dubai International Airport, although there is occasionally an epic queue at passport control with which to contend. If you are very keen to avoid this possibility, then try to make sure you sit at the front of the aeroplane and adopt a fast pace to the arrivals terminal. Don't try to queue-jump or get cute with the counter attendants – they are famously stony-faced, and you will be reprimanded and sent right to the back. You will need to tell the official where you are staying, and they may ask for your mobile number and the phone number of the hotel. If you would like to ensure no standing in line, Dnata offers a Marhaba Service (meaning 'welcome' in Arabic). You can book it online at **dnatatravel.com,** and it costs from AED 90 per adult (extras including a local mobile phone SIM card or even 20 red roses can also be arranged). Once you have been through passport control, your cabin bags will be X-ray scanned before you are allowed to collect your suitcases.

You are allowed to bring AED 3,000 (approximately £514 or US $817) worth of gifts; 400 cigarettes; cigars up to AED 3,000 in value; and 2 litres of wine plus 2 litres of spirits *or* 24 cans of beer into the country. Duty-free shops are at all Dubai terminals and, as a tourist, these are the only shops in the emirate where you will be able to buy alcohol legally. You are also allowed to bring in AED 40,000 (approximately £6,854 or US $10,890) in local or foreign currency or traveller's cheques.

Once you are through, it should take you no time to get to your hotel. It's very easy to hail a cab from the airport (four- and seven-seater Dubai taxis, always in plentiful supply, wait outside). Hotels are prone to charging over the odds for transfers (sometimes up to four times), so we would recommend you hail one of your own

– these special airport taxis know where all the big hotels are. If you haven't changed your money into dirhams before arriving in the city, you can find several places at the airport where you can exchange currency, as well as ATMs that will accept international debit and credit cards. Hire cars can be picked up from the airport, but we really wouldn't advise this, as you'll be tired from the trip and you won't yet have your bearings. You'd be far better off getting a quick and cheap taxi and having the car delivered to your hotel. Although the airport is served by the Dubai Metro, it is all but useless for holidaying tourists, as heavy and bulky suitcases are not allowed on the trains. There are no airport buses of which to speak. You will, of course, need cash to pay for the journey.

BEATING JET LAG

ONE OF DUBAI'S BIGGEST DRAWS FOR BRITISH and South African tourists for short breaks is the fact that jet lag isn't really a feature on a trip here. Sure, the three- or four-hour time difference can throw you a bit off-kilter, but it's nothing plenty of water and a good night's sleep won't fix. Sadly, the jet lag for Australians, Americans and Canadians may take a couple of days to get over. Try to stay away from alcohol and caffeine on the plane, and, if you have arrived during daylight hours, spend some time in the sun, as this should help to reset your body clock. Many hotel spas also offer tailored jet lag massages that should help you get off to sleep should you be struggling. Do not be tempted to bring non-prescription sleeping pills into the country (see page 31 for a list of drugs that are banned here), as this can lead to a prison sentence. Even having them in your system is considered possession.

DEPARTING

DEPARTING FROM DUBAI AIRPORT COULDN'T BE EASIER. Make sure you know which terminal you are departing from (it's Terminal 1 for all airlines apart from Emirates), as they are quite a distance from each other, and do make sure you allow yourself enough time, as rush-hour traffic around that area can be quite heavy. If you are getting a taxi, they will drop you right outside the terminal building – porters will be on hand to help you with your luggage for AED 5–10. Many car hire firms allow you to drop your car directly at the airport, although do check with them how long the process will take and adjust your timings accordingly. You do not need extra time to pay departure tax as there is none, or to claim back VAT on your purchases as, again, it isn't levied here. You should be at the airport at least two hours before your flight is due to depart, but even if you arrive earlier, you won't struggle for something to do. Terminal 1 and Terminal 3 both have ample shops, bars and restaurants to keep you occupied.

TELEPHONES, E-MAIL *and* POSTAL SERVICES

AS THERE ARE NO HOME ADDRESSES IN DUBAI (everything operates on a PO Box service), there isn't what we would recognise as a nationalised postal service. If you are keen to ship large purchases home, check in-store whether they can arrange shipping and handling for you. If not, DHL counters are in Festival Centre, Mall of the Emirates, Dubai Mall and Deira City Centre Mall (visit **dhl.co.ae** for more information). Empost (**empostuae.com;** ☎ 600-56-5555) also ships worldwide and offers an express service that promises to deliver to more than 200 countries within 72 hours.

The Internet is widely available in Dubai. Many cafes, malls and restaurants have free Wi-Fi (although you will need your own laptop), and it will usually be a pretty fast connection. It will be at your hotel's discretion whether they charge for the Internet, and whether it is a Wi-Fi or an in-room connection. Most will also have PCs in the business centres for general use. What is nonnegotiable, however, is access to Web sites that are forbidden by the Internet Access Management Regulatory Policy of the U.A.E. If you try to visit a site with any of the following content, it will be instantly blocked:

- Dating or matchmaking sites
- Sites containing pornography and nudity
- Internet gambling content
- Sites that are offensive to religions

Although not specifically stated, access to anything derogatory about the U.A.E. government will also be heavily censored.

Some hotels offer free local calls within Dubai from your room – check with your concierge. If you want to use your own mobile phone within the U.A.E., make sure your normal service provider has allowed international roaming on your price plan. There are two mobile networks here, Etisalat and Du, and as a tourist you will notice little difference between the two (both are state owned). If you would like to have a local mobile phone while you are here, both networks offer packages for visitors. You should bring an unlocked handset to the U.A.E. with you for this (or make sure your own phone is unlocked and you are able to switch SIM cards – your home service provider will be able to tell you whether this is the case). Etisalat offers an Ahlan (hello) package that costs AED 60. For this, you get a SIM card loaded with AED 25 credit upon line activation, and you can make calls locally and internationally. Credit can be bought in denominations of AED 25 from supermarkets, petrol stations and Etisalat shops and comes either in the form of printed receipts or scratch cards. Du offers a similar package – for AED 55 you will get a local SIM card with AED 10 credit (visit **du.ae** for more details). Both companies have outlets in the arrival terminals of Dubai airport.

To call Dubai from the U.K., dial 00 then 971 (the country code) and then the number. From the U.S., dial 011, then 971 and then the number.

UNDERSTANDING *the* U.A.E. CURRENCY

THE CURRENCY IN DUBAI IS THE DIRHAM, which is pegged to the U.S. dollar. Officially, the currency is abbreviated to AED (Arab Emirates Dirham), but locally it is written as Dhs. A dirham is divided into 100 fils, although the smallest physical denomination is the 25 fil coin. There are also 50 fil and 1 dirham coins. Bills will be rounded up (or down) to the closest 25 fil. Notes come in 5, 10, 20, 50, 100, 200, 500 and 1,000 – do be careful when paying, though, as some of the notes (particularly the 5 and 200 and the 20 and 500) are close in colour. Copious ATMs can be found in malls, bank foyers, hotel lobbies and at many service stations where international credit and debit cards are accepted. Credit cards are also accepted almost everywhere – American Express, Visa and MasterCard are the most common, and most hotels have their own bureau de change.

THINGS *the* LOCALS ALREADY KNOW

TIPPING

THERE IS NO FORMALISED TIPPING CULTURE HERE. Taxi drivers will expect you to round up to the nearest 5 or 10 (they will look confused if you expect change in coins). Beauty salons and hairdressers will expect around 10% of the price of the treatment if you are happy with it – make sure you give this directly to the therapist. If you are ordering drinks at a bar, the barmen won't necessarily expect a tip but will be grateful for it. In restaurants, 10–15% is standard. In some of the larger establishments, a service charge will already have been added to the bill, so do make sure you're not paying twice.

RADIO AND TV STATIONS

A NUMBER OF ENGLISH-LANGUAGE COMMERCIAL RADIO stations are in Dubai. The most popular are Dubai 92 (92.0 FM), Virgin Radio (104.4 FM), Eye of Dubai (103.8 FM) and Coast (103.2 FM). The standard of the DJs varies wildly – from genuinely dreadful to merely dubious – but these stations can be handy for traffic updates and local news. The BBC World Service can also be found at 87.9 FM. Local English-language TV channels are City7 and Dubai One, which air a mix of international and locally-made programmes (the latter mostly look as if they were made by a bunch of sixth-formers with a camcorder). Hotels usually also have a selection of satellite stations playing music, movies and news.

TOILETS

[handwritten: must have – revers. for tea n drink ahead]

APART FROM THE BURJ AL ARAB and the Armani Hotel, you can walk into any hotel in the city. This means that, in practice, tourists are free to use the conveniences in all of them free of charge. All beach parks have toilets, as do the parks, and they are all very well kept. Toilets in the malls are also plentiful and very well attended to. The only thing you many notice is that floors are often wet – this is because, instead of the European bidets, hoses are plumbed into the wall next to the cisterns used to perform ablutions. Some users are more skilful at refraining from spraying the floor than others. In men's toilets, there is usually a mix of urinals and cubicles, although there are very occasionally old-style squat toilets. Men should, under no circumstances, relieve themselves in public, as this could lead to arrest.

RIP-OFFS AND SCAMS

DUBAI IS A VERY TIGHTLY-CONTROLLED CITY, so you really aren't likely to get seriously ripped off, as the penalties are too severe. The only widely-practised mini-scam is run by taxi drivers – you should always have change for them. They do often claim to have none, thus tipping themselves. Also, many expensive restaurants will try to rip you off by upselling imported water (Voss, Evian, San Pellegrino), which often costs as much as a glass of wine (AED 30+), so do ask for local bottled water – Masafi or Arwa are best-known brands – to keep costs down.

SLOW SERVICE

FROM RESTAURANTS TO SHOPS, although service is well meaning, it can often be painfully slow and inept. There's nothing you can do about this really – locals have just learned to grin and bear it. It can sometimes also be wilfully obstructive or lazy – you sometimes get the feeling that the standard answer is no, whether the question is 'Do you have this in another size?' or 'Can you make that without cheese please?' You'll often find that if you push, the answer will change from a negative to a positive. Just try to keep your cool.

SMOKING

THE LAWS HERE REGARDING SMOKING are a little confused. In 2007 it was banned in public places, but in practice, you can still smoke in nearly all bars and nightclubs, both indoors and out. Upmarket restaurants will often have a total ban on it, apart from maybe in the bar, but there will usually be an outdoor terrace for smokers. Do not, under any circumstances, smoke outside on the street during Ramadan – it is an offence punishable by a fine or prison sentence.

BUSINESS HOURS

THE WORKING WEEK HERE IS SUNDAY to Thursday. Friday is the Islamic holy day, so you will find many small shops, malls and restaurants, especially in the older parts of town, shut for at least half of the day. Hotels and large malls are open as usual, however. Stores tend to open at 10 a.m. and stay that way until 10 p.m., sometimes midnight (especially at weekends), and hours are extended during Ramadan.

PUBLIC HOLIDAYS AND MOURNING DAYS

THE DATES OF EID AL-FITR, which signals the end of the month-long Ramadan (see page 27 for more information on the festival), and Eid al-Adha, around two months later, are judged on the lunar calendar, so the dates change each year. The same goes for the festivals celebrating the birth of the Prophet, the ascension of the Prophet and Islamic new year. New Year's Day (1 January) and the U.A.E. National Day (2 December) are fixed dates. The night before Ramadan begins is usually alcohol-free in the city, as are periods of mourning (usually one to three days) after an important member of the U.A.E. royal family has died. You will also find that radio stations are forced to play bland lift music during these periods.

WATER

THE TAP WATER HERE IS DESALINATED, so it can make your skin and hair dry. Drinking it won't harm you, but it just does not taste very nice.

TRAVELLING *with* CHILDREN

DUBAI IS AN EXTREMELY CHILD-FRIENDLY PLACE – from tourist attractions to restaurants, shops to cinemas, there are very few places where they aren't welcome. In fact, travelling en famille will give you an excuse to visit attractions that might otherwise make you feel a bit like Peter Pan. The Dubai Mall's SEGA Republic and Kidzania indoor play zones, the Atlantis hotel's fishy theme parks – Aquaventure and The Lost Chambers – Ski Dubai and the Wild Wadi waterpark are all specifically designed to keep little ones happy. There are also malls that offer a crèche where children can play under professional supervision while you shop – Peekaboo is one of the best for these (**peekaboo.ae**). Many also rent out kiddie cars in which you can push around offspring while you peruse the rails. Many restaurants offer entertainment during their weekly brunches, alongside special child-friendly menus. Most have high chairs.

If you do want some downtime by the pool without the kids, many of the larger hotels – especially those on the beach – have supervised children's clubs. The Atlantis tops the lot, with a Command Centre stuffed with games consoles and Internet-enabled computers, an Underwater Theatre where children can watch the fish during the day and movies in the evening. A Play Zone is complete with a climbing wall and shipwreck, and a Creation Zone hosts arts, crafts and baking classes. They do charge per session for the privilege, though. The Jumeirah Beach Hotel also has the Sinbad's Kids Club for children under age 12, which runs sessions daily 8 a.m.–8 p.m., and the One&Only Royal Mirage also has a daily programme of activities. In fact, nearly all of the large resorts offer something to keep children from getting bored (although do check when booking whether these are complimentary or charged per session, as they can rack up your hotel bill considerably). Nearly all offer babysitting services too. The men and women running the kids' clubs usually have a very high level of English, and in fact many of them are from the U.K. With babysitters it can vary, although most have a very good grasp of the language.

MEDICAL *and* DENTAL PROBLEMS

IN THE CASE OF ILLNESS OR MEDICAL EMERGENCIES, your hotel may well have a doctor on call, or at the least be able to direct you to the nearest hospital. Hospitals are clean and efficient, although most are private, so you will have to pay for your treatment, so do make sure you take out medical insurance. The **American Hospital** (**ahdubai.com;** ☎ 04-309-6700) runs an Easy Access Clinic 10 a.m–10 p.m. seven days a week, where a paediatrician and family medicine specialist is always on call. The **Welcare Hospital** (**ehl.ae;** ☎ 04-282-7788) and the **Medcare Hospital** (☎ 04-407-9101) also have dedicated emergency medicine clinics.

DISABLED TRAVELLERS

ALTHOUGH NOT PERFECT, as a new city Dubai has tried to take disabled tourists into account wherever possible. There is 24-hour assistance, including a taxi service, available at the Dubai airport. The newly-opened Metro is a shining example of assistance for the disabled, with lowered ticket counters and lifts designed with wheelchair access in mind, and textured tiles on platform floors to guide the visually impaired. Unfortunately, in many cases the station spits you out somewhere it would be impossible to manoeuvre a wheelchair, and while it is possible to book a wheelchair-friendly taxi, in practice it is very hard to get the call centre operator to understand what it is you are requesting, so do try to book with **Dubai Taxi** (☎ 04-224-5331) well in advance.

Many hotels are well versed in catering to those with disabilities – do contact yours to check the available facilities first. In terms of attractions, the **Dubai Museum** (☎ 04-353-1862) and **Heritage Village** (☎ 04-393-7151) are accessible to wheelchairs. Dubai and Al Mamzar beach parks, as well as Dubai Creek and Al Safa parks, are all wheelchair accessible. **Orient Tours** (**orienttours.ae**; ☎ 04-282-8238) offers desert tours for access-impaired tourists – its camp, where you can enjoy dinner and a belly dance performance, is wheelchair accessible too – as long as your group is happy to rent out the whole 4x4 vehicle. **North Tours** (**northtours.net**; ☎ 04-222-2808) also offers dhow dinner cruises to disabled passengers. The Spice Souk and Bur Dubai's Meena Bazaar are all but off-limits to wheelchairs, but all of the large malls have very adequate facilities. Most of the restaurants included in the guide have a disabled access rating, but if you decide to go off-piste, phone first. The rule of thumb is that larger hotels are usually fine, while smaller, independent cafes and restaurants may suffer from access issues. For up-to-date information, take a look at the **Department of Tourism and Commerce Marketing** Web site, **dubaitourism.ae,** where you will find a dedicated Special Needs Tourism section.

PART FIVE

GETTING AROUND

VISUALISING *the* CITY

TO UNDERSTAND DUBAI'S ROADS, you must keep firmly in mind the fact that this is not a city that has been centrally planned. To the visitor, routes will seem circuitous, one-way systems incomprehensible and roadworks maddening. We would love to say that there is method in the madness, but if there is, we have failed to decipher it. On the plus side, the traffic that used to blight the main roads during the rush hours of 8–9 a.m. and 5–7 p.m. has calmed down considerably and, as construction slows, the endless re-routings and diversions have become less frequent. Taxis have also become much easier to hail.

Many visitors to Dubai are happy to stay ensconced in their beach-side hotels, especially in the larger complexes such as the Madinat Jumeirah or the Atlantis, where you can easily amuse yourself in their environs for a whole week. It would be a shame not to see any of the emirate, though, and to this end, many of the larger hotels have shuttle buses that will take you at least to Dubai Mall and the Mall of the Emirates. The Big Bus Tours company (**bigbustours.com**) is certainly an option if you would like to see the city in a manageable, one-day chunk without having to deal with cars, taxis or the Metro – take a look at page 135, where we go into more detail.

If you are keen to go out under your own steam, we would suggest reading the following chapters. What can make things especially tricky for the uninitiated is the fact that addresses here are a rarity. This may sound ludicrous, but even when roads do have official names, they are often known locally by something else entirely, so even directing taxis can be hard. This is before you even consider hiring a car and driving yourself.

To get a handle on the city, it helps to think of its beating heart as Dubai Creek, which runs northeast to southwest and splits Dubai's oldest areas, Deira and Bur Dubai, into two. Dubai Creek played a major role in the city's growth as a trading port, especially after it was dredged in 1963 to get rid of the silt that had built up, thus allowing larger trading boats access to the port. As a tourist, you are likely to spend most of your time on the Bur Dubai side. You will, however, likely arrive on the Deira side, as this is where the airport is located, with the shopping and hotel complex of Dubai Festival City sitting nearby. Just behind the international airport lies the border with the neighbouring coastal emirate of Sharjah. Four bridges will take you across Dubai Creek — the recently-widened Garhoud Bridge, Maktoum Bridge, Floating Bridge and Business Bay Crossing, and also Al Shindagha tunnel, which runs straight into Deira and can get supercongested at rush hour.

Five main routes run through Dubai, although by far the most important is the **Sheikh Zayed Road** (E11), the longest road in the U.A.E., which runs from the World Trade Centre roundabout right through the centre of the city and continues on to Jebel Ali and Abu Dhabi (where it becomes Sheikh Maktoum Road). It runs roughly parallel to the coast and widens from four to six lanes in each direction at points. If you want to drive it yourself, you really do need to keep your wits about you on this road as it is the most widely-used highway in the Arab world, and there is, how shall we put it, a rather large international melting pot of driving styles. It was also the scene of the famous 200-car pileup in 2008 due to very thick early-morning fog.

At the Trade Centre roundabout end of the E11, you will find the largest concentration of Dubai's business hotels, flanking the road near the Dubai International Financial Centre. As you drive farther down towards Dubai Marina, you will pass the Burj Khalifa, the Dubai Mall and the surrounding Downtown residential development. The area that currently looks like a skyscraper farm, with towers in varying stages of infancy, is Business Bay, a cluster of office and residential developments that were originally meant to line the extension of Dubai Creek from Ras Al Khor to Sheikh Zayed Road (although the scope of this development will likely be curtailed due to the financial crash, with many of the most impressive planned buildings indefinitely on hold). Past this lie various small malls, car showrooms and the industrial warehouses of Al Quoz, before you pass the Mall of the Emirates, roughly parallel to the Burj Al Arab, which you can see rising out of the sea as you're driving down the six-lane highway. Past this rise the skyscrapers of Dubai Marina, then past that iron smelting plants, Ibn Battuta Mall, the Jebel Ali Resort & Spa and then on eventually to Abu Dhabi.

You will probably have much less cause to use the other main roads. One such road is the **Emirates Road** (**E311**), a six-lane highway that runs from the Jebel Ali Free Zone, extends eastward through Dubai, past the Arabian Ranches, Global Village and Sports City, and through the neighbouring emirates of Sharjah, Umm Al Quwain, Ajman and Ras Al-Khaimah. The **Dubai-Hatta Highway** (**E44**), locally known as Al Khail Road, runs to Hatta and Oman, and the **E66**, also called **Al Ain Road,** runs southward from the Oud Metha area to Al Ain, the second city of the emirate of Abu Dhabi. Two minor roads that you are most likely to use regularly are **Al Wasl Road,** which runs parallel to the Sheikh Zayed Road for a long stretch from around the World Trade Centre roundabout to the Madinat Jumeirah, and the **Jumeirah Beach Road,** which runs along the coast, from the Dubai Marine Resort to the Madinat Jumeirah, where it turns into Al Sufuoh Road before terminating at Dubai Marina.

DRIVING *in* DUBAI

THERE IS NO DOUBT THAT DUBAI IS A DRIVING CITY, and so an obvious way to get around as a visitor is to hire a car. This comes with a caveat – driving in this city is not for the faint-hearted or easily agitated. Having said that, hiring a car is quite hassle-free. Most of the big companies have operations in the U.A.E., and the service is generally good. For peace of mind, we would suggest sticking to the biggest companies, but do shop around for the best rate as they can vary wildly. Some to try are Budget (☎ 04-282-2727, **budget-uae.com**); Avis (☎ 04-224-5219, **avisuae.ae**); Hertz (☎ 800-HERTZ, **hertz-uae.com**); or Thrifty (☎ 04-347-9001, **thriftyuae.com**). Many large hotels also have car hire offices on-site.

When selecting a car, think like a local – the bigger, or at least the safer, the better. It's worth checking the safety record of the car online before confirming – it may not be particularly eco-friendly, but a supersize Hummer is likely to come off better than a three-door Mini in an altercation. You'll need to be over the age of 21 and have a valid international driving licence and your passport. You will be given the option of picking up the car from the airport or having it delivered to your hotel – we would suggest the latter, as negotiating Dubai's roads after a long flight will be draining and potentially dangerous. Most will also offer GPS systems and child seats. Driving is on the right-hand side.

You will be offered various insurance plans, and the advice from a seasoned Dubai driver is to take out the most expensive and comprehensive. Minor prangs are a way of life here, and you don't want to be landed with a huge bill for the excess. Highway etiquette here can be lacking at the best of times, but we have to include an extra word of warning about Ramadan driving. If possible, try to stay off the roads at around sunset, as the actions of near-delirious drivers racing home to break fast can be erratic to say the least. If you do get involved in an accident, it is not enough simply to take the details of the other parties. You will need to call the police at ☎ 999. When they arrive and assess the damage, you will be handed a form in Arabic that you need to give to the car hire company (pink if you are at fault, green if the other driver is). This is a tedious process that can take a while, but it is the law, and you will be fined if you try to dodge it.

You shouldn't need to pay any extra fees for driving to other emirates if you want to do some exploring, but extra charges are involved in driving to Oman, so enquire at the time of booking. There are also Salik (road toll) fees to pay at various points of the city, including the bridges. The car-hire company should pay these as you go along – they can be tracked online – and you will be expected to reimburse them at the end. The same applies to fines for speeding or for breaking traffic regulations.

When driving to a new location, it will pay to get directions that are as detailed as possible – and be prepared to be told to 'make U-turn' multiple times – they aren't big on roundabouts here, so it is a very accepted way of changing direction. Do try to avoid the rush hours Sunday–Thursday of 8–9 a.m. on the Sheikh Zayed Road going towards Abu Dhabi and 5–7 p.m. coming back from the Marina/Abu Dhabi direction towards Dubai on the same road. Also avoid going into and out of Sharjah at these times, as there is invariably a serious bottleneck. Sightseeing visits to Bur Dubai and Deira are best done during the daytime when everyone else is at work – the roads here are even prone to getting snarled up on a Friday and Saturday. Bar the occasional gridlock due to accidents, you should have a pretty free run of the roads outside of these hours. Although it may seem like a good idea to try and find a shortcut when you do encounter traffic, our advice is just grin and bear it – you will spend more time getting lost than you would just waiting where you are. If in doubt, sit it out.

There are some things that make driving here easier than in many major cities – valet parking is plentiful and, for the most part, free. Parking on the street is legal and cheap (AED 2 per hour, rising higher for longer stays, up to a maximum of AED 11), but being caught without a ticket is not, so make sure you pay at the meter. All of the big malls and tourist attractions have more than ample parking (do make sure you remember where you parked, though, as finding your car can be a nightmare). Petrol is also very cheap compared to many other countries, and you don't even have to get out of your car to fill up. And, of course, driving affords you the freedom you simply won't have if relying on taxis and public transport.

DRIVE LIKE A LOCAL

IF YOU ARE KEEN TO GET BEHIND THE wheel, here are a few tips from Dubai drivers on negotiating the city's roads:

1. Don't let your petrol tank get dangerously empty, as seeking out petrol stations can be tricky. It's much better to fill up as and when you see them. Bring cash, as many do not accept credit cards.

2. Many drivers in Dubai consider indicators irrelevant – using them prior to switching lanes is rare.

3. The concept of right of way when minor roads join major roads is rarely observed. Anticipate that drivers merging onto main roads may not stop, signal or even look.

4. Avoid crossing the yellow lines. Police don't like it and fines are severe.

5. Speed cameras have a 10% tolerance in most places but not all. It's best not to take the chance.

6. There are very few roundabouts, so changing direction is done by making a U-turn. People do it all the time, everywhere.

7. There is a zero-tolerance policy for drink driv-ing. Even if you feel fine to drive, don't. Even if someone else causes an accident, you could end up in prison for it.

8. Do not short-cut across sandbanks even if you see others doing so, as it will result in a hefty fine.

9. Never, ever make an offensive hand gesture to a fellow road user, even one who is driving like a chimpanzee. Flipping the bird or even raising your hands heavenwards in a 'What the . . . ?' motion could land you deportation or even a prison sentence.

10. Drivers in Dubai tend to hang in lanes, whether overtaking or not. Undertaking is therefore commonplace, although illegal, so remem-ber to check inside and out if changing lanes.

11. Tailgating is common but is, again, illegal – the police are clamping down on it, and it comes with a heavy fine if you are charged. If someone is doing it to you, just get out of the way. Trust us; it's easier.

unofficial **TIP**
Hiring a 4x4 will tempt some more adventur-ous drivers to off-road in Dubai's surrounding dunes. It's far trickier than it looks, though, so if you are deter-mined to do it, try a one-day course with the Emirates Driving Institute in a company-owned car, from AED 500. Call ☎ 04-263-1100 or visit **edi-uae.com.**

unofficial **TIP**
If you have had a drink, do not even think about getting behind the wheel. Saferdriver (☎ 04-268-8797; **saferdriver.ae**) will send a driver to transport your car (and you) home.

TAXIS

ASK ANY DUBAI RESIDENT how he or she knew that the credit crisis had finally washed up on Dubai's shores and the answer is universal – 'We could actually get a taxi within the hour'. Pre-crunch, the 6,000 or so five- and seven-seater Toyota Camry cars could barely keep up with the demand. Now, it couldn't be easier to grab a cab. These taxis are very easily identifiable, with their sand-coloured exteriors and rainbow-coloured roofs, operated by one of six companies:

Dubai Transport (red roof) ☎ 04-208-0808	**National Taxi** (yellow roof) ☎ 04-339-0002
Ladies Taxi (pink roof) ☎ 04-208-0808	**Arabia Taxis** (green roof) ☎ 04-285-5111
Metro Taxi (orange roof) ☎ 04-267-3222	**Cars Taxis** (blue roof) ☎ 04-269-2900

The Ladies Taxis are driven by women and, predictably, only take women (they won't even accept families with men). They drive about 50% slower than other cars, but at least they smell nice. As all of these cabs are company owned and operated, there is no need to look for an identification badge on the driver – the fact they are driving the car is proof enough that they are on the level.

Your first encounter with a taxi will likely be at the airport. Finding one won't be a problem; there's rarely a long queue, and as it is quite heavily policed, you'll never be approached by an unlicensed cab. These designated airport taxis are metered at the same rate as all the others – AED 1.6 per kilometre (AED 1.7 for the larger people-carriers) – but the fare starts at AED 25.

Your hotel should always have a plentiful supply of cabs waiting outside the lobby, and if not, then the concierge will be happy to call one – although if this is the case, the fare will start at AED 6 instead of AED 3 (this is the same for all taxis booked through the call centre). If you can adequately explain where you are, call one of the numbers listed above to book it yourself. The driver will call you from a Dubai mobile number (starting 050) when he arrives, but most of the time will immediately ring off so he doesn't get charged for the call. Call him back if you can't find him.

You'll be offered the services of a hotel taxi at some point, which the driver will almost certainly tell you costs the same (in our experience, not true). However, these vary wildly in the rip-off stakes – some have meters, which rack up the dirhams at an alarming rate, especially when you are stuck in traffic. Some will agree on a price with you, only to inform you on arrival that they 'got the rate wrong' and it's actually significantly more. These cars are also subject to the AED 4 Salik toll, which official taxis are exempt from – depending on where and how far you are going, this can add up to AED 20+ in a single journey. Our advice is to avoid these unless you are in a desperate hurry and there are no other available options.

Most tourist attractions are also taxi hubs, so even if there is a bit of a queue, it should move quickly. The Dubai Mall, for example, usually has hordes of people all leaving at the same time of the evening – usually around 5 p.m., which is exacerbated by the fact that this is the hour when the drivers' shifts change over. As for hailing a taxi on the street, it couldn't be simpler – stick your arm out and they will stop. Some might even stop when all you are trying to do is cross the road, in which case just wave them away. If they are for hire, the yellow light on top of the car should be lit, but this won't always be the case. If the light is off but you can't see anyone sitting in the cab, stick your arm out regardless and hope for the best.

The tough part, sadly, can come when you try to explain your destination to the driver. As a rule of thumb, the only street name that he will definitely know is the Sheikh Zayed Road, the main artery that runs through the city. People here navigate by landmarks, so if you can find out what the nearest one is (a large hotel, hospital, mall, supermarket and so on), you'll have a better chance of getting there. It also pays to come armed with the phone number of your destination, so if you get lost, you can call for directions. There are four words you need to be wary of: 'I am new driver'. If this is what greets you when you get in the cab, get out. If you get in a taxi and the driver seems to have no idea where your stated destination is, get out then too. It can be expensive and annoying to circle the city while he phones a selection of friends and relatives to try and locate the right road, and there will almost always be another taxi five minutes behind.

One thing that tourists may also be disconcerted by is the fact that many taxi drivers won't speak to you. We're not talking passing-the-time-of-day, what-about-this-weather type chat. A vast majority won't even acknowledge you when you jump into the back seat and bark your destination, instead just speeding off. This doesn't necessarily mean that they don't know where they are going, but if you are concerned, press them for a sign they definitely do. Of course, there is also occasionally the converse problem – we've had drivers try to convert us to Islam, spend the entire journey singing tunelessly in Urdu or enquire loudly why we are 'not married when you so old, madam'.

It's a bit of a myth here that taxis are dirt cheap. Given that most tourists will use them to go everywhere, the cost can add up over a holiday. To get from the new heart of Dubai, the Burj Khalifa, down to Dubai Marina costs around AED 50, and even short journeys can cost, as the road system is counterintuitive, with its maze of one-ways, diversions and U-turns. Taxi drivers can sometimes use this to their advantage and take you around the houses a bit, to up the fare. Unless you know the city well, there is very little you can do about this. If you plan to be visiting multiple places in one day, you can hire a taxi for 6 hours at AED 300 or 12 hours at AED 500. This will be easier, although not really cheaper. Most will also expect a tip – 10% is usual, or for smaller fares round up to the nearest AED 5 or AED 10. Keep a supply of small notes for taxis, as drivers do like tipping themselves, with a cry of 'no change' when faced with AED 100+ notes.

Although it is frowned upon here, it is not unusual for your driver to spend the majority of the ride bellowing into his phone. If he employs the hands-free option, then – depending on the decibels – you might want to ignore this for the sake of an easy (if not quiet) life. If, however, he is juggling gearstick and handset – we have actually experienced a driver steering with his knees while swigging a bottle of water and nattering away merrily to his mate – then you are totally within your rights to demand he desist immediately. Depending on his level of English, and how determined he is to ignore you, a light tap on the shoulder and a 'no phone' mime should do the trick.

The quality of driving varies quite a lot. Tailgating is a common practice, as is breaking the speed limit. If this happens, a warning beep will start emanating from the dashboard – and if you'd rather your driver slowed down, then tell him so. You should also give him plenty of warning if you want him to stop, take a slip road or do a U-turn, as it's standard to cut across four lanes of traffic to reach any motorway exit, which can be seat-of-the-pants stuff. In many taxis, you will spot an electronic pad on the headrests of the driver and passenger seat on which, in theory, you can record your level of satisfaction with the journey (questions such as, 'How polite was my driver?'). They rarely work. If you are genuinely dissatisfied by the standard of driving, the attitude of the driver or the state of the car, make a note of this; then you can call the dedicated freephone number ☎ 800-9090. Threatening to do so will usually mean that the driver falls into line – and is particularly useful if he has refused to pick you up from the side of the road, which he is legally required to do even if the journey is short.

PUBLIC T

THERE ARE THREE
bus or boat. If you
a NOL card – a p
buy, will allow you t
public transport or
more complicated sy
of NOL card – red,
one mode of transp
trips. Cards can be u
single journeys within
to use multiple modes
offices, many superm
includes AED 14 of cr
you can use it for the
able online and only s
nol.ae for more details

then travelling down to Bur Dubai, De
and then back to Al Shindagha, ta
for adults and AED 25 for chil
information.

BUSES

IN A BID TO IMPRO
government introd
how well this
viable mode
which are
The
wai

BOATS

FOR A VISITOR, boats should be considered more of a tourist attraction than a method of getting from A to B in a timely fashion. The most common form of boat travel in Dubai is the diesel-fuelled *abra* that crosses the creek – in fact, in 2009, usage totalled more than 16.5 million journeys. They are a useful way of avoiding the Bur Dubai to Deira traffic if you want to visit the Gold or Spice souks on the Deira side.

They're not the most comfortable things you'll ever ride on, and the benches can get quite packed, but the trips are short. A direct ride across Dubai Creek costs AED 1 (you can't use a NOL card) if you buy a ticket at the designated boarding stations. There are 149 motorised *abras*, which arrive and depart constantly on two main routes – Al Sabkha to Dubai Old Souk (5 a.m.–midnight) and Bur Dubai to Deira Old Souk (24 hours). If you'd like the boat to yourself, the fare should be not more than AED 100 per hour for tourists – but be aware that the driver will probably throw existing passengers off the boat, which can be mortifying. He may ask for more money at the end of the trip.

Another aquatic option is the Dubai water bus, launched in 2007. Although not quite as atmospheric and slightly more expensive at AED 4 for a single trip (they accept prepaid NOL cards), they are air conditioned, so a bit more bearable in the summer months. The best line for sightseeing is the B5, operated specially for visitors, which stops at five of the nine stations, starting at Al Shindagha,

ra, Al Seef, Dubai Creek Park
ing 90 minutes. It costs AED 50
ren. Call ☎ 04-396-3135 for more

E THE JOURNEY TIMES of Dubai's buses, the
uced bus lanes in mid-2010. It remains to be seen
orks, but if successful, it could make them a more
of transport, as it should cut down on journey times,
currently over-long due to traffic congestion.

buses are clean and new, and the air-conditioned stops make
ing in the heat more bearable. But unless you are very dedicated
saving either money (trips cost AED 1.80–5.80) or the environment, then avoid, as the network of 79 bus routes can be very tricky
to use. Stops and stations are hard to locate, most drivers will only
accept the prepaid NOL cards, and buses can get very overcrowded.
The only exception to the rule is when you are only taking a short
journey from a Metro stop to your destination (for example, the five-
minute trip from the Burj Khalifa Metro stop to the Dubai Mall).

Routes and timetables can be downloaded from **rta.ae,** a journey
planner can be found at **wojhati.rta.ae,** or you can call ☎ 800-9090.
Probably the most useful service for the visitor is the Emirates Express
E100 bus to and from Abu Dhabi, which departs from Al Ghubaibah bus
station in Bur Dubai every 40 minutes Saturday–Thursday 6:20 a.m.–
9:40 p.m. It takes two hours and costs AED 20 – considerably less
than the AED 300 taxi fare.

METRO

THE NEWEST ADDITION (as of 9 September 2009, or 09/09/09) to
Dubai's public transport system is the Dubai Metro, and a rather
mighty thing it is too. Stations have so far opened in dribs and drabs,
but 26 of the 29 stations on the Red Line are now open, and the last
3 are expected to open in early 2011. The track, much of which runs
parallel to the Sheikh Zayed Road, is 52.1 kilometres (32.4 miles)
long, 4.7 kilometres (2.9 miles) of which is underground, and the
state-of-the-art trains are driverless. It starts at Rashidiya, just past
the Airport Terminal 3, and goes all the way to Jebel Ali. The Green
Line, which will run from Al Qusais to Al Jadaf, will eventually
intersect the Red Line at Khalid Bin Al Waleed (locally known as the
BurJuman station) and Union Square stations, although the opening
date for this has already been pushed back several times. There were
originally plans for Blue and Purple lines, but these have been put on
hold indefinitely, as plans for the buildings they were intended to serve
have been almost universally binned.

Compared to the London Underground, this is Dubai's first baby step towards a useful transport system – as there are as yet no intersecting lines, you really do just need to buy a ticket, work out which direction you are going and stand on the right platform. The platforms are well signposted, with video screens that tell you how long you will have to wait until the next train arrives (usually a maximum of ten minutes). A disembodied voice announces each stop a couple of seconds before you reach it, so there is no unseemly scrum for the door. Do listen out for it, though, as since the Metro opened, the stopping times have been shortened to speed up the service. Most stations have lifts and escalators (as well as free Wi-Fi), and all have disabled access and are open 6 a.m.–11 p.m. Saturday–Thursday and 2 p.m.–midnight Friday.

Buying a ticket in the stations is easy – in fact, probably easier than on the London Underground. Staff are standing by the ticket machines to help you figure them out (the buttons are in English, so you shouldn't have trouble deciphering them), but unless you have exact change or want to use a credit card, you should go directly to the booths. Three or four of these are in each station, manned with staff behind the glass, all of whom will speak English to varying degrees. Make sure you tell them exactly where you are going, for if your journey involves an added road journey at the other end (as it does, for example, at the Dubai Mall), you will need a ticket that will also allow you onto the bus.

Tickets are priced by journey length, and if you are unsure of which you need, it is best to go to the counter to speak to an assistant. Prices start at AED 2.5 for a single journey within one zone to AED 6.5 for a single for five zones. Double this for return tickets or for gold class. Fares are slightly less if you are loading them onto a silver or a gold NOL card. Children under the age of 5 travel free. Unless you are allergic to other people or travelling during rush hour, don't bother with gold. It's hard to tell where the carriage is (it's actually the front if you are headed to Dubai Marina and the back if you're headed to the airport) and not significantly more comfortable. When we have travelled gold during the daytime, the carriage has been almost empty, but then so were the normal carriages. If you are a single woman travelling on your own and feel uncomfortable, the ladies-only carriage is next to the gold-class carriage – this is especially useful at busy times.

If you already have a NOL card, you just need to touch it to the reader at the barriers, which will slide back to allow you to pass if you have enough credit and also tell you your balance. The same is true of the single paper tickets – the machine will not swallow them when you leave the station, so if you have more than one in your wallet, do try to keep track. In terms of etiquette, if you are feeling polite, then do allow pregnant women and the elderly to sit, although it won't actually be expected of you, as it would in some other countries. If you have luggage, try to keep it out of the way in the areas designated for it. You will actually be stopped from getting on the train if you have very bulky bags.

Try to get a window seat, as the carriages give a great vantage point above the city, or sit at the front if you want to pretend you are at the helm of the driverless train. Two things to remember though: the powers that be sold off the station names to the highest bidder in some areas, hence First Gulf Bank and Sharaf DG stations give little idea of actual location. Also, some were named at the height of the property boom – so Nakheel Harbour & Tower doesn't actually exist, despite having a namesake stop.

Also, at most stations, you will probably still need to get a taxi to your final destination, as you tend to be spat out in rather random locations. Realistically, as a tourist, you will find the most useful stations are those in or near shopping centres. If you want to do a whole day at the malls without having to resort to taxis, you can hit the stores at Deira City Centre, Khalid Bin Al Waleed (for BurJuman Centre), Emirate Towers, Burj Khalifa (for the Dubai Mall) and Ibn Battuta Mall. Al Karama is also useful if you don't want to battle the area's traffic but fancy a stroll around its fake handbag and DVD emporia.

PALM JUMEIRAH MONORAIL

THE PALM JUMEIRAH MONORAIL would be truly useful if it connected in some way to the Dubai Metro, but as you might have already gathered, things rarely work like that here. So instead, it is essentially a park-and-ride for Aquaventure at the Atlantis. Tickets cost AED 15 one way and AED 25 return and are operated seven days a week, 8 a.m.–10 p.m. Covered parking is at the Gateway Towers station at the base of the Palm. From there, it is only 5.45 kilometres (3.4 miles) to the Atlantis and takes five minutes.

WALKING

WE WERE TEMPTED TO LEAVE THIS SECTION AT ONE WORD: don't. But that's not entirely fair. Certainly, you can't expect to cover large areas on foot, but there are pedestrian-friendly pockets of the city that can be pleasant to walk around when the weather is bearable. Luckily, it's also not really possible to stray into a dangerous zone of the city, as there isn't one. Sure, it's not a great idea to walk around a deserted industrial district such as Al Quoz on your own at night, but there is scant chance of you ever ending up there by accident. The other rule of thumb is that if there is no path or pavement, give up. Shortcuts across sand and stones will nearly always leave you sweating, swearing and lost. And one last golden rule: do not underestimate a Dubai summer. Try to walk anywhere – *anywhere* – in the August heat, and you will be drenched in seconds.

Bur Dubai is a good starting point for your walking tour. The Dubai Museum is flanked by Bastakiya on one side (see page 145 for more detailed information), a pretty if sanitised tourist village that aims to re-create the flavour of Dubai when it was just a desert trading port, and on the other by Meena Bazaar, a maze of alleys and one wide cobbled street that runs along Dubai Creek, with shops selling fabric, Indian clothing, jewellery and kitschy souvenirs. Keep walking along Dubai Creek and you will find the nouveau-quaint Heritage and Diving Villages. To explore Deira, with its Gold and Spice souks, take an *abra* (traditional boat) for AED 1 across Dubai Creek from here. If at any point you get seriously lost, the best thing to do is flag down a taxi and get them to take you back to your starting point – asking directions is rarely fruitful, as people won't know street names (or, in these areas, English).

If you like your souks a bit more sanitised, the area around the Burj Kahlifa, the Dubai Mall and the boutique shopping mall and dining destination Souk Al Bahar just opposite are also navigable on foot, and especially pleasant in the early evening when the Dubai Fountain starts up. For shopping and eating, The Walk at Jumeirah Beach Residence, in the Marina, and Marina Walk, just next door, are nice places for an afternoon stroll. Both of these areas have ample parking and lots of taxis.

PART SIX

SIGHTSEEING, TOURS *and* ATTRACTIONS

PLANNING *for* DUBAI TOURING

DUBAI HAS A PLETHORA OF ATTRACTIONS for every type and every age of sightseer. The challenge isn't trying to work out *what* you want to do, but *when* you're going to fit it all in. Inevitably, you'll want to relax for a day or three on the beach, sip a cocktail at sunset, indulge in a spot of shopping and decide where you're going to eat. But it's well worth taking some time to explore beyond these obvious pleasures, as Dubai has a rich history and heritage, a prolific art scene, the most fantastic architecture, old traditional souks and streets in which to lose yourself, waterways to travel down and a beautiful desert in which you can experience a multitude of thrilling activities and adventures. Dubai is not synonymous with culture and heritage, and most people do not come on holiday to Dubai to explore its fascinating historical past. However, scratch beneath its glossy surface, and you will be agreeably surprised to find pockets of Dubai that still retain its traditions and culture and areas that are rich in history. You might want to take in the futuristic skyline of skyscrapers by car; explore the backstreets on foot and see an older, hidden side to Dubai; learn about its heritage at museums and mosques; or travel down Dubai Creek on an *abra* (water taxi). Or you might want to spend an afternoon and evening in the desert on safari or try out dune bashing. Whatever it is that appeals most to you, you can be sure that the diverse contrasts will cause the most surprise and give a gentle but comprehensive introduction to life in Dubai.

Perhaps the most important thing to take into consideration when planning your sightseeing in Dubai is the weather. It's either hot or very hot. Winter, which is November–April, is cooler, with temperatures ranging between the low 20s and mid-30s (about 68–95°F). May–October, you can expect temperatures to reach mid- to high

40s (113–120°F) and the humidity to be very high. Our advice is to make sure that everyone in your party always carries a bottle of water with them. This sounds obvious, but you dehydrate so rapidly here, and once a headache sets in, your day will be spoilt. Take your sunscreen with you. Everywhere. And reapply liberally. Even when it doesn't feel that hot, the sun is so much closer than in Europe, and even the most olive-skinned are at risk of burning in minutes. Wear comfortable shoes. Fashion sandals that work in European climates become hot and sweaty and will rub and cause blisters when you're walking around in 30°C (86°F) heat for any length of time. We find rubber flip-flops keep you coolest, and brands such as Fitflop and Birkenstock are fantastic for these climates. Or if you prefer trainers or pumps, remember, your feet will swell in the heat, so make sure they're up a size for comfort.

Dubai sells itself as a premium tourist destination. However, it is important to remember that it is in the Middle East. The United Arab Emirates is a Muslim country, and Dubai, however liberal it appears, follows strict Islamic laws that should be respected by all travellers. We don't want to labour the point, as we have talked about dress code in detail in Part Three; however, for your own peace of mind, it is worth remembering that if you are visiting a mosque – or some of the older areas such as Karama, Deira and Bur Dubai, where the streets are full of men, especially on evenings and weekends – then women are advised to cover arms and legs. One other thing to remember: Public displays of affection of any sort are illegal. Unless one of you is the parent and the other is your child, just restrain yourselves!

Children are particularly welcomed everywhere in Dubai, and plenty of attractions will really appeal to them as well as to you. There is an amazing amount for children to do in Dubai: there are numerous indoor themed attractions, waterparks and 'edu-tainment'-type museums, and if they want to toboggan on snow in the morning and sandboard in the desert in the afternoon, then that is totally possible too. After all, this is Dubai. Desert activities have their own section in this guide, but we think a lot of them will appeal to children of all ages. It did occur to us, when researching this section, that an inordinate number of indoor theme parks are in Dubai, all vying to be bigger and better than the next. But taking into account the climate, which in effect cancels out outdoor activities for five months of the year, we do see why there is a need for them. Sort of.

If you have young children in your party who get up early, it is worth considering that when planning your itinerary. If you're going to a museum in the morning, it's good to spend an afternoon by a pool or on the beach. Do the outdoor sightseeing in the coolest part of the day, and spend the rest of the day at one of the attractions for children that are indoors and air-conditioned, ending up on the beach or at the pool for a refreshing swim as the sun goes down at 6 or 7 p.m. The wonderful thing about Dubai is that shopping malls, restaurants and many of the attractions for children stay open until 10 p.m. and much later, so there is never a great rush to fit everything in 9 a.m.–5 p.m. Some sites and attractions close at lunchtime for a couple of hours; others stay open all day. We attempt where possible to advise you of this, but it is always worth ringing and checking before you get there to avoid having to wait until opening time again. The souks and older shopping areas tend to close in the middle of the day but do stay open until late at night.

If you are visiting Dubai during the holy month of Ramadan, be aware that there may be restricted opening times of all tourist attractions; and whilst you are not permitted to eat, drink, smoke or chew gum in public during daylight hours, the rules are slightly more flexible, we discovered, if you are travelling on the **Big Bus Tour** – where we were allowed to eat and drink surreptitiously! It tends to be quieter during the daytime when visiting Dubai during Ramadan, when you also have the opportunity to experience the excitement of the *Iftar* banquets and buffets to break the fast at sunset.

Dubai is very easy to negotiate autonomously but is equally as pleasurable to discover with a guide or on a tour. There are tours of all sorts in the city – by foot, by boat or by car. If you don't wish to take a taxi everywhere, and you have no desire to drive yourself, consider hiring a driver or guide for the day to show you around. We list tour companies that we know are efficient and reputable.

The weekend in Dubai is Friday and Saturday. Consequently, from Thursday evening to Saturday evening, it gets very busy in malls, parks, waterparks and restaurants, as well as on tours and desert activities. If you can do some of these activities during the week – Sunday through Thursday – then you will find them less crowded and much more pleasurable.

Before planning what you want to do and where you want to go, consider obtaining one of the following maps once you are in Dubai: The Big Bus Company's map is excellent and can often be found in the larger hotels. The bus tour itself is really worthwhile if you want to check out all the main tourist sites in a few hours and get a feel for the city, but even if you don't decide to take the tour, the map is really useful for highlighting the best things to see and do. Another map that is invaluable is called Dubai Mini Map, by Explorer Publishing, and can be found in most bookshops, larger supermarkets and large hotel shops. It is detailed, splits the city up into the main areas and highlights the best things to see and do, as well as being tiny enough to slip into your pocket. If you prefer a meaty, larger map with the whole of Dubai on page, again Explorer Publishing has come up trumps with its north-oriented, water-resistant and tear-proof Dubai map. Larger in scale, it is excellent for detail and virtually indestructible. To purchase these maps, visit **explorerpublishing.com** or any supermarket or bookshop in Dubai.

EXPLORING:
Useful Tips Summarised

SIGHTSEEING IN DUBAI REQUIRES a little planning in order to ensure that you have the best possible time and the least possible hassle. Here are a few tips.

1. **Water** Carry at least a small bottle each, and refill during the day if necessary. The sun, the heat and the air conditioning, along with all the walking and touring you will do, will make you very thirsty. If you don't drink regularly, you will become dehydrated.

2. **Small-denomination banknotes** Shops, cafes and taxis are notoriously bad about giving change or having change for large banknotes. If the ATM only gives you AED 500, change it into 100s, 50s and lots of 10s before you set out for the day.

3. **Sunscreen** We have all made the mistake of thinking we have acclimatised and that the sun isn't so hot today. It is, and you will burn without protection. We all have. And we felt foolish. Don't make the same mistake.

4. **Hats** It is a good idea, if you plan to be in the sun for any length of time, to cover up with a hat of some description. And if any children, especially young ones in buggies, are in the party, it's imperative that their heads are covered or that a sun parasol protects them.

5. **Public displays of affection** We can't reiterate it enough. They are not tolerated. In the street, in the malls, on the beach, in restaurants or in hotels. Anywhere. Emiratis do get offended and have been known to call the police if they witness any untoward behaviour. Save it for the privacy of your room. It's not worth being arrested.

6. **Visiting a mosque** You will need to cover your arms, legs and head. Normally women will be loaned an *abaya* (robe) and a *hijab* (headscarf) to wear in the mosque, but it is respectful, if you know you are going to be visiting the mosque, to wear modest clothes as well.

7. **Ramadan** The holy month of Ramadan falls earlier each year than the year before. In 2011 it will start at 1 August; in 2012, 20 July; in 2013, 9 July; and so on. It depends on the moon, and it lasts for 30 days. Each day the fast is broken with a big *Iftar* feast. During Ramadan it is illegal to eat, drink, chew gum or smoke in public during daylight hours. At the least, if you are caught, police will caution you. At the worst, you can be arrested. Cafes and restaurants are closed – except in hotels, where special screens are erected at

the entrances so that non-Muslims can eat without offending fasting Muslims. Opening times of everything might be different from normal, so check first before setting out. Be aware that if you are planning to do a lot of physical activities, you are not allowed to drink water in public during daylight hours. Just plan your itinerary accordingly, and while it is permitted for young children under the ages of 11 or 12 to eat and drink in public, there won't be any eateries open to refuel them at lunchtime. Probably better either to take a picnic to eat discreetly out of public sight, or stay close to the larger hotels where food is still being served.

TOP ATTRACTIONS:

Visitors' Checklist

FOR ADDITIONAL MUST-VISIT ATTRACTIONS, look for the .

ABRA RIDE

THE BEST WAY TO GET FROM THE SOUKS in Deira to Bastakiya and Dubai Museum is to take these water taxis across Dubai Creek – efficient, speedy and fun. Buy tickets either side of Dubai Creek at *abra* ticket stations or onboard. Bear in mind that if you're wearing a skirt, it will fly up as the boat takes off. Tuck it in around you, and beware of the splashes. Tickets cost AED 1, and the ride takes 10–15 minutes depending on where you want to stop.

ATLANTIS

WHETHER THEMED HOTELS AND WATERPARKS are your thing or not, Atlantis, the majestic focal point of Palm Jumeirah, is well worth a visit for its magnificent scale and ingenuity. The resort includes a landmark hotel, Dolphin Bay, Aquaventure Water Park, The Lost Chambers Aquarium and Atlantis Dive Centre. Add to that pristine white beaches, world-class cuisine, a luxurious spa and designer boutiques, and this is a day out (albeit very expensive) for all the family. (☎ 04-426-0000; **atlantisthepalm.com**)

BASTAKIYA

THE ANTITHESIS OF ATLANTIS, Bastakiya is one of Dubai's oldest residential areas, now beautifully restored, with historical, windy, shady streets; courtyard houses with traditional wind towers; museums; art galleries; boutique hotels; and delightful restaurants and cafes. Dubai Museum and the Textile Souk are within easy walking distance. For guided walks and information about the area, contact The Sheikh Mohammed Centre for Cultural Understanding situated in Bastakiya. (☎ 04-353-6666; **cultures.ae**)

CREEK DINNER CRUISE

YOU CAN'T FAIL TO NOTICE THE FLOATING RESTAURANTS when you stroll along Dubai Creek, on the Bastakiya/Bur Dubai side, moored along the Creek's edge opposite the British Embassy. At night, these dhows, converted into restaurants, sail up and down the Creek whilst dinner is served. Quality definitely varies between the dhows, and certainly some look a bit basic. However, the following are elegant, the food is excellent and the experience is delightful. Be sure to book in advance.

We think the best is *Bateaux Dubai* (see page 139), and we also recommend *Al Mansour Dhow* (see page 138).

DESERT SAFARIS

NO TRIP TO DUBAI IS COMPLETE without a desert safari. Tour companies have been quick to jump on the bandwagon. A safari is usually half a day, a full day or an overnight stay. Most include dune bashing (tearing wildly up and down sand dunes in 4x4s), a buffet dinner and drinks at a desert camp; sandboarding; camel riding; music; belly dancing; and henna painting. If you get carsick, consider taking travel sickness tablets before you set off – it can be hair-raising. The camps are well equipped with toilets and washbasins. See page 141 for the tour operators we recommend.

DHOW BUILDING YARD

LOCATED CLOSE TO AL GARHOUD BRIDGE and along the Dubai Creek, this shipyard is a fascinating place to see how the traditional dhows are made. It's an incredible sight to see a full-size dhow being transported on the back of a trailer by road. Their size, beauty and wooden construction make them a work of craftsmanship, compared to their modern fibreglass counterparts, and the boats never cease to impress and please. See how they are made, and then walk along Dubai Creek and see the dhows in use. We love the contrast of age-old tradition juxtaposed with all that is new and shiny in Dubai.

DUBAI CREEK

MAKE TIME TO EXPLORE ON FOOT BOTH SIDES of Dubai Creek. Start on the Deira bank, and be transported back in time as sailors load and unload huge blue wooden dhows with cargo. The docks are piled high with boxed shipments for abroad. There is such a sense of romance and excitement about these dhows that it makes you wish that you could stow away and sail off for an adventure. Walk along to the souks and immerse yourself in traditional Arabic life. Be prepared to haggle; the shopkeepers expect it. Then hop onboard an *abra* and cross the water to the Bur Dubai side, where dhows converted into floating restaurants are moored. Here you will discover the delights of one of Dubai's oldest neighbourhoods – Bastakiya and the Textile

Souk. This is an area steeped in tradition, as far removed from one's preconceived idea of Dubai as is possible.

DUBAI FOUNTAIN

ONLY IN DUBAI WOULD YOU HAVE FOUNTAINS THAT DANCE. We admit that it's a little cheesy, but there's something strangely beautiful, almost moving, certainly hypnotic, watching jets of water perform with synchronised accuracy to rousing music and beams of light. Either stand and watch for free from the terraces of Dubai Mall and the bridge that crosses from Dubai Mall to Souk Al Bahar, as the fountains perform every 30 minutes each evening, or reserve a table on the balcony of any restaurant overlooking the water and be entertained as you dine. (**thedubaimall.com;** every half hour: Sunday–Wednesday, 6–10 p.m.; Thursday–Saturday, 4–11 p.m.)

MADINAT JUMEIRAH

ESSENTIALLY, THIS IS AN ARCHITECT'S CONCEPT of an Arabian-style hotel resort for Western tourists, complete with artificial Venetian-style canals and cobblestones, a 'traditional' souk, *abras*, waterfront cafes and restaurants, a theatre and an open-air amphitheatre. The atmosphere's buzzing, and it's fun to take a boat down the little river and visit the turtle sanctuary at the Mina A'Salam. The open-fronted bazaar shops are charming to wander through, but for a bargain you're far better off visiting the real souks and Karama. The Madinat Theatre has very good shows, and the amphitheatre has occasional food festivals and concerts. This is worth a visit for the people-watching. (Jumeirah Beach Road; ☎ 04-366-8888; **jumeirah.com**)

SOUKS

NOTHING BEATS WANDERING through the bustling souks, or markets, in the traditional areas of Deira and Bur Dubai across Dubai Creek. Spices, textiles, gold, perfume, pots and pans, electrical goods and kitsch tourist souvenirs – this is a feast for all the senses. Revel in the aromas of the spices, the calls of the shop owners and the sights of the jewel-coloured textiles. Meander through the windy streets, be prepared to bargain and experience a slice of traditional Dubai life. Visit the Fish Market – you'll smell it before you see it – and be amazed at the variety of species on sale. Take a water taxi to cross from one side of the Creek to the other. Women should dress conservatively. Take cash to pay, as cards are not accepted. In the summer go early or late, as it gets very hot wandering around. Hours vary, but the souks are generally open Saturday–Thursday, 7 a.m.–noon and 5–7 p.m., and on Friday, 5–7 p.m. See Part Nine, Shopping, for more information.

THE WONDER BUS

THE WONDER BUS (☎ 04-359-5656; **wonderbustours.net**) from America is a bus tour option – with a difference. Not only is it capable of doing

Best Views

THE GULF and **BURJ AL ARAB** from **Madinat Jumeirah**	
BIRDS and **BUILDINGS** from **Ras Al Khor Wildlife Sanctuary**	
BURJ AL ARAB and **JUMEIRAH BEACH HOTEL** from public beach	
DUBAI CREEK PARK from the cable cars	
The **DUBAI FOUNTAIN** from **the bridge between Souk Al Bahar** and **Dubai Mall**	
DUBAI from **Burj Khalifa**	
The **DUNES** around **Big Red**	
The **PALM JUMEIRAH** from the **Monorail**	
SHEIKH ZAYED ROAD from the **Metro**	
The **SKYLINE** along **Sheikh Zayed Road**	
The **SKYLINE** from either side of **Dubai Creek**	

120 kilometres (75 miles) per hour on land, but it's also able to do 7 knots on water. The trips are 1½-hour mini-tours of Dubai, around the Dubai Creek area and down the Creek. The bus has onboard TV and toilet, and refreshments are served. Watch the video on the Web site, and thoughts of *Chitty Chitty Bang Bang* will spring to mind.

ACTIVITIES *and* TOURS

TOP TOUR COMPANIES

DUBAI HAS NUMEROUS TOUR COMPANIES for every type of activity. We have selected the following because we feel that they are the best at what they do and cover the widest range of activities on offer in the emirate.

ARABIAN ADVENTURES (☎ 04-303-4888; **arabian-adventures.com**)

THIS TOUR COMPANY WILL CREATE AN ITINERARY to suit you and ensure that you come away with a host of unique experiences – dining in the desert, sandboarding down the dunes, taking a moon-lit cruise by dhow and many more. It splits its tours into different categories – sightseeing, special interest and safaris – and will also organise car rental for you.

You might want to try an orientation tour of Dubai City, take a *Bateaux Dubai* cruise, 'Experience the Future of Dubai', go to Wild

Wadi, or visit Ski Dubai when it's 40°C (104°F) outside. Perhaps you'd like to try a mountain safari to Wadi Hatta, or a camel-riding and sandboarding safari. Whatever it is you're interested in, Arabian Adventures can arrange it for you. Not only does it organise its own tours, but it will also organise trips to attractions in and around Dubai. We have found that this company, used by most of the hotels as their first choice of tour operator, excels in organising first-rate tours and experiences and has an in-depth knowledge of Dubai and its environs. Check out its Web site for all its reservation numbers and detailed information on the activities it offers.

THE BIG BUS COMPANY DUBAI
(☎ 04-340-7709; **bigbustours.com**)

WE LIKE THE BIG BUS COMPANY for several reasons: it makes us smile to see big red open-top London double-decker buses driving round Dubai; it is an excellent way to discover and see an enormous number of sites and areas in Dubai in a few hours; and it is delightful to be able to sit on the top of an open-top bus and not feel freezing cold. Informative and interesting, the tour provides the opportunity to hop on and off all over Dubai; visit museums, malls and beaches; and take a dhow cruise down Dubai Creek. We think The Big Bus offers excellent value for money, with two routes for one ticket – City Tour and Beach Tour – which can be done one at a time, one after the other or one merged into the other within 24 hours of purchasing your ticket. Options are endless.

The ticket also includes:

- opportunities to hop on and off at any of the Big Bus stops to sightsee at your leisure
- free entry to Dubai Museum
- free entry to the Sheikh Saeed Al Maktoum House
- free Arabian dhow cruise
- free walking tour daily October–April
- free three-hour Beach Tour
- free Wafi Welcome Card, offering various discounts at more than 150 shops
- free Mercato Advantage Booklet, offering 10%–50% discount at various shops and restaurants.

Buses operate seven days a week, all the major sights are covered, and there is a recorded commentary in a choice of eight languages. You can purchase your tickets from any Big Bus stop, from your hotel, via the Internet or by telephone at the number listed above.

If you just can't bear the thought of wasting the beautiful weather on a bus, but you still want to take in all the sites, it's really worth

DAY TOUR: 24-HOUR TICKET	
Adult	AED 220
Child (ages 5–15)	AED 100
Family (two adults and two children)	AED 540
DAY TOUR: 48-HOUR TICKET	
Adult	AED 285
Child (ages 5–15)	AED 130
Family (two adults and two children)	AED 700
NIGHT TOUR	**COMBO PACKAGE TOUR***
Adult AED 100	AED 75
Child (ages 5–15) AED 75	AED 50
Family (two adults and two children) AED 275	AED 200

*Purchase your Night Tour ticket at the same time as you buy your Big Bus Day Tour ticket to benefit from the combo package deal. The price listed does not include the Day Tour ticket price.

taking the Night Tour of Dubai. This will give you a completely different perspective of the city as the sun sets and the entire city lights up and sparkles. This tour is two hours long and features a live commentary from a fully-trained guide. The tour departs from Deira City Centre at 7:30 p.m., returning at 9:30 p.m., or from Souk Madinat Jumeirah at 8:30 p.m., returning at 10:30 p.m.

DESERT RANGERS (☎ 04-357-2233; ☎ 050-276-8111; **desertrangers.com**)

A TRAVEL, TOURS AND ADVENTURE SAFARI operator, this company offers an enormous selection and variety of tours, activities and desert adventures. Not only does it cater to individuals and families, but it will also tailor-make any adventure programme for you. This company is outstanding at providing activities – from deep-sea fishing to dune buggy safaris, camel trekking by night to a helicopter tour of Dubai – that are fantastic and exciting, that may take you out of your comfort zone and that all pay excellent attention to detail and safety.

Apart from the activities mentioned above, the company also offers eight different types of safari, a desert driving course, dhow cruise with dinner, Dubai city tour, canoeing expedition, trekking, rock climbing and a desert balloon safari. It also works closely with schools throughout Dubai and offers a range of overnight adventure programmes, so it is very comfortable with children of all ages and abilities, making it an ideal company to use if you are travelling with children. We love its

Dune Buggy Safari with barbecue dinner. It involves spending time in the desert, driving through the sand dunes in dune buggies – which are better than any fairground ride – watching the sun set over the stunning orange desert, riding a camel, trying shisha pipes, enjoying a sumptuous barbecue dinner and watching a belly dancer. The atmosphere is convivial, the staff are fantastically professional and the experience is magical. It's touristy but amazing fun.

Prices vary according to the activity, the time you choose to spend on the activity and whether children are in the party. On average, you're looking at spending around AED 450 per activity, but it can be as little as AED 150 per person for the city tour to more than AED 1,000 per person for the helicopter tour. All information can be found on the company's Web site. Or if you prefer to phone, staff are excellent at helping you work out which activities you want to do and which are suitable for your party.

[TICKET_DXB] (☎ 04-321-4977; ticket-dxb.com)

THIS IS A TOUR COMPANY WITH A DIFFERENCE. If architecture is your thing, then you will love the tours organised by this agency established by the German architects Dominic Wanders and Hannes Werner. Their mission is to present architecture and urban development in Dubai in an informative and highly entertaining manner. Programme lengths can be from one to five days, and whilst we're not suggesting that you would want to spend your entire holiday looking at the architectural delights Dubai has in abundance, we do think that an opportunity to see the Palm Jumeirah, Dubai Marina, Madinat Jumeirah and its souk, the half-finished Dubailand, Burj Khalifa (the world's tallest building), Souk Al Bahar, Dubai Mall's Aquarium, the Dubai International Financial Centre (DIFC) and Dubai Creek Golf & Yacht Club might be made all the more fascinating if experienced architects are your tour guides.

In addition to lending their expertise to these specialised tours, the team of [ticket_dXb] is also happy to help you choose your hotel and organise additional non-architectural trips and activities as well.

BOAT AND YACHT CHARTERS

FOR A DIFFERENT EXPERIENCE, consider chartering your own boat or yacht. We have selected charter companies to suit all pockets.

ARABIAN ADVENTURES (☎ 04-303-4888; arabian-adventures.com)

ARABIAN ADVENTURES WILL CHARTER YOU A LUXURY YACHT manned by a full crew for whatever you'd like to do: a private excursion to sea, water sports, a fishing trip, a dinner cruise and so on. The crew will ensure that you make the most of your time onboard, and Arabian Adventures can also arrange for personalised catering and refreshments during your charter.

BRISTOL MIDDLE EAST (Marina Walk, Dubai Marina; ☎ 04-366-3538; ☎ 050-473-2988/98; **bristol-middleeast.com**)

BRISTOL MIDDLE EAST HAS A large fleet of different sea craft to charter, from luxury yachts to catamarans. Boats can be hired for any event, and the company will organise fishing trips and water sports too.

LUXURY YACHTING CATAMARAN (LYC) (Bur Dubai side of the Creek; ☎ 050-586-9746; **lycatamaran.com**)

ON VERRA CONCEPT BOATS have sailed around the Caribbean, the Côte d'Azur and the Seychelles and are now in Dubai. *On Verra VI* is located in the Creek on the Bur Dubai side, in front of Bastakiya. With the catamaran's 82-man capacity, this company caters to parties with DJs, cocktail food and drinks. All departures are from Bur Dubai to the Burj Al Arab and the Palm Jumeirah. There is a choice of scheduled cruises lasting from three to six hours, or the catamaran can be rented privately by the hour. For details and prices, call LYC or check their Web site. This is a perfect ship for a party.

EL MUNDO (☎ 050-240-1465; **elmundodubai.com**)

ANDORRA IS A 15.24-METRE (50-FOOT), 15-man luxury yacht, moored at Dubai International Marine Club at Le Méridien Hotel and Beach Resort. It is available for all types of sailing charters. *Andorra*'s captain has been sailing the Gulf and European waters for more than 35 years and is a qualified yacht master. Fully comprehensive insurance is included, and the yacht can be rented by the hour for private charters, or for morning and sunset cruises.

ULTIMATE CHARTER (☎ 04-331-1483; ☎ 050-865-0765; **dubaiultimatecharter.com**)

PRIVATE CHARTERS WITH ULTIMATE CHARTER'S yachts range from a 7-man fishing and cruising boat to a 30-man yacht with hot tub. An experienced and qualified crew mans the boats, and pickup and drop-off before and after the cruise can be arranged.

CRUISES

MANY COMPANIES OFFER CRUISES around Dubai's coastline and up and down Dubai Creek. As with everything else, the quality and the prices vary enormously. Here we recommend five of the best. Prices are subject to change and vary according to season.

ARABIAN ADVENTURES (☎ 04-303-4888; **arabian-adventures.com**)

IN ITS PORTFOLIO OF TOURS, Arabian Adventures includes a dhow cruise along Dubai Creek with dinner. The company will collect you from your hotel and take you to the dhow, moored on the Creek. There is an International buffet with soft drinks and a cash bar serving alcoholic drinks. This cruise does not offer live entertainment. As the dhow sails up and down the Creek, you will see old wooden dhows and luxury yachts and spectacular modern architecture, such as the National Bank of Dubai and the Chamber of Commerce & Industry buildings, whilst Sheikh Saeed's House, the birthplace of Sheikh Rashid and the Heritage Village are reminiscent of days gone by. The price, which includes a buffet dinner, two soft drinks and Arabic coffee, is AED 285 for adults and half price for children ages 2–12.

BATEAUX DUBAI (moored on the Bur Dubai side of the Dubai Creek opposite the British Embassy; ☎ 04-399-4994; **bateauxdubai.com**)

BATEAUX DUBAI IS A LUXURY CRUISE SHIP, with a 360-degree glass-enclosed restaurant, owned by Jebel Ali International Hotels. It is made up of a two-tiered outdoor deck, an indoor lounge and the restaurant. The restaurant can host up to 200 guests for dining cruises, and the outdoor deck is perfect for a sundowner before the meal. Known for their sophistication and atmosphere, *Bateaux Dubai*'s dinner cruises combine good food with the opportunity to sail down the Creek. You are served an excellent four-course meal from an à la carte menu offering a fusion of Eastern and Western cuisine. Alcohol is available and charged separately. Live music is played (a pianist accompanied our meal), and as the boat meanders down the Creek, you have fantastic views of old and new Dubai. The experience is more like going to an excellent restaurant that happens to be on a boat, as opposed to going on a cruise with food thrown in. The cost, including a four-course meal *$80* and soft drinks on arrival, is AED 295 for adults and AED 220 for children. The cruise is not suitable for children under age 5.

AL MANSOUR DHOW (moored in front of the Radisson Blu hotel on the Deira side of Dubai Creek; ☎ 04-222-7171; **radissonblu.com**)

AL MANSOUR DHOW IS OWNED by the Radisson Blu hotel and is a traditional wooden dhow. Not quite as elegant or sophisticated as its glass-panelled rival *Bateaux Dubai*, it offers tradition and charm instead. The dhow has two decks: the air-conditioned lower deck seats 60 persons; the upper deck, with a *Majlis* setup, is open and seats 70. During cooler months, the best place to reserve your table is on the upper deck, where you have great views, even though you have to traipse downstairs for the food, which is a serve-yourself buffet. *$50* The Arabic and International food, whilst not haute cuisine, is good, and a bar serves alcoholic drinks. The cost, which includes a buffet and fruit punch, is AED 185 for adults, half price for children ages 4–11 and free for children age 3 and under.

EL MUNDO (berthed at the Dubai International Marine Club at Le Méridien Mina Seyahi, Al Sufouh Road; ☎ 050-240-1465; **elmundo dubai.com**)

FOR AN ALTOGETHER MORE CASUAL CRUISE EXPERIENCE, possibly appealing to a younger crowd, *El Mundo* offers a lively, fun-filled Friday in the Sun four-hour cruise. The boat has a large air-conditioned lounge with bar area, an open deck area and seating on top of the main cabin roof and on the foredeck, so guests may kick back, relax and later watch the sun set across the Gulf. Amenities include ladies' and gents' bathroom facilities and deck shower. Guests board at Dubai International Marine Club (DIMC) and take a sightseeing cruise around the Palm. The ship then drops anchor in sight of the iconic Burj Al Arab hotel. You can then swim, snorkel, enjoy banana boat rides or sunbathe on deck. An informal lunch of gourmet burgers made at the live cooking station is served, and the ship has a licensed bar. Just before sunset, you return to DIMC, where guests are treated to a complimentary beverage at the Barasti Bar. For AED 240 for adults and AED 190 for children, the cruise includes water, soft drinks, gourmet burgers, four alcoholic drinks and all water sports.

Note: All passengers departing on a cruise with *El Mundo* are required to bring an original as well as a copy of a form of photographic identity (for example, a passport). Any persons not doing so will unfortunately not be allowed to sail.

YELLOW BOATS (☎ 800-4034; **theyellowboats.com**)

THIS IS ONE FOR ADRENALINE JUNKIES. Yellow Boats offers high-speed boat tours along the Dubai coast, so while not officially a cruise, it is a wildly exhilarating boat ride nonetheless. The Yellow Boats are top-of-the-line rigid inflatable crafts, manned by experienced and fully-qualified boat crews. Each boat is equipped with the latest GPS navigation and safety equipment. Four tours – ranging from an adrenaline-filled thrill ride to tours around the Palm Jumeirah, Burj Al Arab and Dubai Marina – are on offer and last 20–90 minutes. Prices range AED 90–200 for adults, AED 70–140 for children ages 5–12 or AED 300–580 per family (two adults and two children), depending on the tour and its duration. Unfortunately, children under age 5 and/ or less than 15 kilograms (about 33 pounds) are not allowed to travel on the boats. The Yellow Boats are fantastic fun and very exciting. Teenagers will love them.

For full prices and schedules, contact Yellow Boats, or visit the Web site.

DESERT ACTIVITIES

A LOT OF COMPANIES IN DUBAI ORGANISE a wide range of desert activities. How do you know which is better than another? Most desert activities include refreshments (normally a barbecue), music, shisha, sometimes henna painting and all drinks. All desert camps are fully equipped with toilets and wash facilities.

As with all desert activities, our main concern is that the tour operator is licensed and insured, and that all vehicles are fitted with the regulation safety equipment – especially seat belts. When you make the booking, it's worth finding out what time you will be returning (particularly if you have young children in the party); how child-friendly it is – if that is relevant to you; whether the drivers have the necessary licence for safari; and what the facilities are like at the camp. Also find out what show or performance will be taking place at the camp – some have a belly dance; others have a full programme – what kind of food, buffet or barbecue will be served, and at what time; how many people will be in each car; how long the journey will take; if there will be stops en route; if you will be going dune bashing (if you get carsick, it's worth taking travel sickness pills, as it can be a little wild); and if you will have water supplied on the journey.

Most tour operators offer the standard desert safari, but prices do vary quite a lot, and the cheapest aren't necessarily the best – so shop around until you're happy.

The ubiquitous desert safaris are half days, full days or overnight safaris. You will be picked up from your hotel and will travel to your desert camp in 4x4s. It will be a scenic drive, and once you reach the desert, your driver will normally take you across some fairly-exciting dunes. The safari normally starts in the afternoon so that you arrive at the camp early evening. The camp is laid out like a Bedouin camp, with rugs and cushions. Usually a buffet or barbecue dinner and drinks are served, and you will have the chance to go sandboarding, camel riding and smoke shisha or have your hands painted with henna and watch some belly dancing. The bathrooms are perfectly civilized, with proper toilets, tiled floors and washbasins. If you're staying overnight, there should be showers as well, and you will have breakfast in the morning and the chance to do some more sandboarding and dune bashing before being driven back to your hotel. Confirm the prices when you book, as they change according to season.

ALPHA TOURS (☎ 04-294-9888; alphatoursdubai.com)

THIS IS A VERY COMPREHENSIVE TOUR COMPANY that has extremely well-organised tours. Long-term knowledge of the region has given Alpha Tours a lot of experience in fine-tuning their activities. Desert safaris are action packed – the Bedouin campsite is five-star, and you can do all the usual – ride camels, smoke shisha, sandboard, have henna painting done and enjoy a three-course barbecue dinner buffet with a belly dancer to entertain you. The overnight safari extends this.

ARABIAN ADVENTURES (part of Emirates Airlines; ☎ 04-303-4888; arabian-adventures.com)

USED BY ALL THE MAJOR HOTELS as their tour operator of choice when it comes to organising desert tours, safaris, exploring wadis, desert driving, sandboarding, riding camels and anything else you can do in the desert, this company has informative guides. They can arrange any itinerary you like, and a selection of their desert tours includes Sundowner – a dinner safari in the sand dunes; Riddle of the Sands – a full-day safari; Rise & Shine – a taste of desert tradition; An Off-Road Adventure – wadi and desert tour; Rides and Slides – camel riding and sandboarding; Up the Wadi – a mountain safari to Wadi Hatta; Desert Driving Course . . . and the list goes on. The Sundowner prices are AED 330 for adults, AED 295 for children and a discounted rate for children under age 12. We would recommend this tour company as your first choice; compare tours and prices of other companies with theirs.

ARABIAN DESERT TOURS (☎ 04-268 2880; ☎ 055-874-3891; ☎ 050-758-8911; **adtuae.com**)

THIS WELL-ESTABLISHED COMPANY offers a range of tours, such as Hummer safari, desert safari, quad biking or overnight desert safari, and some are slightly more unusual than the other tour operators. It has two desert camps, one located within the secure location of Dubai Desert Conservation Reserve (for exclusive usage) and the other located in the Margham area in the Big Red (VIP usage). Staff are experienced, knowledgeable and hospitable.

ARABIAN NIGHTS TOURS (☎ 04-321-6565/6500; **arabiannightstours.com**)

THE DESERT SAFARI: FOOTPRINTS IN THE SAND takes you into the heart of the desert, where you will experience dune bashing. You then watch the sunset over the desert before moving on to the Bedouin-style campsite. You will relax in carpeted tents; smoke shisha; attempt riding a camel; try on some local costumes; consume tea, coffee, soft drinks and dates; and have henna painting if you wish. There will also be a photo opportunity with a falcon. A belly dancer will entertain you, and an Arabic-style barbecue with meats, salads, vegetarian dishes, rice, fruit and sweets will be served round the campfire under the stars. You will be driven back to Dubai later. Ample soft drinks, mineral water, tea and coffee will be provided at the campsite, and a cash bar serves alcohol. The prices for this safari are AED 300 for adults and AED 200 for children age 11 and under.

DESERT ADVENTURES (☎ 04-224-2800; **desertadventures.com**)

THE 4X4S TAKE YOU ON A ROLLER COASTER RIDE on the sand dunes on the Desert Safari with Barbecue excursion. You stop on the highest sand dune to watch the sunset. You then continue your journey to the Bedouin campsite in the heart of the desert, where you can have henna designs painted, try on local costumes and enjoy soft drinks, water, tea or coffee. Then it is time to try camel rides and shisha. A belly dancer will perform to Arabic music, and there is a delicious barbecue buffet. This company provides the following warning: the tour is not recommended for heart patients or people with neck or back problems. The half-day tour costs AED 290 for adults and AED 196 for children.

DESERT RANGERS (☎ 04-357-2233; ☎ 050-276-8111; desertrangers.com)

DESERT RANGERS MARKETS ITSELF as a Desert Adventure Tour operator, and its range of activities is extremely comprehensive. Not only does it provide itineraries for pleasure, but it also has a record of creating extremely successful corporate team-building activities. It has a fleet of its own 4x4 Land Cruisers, it pays huge attention to detail, and its staff are very well trained. Activities include a variety of different desert safaris with barbecues and entertainment – such as desert balloon safaris, dune buggy safaris, Hatta pool safaris, mountain safaris and sandboarding safaris – as well as desert driving courses and camel trekking by night (this is just a selection). For the half-day Dune Dinner Safari, the trip stops at a camel-breeding farm, as well as stopping for photo opportunities and refreshments at the more spectacular dunes, in addition to the other typical safari activities. Prices are AED 295 for adults and AED 195 for children.

The Dune Buggy Safari lasts a half-day, and after basic instruction and a safety briefing, you will head off on a roller coaster drive through the sand dunes, where you will have the opportunity to lead the convoy if you feel the urge. For your comfort and safety, each dune buggy comes equipped with a full roll cage, bucket seats and full safety harnesses. The minimum age for driving is 15. Helmet and goggles are provided. You are required to sign a disclaimer form against damage and personal injury, and a certificate will be provided at the end of the safari. For a 60-minute ride, the cost is AED 425. For a 45-minute ride sharing with another person, the cost is AED 325. Spectators pay AED 150. This company is also highly recommended.

EXPLORER TOURS (☎ 04-286-1991; explorertours.ae)

THIS COMPANY PUTS TOGETHER outside activity tours for people with a sense of adventure. The sort of tours it offers include dune buggy safaris, desert safaris, desert driving courses, overnight safaris, sandboarding safaris, camel trekking by night and Liwa Desert safaris. For the very adventurous it offers Extreme Explorer tours, which might last several days. The staff are extremely experienced, and the tours are very well organised. The emphasis is on getting the best out of yourself, and having fun in the process. This company also does a lot of work with schools, including organising Duke of Edinburgh Award programmes and Desert Explorer programmes, which give students an opportunity to have a unique day in the desert hunting fossils, sand dune boarding, camel trekking and playing desert cricket. Staff are extremely experienced at working with children between the ages of 8 and 18.

If you choose the Desert Safari, you will visit a camel-breeding farm and have the chance to ride a camel, unwind by smoking an aromatic shisha, or enjoy a chilled drink before eating a delicious barbecue dinner. A belly dancer will introduce you to the art of Arabian entertainment before you leave the desert and head back to Dubai. Prices are AED 270 for adults and AED 180 for children.

In comparison to quad bikes, dune buggies are more powerful and reliable on sand and at the same time are safer, as they are equipped with a full roll cage, bucket seats and safety harness. You need to be at least 16 years old and sign a disclaimer form against damage and personal injury. You will be provided with a safety helmet and goggles. The Dune Buggy Safari costs AED 500 per person, or, if you are sharing a buggy, AED 375 per person.

AERIAL TOURS

IF YOU HAVE A HEAD FOR HEIGHTS and want to experience a truly unique way to tour Dubai, then consider taking a helicopter or aeroplane ride above the city.

ALPHA TOURS (☎ 04-294-9888; **alphatoursdubai.com**)

ALPHA TOURS OFFERS DAILY CITY HELICOPTER TOURS of varying lengths, taking in different sights and flying over the main attractions of Dubai. The shortest tour is 20 minutes; the longest is one hour. You can either share a helicopter with five other people, or have it for your exclusive use. All passengers must carry an ID document with them – preferably a passport.

AEROGULF HELICOPTER SERVICES (☎ 04-220-0331; **aerogulfservices.com**)

AEROGULF HAS BEEN ESTABLISHED in Dubai for more than 30 years, providing helicopter support to Dubai's oil and gas industry and aerial work for a variety of other industries throughout the Middle East. In recent years, the company has diversified by offering its unique heli-touring experience, Fly Dubai.

Aerogulf Helicopter Services is based at Dubai International Airport, and pickup can be arranged from your hotel. You will arrive at a dedicated VIP check-in area, from which you will then board the helicopter. You can either organise a private charter or take one of the scheduled city tours, lasting either 30 or 45 minutes.

SEAWINGS (☎ 04-807-0708; **seawings.ae**)

IS IT A BOAT? IS IT A PLANE? IT'S BOTH. It's a plane that takes off from water. It operates up to 16 flights daily, offering guests the chance to travel 457 metres (almost 1,500 feet) above Dubai for a fantastic aerial city tour. Seeing the sights from a bird's-eye view is a thrilling experience. Flights include Seawings Silver, a 40-minute dock-to-dock excursion providing views of Dubai's most iconic landmarks, and The Burj Experience, also a 40-minute dock-to-dock aerial experience, focusing on the Burj Khalifa and the Burj Al Arab. You depart from Jebel Ali and land at Dubai Creek. Prices are AED 1,225 per adult and AED 1,040 per child ages 2–11. Children under age 2 are free.

WALKING TOURS

DUBAI IS A FASCINATING CITY to explore on foot, and with a good map you will be able to discover areas with great ease. You will find people helpful and friendly, and it is safe to wander pretty much everywhere. The best times to go walking are anytime during the winter months, or if that's not possible, either very early morning between 7 and 9 a.m., or late afternoon and evening, from 5 p.m. onwards. Take plenty of water, apply your sunscreen, wear comfortable shoes, and you're ready to go. On your own, you might like to explore Dubai Marina, Jumeirah Beach Walk, Satwa, Karama, Dubai Creek and any of the long stretches of beach parallel to Jumeirah Road in the Jumeirah–Umm Suqeim stretch.

Bastakiya

The Sheikh Mohammed Centre for Cultural Understanding (SMCCU), based in Bastakiya, organises walks through Bastakiya, one of the oldest, most traditional districts in Dubai. The guides are knowledgeable, informal and very friendly. You will be led through the narrow winding streets and into old restored houses with traditional wind towers. You will have a chance to find out about the history of Dubai and this neighbourhood in particular. After the tour, you will be invited to the SMCCU, a traditional wind tower house with courtyard, for coffee and dates and the opportunity to have all your questions answered. For information and bookings, call ☎ 04-353-6666, or view the SMCCU's Web site at **cultures.ae.**

Arabian Treasures Walk

If you take the Big Bus Tour (see page 135), then this guided walk is included in the ticket. It starts at Dubai Museum and ends at Dubai Gold Souk. You will wander through some of the oldest trading districts of Deira and into the Textile Souk, and you'll then take a traditional *abra* ride across Dubai Creek into the bustling trade route of the city – to the Spice Souk, the Old Souk and the Gold Souk. You'll have the chance to try your haggling skills and maybe come away with a bargain or two. This is a lovely walk, full of hidden treasures and mysteries. It shows a very different side to Dubai. The walk takes place daily from mid-October to April at midday and 3 p.m. It lasts an hour. For information about the Big Bus Tour, call ☎ 04-340-7709, or view its Web site at **bigbustours.com.**

ORGANISED TOURS

DUBAI WATER BUS (☎ 800-9090; **rta.ae**)

DUBAI HAS RECENTLY SEEN THE INTRODUCTION of a new type of water transport – the Water Bus. It is spacious and comfortable with panoramic windows and wheelchair access. It services five routes along Dubai Creek, enabling commuters, residents and tourists faster and more efficient journeys by water. Each Dubai Water Bus has a sales kiosk selling snacks, magazines and newspapers, as well as prepaid cards for use on the Water Bus. While the Water Bus offers commuter service, the tourist service is a special sightseeing cruise and guided tour of Dubai Creek. Every hour, 8 a.m.–midnight, the Water Bus takes tourists on a 45-minute ride from Al Shindagha Station to Al Seef Station and back. The cost is AED 25 per person.

DREAMDAYS (☎ 800-2080; **dreamdays.ae**)

JUST WHEN WE THOUGHT THAT WE COULDN'T FIND anything bigger, better or more fanciful than the world's largest, tallest, first . . . we discovered Dreamdays, a company that makes all your dreams come true. And in Dubai, where excess and extravagance are lauded, and modesty is not a virtue, how apt to find a company that is considered 'the first and leading provider of gift experiences in the U.A.E.', whose aim it is 'to meet the wishes of customers looking to fulfil their lifetime's fantasies'. This is an Internet-based business; choose the experience you desire and book it through the dedicated call centre (☎ 800-2080).

Finally, if all the tours in this guide have failed to inspire you – if open-top buses, guided walks, dhow cruises, water taxis, helicopters and seaplanes have left you underwhelmed – we have one last suggestion: an exclusive luxury limousine city tour. Dreamdays will arrange for your own professional chauffeur to collect you from your hotel in one of a choice of limos – a Hummer H2 or H1 limo, Cadillac Escalade limo or Ford Excursion SUV limo, all with an entertainment system – and for the next three hours Dubai will be your oyster. You will be treated like royalty, and service will be lavish – all you have to do is sit back and relax. The limousine will hold a maximum of 18 people, and the price is AED 1,349. If you wish to have an extra hour after your three hours are up, add AED 650 per hour.

ART GALLERIES AND EVENTS

DUBAI HAS A PROLIFIC ART SCENE. For a comprehensive overview of all that's happening in the art world in Dubai, check **artinthecity. com** (☎ 04-341-7303), and pick up a copy of *ArtMap*. Both are excellent sources of information. Additionally we recommend *Brownbook* (**brownbookmag.com**), an urban lifestyle guide published six times a year focusing on art, design and travel across the Middle East and North Africa. Also useful is *Canvas* (**canvasonline.com**), a bimonthly magazine offering the latest news on art and culture from the Middle East and the Arab world. The government of Dubai has created its own Web site, **dubaiculture.ae**, which has two useful sections: Live Our Heritage and Calendar and Events.

Al Quoz Industrial Route

The industrial area of Al Quoz is not immediately a place that would seem to attract a buzzing developing art scene, but it is fast becoming home to some of Dubai's most exciting contemporary art galleries, alternative venues and unique cultural institutions, offering an insight into the active development of Dubai's art scene. The great thing about this area is that the galleries are centred around a few streets and are close to quirky, inexpensive restaurants such as **More Cafe** (☎ 04-323-4350; **morecafe. biz**) in the Gold & Diamond Park – which not only serves delicious light meals but also showcases artwork from artists based in the Middle East – and **The Courtyard Gallery & Café** (☎ 04-347-9090; **courtyardgallerydubai. com**) in Al Quoz 3. The cafe features a spacious courtyard, richly Oriental in design, with traditional buildings housing modern galleries surrounding it. Frequently-changing exhibitions showcasing a range of international and local artists, evening concerts and a delightful cafe make this a lively and interesting venue worth visiting on your tour of Al Quoz.

unofficial **TIP**
If you're interested in all things art-related and love an auction, then twice a year – in April and October – the Christie's Dubai auctions continue to act as a major catalyst in the development of the contemporary art market in the Middle East. Call ☎ 04-425-5647 or visit **christies.com**.

Of Al Quoz galleries, **thejamjar** is the creative hub for both **art inthecity.com**, whose aim is to promote art and culture across Dubai through an informative, up-to-date, easy-to-use Web site, and ArtBus, an excellent bus tour with a difference.

DIFC Arts Area

Dubai's newest art spot, the DIFC, is the city's centre of high-end fashion brands, interior design and fine art. Compared to the grittiness of Al Quoz, this is an area that oozes sophistication and polish. It juxtaposes the modern financial world with cutting-edge contemporary international and regional art in a dynamic architectural setting. For a lively, interesting evening out, don't miss **Art Nights @ Gate Village** (☎ 04-362-2395; **registerwithdifc.com/artnights**). Every month, Art Nights @ Gate Village brings together the galleries and retailers of the Gate Village to combine elements of art, film, fashion, design and cuisine through a variety of indoor and outdoor activities. The event is free and open to the public from 7 p.m. to late.

Bastakiya Galleries

Al Bastakiya is a beautifully-restored heritage site and is Dubai's original artistic and cultural hub. Not only is it home to several of Dubai's long-established art galleries, but the historical houses, which are open to the public, also provide a platform for emerging artistic talent as part of Dubai's independent fringe-art fair – Bastakiya Art Fair. The boutique hotels in this district also showcase upcoming talent in their integrated galleries. Bastakiya has the informality of Al Quoz and the glorious natural sophistication of an area steeped in history, heritage and culture. Small collections of art are in most houses into which you poke your head – and all have their doors open for viewers to enter as they please.

TOURING NEIGHBOURHOODS

DUBAI IS SPLIT UP INTO DIFFERENT AREAS, each with its own particular set of characteristics. The contrast between the old and the new is striking, and whilst the skyline is no longer dominated by cranes, you can't fail to notice pockets where development and construction are still ongoing, and other places where it has all ground to a halt. The recession has struck a mighty blow to certain ambitious projects, and many construction sites are eerily quiet, certainly for the foreseeable future.

Originally Dubai centred on Dubai Creek, to the north of the city, a 15-kilometre (9.3-mile) inlet that runs through the centre of the older areas – Deira and Bur Dubai. This is the traditional part of the city, where you will experience the true hustle and bustle of Arabic life and which is as thrilling to visit as any of the new developments. Jumeirah Road, 16 kilometres (9.9 miles) long, runs parallel to the coast, starting at Al Mina and Dubai Dry Docks in the north, taking you sedately from old Dubai, through the attractive residential areas of Jumeirah and Umm Suqeim, to Al Sufouh and into new Dubai, comprising the luxury beach hotel resorts, the Palm Jumeirah, Dubai Marina and the buzz of Media and Internet cities. Parallel to Jumeirah Road, and one block inland, the more frenetic Al Wasl Road takes you through the urban and industrial areas via Satwa and Safa Park to Mall of the Emirates. And parallel to this, one block inland again, is Sheikh Zayed Road, commencing near Karama and Bur Dubai in the north. Lined with iconic skyscrapers, this multilane highway takes you from Za'abeel Park, past Downtown Dubai and the financial district, through the industrial area of Al Quoz – which is fast becoming an artistic hub – and into the sprawling green new residential developments of Emirates Hills, the Lakes, the Greens and down to Jebel Ali.

This section is intentionally not in alphabetical order; rather, we works our way, where possible, through the districts going from north to south.

Garhoud

Previously not known for much more than being the site of Dubai International Airport, Garhoud was zapped to life by the construction of Dubai Festival City, opened in 2007. A true juxtaposition of old and new, Garhoud is an established residential area, popular with airport staff and airline crews for its proximity to the airport. You do need a car to visit this area, or grab a taxi from one of the Metro stops. There are several well-known hotels here, useful for the airport, and whilst there aren't any particularly interesting tourist sites of note, Dubai Festival City (☎ 04-213-6213; **dubaifestivalcity.com**) is a beautifully-landscaped waterfront residential community incorporating the massive shopping mall Festival Centre (☎ 04-232-5444; **festivalcentre.com**) with its huge choice of international retailers, restaurants and entertainment venues. Eat al fresco at Canal Walk, or enjoy a ride on an *abra*. Walk along Festival Marina, where luxury yachts are moored, or catch live concerts in the centre. Irish Village (☎ 04-282-4750/2; **theirishvillage.ae**) is a great bar if you're after a dose of normality, inexpensive drinks and live music, whilst next door in Century Village (☎ 04-282-4122; **centuryvillage.ae**), you can choose from a range of restaurants with cuisines from around the world. The new state-of-the-art Dubai Tennis Stadium (☎ 04-282-4122; **aviationclub.ae**), home to the star-studded annual Dubai Tennis Championships, is also located here. This is a great area if you need to be close to the airport or work in the area; apart from that, it can feel a little remote.

Dubai Creek (Deira side)

The Creek is a natural seawater inlet that separates Deira on the east side of the Creek from Bur Dubai on the west. Life along the Creek retains a sense of Dubai's historical past and its traditions. This area has played a central role in Dubai's development and is an important starting point if you wish to discover what life was like before modernisation took precedence. Trade stemmed from Dubai Creek and is still part of the vibrant way of life here. There are five crossing points across the Creek: Business Bay Crossing, nearest Dubai Festival City; Al Garhoud Bridge, next to Dubai Creek Golf & Yacht Club; Floating Bridge; Maktoum Bridge; and Shindagha Tunnel, which is closest to the sea.

Starting at the inland end of the Creek is **Ras Al Khor Wildlife Sanctuary,** the city's only nature reserve, which attracts an impressive range of bird species, including flamingos, as well as being a site for many native plant species. Call ☎ 04-606-6822/6 or visit **wildlife.ae** to obtain a permit to enter the sanctuary.

Continuing past Dubai Festival City and up the Creek, you reach Dubai Creek Golf & Yacht Club (☎ 04-295-6000; **dubaigolf.com**), voted one of the world's top 100 must-play golf courses. The marina here is home to some truly luxurious yachts, but it is the Boardwalk

Restaurant, built out over the Creek, that we like to head to when we fancy some really decent fish-and-chips. The views are lovely, but we advise you to watch out for bombing seagulls.

It is worth exploring as much of the Creek as you can on foot if possible, especially when you reach the dhow wharf, where stunning blue dhows are moored and sailors load and unload their cargo. The dockside is piled high with crates, the Creek banks are chaotic, and there is an air of excitement and adventure that makes you wish you could hop on board and sail away.

The *abra* ticket office and station is located here. *Abras* are the water taxis and are the most popular form of transport up and down the Creek and over to Bur Dubai, Bastakiya and the souks on the other side. To cross to the other side it will only cost you AED 1. Many people use the *abras* to go to work, and they are considerably cheaper and faster than buses or taxis. Don't make the mistake of taking a private boat – they will charge you AED 20 or more. The *abras* fill up quickly – they seat up to 30 people – and be careful as you hop on board; you don't want to fall into the Creek. Men should try and avoid sitting too close to women on the *abra* unless you are travelling together in the first place. The *abra* ride is breezy and you may get splashed, so sit back and hold onto loose clothing. The crossing from one side to the other takes between five and ten minutes.

You may be offered a private tour up and down the Creek, which is a wonderful way to view the spectacular modern skyline on the Deira side, in contrast to the traditional, historical buildings on the Bur Dubai side. You will be asked for AED 50 one way, AED 100 for both. But you should try and bargain it down to AED 40 and AED 80 at most.

Past the *abra* station you will reach the souk area in Deira. This is a wonderful place to wander around and experience the hustle and bustle of daily Arabic life. It feels a little as if you're entering a time warp, especially if you've come from the newer parts of Dubai. Men in *dhotis* and *dishdashas* throng the streets; women in *abayas* come here to buy their spices and, farther along, their fresh fish.

Meander through the **Spice, Gold** and **Old souks** towards the **Fish Market,** which you will probably smell before you see it. Be prepared to barter, and watch out for men on bikes weaving their way through the narrow streets. The shopkeepers will try and draw you into their shops and will love to chat to you if you let them.

Deira

Once you are in the souks and you wander back a street or two, you are in Deira proper. With its narrow, crowded streets – a little slice of India rather than Arabia – this area oozes personality. This district is full of budget hotels and fantastic, inexpensive places to eat, with every type of Eastern cuisine imaginable – Arabic, Indian, Chinese, Japanese, Iraqi, Iranian and Thai – the choice is endless. On weekends, locals and expats of all nationalities spill out onto the pavements of these small cafes and restaurants. If you're looking for a bargain, this is the area to visit. Apart from the souks, which sell everything from the aforementioned spices, gold and electrical goods, you will also discover clothes, perfumes and quirky tourist souvenirs. For a vast selection of rugs, visit Deira Tower on Al Nasr Square, where about 40 shops sell carpets from Iran, Pakistan, Turkey and Afghanistan. For a more modern shopping experience, Deira City Centre Mall (☎ 04-295-4486; **deiracitycentre. com**), which opened in 1995, changed the concept of shopping in Dubai, with the now familiar mix of high-end shops, restaurants and entertainment facilities. The streets in Deira come alive in the evenings when it cools down. Well worth a visit is the Fish Market near Al Shindagha Tunnel, though best to go early in the morning, when the fish has just been caught and the heat of the day has not had a chance to ripen the pungent odours. Next door is the Fruit and Vegetable Market, piled high with stunning displays of the freshest produce. Once again, it is expected that you will barter when you buy.

As you make your way towards the sea, you'll discover **Al Ahmadiya School** – now a museum of education (☎ 04-226-0286; **dubaitourism. ae**). It was the first school to be built in Dubai, in 1912, and is now an important heritage site. Adjacent is Heritage House, another historical landmark, built in 1890. This is a beautiful house and an excellent example of a traditional Emirati home, constructed from coral and gypsum, with simple architecture and intricate carvings within the arches of the courtyard inside.

Al Hamriya Port sits on the seafront overlooking the unfinished Palm Deira, and a little farther north is Al Mamzar Beach Park (☎ 04-296-6201), covering an area of 106 hectares (262 acres) with barbecue sites, private chalets for hire, a swimming pool, food kiosks, a sheltered beach and safe lagoon, a scenic train and many children's play areas.

Bur Dubai

Bur Dubai, on the western side of the Creek, is an area steeped in history. Explore souks and old neighbourhoods, and if you are interested in finding out what life in Dubai was like long before it was transformed into the Dubai of today, you will discover an altogether more traditional pace of life here, seemingly unaffected by the rapid transformations that have taken place elsewhere.

Although not strictly in Bur Dubai, **Dubai Creek Park** (☎ 04-336-7633) is adjacent to it, facing Dubai Creek Golf & Yacht Club on the other side of the water. It is a magnificent expanse of green space overlooking the Creek and is the second-largest park in Dubai after **Mushrif Park** (☎ 04-288-3624). Dubai Creek Park offers a multitude of interesting activities, including a **Dolphinarium** (☎ 04-336-9773; **dubaidolphinarium.ae**) with live shows; **Children's City** (☎ 04-334-0808; **childrencity.ae**), an interactive science museum; a cable car with fantastic views out across the Creek; a miniature train; mini-golf course; bike hire; a fishing pier; and food outlets. If you visit on a Friday, the delicious aromas of barbecued food will tantalise you as the park fills with locals and expats picnicking at the water's edge. Next to the park you will find **Wonderland Theme Park and Splashland Water Park** (☎ 04-324-1222; **wonderlanduae.com**). With a mix of fairground rides and a waterpark, this is one of Dubai's older parks of this type. It now has to compete with the likes of Aquaventure and Wild Wadi, but it is a cheaper alternative.

As you wander up the Creek, views across to Deira are spectacular, with modern skyscrapers dominating the skyline. Pass the British Embassy (☎ 04-309-4444; **ukinuae.fco.gov.uk**) on your left and you will see cruisers, yachts and dhows moored on your right. Many of the dhows have now been converted into floating restaurants. Sailors will badger you to take a private dhow up the Creek for AED 100. If you're interested, then barter to reduce the price to no more than AED 80. At the mouth of the Creek, you will see the splendid entrance to the Ruler's Court. If you continue up the Creek a little farther, you will reach the Textile Souk, with its glorious array of fabrics of every variety, in every colour. This really is a very pretty area, which has been recently restored, along with the adjacent **Bastakiya.** The stunning textiles will dazzle you, and it's fascinating to watch the tailors working on their old-fashioned sewing machines. Remember to barter for anything you wish to buy, though if you're after a really good bargain, we would also recommend going to **Satwa** for your textiles. Here, however, you can find stunning jewel-coloured pashminas and saris, as well as unusual jewellery and gifts. Once you have found the fabric, if you need an excellent tailor, we would recommend **Lobo Tailor** (☎ 04-352-3760/3345) in Souk Al Kabeer. If you're feeling thirsty, there's a great little place with a wheelbarrow outside that sells the best fresh fruit juices. It's located between the Textile Souk and the *abra* station.

A street away from the Textile Souk is **Souk Al Kabeer,** or Meena Bazaar, as it is known to its predominantly Indian population, which started settling here in the early 1900s. This is one of the oldest residential districts in the city, and you can be sure to find fantastic bargains here. Don't miss a wander down Al Fahidi Street, bordering the Textile Souk. This is the location of Dubai's electronics souk and really comes to life at night. You can't miss it; just look out for the neon lights. This is a fantastic area for delicious, inexpensive Indian food, and you'll find a good selection of restaurants near Dubai Museum and in the nearby Astoria and Ambassador hotels.

A short walk inland and you arrive at **Dubai Museum** (☎ 04-353-1862; **dubaitourism.ae**), a fascinating museum within beautifully-restored Al Fahidi Fort, erected in 1787 to defend the city against invasion. The museum tells the story of the development of Dubai, its history and its traditions. This area is rich in heritage, and as you reach the mouth of the Creek to the area called Shindagha, you can visit the **Sheikh Saeed Al Maktoum House** (☎ 04-393-7139), the official residence of Sheikh Saeed Al Maktoum, ruler of Dubai (1912–1958) and grandfather of the present ruler, Sheikh Mohammed bin Rashid Al Maktoum. The building, which dates from 1896, today houses a rare collection of historical photographs, coins, stamps and documents that record Dubai's history. We would recommend a visit to the **Heritage and Diving Villages** (☎ 04-393-7151), a two-minute walk away. This is a 'living' village, and more than 30 traditional handicrafts are demonstrated here.

As you walk back down towards the Textile Souk and the Creek, you come into Bastakiya, one of the loveliest, most atmospheric areas in Dubai. Bastakiya was Dubai's first commercial district, dating back to the early 1900s, and in recent years many of the buildings have been restored and converted into art galleries, shops, small museums, cafes and boutique hotels. All are free of charge to enter, and you can quite easily spend a day meandering through the winding narrow streets and alleyways, where you may explore old houses with their distinctive wind towers, traditional Arabic architecture and cool, shady courtyards.

The area is close to the docks, with old souks, beautiful architecture and traditional houses with wind towers and shady courtyards. Particularly worth a visit – and not just for their architecture – are a couple of lovely boutique hotels: XVA (☎ 04-353-5383; **xvahotel. com**), an art hotel with an award-winning vegetarian restaurant, and Orient Guest House (☎ 04-351-9111; **orientguesthouse.com**). Basta Art Cafe (☎ 04-353-5071) is a welcome oasis after walking around in the heat. It has a delightful leafy courtyard, and the food is delicious – enormous salads and light snacks, a children's menu and refreshing juices. You could sit here all afternoon. It also sells art and jewellery. Make a point of visiting Local House Restaurant (☎ 04-354-0705), where traditional Arabic food is served and the speciality is camel! Dip in and out of a choice of galleries to suit every taste and pocket; whether you want art, jewellery, spices, antiques or gifts, you will find them here. Other converted houses of note are Calligraphy House, Philately House, the Coins Museum, the Architectural Heritage Department, Innovation Gallery, the Majlis Gallery and Siwar Arts & Handicraft. Between mid-January and the end of February, don't miss the winter market (Saturday, 10 a.m.–5 p.m.; ☎ 04-321-7114) set up in the streets of Bastakiya, with live music and about 50 stalls displaying arts and crafts, antiques, refreshments and a kids' corner.

If you prefer, you can take a delightfully-informal guided walk of Bastakiya organised by the **Sheikh Mohammed Centre for Cultural Understanding** (☎ 04-353-6666; **cultures.ae**).

Karama

Once you have tested your bargaining skills in the souks, you will be more than ready to visit Karama. This is mainly a residential area, but it is renowned for its shopping complex, consisting of two central streets lined with small shops selling extremely good quality but less-than-authentic 'designer' bags, shoes, sunglasses, watches and clothes. If you have teenagers with you, they will love the bargains they can find here. Be prepared to be pestered by the salesmen, and drive a hard bargain. And if you don't think the price is fair, be strong-minded and walk away; you will inevitably get a further reduction. Take plenty of cash with you; credit cards are not always accepted, and cash sometimes means better discounts. Particularly good shops to visit are Green Eye (☎ 04-337-7721) and Walencia (☎ 050-958-0779). They really are Aladdin's caves, especially if you are invited to enter the ominous-sounding back room to see yet more stock. Go for it! You may discover exactly what you didn't realise you were looking for. If all that shopping makes you hungry, food is cheap and tasty at any of the roadside restaurants. Try Pakistani food at Karachi Darbar, Sri Lankan food at Chef Lanka or Filipino food at Tagpuan. You may prefer a set-price thali at any of the Indian restaurants, or *shawarma*, falafel and fresh fruit juices in the small Arabic restaurants.

South of Karama is the beautiful **Za'abeel Park** (☎ 04-398-6888). As always, it is so lovely to find such a fantastic green oasis in this busy city, and the park is never manically busy. We think it has the best children's playground in Dubai.

Oud Metha and Um Hurair

This is the area located in the centre of Dubai, adjacent to Karama. It has good shopping and entertainment facilities but is not necessarily the most interesting of tourist areas if you're short of time. Just south of Dubai Healthcare City, a state-of-the-art medical facility developed in conjunction with top international medical organisations, is **Wafi** (☎ 04-324-4555; **wafi.com**), an Egyptian-themed mall that looks like a pyramid. It has its own souk with a magnificent stained-glass window that dominates the ceiling, bathing the alleyways below in a kaleidoscope of coloured light. It is one of the largest windows of its kind in the world and really is worth seeing. The **Encounter Zone** (☎ 04-324-7747) – which has a huge soft play area and a skate park, three-dimensional cinema and Crystal Maze – is a great venue for families. Nearby is **Lamcy Plaza** (☎ 04-335-9999; **lamcyplaza.com**), another mall with a wide selection of shopping outlets and restaurants and the excellent children's play area Lou Lou Al Dugongs (☎ 04-295-4333). If you're keen to take in a local football match, Al Nasr Football Club (**alnasrclub.com**), a great venue to catch a game, has a real family atmosphere. Al Nasr Leisureland (☎ 04-337-1234; **alnasrll.com**) includes an ice rink, bowling alley, swimming pool and Luna Park, the Fruit Garden with little fairground attractions. Again, you won't go hungry there, as there's a wide selection of restaurants from which to choose.

Al Boom Tourist Village (☎ 04-324-3000/1444; **alboom.ae**), sandwiched between Al Garhoud Bridge and Dubai Creek Park, is a popular wedding venue for couples. You can sample local cuisine in Al Dahleez Restaurant or take a dinner cruise on one of its dhows. Just across the road you can see traditional wooden dhows being built.

Sheikh Zayed Road

This six-lane highway commences at Za'abeel Park, and as you travel south towards Jebel Ali, you can't help but be awed and inspired by the stunning architecture that creates new Dubai. On both sides of the highway you will be captivated by the mass of iconic skyscrapers, including the Burj Khalifa, which dwarfs every other tower; Emirates Office Towers; Shangri-La hotel; the Dusit; the Rose Tower; and The Fairmont. It's well worth taking a drive along Sheikh Zayed Road just to see the futuristic skyline, or travel above it by Metro for a thrilling tour of this exciting city. It really is a stunning skyline and a fascinating example of what happens when the world's architects are let loose in one area.

World Trade Centre to Downtown Dubai

When the Dubai World Trade Centre (☎ 04-332-1000; **dwtc.com**) was built in 1978, it was Dubai's tallest building at 149 metres (488.8 feet) and the first high-rise along Sheikh Zayed Road. This area marks the first stretch of the Sheikh Zayed Road, and the World Trade Centre is the landmark of Dubai's business district, with its hotels, exhibition halls, convention centre and serviced apartment blocks. Although there are now higher, more modern buildings to scale, a trip to the Trade Centre's Observation Deck is worth a visit for its panoramic view of the city.

Two of the most iconic towers in Dubai, which stand opposite each other and change in dynamic depending on where you look at them from, are Jumeirah Emirates Towers (☎ 04-330-0000; **jumeirah. com**). Containing the Emirates Office Tower and Jumeirah Emirates Hotel, they are adjoined by a two-storey complex – The Boulevard at Emirates Towers – which is *the* shopping destination of choice for Dubai's well-to-do. Views are stunning from Vu's Bar on the 51st floor, a venue worth visiting for some serious people-watching.

Behind the towers is **Dubai International Finance Centre** (☎ 800-3432; **difc.ae**), home to Dubai's own financial exchange. We think that the Gate Village – the lifestyle heart of DIFC – is well worth a visit in its own right. This ultra-contemporary area contains innumerable business offices, but it is also a buzzing enclave of art, culture and fashion. The art quarter is fast becoming the hub of Dubai's art world, whilst a number of international fashion boutiques make this shopping area a little more interesting than many. Worth knowing is that during Ramadan, a lot of the restaurants here, which offer a wide and interesting choice to suit all pockets, still serve food during the day. There is very much a feel about this area of any one of Europe's capital cities.

One of the most exciting developments to be found a little farther south is **Downtown Dubai,** where the skyline of already impressive skyscrapers is dwarfed by **Burj Khalifa** (☎ 04-888-8124; **burjkhalifa. ae**), the world's tallest building, and shoppers can shop to their hearts' content in the world's largest shopping mall – **Dubai Mall** (☎ 800-DUBAI-MALL or 800-382-246-255; **thedubaimall.com**).

But more than that, Downtown Dubai is an inspirational urban concept. Architecturally designed to complement the traditional buildings found in Bastakiya and Bur Dubai, **Old Town** is its residential area, where many of Dubai's bright young expats live, work and play. Make time to go and see the **Dubai Fountain** (☎ 04-366-1688). Spectacular fountains that spray to heights more than 150 metres (492 feet) and perform to music and light every evening, they are strangely moving. Enjoy a stroll or a picnic at Burj Park Island, a beautifully-landscaped waterside park, or take the state-of-the-art lift up Burj Khalifa, ascending at 10 metres (32.8 feet) per second, to obtain the best panoramic views of Dubai. Whether you like shopping malls or not, Dubai Mall is still worth a visit. Not only will you get a lot of exercise – the place is huge, with 1,200 shops, two department stores, Fashion Avenue (dedicated to haute couture), a Gold Souk and more than 150 cafes and restaurants to tempt you – but there are some excellent leisure attractions for families for when you've had enough of the beach for a day or so: the world's largest aquarium, **The Dubai Aquarium and Underwater Zoo** (☎ 04-448-5200; **thedubaiaquarium. com**) – well worth a visit and beautifully designed; **KidZania** (☎ 04-448-5222; **kidzania.com**) – you will lose your children for three or four hours, at the very least, to the best-designed children's 'edu-tainment' city concept we've come across; and **SEGA Republic** (☎ 04-448-8484; **segarepublic.com**) – an indoor theme park, an Olympic-size ice rink and the ubiquitous multi-screen cinema complex.

To offset the commercialism of the mall, we suggest that you wander over to the elegant **Souk Al Bahar** (**theoldtownisland.com**) overlooking the fountains. Linked to the mall by a bridge, and to the stunning **Palace hotel** (☎ 04-428-7888; **theaddress.com**), it is a delightful mix of eclectic shops and excellent restaurants and cafes. We recommend eating dinner on one of the many restaurant terraces and enjoying the Dubai Fountain whilst you eat. This area comes alive and is buzzing at night.

Satwa

The other side of Sheikh Zayed Road, east towards the sea and on level with the Trade Centre, is a district of Dubai that couldn't be more different from Downtown Dubai. It is an area of contrasts. At one end of Al Satwa Road, it is a wide, green and leafy residential avenue with smart villas. As you travel north it becomes a busy, bustling souk, with small open shops crammed side by side. Carpenters' workshops sit next to car mechanics, shops selling every type of electrical goods next to beauty salons and florist shops, car accessories sold next to a butcher's shop with a carcass hanging in the window – there are shops here overflowing with things you never knew you needed. The streets are crowded with Indians, Filipinos, Pakistanis, well-heeled Western women getting a dress made and the occasional tourist looking for a good deal. This area brims with atmosphere and bargains and is the place to go if you wish to have clothing made. The textiles shops are fantastic, and tailors will copy your favourite dress or suit for a fraction of the price you bought the original for, in any fabric of your choice. For cheap Indian or Arabic food, you won't be disappointed.

Off Al Satwa Road is Hudaiba Street, commonly known as Plant Street. It is famous for its pots and plants and is where expats desperate for a real tree as opposed to a fake one go at Christmastime. Be sure to walk down to **Book World** (☎ 04-349-1914), near the end of Hudaiba Street on the right. It stocks more than 45,000 mainly second-hand books, from Booker Prize quality to chick lit and beyond.

By now you are sure to be feeling hungry. **Al Mallah** (☎ 04-398-4723), on Al Diyafah Street, serves up some of the best Lebanese food in Dubai. Its falafel and *shawarma* are delicious and generous in portion, and its fresh juices are excellent. **Ravi's** (☎ 04-331-5353), a Pakistani restaurant on the east side of the Satwa Roundabout, is legendary for being incredibly cheap and very tasty. Many restaurants along Satwa Road are worth trying, and if you have the time, we recommend eating a traditional Indian thali at **Vandana Vegetarian Restaurant** (☎ 04-331-5346).

Two other things to look out for when you're in Satwa: If you're on Plant Street, walk along to Al Wasl Road and see the intricate and colourful mosaic architecture of the Iranian Hospital and Iranian Mosque. If you wander down to the far end of Al Diyafah Street, towards the sea where it meets Jumeirah Road, you will have an excellent view of the gigantic flag – the biggest U.A.E. flag in the world – flying above Union House, which is where the treaty uniting all seven emirates into the U.A.E. was signed in 1971.

Jumeirah

Jumeirah begins by the giant flagpole at the end of Al Diyafah Street and is the area sandwiched between Jumeirah Road, or Beach Road as it is informally known, and Al Wasl Road. It stretches about 9 kilometres (5.6 miles) down to Umm Al Sheif Road. Jumeirah Road runs parallel to the coast for about 16 kilometres (9.9 miles) in total, as far as Al Sufouh Road, near **Madinat Jumeirah.** Areas in this strip, after Jumeirah, are Umm Suqeim 1, 2 and 3 and Al Sufouh 1 and 2.

Jumeirah comprises three areas, originally named Jumeirah 1, 2 and 3. It is home to several public beaches, a couple of historical sites and hundreds of luxury villas. Jumeirah is the oldest expat residential area in Dubai and therefore the most established. It is leafy and has pavements, and you will more than likely see maids and gatemen cleaning cars and hosing front pavements as you explore. Jumeirah Road feels like a seaside resort; you can easily access several long golden beaches, and there are lots of cafes, restaurants, boutiques and smaller shopping malls. This road also seems to have more than its fair share of medical clinics of every kind, from dental to plastic surgery, physiotherapy to laser treatment.

The beautiful **Jumeirah Mosque** (☎ 04-353-6666) is well worth a visit, as is **Majlis Ghorfat Um-Al Sheif** (☎ 04-394-6343), an excellent example of a traditional house, constructed in 1955 from coral stone and gypsum and used by the late Sheikh Rashid bin Saeed Al Maktoum as a summer residence. Dating back to the sixth century AD is the **Archaeological Site** in Jumeirah 2 on Street 16, between Jumeirah Road and Al Wasl Road. This was the site of a caravan station along an ancient trade route that linked Iraq to Oman. It's one of the most significant archaeological sites in the United Arab Emirates, with sections of walling, a souk and houses – one of which is thought to have been the governor's palace. The site is surrounded by modern villas, and whilst it's not officially open to the public, you are able to look around if you first obtain a permit.

The beaches are fantastic down Jumeirah Road. Jumeirah Open Beach is free – next to Dubai Marine Beach Resort & Spa – or spend a day at **Jumeirah Beach Park,** with all the facilities of a beach club – restaurants, showers, landscaped gardens, children's play areas and barbecue areas. Sunloungers and umbrellas are for hire for no more than AED 5 per person, or AED 20 per car. Just remember that Monday is ladies' day only.

unofficial **TIP**
We do not recommend visiting the Dubai Zoo, which is small and smelly.

For delicious fresh food and juices we wholeheartedly recommend Lime Tree Café (☎ 04-349-8498) next to Jumeirah Mosque. We love the summer holiday feeling that Jumeirah Road induces.

Umm Suqeim

This is the area adjacent to Jumeirah, between Jumeirah Road and Al Wasl Road as they continue south. Like Jumeirah it is an established, leafy family neighbourhood where many of Dubai's Western expats live. It has long stretches of beach, parks in abundance and an easy, laid-back feel to it. Some of the expat international schools are situated in this area, and you will find Western-style supermarkets with goods from the U.K., the U.S. and the rest of Europe. You will see a predominance of well-heeled yummy mummies (or Jumeirah Janes, as they are familiarly known) driving around in their 4x4s here. Do not be surprised to see mothers trailing round the supermarkets followed by their maids looking after their young children. How quickly expats adapt!

The iconic landmark **Burj Al Arab** (☎ 04-301-7777), Dubai's most luxurious hotel, dominates the coastal skyline here in the shape of a billowing sail. Originally the tallest hotel in Dubai, it has now been pipped by the Rose Tower on Sheikh Zayed Road. At night it is beautifully illuminated, and from the sea, if you look back to shore, the Burj Al Arab is the sail in front of the wave that is **Jumeirah Beach Hotel.** The stretch of beach from Jumeirah Beach Hotel is home to several beach resort hotels and **Wild Wadi** (☎ 04-348-4444; **jumeirah.com**), a waterpark with 30 rides and attractions, themed around the tale of Juha, a well-known character from Arabian folklore.

All the hotels along this stretch are beautiful, but particularly worth a visit, even if you're not staying there, is **Souk Madinat Jumeirah.** It resembles a traditional Arabian souk, and within the resort is a maze of alleyways with open-fronted shops and boutiques. Lively restaurants and cafes line the Venetian-like waterway, where *abras* chug up and down, taking guests for rides. It does have an element of the theme park about it, but with masses of atmosphere it's a great place to spend an evening. The Madinat Theatre, also within the resort, has a regularly-changing, interesting programme of shows and concerts.

Al Safa and Al Quoz

Sheikh Zayed Road cuts through two distinct areas after it passes Downtown Dubai and Business Bay, going south towards Sharjah. To the right – west – in Al Safa, is an unexpected 25.9 hectares (64 acres) of open park. **Safa Park** (☎ 04-349-2111) is an oasis of serenity in the middle of a built-up urban district. It is one of Dubai's oldest and largest parks and has something for everyone.

Across the other side of Sheikh Zayed Road, to the east, is **Al Quoz** industrial area. This is not an immediate contender for best tourist destination in Dubai; however, strangely, it is becoming one of the most interesting areas of Dubai to visit if you love art and the arts. Hidden away in massive warehouses that are often a little difficult to find is a collection of galleries and interior design shops, small cafes, the Gold & Diamond Park and Times Square Centre.

Al Quoz art scene attracts up-and-coming artists and photographers. Galleries here work to promote Arab art on the international scene, and when you find the galleries nestled amongst the industrial warehouses, you feel a real sense of excitement and discovery. Some galleries showcase artists' works; others offer workshops and studio sessions. For comprehensive information about Al Quoz, and all the other art areas in Dubai, we'd recommend visiting the excellent site **artinthecity.com** and getting hold of its *ArtMap*.

For fantastic bargains, and every type of souvenir imaginable, the **Antiques Museum** (☎ 04-347-9935; **fakihcollections.com**) neither sells antiques nor is a museum, but it resembles a rather more ramshackle, chaotic version of Mr Magorium's Wonder Emporium for grown-ups. The most eccentric place to visit, it is piled high and crammed full to the bursting point with everything you would ever find in any tourist shop or souk, and at even better prices. It's worth a visit if only to see how fire, health and safety regulations have been bypassed in the most spectacular of ways.

Al Barsha/Mall of the Emirates

Al Quoz leads into Al Barsha, which is an area of Dubai that seems to have little to recommend it as far as sightseeing is concerned, except that it's where **Mall of the Emirates** (☎ 04-409-9000; **malloftheemirates.com**) is situated. It has an inordinate number of new, cheaper-priced hotels springing up. Part of Al Barsha is an established residential area, with large villas at a fraction of the price of their counterparts in Jumeirah across the Sheikh Zayed Road. Mall of the Emirates is home to **Ski Dubai** – that's what the ski-slope-shape protrusion emerging out the top is – the **Kempinski Hotel,** and as many shops, cafes and restaurants as you could hope to find in one mall, as well as a multi-screen cinema and other entertainment facilities. The mall was recently enlarged by half its size again. Recession? What recession?

New Dubai

This area encompasses everything between Mall of the Emirates and Jebel Ali, including **Palm Jumeirah** and **Dubai Marina, Media City, Internet City, Knowledge Village** and the **Emirates Living Community.** With the exception of a few hotels, everything in this area has been built in the last five years, and most future developments are happening on this side of town.

From the sky, Palm Jumeirah looks like a palm-tree-shaped piece of land sticking out into the sea. Luxury apartments and stunning villas sit on the trunk and the fronds of the Palm. At the end of the Palm rises the majestically-themed **Atlantis** hotel (☎ 04-426-0000; **atlantisthepalm.com**). You have to drive under the sea to reach it. If we are very honest – whilst the Palm is a sensational example of land reclamation, and residents enjoy their own private beaches, happy in the knowledge that they are part of a unique and exclusive community – there is a whiff of the glorified housing estate about it, albeit an exceedingly luxurious one. The Atlantis hotel is enormous and marginally gaudy. The lobby reminds us a little of a gigantic bus or train terminal, with hordes of people constantly milling around. This is not a hotel for the faint-hearted. Everything is done on a gargantuan scale. It is situated on a 46-hectare (113.7-acre) site, with a 17-hectare (42-acre) waterpark – **Aquaventure,** a sensational aquarium – **The Lost Chambers** and **Dolphin Bay,** where you can swim with the dolphins. It also has **Ambassador Lagoon,** home to the largest open-air marine habitat in the Middle East, with 65,000 marine animals. The hotel has 17 restaurants, of which 4 are celebrity chef restaurants; two kilometres (1.2 miles) of private beach and two pools the size of lakes. It would be quite easy to enjoy a holiday here and find enough to keep you entertained for a week without having to go anywhere else in Dubai.

Back on the mainland, the area in front of the Palm is Al Sufouh, home to Media City, Internet City and Knowledge Village. Both tax-free business zones, Media City and Internet City are home to global giants such as CNN, the BBC, Reuters, Bloomberg, *The Times,* Sony, Microsoft, Dell, HP and IBM to name just a few, whilst Dubai Knowledge Village, with more than 450 business partners, enjoys the distinction of being the world's only free zone cluster totally dedicated to human resources management. For a very funky vibe, the new **Media One Hotel** (☎ 04-427-1000; **mediaonehotel.com**) is a stylish venue for a night out if you want to mix with Dubai's hip young media scene. For jazz lovers, Dubai Media City's Open Air Amphitheatre hosts the extremely successful annual **Dubai International Jazz Festival** (☎ 04-391-1196; **dubaijazzfest.com**). It usually takes place around February each year.

Continuing along the coast, past the Palm, you will reach Dubai Marina, the Venice of the Middle East. This area has seen the most enormous amount of development in the last few years. Extremely sought-after high-rise apartment buildings line the man-made Marina, whilst **Jumeirah Beach Residence** (JBR) has 36 towers along the last stretch of beachfront. JBR Walk is full of trendy boutiques and seafront cafes and restaurants. Between October and April, Dubai's very own Covent Garden Market (**coventgardenmarket.ae**) takes place every Wednesday, Thursday, Friday and Saturday just at the end of the Walk near the beach. Elegant beach resort hotels fill the coastline here, and Dubai International Marine Club (**dimc.ae**) is the prime location for sailing and boating in Dubai and hosts legs of the Off-Shore Powerboat Racing Series. Dubai Marina, the largest man-made marina in the world, has a varied selection of restaurants and cafes and is a fun place to visit with children, as the fountains set in the pavement outside Starbucks are great for them to run around and cool off in. You can rent go-karts and take a tour of the walkway from Johnny Rocket's to Dubai Marina Mall, or we can recommend a short sea trip by dhow from Dubai Marina, courtesy of Captain Jack's Cruises (☎ 04-366-3538; **bristol-middleeast.com**).

As you continue along Sheikh Zayed Road, away from Al Barsha, with Media City on your right, you reach a new residential community called Emirates Living. This is a series of gated districts that particularly appeals to the expat community. Reminiscent of Stepford Wives, the communities are immaculate. The Lakes, Emirates Hills, The Meadows, The Springs – all have manicured lawns, landscaped parks, tree-lined streets, flowers in the gardens and perfectly-designed villas. Whilst these developments are extraordinarily well planned, there is something a little eerie about them. They lack soul. Perhaps that will come in time, but drive through them, and you expect at any moment for every front door to open simultaneously and perfectly-pressed families to exit mechanically at the same time – and maybe one child will let its ball drop out of sync and spoil the perfection of the street. Each zone has its own security-gated entrance to prevent non-residents from entering uninvited. In the middle of Emirates Hills there are two golf courses and **The Address Montgomerie Dubai** hotel (☎ 04-390-5600; **theaddress.com**). Why, you might almost forget you were in the Middle East.

Hatta

We decided to include Hatta in this guidebook about Dubai because it is in Dubai – just. To get to it, you have to leave Dubai, enter Oman, leave Oman and re-enter Dubai. And you'll need your passport. But it still is in Dubai. You'll also need a four-wheel-drive, or a driver, or a guide or all three. If you rent a car in Dubai, make sure that you are insured to drive it off-road and in Oman. An easier alternative is to take a tour with a reputable company. We would strongly recommend, if you're planning to drive yourself, that you get hold of an excellent guide by Explorer called *U.A.E. Off-Road: 26 Adventurous Routes*. It takes about an hour to get to Hatta from Dubai and is well worth a visit if you have the time.

Ignore the Hatta Fort Hotel, which is a bit 'pack 'em in and rip 'em off' (☎ 04-809-9333; **hatta-fort-hotel.com**) and isn't nearly as nice as the photos make it seem. When we visited it on a weekend, it was heaving with day-trippers and frenetic tourists, they charged us to use a nearby piece of sand as their overflow car park, and the buffet had seen better days. Instead, either take a picnic with you, or go to the supermarket complex nearby and buy a selection of freshly-made food on which to picnic, and make straight for the Hatta pools. You will have wonderful views of the Hajar Mountains en route, and swimming in these natural clear rock pools known as wadis is unbelievably refreshing, especially in the summer months. Do be careful in and near wadis, though, as flash floods occur, and the speed with which the water rises has to be seen to be believed.

We would also recommend visiting the **Hatta Heritage Village** (☎ 04-852-1374), which is nestled in the Hajar Mountains. It dates back more than 400 years to the 16th century and provides a fine example of traditional-style village architecture. You can wander everywhere in the village, but we'd recommend visiting it in the cooler winter months, as it is outside. It consists of two watchtowers, a mosque and houses constructed of stone, mud, reeds and palm tree trunks, built around the imposing Hatta Fort dominating the village. When you arrive, men in *dishdashas* sitting in the shade will offer you traditional Arabic coffee and dates. If you want to go really off-road and drive into the desert, we suggest you go to Big Red – a big red sand dune, which has become a challenge for most off-roaders to reach the top. Go on a Friday afternoon, especially in winter, when this area becomes one big dune-bashing motor show. Fossil Rock is where many people go camping during the winter months and is a great desert drive for beginners. This large outcrop is known as Fossil Rock after the marine fossils that can be found on its slopes. And whilst you are en route to Hatta, you will pass small shops lining the main road, offering an interesting selection of clay pots and carpets from Iran and Afghanistan. Ladies, watch out – here was the only time in Dubai that we came across some really lecherous salesmen.

If you're feeling peckish on your way back from Hatta and can't wait until you get back into Dubai proper, it's worth making a detour at International City – and we'll explain why. International City lies along the Dubai–Hatta road and between Interchange 5 and 6 of Emirates Road, opposite to the Dubai Central Fruit and Vegetable Market. It is a purpose-built city providing low-cost accommodation built in clusters featuring the architectural design properties of countries from around the world. It's unexciting except for two places of note: **Dragonmart** (☎ 04-428-5665/4; **dragonmart.ae**), a shopping mall with 3,950 shops all selling products from China (the bargains are amazing), and **BritBalti** (☎ 04-432-7528; **britbalti.com**), a very small Indian restaurant serving British-style curries for those Brits who are feeling homesick and are missing their chicken tikka masala on a Saturday night. It's not snazzy, and there's not a lot of atmosphere, but the owners – the Ahmed family, who ran a curry house in Twickenham, near London – are delightful, warm and welcoming. The food is tasty and familiar to British curry aficionados, and you will definitely not be breaking the bank.

MEYDAN RACECOURSE   50 AED → premium seating

THE NEW MEYDAN RACECOURSE (Nad al Sheba; ☎ 04-327-0077; **meydan.ae**) opened in March 2010 with the pinnacle of Dubai's racing calendar, the Dubai World Cup. The venue, which is gigantic and resembles an airport, comprises a 1,750-metre (5,741.5-foot) all-weather surface and 2,400-metre (7,874-foot) turf course. The grandstand accommodates a capacity of 60,000 spectators and incorporates the world's first five-star trackside hotel, known as – wait for it – The Meydan. The racecourse will also be home to the Meydan Museum & Gallery, the Meydan Marina, Meydan Grandstand Suites and the Falcon Commercial Park free zone offices. In addition to this there will be an IMAX cinema, and the Dubai Racing Club and Emirates Racing Authority will have their offices located here. The idea is that Meydan will become a year-round entertainment venue.

Three main horse racing events will take place at Meydan annually: the Winter Racing Challenge, from early November to early January; the Dubai International Racing Carnival, from the middle of January to the beginning of March; and the Dubai World Cup meeting, which traditionally falls on the last Saturday in March.

General admission will be free; grandstand and package prices vary. Races commence at 7 p.m. If you are thinking of being in the grandstand, you will need smart attire, and women are encouraged to wear hats and formal dress. Think Ladies' Day at Royal Ascot and you can't go wrong. If you've only brought holiday gear with you, stick to the free admission areas and you'll be fine in casual wear. For information about future racing events, check the Web site **dubai racingclub.com** or call ☎ 04-223-0000.

DUBAILAND

WE WOULD VERY MUCH LIKE to have included information about the celebrated Dubailand, which should have opened in 2009, will cover an area of about 279 million square metres (about 3 billion square feet) and will house the biggest theme-amusement park in the world. This complex will be divided into seven themed zones called worlds: Attractions & Experience World, Retail & Entertainment World, Themed Leisure & Vacation World, Eco-Tourism World, Sports & Outdoor World, Downtown and Science & Planetariums. Apart from the countless entertainment zones, the complex will also include tourism, real estate, luxury hospitality and retail areas. Conceived as the largest destination for family-oriented tourism and entertainment in the Middle East, Dubailand will have a number of theme parks, including one of the largest waterparks in the world. It will also feature several attractions catering to the entire family. These include The Restless Planet, a dinosaur theme park being developed in cooperation with the Natural History Museum in the U.K.; a Sports City, featuring large state-of-the-art stadiums; the Great Dubai Wheel; the Islamic Culture and Science World; the Mall of Arabia, set to become one of the largest shopping centres in the world; and Tiger Woods Dubai. Universal Studios was also going to open there. Indeed, there are some sensational gates at its entrance, but that's all there is of it so far, as was the case at Legoland.

Exciting and amazing as all this sounds, the aim is that it will become the world's biggest theme park, twice the size of Walt Disney World in America, and will contain a minimum of 55 hotels within its geographical location. The only thing that currently exists is Global Village, which closes for the summer. The rest is mainly sand. Construction has ground to a halt, and it is now anticipated that this ambitious project may not be completed until 2020.

ATTRACTION PROFILES

HAVING LOOKED AT AREAS OF DUBAI and pointed out, in brief, places or attractions that we think may interest you, we now describe in more detail some of the major attractions. Under each profile we inform you of where they are in Dubai, to whom we think they will appeal and into which category they fall. Author's ratings suggest how good the attraction is in its category and whether we think it's really worth seeing in the short space of a holiday.

Al Ahmadiya School and Heritage House ★ ★ ★

APPEAL BY AGE	PRESCHOOL –	PRIMARY SCHOOL ★★	TEENS ★
YOUNG ADULTS ★	OVER 30 ★★		SENIORS ★★★

near Gold House Building, Al Khor Street, Al Ras, Deira;
☎ **04-226-0286; dubaitourism.ae**

Type of attraction Two important heritage sites – the first school in Dubai (now a museum of education) and the house belonging to the pearl merchant who established the school **Admission** Free **Hours** Saturday–Thursday, 8 a.m.–7:30 p.m.; Friday, 2:30–7:30 p.m. **How much time to allow** 1 hour **Special comments** Gives an excellent insight into the architecture and history of Dubai. **Author's rating** ★★★. Well worth a visit to appreciate the history of education in Dubai and the beautiful detail in the construction and architecture of the buildings. Make this visit a part of your tour of the souks in this area to get a real feel for how Dubai used to be.

DESCRIPTION AND COMMENTS Constructed in 1912, Al Ahmadiya School was established by Ahmed Bin Dalmouk, a wealthy pearl merchant who believed in the benefits of education. About 200 boys were taught at the school, learning basic arithmetic, the Qur'an and Islamic studies, the Arabic language and grammar. Pupils were still coming to the school up until 1962, when it moved to larger premises. The school provides information about education at the turn of the century, and the classrooms look as they did when the school was in use. The school is located in what is becoming an established heritage district and is just behind Heritage House, which was Sheikh Ahmed bin Dalmouk's former home. It dates back to 1890 and is an excellent example of a traditional family house. Both buildings have been converted into museums and have been restored using original construction materials – gypsum, coral, shell, stone and sandalwood.

kids Aquaplay ★ ★ ★ ★ ★

APPEAL BY AGE	PRESCHOOL ★★★★★	PRIMARY SCHOOL ★★★★★	TEENS –
YOUNG ADULTS –	OVER 30 ★		SENIORS ★

Mirdif City Centre Mall, Mirdif; ☎ 800-534-7873; aquaplayme.com

Type of attraction Indoor water-based entertainment area **Admission** Rides vary in price between AED 5–30 per ride. **Hours** Daily, 10 a.m.–10 p.m. **How much time to allow** 2 hours **Special comments** You won't need a swimming costume. **Author's rating** ★★★★★. A bit like Willy Wonka's Chocolate Factory with water instead of chocolate. Fun and educational, and you don't have to get wet.

continued on page 168

Dubai Attractions by Type

TYPE AND NAME	AUTHOR'S RATING	NEIGHBOURHOOD
ART EVENTS		
Bastakiya Art Fair	★★★★★	Bastakiya, Bur Dubai
ArtBus	★★★★	Madinat Jumeirah, Al Sufouh
Art Dubai	★★★★	Madinat Jumeirah, Al Sufouh
ART GALLERIES		
Ayyam Gallery	★★★★	Al Quoz
Carbon 12	★★★★	Al Quoz
Cuadro Fine Art Gallery	★★★★	DIFC Gate Village
The Empty Quarter	★★★★	DIFC Gate Village
The Farjam Collection	★★★★	DIFC Gate Village
Gallery Isabelle Van Den Eynde	★★★★	Al Quoz
Majlis Gallery	★★★★	Bastakiya, Bur Dubai
The Third Line	★★★★	Al Quoz
XVA Gallery	★★★★	Bastakiya, Bur Dubai
Art Sawa	★★★	Al Quoz
Mojo Gallery	★★★	Al Quoz
Portfolio Gallery	★★★	Al Quoz
thejamjar	★★★	Al Quoz
1x1 Art Gallery	★★	Al Quoz
CHILDREN'S ATTRACTIONS		
Aquaplay	★★★★★	Mirdif
Cité des Enfants	★★★★★	Mirdif
Dubai Aquarium and Underwater Zoo	★★★★★	Downtown
Jumeirah Beach Park	★★★★★	Jumeirah
KidZania	★★★★★	Downtown
Aquaventure	★★★★	Palm Jumeirah
Children's City	★★★★	Bur Dubai
Safa Park	★★★★	Al Safa
Ski Dubai	★★★★	Al Barsha
Wild Wadi	★★★★	Umm Suqeim
Cable Car Ride	★★★	Bur Dubai

TYPE AND NAME	AUTHOR'S RATING	NEIGHBOURHOOD
Café Céramique	★★★	Al Barsha, Jumeirah and Garhoud
Dolphin Bay	★★★	Palm Jumeirah
Dubai Dolphinarium	★★★	Bur Dubai
Dubai Drums	★★★	Desert
Dubai Kartdrome and Laserdrome	★★★	Motorcity (Al Barsha South)
Encounter Zone	★★★	Oud Metha
Al Saheel: A Thousand and One Horse Tales	★★★	Arabian Ranches
thejamjar	★★★	Al Quoz
iFly Dubai	★★	Mirdif
The Lost Chambers	★★	Palm Jumeirah
Luna Park, the Fruit Garden	★★	Oud Metha
Magic Planet	★★	Al Barsha, Deira and Mirdif
Soccer Circus Dubai and Team Zone	★★	Mirdif
Yalla! Bowling Lanes	★★	Mirdif
SEGA Republic	★	Downtown Dubai
Stargate	★	Za'abeel
Wonderland Theme Park and Splashland Water Park	★	Oud Metha

CULTURAL AND HERITAGE SITES

Burj Khalifa	★★★★★	Downtown
Dubai Museum	★★★★★	Bur Dubai
Hatta Heritage Village	★★★★★	Hatta
The Sheikh Mohammed Centre for Cultural Understanding	★★★★★	Bastakiya
Heritage and Diving Villages	★★★★	Bur Dubai
Al Ahmadiya School and Heritage House	★★★	Deira
Bait Al Wakeel	★★★	Bur Dubai
Majlis Ghorfat Um-Al Sheif	★★★	Jumeirah
Sheikh Saeed Al Maktoum House	★★★	Bur Dubai
Jumeirah Archaeological Site	★★½	Jumeirah

Dubai Attractions by Type (continued)

TYPE AND NAME	AUTHOR'S RATING	NEIGHBOURHOOD
MOSQUES		
Jumeirah Mosque	★★★★★	Jumeirah
Grand Mosque Dubai	★★★	Bur Dubai
PARKS AND GARDENS		
Mushrif Park	★★★★★	Mirdif
Ras Al Khor Wildlife Sanctuary	★★★★	Bur Dubai
Safa Park	★★★★	Al Safa
Za'abeel Park	★★★★	Za'abeel
Dubai Creek Park	★★★	Bur Dubai

continued from page 165

DESCRIPTION AND COMMENTS Water, young children, splashing, no mess for you to clear up – what could be more perfect? This is an indoor entertainment centre at Playnation with a difference – all the interactive games involve water. Children wear plastic overalls and, under the diligent eye of the staff, can splash to their heart's content at Muriel's Aquatraptions – a stand-and-play activity area with mini water tubes, slides, interactive fountains, squirters and boats that children can mess around with while learning about water movement, pressure, currents and hydropower. Oscar's Wave Rider is a kayak-style log-flume ride, and Pelican Bay is a fishing port–themed climbing and soft play area. There's also a bumper-boat ride called Ravi's Slamming Shells, a sea horse carousel, water-themed arcade games, gemstone digging and a tugboat swing ship. If you have older children, send them off to another Playnation attraction and let the little ones have a great time at this excellently designed one.

kids Aquaventure ★★★★

APPEAL BY AGE PRESCHOOL ★★★	PRIMARY SCHOOL ★★★★★	TEENS ★★★★★
YOUNG ADULTS ★★★★	OVER 30 ★★★	SENIORS ★

Atlantis, The Palm, Palm Jumeirah; ☎ 04-426-0000

Type of attraction Outdoor waterpark **Admission** AED 200 for adults and AED 150 for children; discounted admission after 3 p.m. Sunday–Thursday, AED 150 for adults and AED 120 for children. **Hours** Daily, 10 a.m.–sunset **How much time to allow** Half a day **Special comments** Outdoor attractions, even waterparks, are not recommended during high summer due to the heat. **Author's rating ★★★★.**

DESCRIPTION AND COMMENTS Only the very hard of heart could fail to love this completely over-the-top waterpark. It's actually smaller than you might imagine, with fewer rides than competitor Wild Wadi, but the ones it does have are very impressive. The vertical Leap of Faith slide shoots you through a shark tunnel at Formula 1 speeds, but there are more sedate rides too. Bobbing about on the lazy river in a giant tyre is a very pleasant way to spend an afternoon. There is also a beach with sunloungers for when you get bored – beware, though, towel rental for a family can rack up, so think about bringing your own. The ground can get very hot during summer, so do wear flip-flops into the park, and if you are prone to sunburn, wear a T-shirt over your swimsuit, as the rides don't afford much shade.

ArtBus ★★★★

APPEAL BY AGE	PRESCHOOL –	PRIMARY SCHOOL –	TEENS ★
YOUNG ADULTS ★★★	OVER 30 ★★★★		SENIORS ★★★★

To coincide with Art Dubai and Bastakiya Art Fair;
☎ **04-341-7303; artinthecity.com**

Type of attraction Bus tour with an art theme **Admission** AED 50 **Hours** Only runs during Art Dubai and Bastakiya Art Fair, 10 a.m.–5 p.m. **How much time to allow** 1–2 days **Special comments** ArtBus follows two full-day routes. **Author's rating ★★★★.** By the end of a day you will not only have seen some of Dubai's most interesting art galleries, but you will have made new friends as well.

DESCRIPTION AND COMMENTS ArtBus is a fantastic bus tour dedicated to getting enthusiasts to where the art is! The only downside is that it runs for merely three days each year, during Art Dubai, Dubai's annual art fair, which is held in March at the Madinat Jumeirah. ArtBus shuttles passengers on a tour of Dubai's art pockets to and from the fair via Al Quoz galleries, Al Bastakiya arts quarter and Dubai International Financial Centre's (DIFC's) Gate Village. The bus provides guided tours of the city's prominent galleries, studios, art centres, alternative art spaces and art fairs. It's a hassle-free journey through Dubai's changing landscape and developing arts scene. There are two tours, and each tour takes a full day, with pickup and drop-off at the Madinat Jumeirah, where Art Dubai is held. Both tours take place each day of the Art Dubai period. Two knowledgeable guides accompany each bus, and the tour is conducted in English. The guides stay with the passengers for the entire tour, and there is a lunch stop at a lovely restaurant. The atmosphere on the bus is very friendly, and passengers get to know each other over the course of the tour, so by the end of the day, there's a really convivial feeling amongst the group. Seats fill up very fast, so it is important to make a reservation.

Art Dubai ★ ★ ★ ★

APPEAL BY AGE	PRESCHOOL –	PRIMARY SCHOOL –	TEENS ★
YOUNG ADULTS ★★★	OVER 30 ★★★★		SENIORS ★★★★

Madinat Jumeirah, Jumeirah; ☎ 04-323-3434; artdubai.ae

Type of attraction Art fair held annually **Admission** AED 50 **Hours** Usually held for three or four days in March; hours vary. **How much time to allow** 2 hours to 2 days **Special comments** One of the biggest contemporary art events in the Middle East. **Author's rating** ★★★★. A fantastic opportunity to see art from more than 70 galleries and 30 countries in one place.

DESCRIPTION AND COMMENTS Whilst this is not a gallery, it is important to include Art Dubai, the extremely prestigious international art fair that punctuates Dubai's prolific art scene annually. It is now considered the essential gathering place for collectors, artists and art professionals from across the Middle East, South Asia and beyond, and has been instrumental in reviving the city's art culture. Dubai has many small galleries, but Art Dubai provides a focal point for the year for Dubai's art scene and showcases many of the local galleries' works.

Art Sawa ★ ★ ★

APPEAL BY AGE	PRESCHOOL –	PRIMARY SCHOOL ★	TEENS ★
YOUNG ADULTS ★★★	OVER 30 ★★★★		SENIORS ★★★★

Al Rasaas Road, Street 14B, Al Quoz 1; ☎ 04-340-8660; artsawa.com

Type of attraction Art gallery **Admission** Depends on the event; gallery viewing free of charge. **Hours** Saturday–Thursday, 10 a.m.–7 p.m. **How much time to allow** Depends on the event. **Special comments** Particularly focused on exhibiting artists from the North African continent. **Author's rating** ★★★. A spectacular gallery, the largest in Dubai, promoting work from a wide range of artists, in a variety of different media.

DESCRIPTION AND COMMENTS This enormous (1,115 square metres, or about 12,000 square feet) art space devotes itself to showcasing artists from the Middle East, North Africa and neighbouring countries. It hosts innovative exhibitions and educational programmes, as well as offering a range of publications reflecting current issues and practices.

Ayyam Gallery ★ ★ ★ ★

APPEAL BY AGE	PRESCHOOL –	PRIMARY SCHOOL ★	TEENS ★
YOUNG ADULTS ★★★	OVER 30 ★★★★		SENIORS ★★★★

Al Serkal Avenue, Street 8, Al Quoz 1; ☎ 04-323-6242; ayyamgallery.com

Type of attraction Contemporary art gallery **Admission** Free **Hours** Saturday–Thursday, 10 a.m.–8 p.m. **How much time to allow** 30 minutes + **Special**

continued on page 174

What to Do in Deira & Bur Dubai

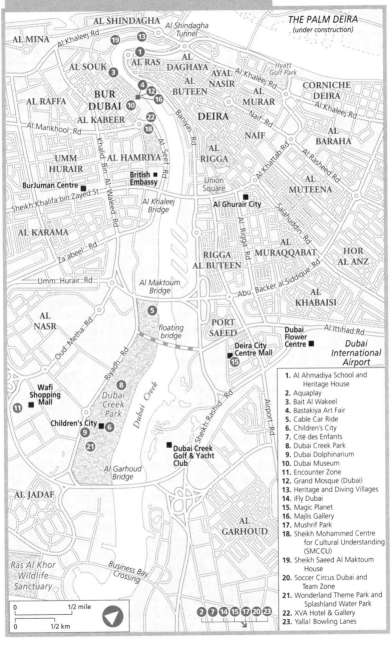

THE PALM DEIRA
(under construction)

AL SHINDAGHA
Al Shindagha Tunnel
AL MINA
Al Khaleej Rd
AL SOUK
AL RAS
AL DAGHAYA
AL BUTEEN
AYAL NASIR
Al Khaleej Rd
Hyatt Golf Park
CORNICHE DEIRA
Al Khaleej Rd
BUR DUBAI
AL RAFFA
AL KABEER
AL MURAR
DEIRA
Naif Rd
AL BARAHA
Al-Mankhool Rd
Banyas Rd
NAIF
Al-Seef Rd
Khalid Bin Al-Waleed Rd
AL HAMRIYA
AL RIGGA
British Embassy
BurJuman Centre
Sheikh Khalifa bin Zayed St
Al Khaleej Bridge
Union Square
Al Ghurair City
Al-Khattab Rd
Al-Rasheed Rd
AL MUTEENA
UMM HURAIR
AL KARAMA
Za'abeel Rd
Al-Rigga Rd
Salahuddin Rd
RIGGA AL BUTEEN
AL MURAQQABAT
HOR AL ANZ
Umm Hurair Rd
Al Maktoum Bridge
Abu Backer al-Siddique Rd
AL KHABAISI
AL NASR
Oud-Metha Rd
Riyadh Rd
floating bridge
PORT SAEED
Dubai Flower Centre
Al-Ittihad Rd
Dubai International Airport
Deira City Centre Mall
Sheikh Rashid Rd
Airport Rd
Wafi Shopping Mall
Dubai Creek Park
Dubai Creek
Children's City
Dubai Creek Golf & Yacht Club
Al Garhoud Bridge
AL JADAF
AL GARHOUD
Ras Al Khor Wildlife Sanctuary
Business Bay Crossing

0   1/2 mile
0   1/2 km

1. Al Ahmadiya School and Heritage House
2. Aquaplay
3. Bait Al Wakeel
4. Bastakiya Art Fair
5. Cable Car Ride
6. Children's City
7. Cité des Enfants
8. Dubai Creek Park
9. Dubai Dolphinarium
10. Dubai Museum
11. Encounter Zone
12. Grand Mosque (Dubai)
13. Heritage and Diving Villages
14. iFly Dubai
15. Magic Planet
16. Majlis Gallery
17. Mushrif Park
18. Sheikh Mohammed Centre for Cultural Understanding (SMCCU)
19. Sheikh Saeed Al Maktoum House
20. Soccer Circus Dubai and Team Zone
21. Wonderland Theme Park and Splashland Water Park
22. XVA Hotel & Gallery
23. Yalla! Bowling Lanes

What to Do in Jumeirah

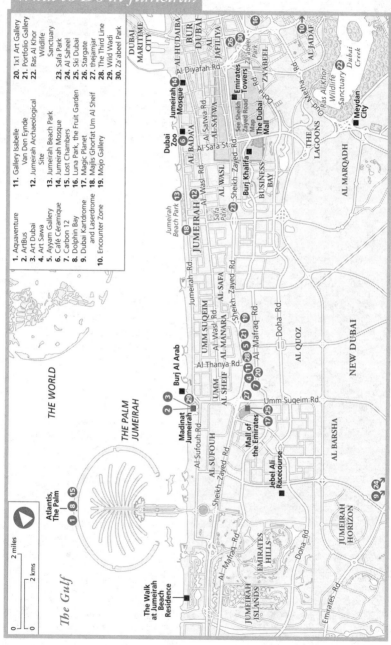

What to Do on Sheikh Zayed Road

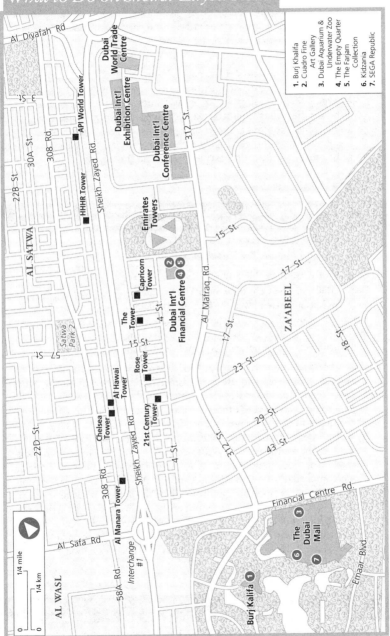

1. Burj Khalifa
2. Cuadro Fine
   Art Gallery
3. Dubai Aquarium &
   Underwater Zoo
4. The Empty Quarter
5. The Farjam
   Collection
6. Kidzania
7. SEGA Republic

continued from page 170

comments A 929-square-metre (almost 10,000-square-foot) space dedicated to promoting contemporary art from Syria and the Levant. **Author's rating** ★★★★. A beautiful space, well curated, providing an excellent introduction to Middle Eastern art.

DESCRIPTION AND COMMENTS This gallery, which also has locations in Damascus and Beirut, concentrates on showcasing works of young, emerging Middle Eastern artists. Several times a year the gallery organises in-house the Young Collectors Auction, which offers an opportunity to a new generation of collectors and patrons in the Middle East to buy sought-after artworks at highly competitive prices. The gallery represents more than 30 artists exclusively around the world.

Bait Al Wakeel ★★★

APPEAL BY AGE	PRESCHOOL ★	PRIMARY SCHOOL ★★	TEENS ★★
YOUNG ADULTS ★★	OVER 30 ★★★		SENIORS ★★★

edge of Dubai Creek, between Bur Dubai Abra Station and Old Souk Abra Station, Bur Dubai; ☎ 04-353-0530

Type of attraction Maritime museum and restaurant **Admission** Free **Hours** Daily, 11:30 a.m.–midnight **How much time to allow** 1 hour including time for lunch **Special comments** It was the first office building in Dubai. **Author's rating** ★★★. For atmosphere, the restaurant is hard to beat, as you sit literally over the Creek, in one of Dubai's oldest buildings, watching life on the river. Decent traditional food, and the museum explains Dubai's maritime history.

DESCRIPTION AND COMMENTS Built in 1935 by the late Sheikh Rashid, Bait Al Wakeel was a shipping office for Gray Mackenzie & Company, who were agents for many of the shipping lines that sailed into Dubai. The lower floor was used as offices, whilst the manager and his family used the upper floor as accommodation. To board the ships, staff only had to walk through the back door and they were on the quayside. The building is a fine example of early-20th-century Arabic architecture and was made from local mud and coral. Mangrove poles to support the roof were imported from East Africa. After Bait Al Wakeel was restored and refurbished, the landing stage, from which the agents' boats used to sail out to visit the cargo ships anchored offshore, was turned into a deck for dining as part of a restaurant within Bait Al Wakeel. Today it also houses a fishing museum depicting Dubai's once-traditional fishing and maritime history and culture. The restaurant serves very decent seafood.

Bastakiya Art Fair ★★★★★

APPEAL BY AGE	PRESCHOOL –	PRIMARY SCHOOL ★	TEENS ★★
YOUNG ADULTS ★★★	OVER 30 ★★★★		SENIORS ★★★★

Bastakiya, Bur Dubai; ☎ 04-353-5383; bastakiyaartfair.com

Type of attraction Annual art fair held for four days only **Admission** Free **Hours** Usually held in March to coincide with Art Dubai; hours vary. **How much time to allow** 2 hours to half a day **Special comments** Located in the galleries and streets of Bastakiya. Take plenty of water; it can get hot. **Author's rating** ★★★★★. Bastakiya is a fascinating area in its own right, so be prepared to get sidetracked. This is a laid-back fringe art fair, in a beautifully-restored heritage area.

DESCRIPTION AND COMMENTS Bastakiya Art Fair runs parallel to Art Dubai annually, and it's altogether a more relaxed and bohemian affair. It provides a wider celebration of the arts in one of Dubai's loveliest heritage areas. Traditional houses within Bastakiya are opened to the public, and participants exhibiting their works are local, regional and international. Exhibitions are hosted by individual participants, galleries and internationally-acclaimed curators. The programme of events includes daily exhibitions, movie screenings, book readings, performance art and a series of brunch talks. Intersperse this with some relaxation in any of Bastakiya's delightful restaurants or cafes, and the chance to wander through some of Dubai's most beautiful restored streets, and you have the recipe for a fun-filled, fascinating day out.

 Burj Khalifa ★★★★★

APPEAL BY AGE	PRESCHOOL ★	PRIMARY SCHOOL ★★	TEENS ★★★★
YOUNG ADULTS ★★★★		OVER 30 ★★★★	SENIORS ★★★★

1 Emaar Boulevard, Downtown Dubai; ☎ 04-888-8124; burjkhalifa.ae

Type of attraction Tallest building in the world with a spectacular observation deck **Admission** Reserved – dated and timed: AED 100 for adults, AED 75 for children ages 4–12, and free for children age 3 and under. Immediate entry: AED 400. **Hours** Sunday–Wednesday, 10 a.m.–10 p.m.; Thursday–Saturday, 10 a.m.–midnight **How much time to allow** 2 hours **Special comments** Book in advance and save AED 300 per person. **Author's rating** ★★★★★. Not strictly a cultural attraction, but may become part of Dubai's heritage.

DESCRIPTION AND COMMENTS The tallest building in the world towers over every other building in Dubai and can be seen for miles around; it majestically dominates Dubai's skyline and is home to residential apartments, offices and shops. It's very difficult to get a sense of just how tall it is, but bear in mind that at 800 metres (2,624.7 feet) tall, it is almost half a kilometre taller than the next tallest building in Dubai, the Emirates Office Tower at 355 metres (1,164.7 feet). Its opening in January 2010 was televised around the world. It holds several other records apart from those already mentioned – it has the highest number of storeys in the world, the highest occupied floor in the world, the highest outdoor observation deck in the world and the lift with the longest travel distance in the world. Up close you can't fail to be overwhelmed by its sheer immensity.

The Burj houses the Armani Hotel Dubai and Armani Residences (see page 55) as well as private ultra-luxurious residences and corporate suites. On level 122 is a restaurant, and the tower's public observatory is on level

124. Burj Khalifa's At the Top experience is literally out of this world. Best to book in advance to avoid queuing and to cut your costs considerably. Pitch-black, high-speed lifts whisk you 124 floors above the ground for an awe-inspiring view from the observation deck. A typical visit will last about an hour, although you are welcome to stand gawping for as long as you like, and the views are some of the most stunning you will find of Dubai. On a very clear day, you can see the coastline of Iran; but even if it's hazy, you'll get a wonderful bird's-eye view of Sheikh Mohammed's palaces and the desert beyond.

The journey begins in the lower ground level. You'll leave the reception area aboard the 65-metre-long (213.3-foot-long) 'travelator' on a trip that portrays, through multi-media presentations, a history of Dubai up to the present day. A viewing point at this stage allows you to look at the tower close up through a skylight. You'll then enter the lift, which fits about 20 people. It travels incredibly fast – at 10 metres (32.8 feet) per second – but you are not aware of the speed at which you're travelling, and during your journey, a light show and music play in the lift. The observation deck is very large and is split into two parts – one roofed, one open-air. Floor-to-ceiling glass walls provide a breathtaking unobstructed 360-degree view of the city, desert and ocean, but if you suffer from vertigo, don't worry: the sheer size of the observation deck seems to minimise how scarily high you actually are.

Dubai looks particularly lovely at night, with sparkling lights and stars vying for attention. Special telescopes provide virtual time-travel visions of the scenes beyond and below. You'll see close-up, real-time views as well as the past and the future, by day and by night. You can also walk the entire perimeter for the most comprehensive views. Windows are louvred so that you can take photos without getting a reflection from the glass. We were surprised to find that we stayed up there an hour; it was so intriguing.

 kids **Cable Car Ride** ★ ★ ★

APPEAL BY AGE	PRESCHOOL ★★	PRIMARY SCHOOL ★★★	TEENS ★★
YOUNG ADULTS ★		OVER 30 ★	SENIORS ★

Dubai Creek Park – located between Al Maktoum and Al Garhoud bridges in the heart of Bur Dubai; ☎ 04-336-7633 (park) and ☎ 050-624-9642 (cable car)

Type of attraction Outdoor cable car ride **Admission** Park: AED 5 per person. Cable car ride: An additional AED 25 for adults and AED 15 for children. **Hours** Sunday–Wednesday, 8 a.m.–11 p.m.; Thursday–Saturday, 8 a.m.–11:30 p.m. **How much time to allow** 1 hour **Special comments** It does get hot, and during the summer the cable car runs at variable times because of the heat. During the winter it runs all day. **Author's rating** ★★★. This is definitely an attraction to do with younger children. The trouble is that there are so many sensational things to do in Dubai that this seems a little mundane in comparison because it is older. Nevertheless it is fun and, if you're in Dubai Creek Park, worth doing.

DESCRIPTION AND COMMENTS Another way to see how Dubai is developing is to take the 2.5-kilometre (1.6-mile) cable car ride, 30 metres (98.4 feet) above the shore of the Creek. The Dubai cable car ride system connects the park's amphitheatre and Al Maktoum Bridge. There are three stations en route, and passengers can embark or disembark from any of them.

Dubai Creek is fascinating from any viewpoint, and being up high only enhances it. Watching the busy road network from above is strangely mesmerising as well. We probably wouldn't recommend this ride if you are afraid of heights.

kids Café Céramique ★★★

APPEAL BY AGE	PRESCHOOL –	PRIMARY SCHOOL ★★★★	TEENS ★★★★
YOUNG ADULTS ★		OVER 30 ★	SENIORS ★

Town Centre Mall, Jumeirah Road, Jumeirah; ☎ 04-344-7331; Festival Centre, Festival City; ☎ 04-232-8616; cafe-ceramique.com

Type of attraction Concept cafe – paint your own ceramics **Admission** AED 50–200, depending on how many pieces of pottery you choose to paint and what you have to eat. **Hours** Daily, 9 a.m.–midnight **How much time to allow** 1–1½ hours **Special comments** Bear in mind that you'll need to leave your ceramics to be fired, and then pick them up a few days later, so don't visit this cafe at the end of your holiday. **Author's rating** ★★★. A franchise, similar to many that are now seen on the high streets in the U.K. Go for the ceramic painting rather than the food.

DESCRIPTION AND COMMENTS Part cafe, part studio, the cafe walls are lined with bisque ceramics of all description, from crockery to sculpture. Paints, brushes and ideas are provided; all you need to do is select which piece of pottery you like and sit and paint it. You don't need to be artistic or a whizz with a paintbrush. This will keep the children occupied whilst you have a bite to eat. The food sounds better than it tastes but is perfectly pleasant, and this is a good place to while away an hour or so in the cool.

Carbon 12 ★★★★

APPEAL BY AGE	PRESCHOOL –	PRIMARY SCHOOL ★	TEENS ★
YOUNG ADULTS ★★★	OVER 30 ★★★★	SENIORS ★★★★	

Warehouse D37, Alserkal Avenue, Street 8, Al Quoz 1; ☎ 050-464-4392 or 050-873-9623; carbon12dubai.com

Type of attraction Eclectic art gallery **Admission** Free **Hours** Saturday–Thursday, 11:30 a.m.–7 p.m. **How much time to allow** 30 minutes + **Special comments** Contemporary, simple white cube space enhances the art on display to great effect. **Author's rating** ★★★★. A gallery with a mix of international artists, including some from the Middle East, showcasing works in all media.

DESCRIPTION AND COMMENTS Carbon 12 represents both newly-discovered artists and internationally-recognised names whose works already hang in museums. The gallery exhibits paintings, sculptures, photography and media art. The artists represented are often being seen for the first time in the region.

 Children's City ★★★★

APPEAL BY AGE	PRESCHOOL ★★	PRIMARY SCHOOL ★★★★★	TEENS ★★★★★
YOUNG ADULTS ★★		OVER 30 ★★★	SENIORS ★★★

Gate 1, Dubai Creek Park, Bur Dubai; ☎ 04-334-0808; childrencity.ae

Type of attraction Interactive science-centred children's museum **Admission** AED 15 for adults, AED 10 for children, and free for children under age 2. **Hours** Saturday–Thursday, 9 a.m.–7:30 p.m.; Friday 3–7:30 p.m. **How much time to allow** 2 hours **Special comments** A great museum that will keep children occupied for a few hours during the heat of the day. **Author's rating** ★★★★. We think that this is a gem of a museum; loads of interesting hands-on displays will interest a wide spectrum of ages – and unlike London's Science Museum, practically empty, so children have lots of time to try everything.

DESCRIPTION AND COMMENTS If you've visited Launch Pad gallery at the Science Museum in London, then you will have a fair idea of what Children's City is like. It is the first educational city in the U.A.E. devoted to children between 2 and 15 years old, where they can investigate, explore, play, discover and learn about the world in which they live. It takes the children on a journey through the human body, science and space with the help of different zones. More than 50 exhibits, many of which are interactive, appeal to all ages of children. Our favourites are trying the simulator, where you can try flying on a magic carpet or riding on a camel; dressing up in clothes from around the world; and using the giant computer to send messages. Other facilities include a special play area for those under the age of 5, a theatre, a planetarium, a souvenir shop and a cafe.

kids **Cité des Enfants** ★★★★★

APPEAL BY AGE	PRESCHOOL ★★★★★	PRIMARY SCHOOL ★★★★★	TEENS –
YOUNG ADULTS –		OVER 30 –	SENIORS –

Mirdif City Centre Mall, Mirdif; ☎ 800-534-7873; citedesenfantsme.com

Type of attraction Children's educational play centre **Admission** AED 130 for one adult and one child, AED 190 for one adult and two children, and AED 245 for one adult and three children. Each additional guest over a group of four will be charged AED 50. **Hours** Saturday–Wednesday, 10 a.m.– 11 p.m.; Thursday–Friday, 10 a.m.–midnight. **How much time to allow** 1 hour + **Special comments** New from France, this is a delightful educational play zone, beautifully designed. **Author's rating** ★★★★★. A mix between a science-type museum and a really good play centre, with very beautifully-designed exhibits. A real treat for little ones.

DESCRIPTION AND COMMENTS Cité des Enfants is an 'edu-tainment' play area at Playnation with 97 different exhibits across five zones, designed around the principle of learning through play. Once you have paid, you can stay as long as you like. The five zones are called I Discover Myself; I Can Do; I Locate Myself; All Together; and I Experiment. We liked the light-and-colour exhibit in I Experiment, the hut of anger in I Discover Myself and the speaking letters in I Can Do. You'll find some really unusual exhibits here, which are both stimulating and great fun. Also worth looking out for are the monthly workshops, which cover a wide range of subjects such as Science Discoveries, Animal Mania and Our Mother Earth, to name a few. Workshop sessions are AED 75, and you drop your child off for 90 minutes – 45 minutes for the workshop followed by 45 minutes in the exhibition area, supervised by a Cité des Enfants animator.

Cuadro Fine Art Gallery ★ ★ ★ ★

APPEAL BY AGE	PRESCHOOL –	PRIMARY SCHOOL ★	TEENS ★
YOUNG ADULTS ★	OVER 30 ★ ★ ★ ★		SENIORS ★ ★ ★ ★

Gate Village, DIFC; ☎ 04-425-0400; cuadroart.com

Type of attraction A gallery for the serious art lover **Admission** Free **Hours** Sunday–Thursday, 10 a.m.–8 p.m.; Saturday, midday–6 p.m. **How much time to allow** 1 hour **Special comments** A serious player in the Dubai art world. **Author's rating** ★ ★ ★ ★. Cuadro is an impressive gallery with a beautiful space, and it takes itself very seriously, showcasing a range of really top-notch artists.

DESCRIPTION AND COMMENTS This sophisticated gallery represents sought-after artists who boast work represented in permanent collections of museums such as MoMa, the Tate Britain and the Guggenheim. The gallery is equally committed to discovering, exhibiting and promoting artists from the Gulf and the Middle East, and working closely with international partners to exhibit the works of Middle Eastern artists in international venues.

kids Dolphin Bay ★ ★ ★

APPEAL BY AGE	PRESCHOOL –	PRIMARY SCHOOL ★ ★ ★ ★	TEENS ★ ★ ★ ★
YOUNG ADULTS ★ ★ ★ ★	OVER 30 ★ ★ ★		SENIORS ★ ★

Atlantis, The Palm, Palm Jumeirah; ☎ 04-426-1030; atlantisthepalm.com

Type of attraction In-water interactive dolphin experience **Admission** Dolphin Encounter: AED 595; Dolphin Adventure: AED 890; Royal Swim: AED 975; observer pass: AED 300 **Hours** Daily, 9 a.m.–3:10 p.m. **How much time to allow** 90 minutes **Special comments** Admission price also includes access to the Aquaventure theme park and beach. **Author's rating** ★ ★ ★. There's no getting around the fact that taking your family to get up-close and personal with these beautiful mammals is expensive, but it is a unique experience.

DESCRIPTION AND COMMENTS There are a number of packages available here, all of them very expensive and, unfortunately, quite short. These are booked in time slots, so do allow yourself enough time to get there, as Dolphin Bay itself is quite some distance from the car park and you will hold up a whole group if you're late. On arrival, you are given lockers and towels and are issued wetsuits – don't wear jewellery, as you will be sternly told to take everything off, even small stud earrings. The trainers will then show a short video and walk you through what is about to happen. Then you'll be led into the water. If you are paying for the Dolphin Encounter, you'll wade to waist height in the water, where you can touch, play with and 'kiss' the dolphin – the whole experience lasts 30 minutes. Adults might find this a bit embarrassing, as you will be made to sing, clap and dance for the dolphin. Yes, really. The next tier, the Dolphin Adventure, will lead guests out to water up to 3 metres (9.8 feet) in depth and will be allowed to hold onto the dolphin's fin while it gives you a ride back into shore. The newest experience to be added to the list is the Royal Swim, where two dolphins lead you around the pool and also jump over your head. Children under age 12 are not allowed out into the water on their own, but there is no lower age limit for the Dolphin Encounter if a guardian is in the water too. For the other experiences, children must be aged over 12 and competent swimmers.

 kids ## Dubai Aquarium and Underwater Zoo ★★★★★

APPEAL BY AGE	PRESCHOOL ★★	PRIMARY SCHOOL ★★★★★	TEENS ★★★★★
YOUNG ADULTS ★★★★★		OVER 30 ★★★★★	SENIORS ★★★★★

Dubai Mall, Downtown Dubai; ☎ 04-448-5200; thedubaiaquarium.com

Type of attraction Aquarium **Admission** Aquarium Tunnel: AED 25 for adults and AED 20 for children ages 3–16. Tunnel and Underwater Zoo: AED 50. **Hours** Sunday–Wednesday, 10 a.m.–10 p.m.; Thursday–Saturday, 10 a.m.–midnight **How much time to allow** 2 hours **Special comments** An aquarium marketed as an underwater zoo with a rain forest theme; beautiful in every way. **Author's rating** ★★★★★. This is an excellent aquarium – very well laid out and themed, with informative panels, very friendly and knowledgeable staff and out-of-the-ordinary attractions to make it just that little bit different.

DESCRIPTION AND COMMENTS It has the largest viewing panel on the planet, a fascinating cage-snorkelling experience, more than 150 aquatic species and 33,000 aquatic animals, shark dives, glass-bottom boat rides and the world's largest suspended tank containing 10 million litres (about 2.6 million gallons) of water. And it is in a shopping mall. This is the most interesting aquarium we've visited. The facts alone are quite jaw-dropping, but the design is pretty spectacular as well. You have the choice of either just taking a walk under the water through the 48-metre-long (157.5-foot-long) Aquarium Tunnel – with sharks and rays swimming just above your head – or also visiting the Underwater Zoo, part rain forest, part aquarium, with 36 aquatic displays. At the Underwater Zoo you will see otters, penguins, water rats and piranha amongst other things; you can reach out and touch the Rock Pool creatures; and you can enjoy the slightly scary sensation of standing on top of the Aquarium Viewing Panel. It is fascinating to learn about what goes on behind the scenes at the aquarium – the logistics are mind-blowing. If that's not enough, you can dive and swim with the fish – if the thought of being in a giant fishbowl with the entire mall watching you doesn't put you off. A glass-bottom boat ride, which lasts about 15 minutes, will set you back an extra AED 25, the cage-snorkelling experience costs AED 225 and the shark dive, depending on whether you are already a licensed diver or need training, costs between AED 625 and AED 1,025. To find out more about these activities, call ☎ 04-342-2993. We think this is one of Dubai's best-value themed attractions.

Dubai Creek Park ★ ★ ★

APPEAL BY AGE	PRESCHOOL ★ ★ ★	PRIMARY SCHOOL ★ ★ ★ ★	TEENS ★ ★ ★
YOUNG ADULTS ★ ★		OVER 30 ★ ★ ★ ★	SENIORS ★ ★ ★ ★

located between Al Maktoum and Al Garhoud bridges in the heart of Bur Dubai; ☎ 04-336-7633

Type of attraction A park with a myriad of activities for all ages **Admission** AED 5 per person **Hours** Sunday–Wednesday, 8 a.m.–11 p.m.; Thursday–Saturday, 8 a.m.–11:30 p.m. **How much time to allow** 2–4 hours **Special comments** Masses to do here. **Author's rating** ★ ★ ★. An excellent park in which to while away the time; probably too much to do in one day. Decide whether to do the outside activities or inside ones, not both, unless you plan to spend a day there.

DESCRIPTION AND COMMENTS A beautiful park set in 96 hectares (237.2 acres) of lawns features 280 types of plants, a desert garden with a traditional irrigation system and lots of beautiful flower gardens. Set on Dubai Creek, it's the second-largest park in Dubai after Mushrif Park and has wonderful views. With designated barbecue areas, shady picnic spots and a variety of restaurants and cafes, this park is an excellent place in which to spend a few hours. There are playgrounds, a miniature train and a cable car (see page 176), if you fancy having an aerial view of the Creek. The park has an amphitheatre, and you can fish from a designated pier. You can take *abra* rides and dhow cruises from the park, creekside, and there is a small 18-hole mini-golf course. There is also a jogging track. If it all gets too hot to be outside, the park has an excellent Dolphinarium (see page 182) with live shows daily and a terrific children's science (sort of) museum – Children's City (see page 178).

If you're hankering after some green space, Dubai Creek Park is well worth a visit. Situated in the heart of the city but blessed with acres of gardens, this is the ultimate in park life. From Gate 2, four-wheel cycles can be hired (you can't use your own bike in the park). In-line skating is allowed, if you by any chance thought to pack your skates.

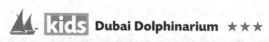 **Dubai Dolphinarium** ★★★

APPEAL BY AGE	PRESCHOOL ★★★	PRIMARY SCHOOL ★★★★★	TEENS ★★★★
YOUNG ADULTS ★★★		OVER 30 ★★	SENIORS ★★

Dubai Creek Park, Entrance 1, Bur Dubai;
☎ **04-336-9773; dubaidolphinarium.ae**

Type of attraction Dolphin and seal show **Admission** VIP seating: AED 120 for adults and AED 80 for children; circus: AED 140 for adults and AED 100 for children. Standard seating: AED 100 for adults and AED 50 for children; circus: AED 120 for adults and AED 70 for children. **Hours** Showtimes: Monday–Thursday, 11 a.m. and 6 p.m.; Friday–Saturday, 11 a.m., 3 p.m. and 6 p.m. Swimming with dolphins: Monday–Thursday, 1 p.m., 2 p.m., 3 p.m. and 4 p.m. **How much time to allow** 2 hours **Special comments** For limited periods throughout the year, other shows – such as the Dolphin Spectacular Chinese Circus – take place at the Dolphinarium. Ring to find out. **Author's rating** ★★★. An easy, entertaining way to spend a couple of hours if you like performing dolphins and seals.

DESCRIPTION AND COMMENTS Three Black Sea bottlenose dolphins perform displays and sequences and impress with their skill and obedience, whilst four fur seals perform on land. This is a sizeable dolphinarium, and the shows are great fun. After the show you can have your photo taken with the dolphins, with prices ranging AED 80–120 depending on how you pose with the dolphins. There is also an opportunity to swim for 20 minutes with the dolphins, which is a wonderful experience. Prices range from AED 400 for up to six people to AED 1,600 for up to three people.

Dubai Drums ★★★

APPEAL BY AGE	PRESCHOOL ★★	PRIMARY SCHOOL ★★★★	TEENS ★★★★
YOUNG ADULTS ★★★★		OVER 30 ★★★	SENIORS ★★

Gulf Ventures Desert Camp – see Web site for map and details;
☎ **050-659-2874; dubaidrums.com**

Type of attraction Full-moon desert drumming **Admission** AED 190 (alcohol extra) for adults, AED 85 for children ages 5–14, and free for children under age 5. **Hours** Dependent on the weather, so September and October and then each full moon, 6:30 p.m.–midnight. **How much time to allow** 5–6 hours **Special comments** This takes place at full moon, outside in the desert, when the weather's not too hot. Check the Web site for details. You can leave after dinner if you can't manage the whole six hours. **Author's rating** ★★★. A very unusual but cool way to spend an evening in the desert. Very magical to play the drums under the stars.

DESCRIPTION AND COMMENTS Full-moon desert drumming is an activity organised by Dubai Drums. You head out to the desert camp and will find African drumming experts, lots and lots of drums, a barbecue, dancing music and plenty of good company. It's an event that is surreal but lovely and suits all ages. You will be taught how to drum and will have lots of opportunity to do so, and when you're not drumming, you'll be having a barbecue and a few drinks, making new friends, relaxing or dancing as you desire. Remember to take some warm clothes, as it gets chilly in the desert at night in the winter.

kids Dubai Kartdrome and Laserdrome ★ ★ ★

APPEAL BY AGE	PRESCHOOL —	PRIMARY SCHOOL ★★★	TEENS ★★★★★
YOUNG ADULTS ★★★★★		OVER 30 ★★★★	SENIORS ★

Dubai Autodrome, Motorcity, south of Al Barsha;
☎ **04-367-8744; motorcity.ae**

Kartdrome

Type of attraction Karting **Admission** AED 100 per 15-minute session **Hours** Vary seasonally; call telephone number listed above for daily availability of Arrive & Drive sessions; usually opens between 2 and 4 p.m. and closes 8:30–midnight. **How much time to allow** 1 hour + **Special comments** Ages 7–12 use the indoor track; age 13 and above use the outdoor track. Always phone first to find out timings and availability. **Author's rating** ★★★. Great fun if there are a few of you to race against. In summer check if you can use the indoor track, as it will be unbearable outdoors once you are bundled up in your balaclavas and overalls!

DESCRIPTION AND COMMENTS   Dubai Kartdrome is based at Motorcity and has both an indoor and outdoor karting track for anyone over the age of 7 who wishes to come and race karts. There are special Arrive & Drive karts and karting sessions for children ages 7–12 every day in the Indoor Kartdrome. Check timings by phone for the daily schedule, as corporate parties sometimes take over the facility. You need to wear closed sports shoes or trainers but will be loaned helmets, balaclavas, gloves and kart suits, all of which are included in the price. You will be given a briefing when you arrive so that you know how to drive the karts safely and will then have a 15-minute session on the track. You can book as many sessions as you like, as long as there is space. Fully-trained staff monitor the children's safety and offer advice as necessary. The karts are very easy to get to grips with; the problem will be stopping the dads trying to take over.

Laserdrome

Type of attraction Laser tag (like paintball without the paint) **Admission** AED 90 per 15-minute game **Hours** 1 hour + **Special comments** For a good adrenaline-fuelled day out, try the Kart and Shoot combo. Phone first to check availability. **Author's rating** ★★★. Seems a bit daft to go to Dubai and do laser tag, but if you must, you must. And if you've got to wait your turn for the Kartdrome track, then you might as well add a laser battle into the mix.

DESCRIPTION AND COMMENTS A unique feature of the Indoor Kartdrome Complex is the Laserdrome game area. Players are sorted into two teams (maximum ten players), and they battle against each other with laser guns. The battles are set in a mediaeval castle–type environment, featuring a huge Day-Glo dungeon-style decoration with lighting and artificial fog aimed at disorienting you and obscuring your vision, making it harder to tag your opponents. Add a pumping soundtrack, and it's like a life-size scene from the latest X-Box or PlayStation game. Might be just the antidote to beautiful golden beaches and tranquil turquoise seas.

 Dubai Museum ★★★★★

APPEAL BY AGE	PRESCHOOL –	PRIMARY SCHOOL ★★	TEENS ★★
YOUNG ADULTS ★★★	OVER 30 ★★★★		SENIORS ★★★★

near Bastakiya and Dubai Creek, Bur Dubai;
☎ **04-353-1862; dubaitourism.ae**

Type of attraction Museum focusing on the history of Dubai Admission AED 3 for adults and AED 1 for children Hours Saturday–Thursday, 8:30 a.m.–8:30 p.m.; Friday, 2:30–8:30 p.m. Check the timings at Ramadan. How much time to allow 1–2 hours Special comments It can get crowded if busloads of tourists are dropped off. Not wheelchair-friendly. Author's rating ★★★★★. This is a really interesting museum – be aware that the main part of it is underground. We've seen people leave after the first section, not realising that it continues!

DESCRIPTION AND COMMENTS Located in the beautifully-restored Al Fahidi Fort, this museum gives a fascinating insight into Dubai's history, its development and traditional Emirati life. It is always surprising and lovely to find old parts of Dubai and to realise that it does indeed have a rich history. Al Fahidi Fort was built in 1787 and once guarded the landward approaches to the town. Outside the fort you can see the traditional city walls and an enormous wooden dhow. You enter an open courtyard, which has a display of miniature dhows. Rooms off the courtyard display weapons and musical instruments, and a film shows traditional dancing. Enter the turret in the corner and go downstairs – underground – to enter the main museum. In the first hall watch the fascinating film with three-dimensional displays showing the history of Dubai, its development and growth so far and future projects. It helps you understand why the Emiratis are justifiably proud of what they've achieved when you realise that until relatively recently, Dubai was a fishing village surrounded by desert. Hands-on exhibits and life-size dioramas lead you gently through the lives and times of the city and its people from the third century BC to the present day. There are re-creations of a souk and typical homes, as well as tableaux that bring to life the occupations, costumes and social customs of the day. Background soundtracks provide atmosphere, and children as well as adults will enjoy walking around and through the exhibits.

The Empty Quarter ★ ★ ★ ★

APPEAL BY AGE	PRESCHOOL –	PRIMARY SCHOOL ★	TEENS ★★
YOUNG ADULTS ★★	OVER 30 ★★★★		SENIORS ★★★★

Building 2, Gate Village, DIFC; ☎ 04-323-1210; theemptyquarter.com

Type of attraction Photography gallery **Admission** Free **Hours** Saturday–Thursday, 9 a.m.–10 p.m.; Friday, 3–10 p.m. **How much time to allow** 1 hour **Special comments** An excellent gallery for photographers and photography enthusiasts alike. **Author's rating** ★★★★. Interesting exhibitions that focus on transcending cultures and political issues. The quality of the photography on show is consistently excellent.

DESCRIPTION AND COMMENTS   The Empty Quarter is the only gallery in Dubai devoted exclusively to fine art photography, and it serves a rapidly-growing membership of artists and photography enthusiasts. The gallery aims to expand the understanding and appreciation of photography as an artistic medium and showcases the works of young emerging and established photographers. Photography exhibited is from all continents and various points of views: documentary, fine art, photojournalism, poetic, personal, abstract, human and street photography. An excellent range of rare and special-edition books is available to buy.

kids Encounter Zone ★ ★ ★

APPEAL BY AGE	PRESCHOOL –	PRIMARY SCHOOL ★★★	TEENS ★★★★★
YOUNG ADULTS ★★	OVER 30 ★★		SENIORS ★

Wafi City Mall; ☎ 04-324-7747

Type of attraction Indoor amusement park **Admission** Choose a zone, then pay AED 35 for two hours and AED 25 for every two hours after; some attractions are an additional AED 2. **Hours** Saturday–Tuesday, 10 a.m.–11 p.m.; Wednesday–Thursday, 10 a.m.–midnight; closed Fridays. **Special comments** A state-of-the-art entertainment centre **Author's rating** ★★★. If you're at Wafi and have a spare hour to kill with bored children, you could do worse than visit the Encounter Zone.

DESCRIPTION AND COMMENTS   A family entertainment zone, the Encounter Zone is divided into two separate areas – Galactica and Lunarland. In Galactica teenagers amuse themselves with the famous Crystal Maze, the three-dimensional cinema, an indoor in-line skating area and a 'live' horror show. In Lunarland, younger children will enjoy a soft play area, flying spaceships, an arts and crafts corner and a children's toyshop called Imaginarium with a collection of traditional toys. There is also a roller coaster simulator, which feels remarkably like the real thing, and numerous arcade games.

The Farjam Collection ★★★★

| APPEAL BY AGE | PRESCHOOL – | PRIMARY SCHOOL ★★★ | TEENS ★★ |
| YOUNG ADULTS ★★ | | OVER 30 ★★★★ | SENIORS ★★★★ |

Building 4, Gate Village, DIFC; ☎ 04-323-0303; farjamcollection.org

Type of attraction A privately-owned art collection spanning vast historical and geographical spectra **Admission** Free **Hours** Sunday–Thursday, 10 a.m.– 8 p.m.; Saturday, midday–8 p.m. **How much time to allow** 30 minutes + **Special comments** An impressive collection that includes treasures from ancient Islamic art as well as works by modern Western masters and contemporary Iranian and Arab artists. **Author's rating ★★★★**. Differentiates itself from other galleries as its foremost ambition is art education.

DESCRIPTION AND COMMENTS   The Farjam Collection is an extremely prestigious privately-owned art collection and includes artworks by masters such as Pablo Picasso, Georges Braque, Henri Matisse and Alberto Giacometti, as well as a selection of works by Farhad Moshiri, Mohammad Ehsai, Mostafa El-Razzaz and Ali Omar Ermes, and treasures from ancient Islamic art. Selected works from this distinguished collection are on view to the public through a series of curated exhibitions. A programme of educational events is offered free of charge to the public and includes First Wednesdays – guided lunchtime visits by exhibiting artists – and the monthly Art Nights, in conjunction with the DIFC, when the gallery stays open later than usual and visitors can enjoy the exhibition in a relaxed evening session. Art camps for children are run during the summer holidays.

Gallery Isabelle Van Den Eynde
(formerly B21 Gallery) ★★★★

| APPEAL BY AGE | PRESCHOOL – | PRIMARY SCHOOL ★ | TEENS ★ |
| YOUNG ADULTS ★★ | | OVER 30 ★★★★ | SENIORS ★★★★ |

Al Serkal Avenue, Street 8, Al Quoz 1 (opposite Ayyam Gallery); ☎ 04-323-5052; ivde.net

Type of attraction Middle Eastern art gallery **Admission** Free **Hours** Saturday– Thursday, 10 a.m.–7 p.m. **How much time to allow** 30 minutes + **Special comments** An interesting, elegant space, dedicated to representing a group of artists emerging from the contemporary Arab and Iranian art scenes. **Author's rating ★★★★**. Gallery IVDE showcases artists who practise in all media and who push the boundaries in terms of the conventional understanding of art currently coming out of the Middle East. Some interesting conceptual art is exhibited here.

DESCRIPTION AND COMMENTS   Gallery Isabelle Van Den Eynde, formerly the B21 Gallery, has discovered and nurtured the talent of some of the most promising figures in the Middle East's contemporary art scene. A generation of artists has emerged from the gallery's focused tutelage, attracting the attention of adventurous collectors and curators, as well as prestigious institutions from the region and beyond. These selected rising talents are leading the way in an exciting young art movement and manifest their ideas powerfully in their works.

Grand Mosque Dubai ★ ★ ★

APPEAL BY AGE	PRESCHOOL –	PRIMARY SCHOOL ★	TEENS ★
YOUNG ADULTS ★★	OVER 30 ★★★★		SENIORS ★★★★

near the Ruler's Court, Bur Dubai

Type of attraction Mosque **Admission** Non-Muslims are not permitted to enter the Grand Mosque, but they can visit the minaret and take photos of the mosque from there. **Hours** Any day except Friday or at prayer time. **How much time to allow** As long as it takes you to appreciate it. **Special comments** Dress conservatively; you are in an older neighbourhood visiting a religious site. **Author's rating** ★★★. Whilst you cannot enter the mosque, it is worth seeing, particularly at sunset, as it is so beautiful. Additionally, you are in a particularly interesting neighbourhood, and the Heritage and Diving Villages are adjacent – well worth a visit, especially in the evening.

DESCRIPTION AND COMMENTS The Grand Mosque is counted as one of the largest mosques in the U.A.E., with the capacity to accommodate up to 1,200 worshippers. It was constructed in the traditional Islamic architectural style and opened in 1900 as a *kuttab* (Qur'anic school), where children learnt to recite the Qur'an from memory. The Grand Mosque was rebuilt in 1998, maintaining its original style, and now boasts a 70-metre-high (229-foot-high) minaret – the tallest in Dubai. It has 45 small domes in addition to 9 large ones, with handmade stained-glass panels. Its sand-coloured walls and wooden shutters blend perfectly with the surrounding older neighbourhood of Bur Dubai. It is Dubai's main centre for worship.

Hatta Heritage Village ★ ★ ★ ★ ★

APPEAL BY AGE	PRESCHOOL –	PRIMARY SCHOOL ★	TEENS ★
YOUNG ADULTS ★★	OVER 30 ★★★★		SENIORS ★★★★

in the Hajar Mountains, Hatta; ☎ 04-852-1374; dubaitourism.ae

Type of attraction Old restored village **Admission** Free **Hours** Saturday–Thursday, 8 a.m.–8 p.m.; Friday, 2–8 p.m. Ramadan: Saturday–Thursday, 9 a.m.–5 p.m.; Friday, 2–5 p.m. **How much time to allow** 1 hour + **Special comments** Go in winter – it is outside and will be very hot in summer. **Author's rating** ★★★★★. Fascinating to be able to wander around an old restored village and imagine life as it was 400 years ago. A perfect example of villages of the past, with stunning architecture in a beautiful setting. Make a day of visiting Hatta, and coincide this visit with a trip to the Hatta pools.

DESCRIPTION AND COMMENTS Hatta Heritage Village dates back to the 16th century and provides a perfect example of traditional-style village architecture. It is constructed of stone, mud, reeds and *barasti* (palm leaves and tree trunks). Two watchtowers, a mosque and houses comprising 30 buildings in total surround the impressive Hatta Fort, which dominates the village. As you wander around the site, through the open buildings and in and out of the narrow alleyways, it is easy to see how the village was able to protect itself from hostile invaders from the vantage point of the two towers overlooking the village. Hatta's history goes back more than 3,000 years, and the area includes a 200-year-old mosque and the fortress built by Sheikh Maktoum bin Hasher Al Maktoum in 1896, now used as a weaponry museum.

Heritage and Diving Villages ★ ★ ★ ★

APPEAL BY AGE	PRESCHOOL ★	PRIMARY SCHOOL ★★★★	TEENS ★★★★
YOUNG ADULTS ★★★★		OVER 30 ★★★★	SENIORS ★★★★

Al Shindagha area, next to the Sheikh Saeed Al Maktoum House, Dubai Creek; ☎ 04-393-7139; dubaitourism.ae

Type of attraction A really interesting working village/museum with demonstrations, food tasting, camel rides, restaurants and so on **Admission** Free **Hours** Saturday–Thursday, 8:30 a.m.–10 p.m.; Friday, 3:30–10 p.m. Ramadan: Saturday–Thursday, 9 a.m.–2 p.m. and 8:30 p.m.–midnight; Friday, 8:30 p.m.– midnight **How much time to allow** 2 hours + **Special comments** Particularly fun to visit in the evening, and best to visit in the cooler winter months. Check out the Web site for special events and performances. **Author's rating ★★★★**. Children will enjoy this as much as adults.

DESCRIPTION AND COMMENTS   The Heritage and Diving Villages give excellent insight into Dubai's Bedouin traditions and maritime past. A world away from the glitzy face of new Dubai, this is a chance to discover Dubai's history – the importance of pearl diving, its architecture, its crafts and its food – in an interesting and informal way. This 'living' museum is staffed by real tradespeople who display their crafts and skills as they have been practised for hundreds of years. You can ride on camels, watch falcon displays and horse shows and enjoy occasional performances by local musicians and dancers. The village is particularly lively during the Dubai Shopping Festival and national holidays such as Eid. You will see more than 30 traditional handicrafts, such as pottery, weaving and baking. Next door in the Diving Village you can find out about Dubai's maritime history and learn about its pearl-diving culture. There are models of dhows and pearling boats, demonstrations of boat-building and a small aquarium. Buy souvenirs in the small shops in the village and contribute to the livelihood of the villagers here. Local Arabic women serve up traditionally-cooked bread and Arabic coffee.

This area is actually a very accurate portrayal of what life was like when pearl trading and smuggling were the tiny emirate's main revenues. The best time to go is at night, when it comes alive, especially during the winter months and the Dubai Shopping Festival. This is an ideal way to experience Arabian hospitality and customs.

 iFly Dubai ★ ★

APPEAL BY AGE	PRESCHOOL –	PRIMARY SCHOOL ★★★★★	TEENS ★★★★★
YOUNG ADULTS ★★★		OVER 30 ★★★	SENIORS ★

Mirdif City Centre Mall, Mirdif; ☎ 800-534-7873; www.iflyme.com

Type of attraction Indoor skydiving **Admission** Peak: AED 195 for adults and AED 145 for children. Off peak: AED 165 for adults and AED 125 for children. **Hours** Saturday–Wednesday, 10 a.m.–11 p.m.; Thursday–Friday, 10 a.m.–midnight **How much time to allow** 1 hour **Special comments** Not for people with back or shoulder problems, and we didn't much like having to sign a damage waiver. **Author's rating** ★★. A skydiving experience in a wind tunnel. Unusual and exciting. Very brief.

DESCRIPTION AND COMMENTS First the facts – iFly Dubai at Playnation is not a ride or a simulator. It is a vertical wind tunnel that moves air up in a vertical column, offering the best possible flight experience for indoor skydiving. It is safe for children, exciting for teens and challenging for adults. Skydivers train here as well. The airflow is controlled according to the ability of the people who are skydiving.

Flyers are taken into a training room where a skydive instructor shows you a safety video and explains the positions you need to adopt when skydiving. Chris, the instructor we had the day we were there, had the look of a man who'd been quite an adrenaline junkie in a former life, and was now wondering what he was doing training indulged expat children in the safety drill for skydiving in a wind tunnel. The training took 15 minutes. The group were then provided with padded jump-suits, helmets, shoes, socks and goggles. The children all waited in the outer chamber of the tube, whilst Chris battled his way against the wind into it and then took each child in separately for a couple of minutes, so that they could practise being horizontal on a pillow of air. They then went back in a second time and, like Lois Lane with Superman, were taken up the wind tunnel by Chris, who flew with them. They absolutely loved it. We thought that for the time they were in there, it was just a little bit of a swizz.

Jumeirah Archaeological Site ★ ★ ½

APPEAL BY AGE	PRESCHOOL –	PRIMARY SCHOOL –	TEENS ★
YOUNG ADULTS ★		OVER 30 ★★	SENIORS ★★

Street 16, first left after Al Atthar Street from Safa Park, Jumeirah; ☎ 04-349-6874; dubaitourism.ae

Type of attraction Archaeological site **Admission** Free, but you need a permit **Hours** Sunrise–sunset **How much time to allow** 30 minutes **Special comments** The archaeological site is not officially open, but you can enter and have a look. Obtain a free permit from the Dubai Museum. **Author's rating** ★★½. Unless you are a die-hard fan of archaeological ruins, you probably won't feel the urge to make a special journey to visit this site. However, if you are interested in the history of Dubai, coincide your archaeological trip with a visit to Majlis Ghorfat Um-Al Sheif in the same area, then visit Dubai Museum and the Heritage and Diving Villages in Shindagha, where tools, pottery and coins excavated from the site are on display.

DESCRIPTION AND COMMENTS Archaeological digs during the past 40 years have uncovered pre-Islamic foundations dating back to the sixth century. This was the site of a caravan station along an ancient trade route that linked Iraq to Oman. It is considered one of the most significant archaeological sites in the U.A.E., with sections of walling, a souk and houses, one of which is believed to have been the palace of an earlier ruler. In the heart of Jumeirah, surrounded by villas and streets, this site is enclosed by a metal-link chain fence. Don't let that put you off; simply obtain a permit from the Dubai Museum, and you can look around.

kids Jumeirah Beach Park ★★★★★

APPEAL BY AGE	PRESCHOOL ★★★★★		PRIMARY SCHOOL ★★★★★
TEENS ★★★★★	YOUNG ADULTS ★★★★★	OVER 30 ★★★★★	SENIORS ★★★★★

Jumeirah Road, Jumeirah; ☎ 04-349-2555 or 050-858-9887

Type of attraction Beach park **Admission** AED 5 per person; AED 20 per car **Hours** Daily, 7 a.m.–10:30 p.m. Monday: Ladies' day. **How much time to allow** 1 hour to a full day **Special comments** Beautiful beach park with the facilities of a hotel beach resort. Absolutely packed on Fridays. **Author's rating ★★★★★.** This is a stunning beach park – with excellent facilities that will definitely appeal to all ages.

DESCRIPTION AND COMMENTS Apart from the beautiful beach, pleasant shady gardens, barbecue area, showers, sunloungers for hire, changing rooms and cafes selling the normal junk food, there is also an excellent playground for younger children, which will keep them entertained for at least an hour. Despite the fact that on the weekend – Fridays in particular – it is really crowded, there is very little we don't like about this lovely park.

Jumeirah Mosque ★★★★★

APPEAL BY AGE	PRESCHOOL –		PRIMARY SCHOOL ★	TEENS ★★
YOUNG ADULTS ★★		OVER 30 ★★★★		SENIORS ★★★★

Jumeirah Road, Jumeirah; ☎ 04-353-6666; cultures.ae

Type of attraction Mosque **Admission** AED 10 per person; not suitable for children under the age of 5. **Hours** Saturday, Sunday, Tuesday and Thursday, 10 a.m. During Ramadan, an evening tour is scheduled. **How much time to allow** 2 hours **Special comments** Please make sure that you are suitably dressed to enter the mosque – women will be given an *abaya* and shawl to cover head, arms and legs, but should dress conservatively – trousers or a skirt to the knees.

Men should wear trousers. The tour takes 1¼ hours. Arrive five minutes early; you do not need to pre-book. You can take photos. **Author's rating ★★★★★**. A fascinating introduction to Islam and Arabic traditions and a great opportunity to learn about the Emirati culture and religion.

DESCRIPTION AND COMMENTS Jumeirah Mosque dominates the square at the top of Jumeirah Road. It is a beautiful piece of architecture and is the only mosque in Dubai that non-Muslims are permitted to enter. The Sheikh Mohammed Centre for Cultural Understanding (SMCCU; see page 200) organises visits to the mosque four mornings a week, and you may only enter the mosque with a guide. You don't need to book; just turn up Saturday, Sunday, Tuesday or Thursday at 10 a.m. outside the mosque by The One furniture shop, where the guides will meet you. You will be taken inside, and women will be loaned a traditional *abaya* for the dura- tion of their visit. The guides will help you cover your hair. Once inside, you will be asked to remove your shoes.

The SMCCU's motto is 'Open Doors, Open Minds', and the aim of the 1¼-hour tour is to enable non-Muslims to find out as much as they can about Islam, Emirati culture and religious practices. No question is taboo, and their aim is for you to have fun. Their style is informa- tive and informal, and they are extremely friendly and welcoming. You will have the opportunity to learn about the architecture of the mosque and the religious significance of key design features. Male and female guides explain the origins of the religion and its central tenets – the five pillars of Islam. You will learn that the Arabic word for mosque is *masjid*, or 'place for prostration', and the holy day of the Islamic week is Friday. The call to prayer was traditionally made five times a day by the muezzin from the top of the minaret, but it is now heard with the help of high-powered speakers.

The Jumeirah Mosque is considered to be the most beautiful mosque in Dubai and was built in the medieval Fatimid tradition, using modern building materials. Completed in 1983, the white stone structure has towering twin minarets that frame a large central dome. Its seashell-like finish and colouring fit perfectly with the mosque's position opposite the white sands of Jumeirah Beach. It is particularly worth seeing at night when illuminated and each intricate detail of its artistry is enhanced.

Remember to dress conservatively. After your tour, we recommend eating at the Lime Tree Café, a couple of minutes' walk away. You won't be disappointed.

kids KidZania ★★★★★

APPEAL BY AGE	PRESCHOOL ★★★★★	PRIMARY SCHOOL ★★★★★	TEENS ★★★
YOUNG ADULTS –	OVER 30 –		SENIORS –

Level 2, Dubai Mall, Downtown Dubai; ☎ 04-448-5222; kidzania.ae

Type of attraction Interactive 'edu-tainment' centre, scaled-down city/world for children **Admission** AED 125 for children ages 4–15, AED 95 for children ages 2–3, free for children under age 2 and AED 90 for accompanying adults. **Hours** Sunday–Wednesday, 9 a.m.–10 p.m.; Thursday, 9 a.m.–midnight; Friday–Saturday, 10 a.m.–midnight **How much time to allow** At least 3 hours **Special comments** Best for ages 3–13; adults can only enter accompanied by a child. If the child is less than 120 centimetres (about 47 inches), then he/she must be accompanied by an adult. **Author's rating** ★★★★★. Outstanding concept – a city scaled down to children's size. Here, children can remain entertained for four hours without a peep.

DESCRIPTION AND COMMENTS   Think of the film *The Truman Show*, where Jim Carrey's world was, unknown to him, inside a massive studio, and that is a little bit what KidZania is like. It is a nation for children – a fully-constructed city where a child can become a surgeon, a police officer, a firefighter, a racing car driver, a fashion model, a chef, a journalist, a pilot and a whole lot more – all in the course of a day. There is a choice of 70 professions. The official currency of KidZania is kidZos. On arrival at the entrance to KidZania, you'll find the staff dressed as aircrew, and the ticket you buy is an air ticket. The children are given a wallet with a cheque in it, and after 'landing' in KidZania, they go immediately to the bank to cash their cheque. They are then free to spend their money at whichever outlets they like – outlets such as Waitrose, McDonald's and Emirates Airport, as well as more generic ones. At each outlet they are given the relevant job training, and as they are paid for their services, they then have more money to spend. Security is outstanding here. All children have an electronic bracelet, and if you accompany your child, you also have one. When you leave, it is recorded on your bracelet which children accompanied you, so you can't leave with anyone else's children. If you choose to leave your children inside unaccompanied, you are allocated a number, which is recorded on the children's bracelets. Again when you pick them up, only the children with your number on their bracelet can go with you. All activities are coordinated by Zoopervisors, who are specially trained and extremely patient. And if you find that four hours in a children's world might conceivably be a little trying, there is an excellent Parent's Lounge, with cafe, computers, Internet connection, TV room and comfy sofas on which to relax. Whilst KidZania will predominantly appeal to 6-year-olds and up, there is also an excellent supervised five-room play area for little ones. This theme park really captures the imagination.

kids The Lost Chambers ★ ★

APPEAL BY AGE	PRESCHOOL ★★★★		PRIMARY SCHOOL ★★★★	TEENS ★★★
YOUNG ADULTS ★★		OVER 30 ★★★		SENIORS ★★

Atlantis, The Palm, Palm Jumeirah; ☎ 04-426-0000; atlantisthepalm.com

Type of attraction Themed aquarium **Admission** AED 100 for adults and AED 70 for children **Hours** Daily, 10 a.m.–11 p.m. **How much time to allow** 1 hour

Special comments Only the very young or very credulous will get a lot out of this 21-exhibit aquarium. **Author's rating ★★**.

DESCRIPTION AND COMMENTS Guests at Atlantis get free entry to this mini 'underwater' theme park, and in all honesty we wouldn't recommend paying to get in otherwise. It is actually pretty well done – the Atlantian-themed underwater city is cavelike and has fountains that spew steam, Atlantian warriors guarding the tanks and fake lichen-covered walls – but it barely takes 30 minutes to trot around. Having said that, there is a great view into the Ambassador Lagoon, and it is interesting at feeding times (10 a.m., 2 p.m. and 4 p.m.). Some very cute touches include a small sea horse tank, a lobster 'tunnel' where you can watch them crawling above your head and also a touch pool where kids can get their hands on very ugly horseshoe crabs.

kids Luna Park, the Fruit Garden ★★

APPEAL BY AGE	PRESCHOOL ★★★★	PRIMARY SCHOOL ★★★★	TEENS –
YOUNG ADULTS	–	OVER 30 –	SENIORS –

Al Nasr Leisureland, Oud Metha; ☎ 04-337-1234; alnasrleisureland.ae

Type of attraction Funfair/theme park **Admission** AED 10 for adults and children age 5 and up; AED 5 for children under the age of 5 **Hours** Daily, 9 a.m.–midnight **How much time to allow** 45 minutes **Special comments** Best for ages 3–10. Another themed park, with a fruity theme. **Author's rating ★★**. Perfectly pleasant if you have the time.

DESCRIPTION AND COMMENTS This sweet little park with fairground-type rides will appeal to younger children. However, there are so many other places to visit that are more interesting and more fun that it would really only be worth visiting this park if you were in the area with an hour to spare.

kids Magic Planet ★★

APPEAL BY AGE	PRESCHOOL ★★★	PRIMARY SCHOOL ★★★	TEENS ★★★
YOUNG ADULTS	★	OVER 30 –	SENIORS –

Mall of the Emirates, Al Barsha; ☎ 04-341-4000. Deira City Centre Mall, Deira; ☎ 04-295-4333. Mirdif City Centre Mall, Mirdif; ☎ 04-231-6311; magicplanet.ae

Type of attraction Indoor theme park **Admission** AED 1 for four tickets, redeemable for rides **Hours** Daily, 10 a.m.–midnight **How much time to allow** 1–2 hours **Special comments** Best for ages 3–5 and 10–13. **Author's rating ★★**. If your children like very noisy arcade-style theme parks, then this will appeal to them no end and will keep them amused for an hour or so.

DESCRIPTION AND COMMENTS Magic Planet can be found in Mall of the Emirates and Deira City Centre Mall, and now in a very zingy modern format in Mirdif City Centre Mall. If we were to choose just one to visit, it would be Mirdif's, hands-down. The other two seem to follow the format of the frenetic amusement arcades you might find in any suburban town, whilst the very new one at Mirdif is calmer, with much better attractions. Traditionally in the other two you will find ten-pin bowling, bumper cars, billiards tables, many amusement arcades, carousels and fairground-type rides. The Mirdif branch has a climbing wall and a sky ride – where you are strapped into a harness and make your way around a circuit at roof level. Scary, but exhilarating. There's also Kids Planet (where you pay an hourly rate), which is a soft play centre for younger children; a bowling alley; dance mats; computer games; and a pool table. Mirdif's Magic Planet seemed lighter, more spacious and cleaner than the other two, and is part of Playnation, an outstanding new theme park at Mirdif City Centre Mall.

Majlis Gallery ★ ★ ★ ★

APPEAL BY AGE	PRESCHOOL –	PRIMARY SCHOOL ★★	TEENS ★★
YOUNG ADULTS ★★	OVER 30 ★★★★★		SENIORS ★★★★★

Al Musalla Roundabout, Bastakiya, Bur Dubai;
☎ **04-353-6233; themajlisgallery.com**

Type of attraction A gallery of traveller-artists **Admission** Free **Hours** Saturday–Thursday, 9:30 a.m.–8 p.m. **How much time to allow** 30 minutes + **Special comments** A fine restored *Majlis* and courtyard, showcasing more-traditional, less-conceptual work, normally by traveller-artists who either live here or are staying here temporarily. **Author's rating** ★★★★. An extremely relaxed gallery with very appealing, very affordable work on show and for sale. Artists use the gallery as a base for their travels, and their work is inspired by the Middle East.

DESCRIPTION AND COMMENTS The Majlis Gallery, a haven for artists and art lovers, was established over time by Alison Collins, who came to Dubai in 1976 to work as an interior designer, found the house that is now the Majlis Gallery and moved her family into it for ten years, whilst also hosting many informal soirées there, introducing artists both professional and amateur to a somewhat culturally-bereft community. In 1989, after moving out, she turned the house into a full-time gallery space. The traveller-painters remain a defining part of what the Majlis represents, but it also exhibits and sells sculptures, artefacts, trinkets and shabby-chic wooden furniture, made in India out of limed mango wood. Not to be missed – ARTSHACK, a separate space within walking distance of the gallery, where they have a huge selection of art, furniture and artefacts at unbelievably low prices. Be sure to ask about it when you visit.

Majlis Ghorfat Um-Al Sheif ★ ★ ★

APPEAL BY AGE	PRESCHOOL –	PRIMARY SCHOOL ★	TEENS ★
YOUNG ADULTS ★	OVER 30 ★★★		SENIORS ★★★

17 Street, off Jumeirah Beach Road, Jumeirah 3;
☎ **04-394-6343; dubaitourism.ae**

Type of attraction A former sheikh's summer residence and gardens **Admission** AED 1 for adults and free for children **Hours** Saturday–Thursday, 8:30 a.m.– 1:30 p.m. and 3:30–8:30 p.m.; Friday, 3:30–8:30 p.m. **How much time to allow** 30 minutes + **Special comments** A fine example of how the moneyed classes in Dubai used to live. **Author's rating** ★★★. It's surprising to find this fine old house amongst the modern villas now surrounding it. The gardens are particularly interesting, with a reproduction of a traditional Arabic irrigation system.

DESCRIPTION AND COMMENTS Constructed in 1955, Majlis Ghorfat, a two-storey house, was the summer residence of Sheikh Rashid bin Saeed Al Maktoum. It is well restored and shows how effective the wind tower was in keeping a house cool in summer, without modern air conditioning. Local people who came to air their grievances and discuss their ideas with the sheikh would attend the *Majlis* in the evenings. Traditional building materials were used in the construction of the *Majlis*: gypsum and coral rock, with palm fronds on the roof. The ground floor is an open veranda, whilst upstairs, the *Majlis* is decorated with rugs, low seating, cushions, lanterns, rifles and a traditional coffee set laid out on a low table, as it may have been in Sheikh Rashid's day. The roof terrace was used for drying dates and for sleeping on. The wind tower, a traditional feature of most older houses, was designed to channel even the slightest breeze down the tower into the house to keep it cool during the hottest months. Before the construction of the modern villas, Sheikh Rashid had a beautiful view of the sea from the upper floors. It is interesting to wander around the gardens and see how they would have been irrigated.

Mojo Gallery ★★★

APPEAL BY AGE	PRESCHOOL –	PRIMARY SCHOOL ★	TEENS ★★
YOUNG ADULTS ★★	OVER 30 ★★★★		SENIORS ★★★★

Unit 33, Al Serkal Avenue, Street 8, Al Quoz 1;
☎ **04-347-7388; themojogallery.com**

Type of attraction A dynamic art gallery **Admission** Free **Hours** Sunday–Thursday, 10 a.m.–7 p.m. **How much time to allow** 30 minutes + **Special comments** Focuses on design-based work and conceptual art. **Author's rating** ★★★. It not only showcases the work of established artists but also works closely with local universities, exhibits advanced design students' works and promotes emerging artistic talent from the U.A.E.

DESCRIPTION AND COMMENTS Mojo Gallery is a multifunctional art space that brings together art, design and new media. Exhibitions explore contemporary themes and concepts in fine art and design expressed through different media and formats. The gallery exhibits original paintings, conceptual photography, digital media, works on paper, mixed-media prints, sculpture, illustrations and video art and installations. It also holds workshops designed and led by exhibiting artists and artists associated with the gallery.

Mushrif Park ★ ★ ★ ★ ★

APPEAL BY AGE	PRESCHOOL ★★★★	PRIMARY SCHOOL ★★★★★	TEENS ★★★
YOUNG ADULTS ★★	OVER 30 ★★★★		SENIORS ★★★★

Airport Road, just behind Mirdif; ☎ 04-288-3624

Type of attraction Park **Admission** AED 2 per person; AED 10 per car. Swimming: AED 10 for adults and AED 5 for children. **Hours** Daily, 8 a.m.– 11 p.m. **How much time to allow** 2–4 hours **Special comments** A bit off the beaten track but well worth a visit. **Author's rating** ★★★★★. This is a lovely park, especially as it doesn't feel too landscaped and has lots of unmanicured areas.

DESCRIPTION AND COMMENTS Beyond Mirdif, set in a natural *ghaf* forest, is Dubai's largest and oldest park. It is 500 hectares (about 1,235.5 acres) and is made up of long, sandy plains tufted with grass. It has a substantially-long cycle track on which you can ride your bike, a small aviary, a wooden jungle gym, a fairground with merry-go-rounds, a swinging pirate ship, a miniature train, playgrounds, camel and pony rides and sports courts. The big draw for children, however, is World Village, which is made up of scaled-down houses reflecting architecture from around the world, including a Dutch windmill, a Tudor house, an Arabic house with a wind tower, a tepee and so on. There is plenty of space for children to have a good run around, and lots of natural shaded picnic areas with barbecue facilities where you can picnic. If you're feeling the heat, take a dip in one of the old-fashioned swimming pools.

1x1 Art Gallery ★ ★

APPEAL BY AGE	PRESCHOOL –	PRIMARY SCHOOL ★	TEENS ★
YOUNG ADULTS ★★	OVER 30 ★★★		SENIORS ★★★

Warehouse No 4, Al Quoz 1, PO Box 214723;
☎ 04-348-3873; 1x1artgallery.com

Type of attraction Indian art gallery **Admission** Free **Hours** Sunday–Thursday, 10 a.m.–6 p.m. **How much time to allow** 30 minutes + **Special comments** Specialises in promoting contemporary Indian art. **Author's rating** ★★. Interesting because it promotes Indian art in Dubai, but doesn't change its exhibition as frequently as other galleries in the area.

DESCRIPTION AND COMMENTS 1x1 Art Gallery, established in 2006, has always been at the forefront of the Indian art scene, exhibiting modern and contemporary Indian art. It has a steady calendar of cutting-edge exhibitions and has set new benchmarks for works in installation and new media. Malini Gulrajani, director of the gallery, has won plaudits both in India and internationally, and her extensive knowledge of the Indian art scene has led her to become a consultant for serious collectors.

Portfolio Gallery ★ ★ ★

APPEAL BY AGE	PRESCHOOL –	PRIMARY SCHOOL ★	TEENS ★★★★
YOUNG ADULTS ★★★★		OVER 30 ★★★★	SENIORS ★★★

Al Serkal Avenue, Street 8, Al Quoz 1;
☎ 04-323-2395; portfolio-uae.com

Type of attraction Dubai's first photography-only gallery **Admission** Free **Hours** Sunday–Thursday, 10 a.m.–6 p.m. **How much time to allow** 30 minutes + **Special comments** The gallery space includes a printing station for the city's photographers, a selection of photography books and a pool table! **Author's rating** ★★★. A fun, informal space, which prides itself on not being elitist. Interesting photography as well.

DESCRIPTION AND COMMENTS Portfolio Gallery is the initiative of French photographer Emmanuel Catteau, who has lived in the Middle East for nine years. His works capture the most unexpected images of cultural diversity, timeless sceneries, urban lifestyle and up-to-date photo reports. The gallery showcases his works, which are exceptionally interesting, and provides a space for other photographers whom he feels can bring a different and original view to photography.

Ras Al Khor Wildlife Sanctuary ★ ★ ★ ★

APPEAL BY AGE	PRESCHOOL ★★	PRIMARY SCHOOL ★★	TEENS ★★
YOUNG ADULTS ★★		OVER 30 ★★★★	SENIORS ★★★★

at the inland end of Dubai Creek on the Bur Dubai side; ☎ 04-338-2324

Type of attraction Outdoor habitat and wetland reserve **Admission** Free **Hours** Saturday–Thursday, 9 a.m.–4 p.m. (November–April is the best time for bird-watching) **How much time to allow** 2 hours + **Special comments** To visit the sanctuary you must apply to the Marine Environment and Sanctuaries Unit, Environment Department, for a visitors' entry permit (☎ 04-206-4240/4244/4260). The application form can also be downloaded from **wildlife. ae.** Processing of the permit will take at least two working days. **Author's rating** ★★★★. To see the pink flamingos is spectacular, and it feels as if you've discovered another world in the middle of the urban jungle.

DESCRIPTION AND COMMENTS Ras Al Khor, on Dubai Creek, is a wetland reserve featuring mangroves, lagoons, mudflats, sabkhas (coastal salt flats), reed beds and shrub lands. Spread across 6.2 square kilometres (2.4 square miles), it is one of the few urban protected areas in the region and is unusual because it is surrounded by frenetic urban sprawl. Thousands of different birds migrate here in the winter, and the site is home to a multitude of native plant species, as well as crustaceans, small mammals and various species of fish. The sanctuary is most renowned for its pink flamingos: up to 3,000 of the birds flock here during the winter, and to see them feels like a real privilege. You can spot the birds here from three hides, which have been designed as traditional wind towers and offer a panoramic view of the sanctuary. The hides are equipped with telescopes, binoculars and other gadgets to facilitate bird-viewing. Visitors can enter the hides with the required permits.

kids Safa Park ★ ★ ★ ★

APPEAL BY AGE	PRESCHOOL ★★★	PRIMARY SCHOOL ★★★★	TEENS ★★★
YOUNG ADULTS ★★		OVER 30 ★★★★	SENIORS ★★★★

Al Wasl Road, Al Safa; ☎ 04-349-2111

Type of attraction Park and playground **Admission** AED 3; free for children under age 3 **Hours** Saturday–Wednesday, 8 a.m.–11 p.m.; Thursday–Friday, 8 a.m.–11:30 p.m.; Tuesday: ladies and children only. **How much time to allow** 1–3 hours **Special comments** Lovely park with plenty to keep the offspring occupied for an hour or two. Gets very crowded on Fridays. **Author's rating** ★★★★. Strange as it may seem, ladies' and children's day is actually very pleasant; much less crowded, and with an easy, laid-back atmosphere, but little boys can only enter with their mums on those days. Best for ages 4–7 with energy to burn, and teenagers who want an excuse to wander off.

DESCRIPTION AND COMMENTS It comes as a surprise to find an enormous green and leafy park like this in the middle of one of Dubai's most built-up residential areas, with Sheikh Zayed Road bordering it on one side. Not only is it beautifully landscaped, but it also has something for all age groups. There are electronic games for teenagers in the Pavilion; a little fairground section with bumper cars, a merry-go-round and a Ferris wheel; a miniature train that takes you round the park; boats to hire on the lake; a trampoline; and an old-fashioned maze that is surprisingly difficult to find your way out of. There are acres of grassy lawn, picnic and barbecue areas, children's playgrounds, ducks to be fed – so take some old bread – and large four-wheel bikes to hire. This is a really lovely park for a family afternoon out.

This is one of Dubai's largest and most popular parks and is an unexpected 25.9 hectares (64 acres) of green oasis. It can take about two hours to walk around on foot and has a good 3-kilometre (1.9-mile) spongy running track. On weekends, particularly Fridays, this park is incredibly crowded, full of people with picnics, barbecues and guitars. On the first Saturday of every month it hosts a flea market with great bargains and lots of tat as well. There is a canal and waterfall, a hill with shady trees – great for picnicking – sports courts, football pitches and barbecue areas. When you're feeling peckish, there are snack booths and a restaurant with decent snack food. If you need to escape the male population, there is an enclosed, separate ladies-only park within the park. If it's nature you're after, there are wooded wildlife habitats where you can find more than 200 species of birds.

Al Saheel:
A Thousand and One Horse Tales ★★★

HoofbeatZ Pavilion at the Dubai Polo Equestrian Club, Arabian Ranches;
☎ **04-330-6266; alsaheel.com**

Type of attraction Theatre/horse show **Admission** AED 225 for adults and
AED 100 for children ages 2–12; free for children under age 2. Hospitality (priority
seats and a behind-the-scenes preshow): AED 325. **Hours** Open seasonally; check
Web site for details. Thursday–Friday, 7:30–9:30 p.m. **How much time to allow**
2 hours **Special comments** 44 horses, 30 riders, theatre and stunt riding. Arabian
horsemanship at its best. **Author's rating** ★★★. If you have children who are mad
about horses, this is an excellent show, combining the excitement of the circus with
the drama of the theatre. An unusual and entertaining evening out.

DESCRIPTION AND COMMENTS   A horse show with drama, music, lights and
excitement, this spectacle has 25 acts that include light shows, songs,
fabulous costumes and traditional dances. Al Saheel is the ancient Arab
tradition of storytelling. You will see Spanish dressage, stunt riding
and horse whispering, as well as the horses performing various tricks.
The HoofbeatZ stables house the widest variety of horse breeds in the
country, including Spanish Andalucian dressage horses, black Friesians
from Europe, American Morgans and quarter horses, pintos, miniature
horses and a whole herd of beautiful Arabians, some of which were
rescue horses that have been completely re-trained and rehabilitated
by the HoofbeatZ training team. A variety of live cooking stations and
drinks are available on a cash basis. The show takes place in the air-
conditioned big-top-tented HoofbeatZ Pavilion.

kids **SEGA Republic** ★

Level 2, Dubai Mall, Downtown Dubai; ☎ **04-448-8484; segarepublic.com**

Type of attraction Indoor theme park **Admission** Power Pass (a day pass for
all attractions): AED 140; Platinum Power Pass (day pass for all attractions plus
AED 200 credit for games): AED 220; Pay & Play Pass: buy a minimum charge of
AED 10 and top it up as you go. Attractions have individual prices, ranging between
AED 15 and AED 30. **Hours** Sunday–Wednesday, 10 a.m.–11 p.m.; Thursday–
Saturday, 10 a.m.–1 a.m. **How much time to allow** 1–2 hours **Special comments**
A state-of-the-art amusement arcade with fairground rides best for ages 9–13.
Author's rating ★. Useful for leaving bored teenagers for an hour or two whilst
you indulge in a spot of retail therapy, or take younger children to KidZania.

DESCRIPTION AND COMMENTS   Five zones of entertainment for all ages include
Speed Zone – with motion simulator games; Adventure Zone – with a

roller coaster and other adrenaline-pumping rides; Sports Zone – sports simulation games such as snowboarding and goal shooting; Cyberpop Zone – interactive gaming equipment, with battle zombies, combat jet flying and karaoke singing; and Redemption Zone – games with winnable merchandise. It's loud, it's frenetic and it's a bombardment of the senses. If you're young, what's not to love?

The Sheikh Mohammed Centre for Cultural Understanding (SMCCU) ★★★★★

| APPEAL BY AGE | PRESCHOOL ★ | PRIMARY SCHOOL ★★ | TEENS ★★ |
| YOUNG ADULTS ★★★ | OVER 30 ★★★★★ | | SENIORS ★★★★★ |

Bastakiya; ☎ 04-353-6666; cultures.ae

Type of attraction Organisation that hosts events and tours **Admission** Depends on the event/tour; see below, visit the Web site or call for details **Hours** Depends on the event/tour; see below, visit the Web site or call for details **How much time to allow** Depends on tour you are attending **Special comments** An excellent centre that organises a number of activities designed to increase understanding about life, religion, culture and traditions in Dubai. **Author's rating ★★★★★**. The staff here are incredibly knowledgeable about what to visit, see and do in Dubai – a sort of alternative tourist office. Local volunteers run a series of fascinating and entertaining programmes – walks, meals, tours and so on – and go out of their way to make you feel welcome, to encourage you to ask questions about anything and everything and to dispel the mystery that surrounds Islam and the Arab way of life.

DESCRIPTION AND COMMENTS Based in a traditional restored house in old Bastakiya, SMCCU aims to break down barriers between people of different nationalities and to raise awareness of the local culture, its traditions and customs and the official religion – Islam – among foreign residents and visitors to the U.A.E. The building is well worth visiting for the *Majlis*-style rooms around a large enclosed courtyard. SMCCU organises an excellent guided tour of Jumeirah Mosque (Saturday, Sunday, Tuesday and Thursday at 10 a.m.; see page 190); cultural breakfasts (Monday, 10 a.m.; AED 50 per person; book in advance); cultural lunches (Sunday, 1 p.m.; AED 60 per person; book in advance); guided walking tours of Bastakiya (phone to reserve a place); language classes; and cultural programmes. U.A.E. nationals act as volunteers for these activities and are enthusiastic to explain all aspects of Emirati life. During Ramadan, special *Iftar* dinners are organised. For information about all the events, call the centre or drop in. We can't overemphasise how charming staff are here. We particularly like the fact that they want you to ask questions and want to introduce you to the Arabic way of life.

Sheikh Saeed Al Maktoum House ★ ★ ★

APPEAL BY AGE	PRESCHOOL –	PRIMARY SCHOOL ★	TEENS ★★
YOUNG ADULTS ★★★	OVER 30 ★★★★		SENIORS ★★★★

Al Shindagha area, next to Heritage and Diving Villages, Dubai Creek, Bur Dubai; ☎ 04-393-7139; dubaitourism.ae

Type of attraction A former sheikh's palace rebuilt and turned into a museum **Admission** AED 2 for adults and AED 1 for children; free for children under age 6 **Hours** Saturday–Thursday, 8 a.m.–8 p.m.; Friday, 3–9:30 p.m. **How much time to allow** 30 minutes **Special comments** A beautiful example of what is considered a modest palace. **Author's rating** ★★★. Visit in the evening, when the house is illuminated and looks particularly beautiful.

DESCRIPTION AND COMMENTS Sheikh Saeed Al Maktoum, the architect of modern Dubai and ruler of Dubai 1912–1958, was the grandfather of the present ruler, Sheikh Mohammed bin Rashid Al Maktoum. The original house was built on Dubai Creek in 1896 by Sheikh Saeed's father with magnificent views of the Gulf so he could observe shipping activity from the balconies. However, the significant development along the shoreline in recent years has diminished these views.

It became the seat of the Al Maktoum family and local government, as well as Sheikh Saeed's official residence until his death in 1958. After his death, the house was abandoned and was finally demolished. The current palace was rebuilt adjacent to the original site.

This 30-room house consists of wind towers and rooms built around a central courtyard. There are two entrances into the building – along the Creek side and at the rear of the building, the latter more than likely reserved for family members. Traditional construction techniques were used – coral from the Gulf was treated with lime and plaster to form the walls, and the house was kept cool by four elegant wind towers. Sheikh Saeed's residence is a typical example of late-19th-century Arabian architecture: vaulted high-beamed ceilings, arched doorways, sculpted windows, carved teak doors and windows, wooden lattice screens and gypsum ventilating screens with floral and geometric designs set into the thick walls. On the ground floor you will find a large *Majlis*, living rooms, storerooms and kitchen, which open onto a central courtyard, protected from the hot desert winds by high boundary walls. The upper floor, with its numerous bedrooms and balconies, enjoyed spectacular views over the Creek.

Today the house is open to the public as a museum, and each room displays rare and beautiful photographs, coins, stamps, paintings, lithographs and documents that vividly portray the early development of Dubai.

kids Ski Dubai ★★★★

APPEAL BY AGE	PRESCHOOL ★★★	PRIMARY SCHOOL ★★★★★	TEENS ★★★★★
YOUNG ADULTS ★★★★★		OVER 30 ★★★★	SENIORS ★★

Mall of the Emirates, Al Barsha; ☎ 04-123-4567 or 800-534-7873; skidxb.com

Type of attraction Indoor snow park/ski slopes **Admission** Snow Park: AED 100 for adults and AED 90 for children; Ski Slope (two hours): AED 180 for adults and AED 150 for children. **Hours** Sunday–Wednesday, 10 a.m.–11 p.m.; Thursday, 10 a.m.–midnight; Friday, 9 a.m.–midnight; Saturday, 9 a.m.–11 p.m. **How much time to allow** 2 hours **Special comments** Wear warm clothes if you have them, because even though all ski clothing is given to you, it's still very cold in there, and gloves and hats aren't included with the kit. **Author's rating ★★★★.** Surreal as a ski resort in a shopping mall with real snow is, even by Dubai's standards, it is worth going to for the 'I've been there' kudos.

DESCRIPTION AND COMMENTS   When it's 40°C (104°F) outside, there is nothing more surreal than donning a snowsuit and playing in the snow in a shopping mall. And as for conserving energy, consider that as air conditioning cools the mall down, inside Ski Dubai, 22,500 square metres (equivalent to three football pitches, or 242,187.9 square feet) are covered with real snow all year round, and the temperature is maintained at -1°C to -2°C (or 30.2°F to 28.4°F). It is 85 metres high (approximately 25 storeys, or 278.9 feet) and 80 metres (262.5 feet) wide. And halfway up, Avalanche Cafe has overhead heaters on its terrace to keep you warm. This is a fantastic place to go for any snow enthusiast who has had enough of the heat.

  This indoor ski resort with real snow offers something for all age groups. Included in your Slope Pass are jackets and trousers for adults, all-in-one ski suits with hoods for children, disposable socks and helmets for children, as well as skis, ski boots and ski poles or snowboard and snowboard boots. Younger children will love the Snow Park, where they can play on toboggans and race down snowy hills, go on a bobsled ride, explore a snow cavern, make a snowman or play with snowballs. When they're feeling cold, you can sit in the little cafe, still in the snow, and enjoy a creamy hot chocolate. It really does feel as if you are in a ski resort. Older children will enjoy skiing or snowboarding; there are five different runs for varying abilities with ski lifts. This is a really entertaining way to spend a couple of hours when you need a fix of alpine conditions.

kids Soccer Circus Dubai and Team Zone ★★

APPEAL BY AGE	PRESCHOOL –	PRIMARY SCHOOL ★★★	TEENS ★★★★
YOUNG ADULTS ★★★		OVER 30 –	SENIORS –

Mirdif City Centre Mall, Mirdif; ☎ 800-534-7873; soccercircus.com

Type of attraction Indoor interactive football game **Admission** Soccer Circus: AED 80 for adults and AED 55 for children under 1.2 metres (3.9 feet). Team

Zone, peak times: AED 520 per hour; off-peak times: AED 400 per hour. **Hours** Saturday–Wednesday, 10 a.m.–11 p.m.; Thursday–Friday, 10 a.m.–midnight **How much time to allow** 1 hour + **Special comments** Indoor football pitch with a difference. **Author's rating** ★★. A clever football-themed attraction – full pitches to play a game and a full-size innovative interactive soccer game to train against. Ideal for the Dubai climate; possibly a bit mundane for children from Europe, who can play football outside whenever they wish.

DESCRIPTION AND COMMENTS Soccer Circus at Playnation has two parts to it. The first is Training Academy, made up of four different skill games played by each person in a football-themed arena. The second is Powerplay, where you play a game against an automated team in a stadiumlike atmosphere. Team Zone, meanwhile, comprises three five-a-side pitches that can also be used for badminton, volleyball, hockey, cricket and other sports. Turn up, and you will be formed into a team with other people wanting to play. Coaches will referee your game and will help your performance where necessary.

kids Stargate ★

APPEAL BY AGE	PRESCHOOL ★★	PRIMARY SCHOOL ★★★★	TEENS ★★★★
YOUNG ADULTS ★★	OVER 30 ★★		SENIORS ★★

Area A, Gate 4, Za'abeel Park, south of Karama, off World Trade Centre roundabout; ☎ 04-398-6888; stargatedubai.com

Type of attraction Space theme park **Admission** Entry to Za'abeel Park: AED 5 per person. Entry to Stargate: Free; load a swipe card with as much credit as you want, depending on which attractions you visit. Special promotions: pay AED 100 and receive AED 30 extra; pay AED 200 and receive AED 100 extra, with no expiry date. Attractions vary in price from AED 15 upwards. **Hours** Saturday–Wednesday, 10 a.m.–10 p.m.; Thursday–Friday, 11 a.m.–11 p.m. **How much time to allow** 3 hours + **Special comments** Another family 'edu-tainment' centre; best for ages 5–15. **Author's rating** ★. The space theme is a bit misleading, as the only reference to space is the names of the different domes. The activities themselves are pretty run-of-the-mill theme-park type attractions.

DESCRIPTION AND COMMENTS Stargate comprises five space domes linked to a central pyramid, each with a range of attractions for the entire family. It looks impressive from outside. The domes are UFO Dome, with a go-kart track; Lunar Dome, which houses an ice rink; Saturn Dome, with a three-dimensional cinema; Mars Dome, with a state-of-the-art play and activities area for children; and Earth Dome, containing a 'Spinning Earth' family roller coaster. The central pyramid is the food court, with a range of cafes and restaurants to suit all tastes. It's a perfectly nice theme park, but it's just one of many, and we're a tiny bit dubious about where the 'edu' bit of 'edu-tainment' fits in. Za'abeel Park is, however, lovely and worth a wander round, and Zen Restaurant (☎ 04-358-0099; **zendubai.com**) at Gate 6 is delightful.

kids thejamjar ★★★

APPEAL BY AGE	PRESCHOOL ★	PRIMARY SCHOOL ★★★★	TEENS ★★★★
YOUNG ADULTS ★★★		OVER 30 ★★★★	SENIORS ★★★★

White Warehouse No. 45, Al Quoz; ☎ 04-341-7303; thejamjardubai.com

Type of attraction A gallery, a creative art space, a studio and a venue for special-event evenings **Admission** Depends on the event **Hours** Saturday and Monday–Thursday, 10 a.m.–8 p.m.; Friday, 2–8 p.m.; closed Sunday. **How much time to allow** Depends on the event **Special comments** Slightly off the usual tourist track, and in an interesting area for an arty day out. **Author's rating** ★★★. An exciting venue with activities, exhibitions and events that will appeal to all age groups.

DESCRIPTION AND COMMENTS   A lively, informal gallery, thejamjar exhibits contemporary art from emerging local and international artists. Through its curatorial collaborations and cultural exchange programme, it brings to the forefront cutting-edge art practises with a year-round exhibition and arts calendar. Its creative team – responsible for creating the ArtBus and ArtintheCity.com, and publisher of *ArtMap* – is dynamic, innovative and forward thinking. Not only does the gallery showcase the works of professional artists, but it is also a creative art space that can be used by both professional and amateur artists. The gallery has studio space for people who wish to come and paint for fun and runs workshops for children and adults. It provides everything you need in terms of canvas, paint and professional advice, so you can be as creative as you like. The painting workshops are best for ages 5–15. (Dare we say that girls might prefer this to boys?)

Open every day but Sunday, this is a fantastic place to take children when they are bored in the holidays. It organises corporate team-building days and events and works closely with local charities. This venue also hosts film, music and drama nights and is a popular centre for artists of all genres. Ring the gallery or look at their Web site to see what events are taking place.

The Third Line ★★★★

APPEAL BY AGE	PRESCHOOL	PRIMARY SCHOOL ★	TEENS ★★
YOUNG ADULTS ★★★		OVER 30 ★★★★	SENIORS ★★★★

Al Quoz 3 (next to the Courtyard Gallery & Cafe);
☎ 04-341-1367; thethirdline.com

Type of attraction A serious gallery that only represents Middle Eastern artists **Admission** Free **Hours** Saturday–Thursday, 10 a.m.–7 p.m. **How much time to allow** 30 minutes + **Special comments** This Dubai gallery is well known on the international art scene. **Author's rating** ★★★★. This is a sophisticated art space showcasing interesting, contemporary regional art. Just worth noting: the gallery has a fantastic polished concrete floor!

DESCRIPTION AND COMMENTS This art gallery focuses on promoting contemporary Middle Eastern art and artists locally, regionally and internationally on a long-term basis. In addition to monthly exhibitions, the gallery hosts and organises non-profit alternative programs.

kids Wild Wadi ★ ★ ★ ★

APPEAL BY AGE	PRESCHOOL ★★★★	PRIMARY SCHOOL ★★★★	TEENS ★★★★
YOUNG ADULTS ★★★★	OVER 30	★★★	SENIORS ★★

Jumeirah Road in front of Burj Al Arab, Umm Suqeim, PO Box 26416; ☎ 04-348-4444; wildwadi.com

Type of attraction Outdoor waterpark Admission AED 200 for adults and AED 165 for children; Sundowner entry (two hours before park closes): AED 165 for adults and AED 135 for children. Hours November–February: Daily, 10 a.m.–6 p.m.; March–May: Daily, 10 a.m.–7 p.m.; June–August: Daily, 10 a.m.–8 p.m.; September–October: Daily, 10 a.m.–7 p.m. How much time to allow At least half a day Special comments A wonderful day out in the sun – and do take a look at the photos they snap of you going down the slides; they are often unintentionally hilarious. Author's rating ★★★★. Best for ages 5–15.

DESCRIPTION AND COMMENTS The original and, many would argue, still the best, Wild Wadi may not boast a shark-infested tank, but it is a great day out for the whole family. Teens will love the simulated surfing ride; babies will be thrilled with a bob in the wave pool; toddlers can enjoy a themed water play park; and adults can dare each other to brave the genuinely frightening Jumeirah Sceirah drop, at 80 kilometres (49.7 miles) per hour. There is also a lazy river (which actually becomes wild-water rapids at points, so hold onto those string bikinis), a large beach and a couple of shaded terraces where you can have some downtime. If you load up your wristband with cash on entry, you won't have to return to your locker all day, as you can pay for food, drink and even souvenirs with these.

kids Wonderland Theme Park and Splashland Water Park ★

APPEAL BY AGE	PRESCHOOL ★★	PRIMARY SCHOOL ★★★★	TEENS ★★★★
YOUNG ADULTS ★★	OVER 30 ★★		SENIORS ★★

near Al Garhoud Bridge, alongside Dubai Creek Park, Oud Metha; ☎ 04-324-1222; wonderlanduae.com

Type of attraction Theme park and waterpark Admission Theme park: AED 90 for adults and AED 85 for children ages 5–12. Waterpark: AED 85 for adults and AED 80 for children ages 5–12. Combined ticket: AED 100 for adults and AED 90 for children ages 5–12; free for children under age 5. Hours Theme park: Daily, 10 a.m.–10 p.m. Waterpark: Daily, 10 a.m.–6 p.m. How much time to allow 3 hours + Special comments One of Dubai's older family amusement parks. Not nearly as popular with tourists and expats as Wild Wadi or Aquaventure.

Author's rating ★. Best for ages 5–15. If we were choosing a waterpark to visit for the day, we'd probably not go to this one, as the other two are far more modern and exciting. However, they are also more expensive, so that might be a deciding factor in this park's favour.

DESCRIPTION AND COMMENTS Wonderland, with connotations of Michael Jackson (unintentionally), is a theme park with a Caribbean slant, in three main areas – Main Street, offering a water mist show and videos played on a thin film of water, plus slot machines and arcade games; Theme Park; and Splashland. A selection of restaurants offer fast food, and the theme park is like a fairground with roller coaster rides, slides, bumper cars, go-karts, a pirate ship, a horror house – you get the picture. Splashland is the watery bit, with a lazy river, speed slides, rapids, surf hill and a dragon pool. Whilst it is fine, and the facilities are good, it does feel dated and lacks the pizzazz of Wild Wadi and Aquaventure.

XVA Gallery ★ ★ ★ ★

APPEAL BY AGE	PRESCHOOL ★	PRIMARY SCHOOL ★★	TEENS ★★
YOUNG ADULTS ★★	OVER 30 ★★★★★		SENIORS ★★★★

next to Dubai Creek in Bastakiya, Bur Dubai; ☎ 04-353-5383; xvagallery.com

Type of attraction Art gallery, art hotel, cafe and shops **Admission** Free **Hours** Saturday–Thursday, 9:30 a.m.–8 p.m. **How much time to allow** 45 minutes–1 hour +, if you decide to stop for a drink and some food **Special comments** Part of a really lovely un–Dubai-like boutique hotel in a restored house with courtyards. **Author's rating** ★★★★. We love the fact that this hotel and gallery are as far removed from one's preconceived concept of Dubai as is possible. We recommend this gallery for the beauty of its architecture and its chic and understated luxurious atmosphere. However, the artworks are always exciting and inspiring and are exhibited throughout the gallery and the hotel.

DESCRIPTION AND COMMENTS XVA occupies a renovated traditional *Majlis*-style building, boasting original architectural motifs, wind towers and three open courtyards, in which one can relax and soak up the exceptional atmosphere of this heritage space. Besides being an internationally-acclaimed art gallery, XVA boasts a unique art hotel, an award-winning vegetarian cafe, several shops, an in-house tailor and a traditional dhow. Since 2003, XVA has pioneered contemporary Middle Eastern and international art in Dubai. It participates regularly at international art fairs and is responsible for creating the Bastakiya Art Fair, which runs every March.

kids Yalla! Bowling Lanes ★ ★

APPEAL BY AGE	PRESCHOOL –	PRIMARY SCHOOL ★★★★	TEENS ★★★★
YOUNG ADULTS ★★★★	OVER 30 ★★★★		SENIORS ★★

Mirdif City Centre Mall, Mirdif; ☎ 800-534-7873; yallabowlingme.com or playnationme.com

Type of attraction Bowling **Admission** AED 17–25 per person for one game; AED 30–45 per person for two games; AED 40–65 per person for three games. Prices go up depending on what time of what day you are playing. Best to look at price list or call to find out. **Hours** Daily, 10 a.m.–midnight **How much time to allow** 1 hour + **Special comments** State-of-the-art bowling alley **Author's rating** ★★. Very nicely laid out, even if a bowling alley is pretty similar the world over. To be fair, it is spanking new and has very nice decor.

DESCRIPTION AND COMMENTS This bowling alley features 12 lanes of cosmic ten-pin bowling with advanced video simulation. This Playnation attraction also consists of a pool and billiards area and the latest video games. It has a bit of an urban graffiti look going on. Bowling is always fun for the whole family, and this bowling alley is a little more state-of-the-art than most. This area is also home to Johnny Rocket's diner, which makes it very popular with Dubai's teenagers.

Za'abeel Park ★★★★

APPEAL BY AGE	PRESCHOOL ★★★★	PRIMARY SCHOOL ★★★★	TEENS ★★★★
YOUNG ADULTS ★★★★		OVER 30 ★★★★	SENIORS ★★★★

south of Karama off World Trade Centre roundabout; ☎ 04-398-6888

Type of attraction Park and playground with a multitude of activities **Admission** AED 5 per person **Hours** Saturday–Thursday, 9 a.m.–11 p.m.; Friday, 9 a.m.–11:30 p.m. **How much time to allow** 1–3 hours **Special comments** If you get a chance to try the restaurant at Gate 6 after your day in the park, it's well worth the effort. **Author's rating** ★★★★. A fantastic playground that will appeal to big children as well as little ones.

DESCRIPTION AND COMMENTS More like two parks connected by footbridges, this delightful 51-hectare (126-acre) park sports a large lake where you can hire boats, an amphitheatre, a 4.3-kilometre (2.7-mile) jogging track, manicured cricket pitch and an adventure playground that is enormous and suits children from tiny toddler age to young teenagers. There are even little bikes for hire. There are large expanses of landscaped gardens, covered picnic areas and barbecue facilities. Kiosks sell drinks and ice creams, and we heartily recommend an excellent restaurant just inside Gate 6 called Zen Restaurant, which has stunning views over the water and delicious Thai, Chinese and Indian food on the menu. An entire area is dedicated to inflatables, trampolines, a miniature train and horse rides, which is fun in the cooler months. And at Stargate (see page 203), the space-age theme park (called an 'edu-tainment' centre), you will find five space zones in which you can participate in activities such as go-karts, bumper cars, an ice rink, roller coaster, fun track and the world's biggest soft play area.

PART SEVEN

DINING *and* RESTAURANTS

▪ EAT *the* EMIRATE

FROM HOLE-IN-THE-WALL KEBAB SHOPS in Satwa to gold-leaf sushi at the Cavalli Club, eating out in Dubai offers innumerable options. If you want to drink alcohol with your meal, then you have to stay within the confines of a hotel, but if you are happy to eschew the wine, then the emirate is your oyster. It will shock nobody that the best-represented cuisine here is Arabic, although most of the standout venues are specifically Lebanese or Iranian rather than Emirati. Some of the best hummus, kebabs and fluffy breads in Dubai can be found in the small street-side cafes on Jumeirah Beach Road and around Al Diyafah Street in Satwa. Although the rotating chicken *shawarma* may remind you of lousy kebab shops back home, don't be put off – the AED 7 snacks, loaded with tahini and salad, are delicious across the board, especially when washed down with freshly-squeezed juice (we love pomegranate but are less keen on the unctuous avocado). Indian food from all over the subcontinent and tasty Pakistani cuisine are also extremely popular, and again, the cheapest eats are the best. You will find that the fare differs a lot from the Westernised versions of most high-street curry houses, but being adventurous does pay off. Of course, coffee shops, sushi joints, burger bars and pizza places are everywhere – you could very easily eat your way around the world without damaging your wallet (although your waistline is an entirely different matter). Weirdly, it's often cheaper to eat at these places than it is to cook (the supermarket-bought AED 30 rotting lettuce is a particular bugbear for locals), so even if you have rented an apartment with a kitchen, you would be advised to only use it for breakfast, and head off for a culinary adventure at lunch and dinner.

At the other end of the scale, there are many, many places to drop serious dirhams. A host of Michelin-starred chefs have outposts here, although unfortunately none of them head up their kitchens full time. Vineet Bhatia, Pierre Gagnaire, Giorgio Locatelli, Gordon Ramsay and Gary Rhodes have all put their names to restaurants, although some visit their kitchens more than others. Many places offer added spectacle with their food – from the giant fish tanks at Atlantis's Ossiano to the whirling dervish at Bab Al Shams's Al Hadheerah. If you are keen to dine at any of these, we would recommend booking as soon as you land. You will, in general, be accommodated, although if they are particularly busy, you might only be able to get an early slot (people do tend to eat quite late in Middle Eastern countries). The person taking the booking will generally have a decent command of English, although if you have any specific or unusual requirements, you may have to speak to a supervisor. The same principle can be applied if you have any problems when you arrive at the restaurant – requests for a better table, complaints about dishes or queries about bad wine should all be addressed to a manager, as often you will encounter indifference or confusion from lower-ranking servers. In general, the hardest tables to get will be on the terrace during the pleasant months (November–March) – if you want one of these, do put in your preference when booking.

As well as these superstar joints, all of the large five-star hotels will have an all-day dining restaurant that serves International buffet fare for breakfast, lunch and dinner, often with a live cooking station. These can represent great value, especially if you have children who are fussy eaters. In general, at the higher end of fine dining here, children are tolerated rather than welcomed with open arms. If anyone in your party has allergies, do make sure you are understood by the waiter and the chef – again, call over a manager if you need to. When the bill arrives (which will usually be presented to you with both hands, out of respect), you will often find a service charge already included. If this is not the case, you will usually be able to add it to the credit card total. If you would rather your money went straight to your server, ask for this to be removed and give them cash personally.

*un*official **TIP**
Twice a year, the **Taste of Dubai Festival** (tasteofdubaifestival.com) gathers together chefs from Dubai's top dining spots at the outdoor amphitheatre at Dubai Media City, where they cook their signature dishes for you to sample and offer classes and demonstrations in a three-day epicurean extravaganza.

If you are dining in a hotel, there is no need to ask the staff to call you a taxi when you leave – a line of them will always be waiting outside the lobby.

One thing you need to know: although in Islam it is forbidden to consume pork products or alcohol, you can buy both here. In supermarkets, you will find a room tucked away at the back selling all the sausages your heart desires (and, rather more worryingly, Pop-Tarts), and hotel restaurants are allowed to serve pork, as long as it is marked with a discreet (p) next to the item description. Alcohol is also served only in hotels. As a tourist, the only place you will be able to buy it outside of these establishments is in duty free at the airport – and, when it is included in food, it will be marked with an (a).

While we have made every effort to include the best and the best-value restaurants in Dubai in this chapter, new venues are constantly popping up all over the city. Monthly listings magazines *What's On* and *Time Out* (**timeoutdubai.com/restaurants**) have a weekly round-up available in print and online, with all the new openings and offers. Monthly *What's On* magazine also regularly reviews new venues.

ECO CRED

IN DUBAI, DOUBLE-DIGIT FOOD MILES are something you have to swallow – metaphorically and literally. Eco-debates that rage in more temperate countries simply do not have the same weight here, as received wisdom is that eating locally and seasonally would lead to drastically-limited menus. Some places do valiantly try – **Baker & Spice** (Souk Al Bahar, Downtown Burj Khalifa; ☎ 04-425-2240) is one, showcasing gleaming piles of fruit and vegetables from Sharjah, Al Ain, Oman and Saudi Arabia on its communal table and providing provenance for its ingredients on the menu. The three branches of **Organic Foods & Café,** the biggest of which is in the Dubai Mall (**organicfoodsandcafe.com**), have also been spearheading the movement for several years, but in reality you would be well advised to leave your eco-conscience at the airport, or your gastronomic experience is going to be quite limited.

FIVE STARS *on a* BUDGET

WEEKDAY, DAYTIME DINING IN DUBAI is particularly fruitful for the wallet-conscious epicure. Fixed-price menus at restaurants in business hotels – basically, anywhere without a beach – often offer a 'best of' their signature dishes for bargain basement prices Sunday–Thursday. One of the best is **Zuma,** where the Ebisu lunch, AED 110, and the early-evening Taste of Zuma three-course dinner with a glass of wine, costing AED 195, represent excellent value for the money. **Okku** offers something similar for AED 99, and the normally heart-stoppingly expensive **Reflets par Pierre Gagnaire** has a four-course lunch menu for AED 250. But these are forever being introduced and

*un*official **TIP**
If you are planning on spending more than a couple of days in the city, it is worth investing in a copy of *The Entertainer*, available from all good bookshops, petrol stations and supermarkets (**theentertainerme. com**). For AED 210, you get hundreds of 'buy one, get one free' vouchers for main courses at restaurants across the city, valid for a year. Do check the expiry date of the vouchers before you buy, though, as some unscrupulous shops don't take old copies off the shelves.

re-jigged, so if you fancy eating somewhere that appears out of your price range, do call and enquire if there is a current offer. Free newspaper *7Days* also runs Foodie Fridays, where discounts of up to 50% are offered at one restaurant per week in the city. If you can't find a copy of the paper, vouchers can be printed out from its Web site (**7days.ae**).

UNDERSTANDING EMIRATI FOOD

UNLESS YOU ARE LUCKY ENOUGH to be invited into the home of a native, the truth is that it's unlikely you'll experience great Emirati food in Dubai. The places that pride themselves on providing local fare include **Al Hadheerah** (Bab Al Shams Desert Resort; ☎ 04-809-6100), **Bastakiyah Nights** (Bastakiyah; ☎ 04-353-7772) and **Local House** (Bastakiyah; ☎ 04-354-0705), which in reality offer a selection of pan-Arabic dishes with a couple of Emirati staples thrown in for good measure. It is also worth remembering that you will never see a local in these venues – they are strictly for tourists. Emirati food is cooked, and eaten, at home – until very recently there was no culture of eating out. Dating back 7,000 years, the staple dishes of the Emirates, as the cuisine of a Bedouin culture, were traditionally cooked in large quantities to feed big groups often for several days – so they don't necessarily lend them-

unofficial **TIP**
Sweet tooth? Well, Dubai is the Middle East's cupcake capital. New York City transplant Magnolia Bakery is housed in the basement floor of The Dubai Mall's Bloomingdale's, with local offerings coming from Kitsch Cupcakes (Villa 611, Beach Road; ☎ 04-395-6963) and Sugar Daddy's (☎ 04-344-8204; **sugardaddysbakery.com**) in The Village Mall, also on Beach Road.

selves to small-scale production. This means that the best time to try Emirati food is during Ramadan, at *Iftar* and *Suhoor* feasts.

The staple carbohydrates of the cuisine are rice (usually white basmati rice) and bulghur wheat (*jareesh*). Lamb and goat are the most common meat, and fish comes in the shape of locally-caught *hammour*, shark and stingray, which are sometimes cured in salt. Saffron, cumin and cardamom are popular herbs. In addition, because Dubai was and remains a trading hub, dishes and ingredients from all over the world have been reworked and incorporated into the diet. Desserts, in common with many other Middle Eastern countries, are incredibly sweet and often feature honey, rosewater or nuts. Dates are also widely grown and feature in many of these. Although in times gone by the camel was far too useful to be dinner, camel meat is on the menu at some outré establishments. The Local House (see above) offers low-fat burgers made from the most iconic of Dubai's beasts of burden, while **Al Nassma**

(☎ 04-223-9289; **al-nasma.com**) sells camel-milk chocolates in gift boutiques, including those in Jumeirah hotels, and has a cafe in the food court of Mall of the Emirates, where you can treat yourself to a camel-milk latte (it tastes a bit like soy milk). **Camelicious** (**camelicious.ae**) also sells flavoured camel milk (its highlighter-pink strawberry flavour is a guilty pleasure) in many of Dubai's supermarkets.

Below is a list of traditional Emirati dishes for which to look out.

Aseeda A dessert made from local pumpkins, sugar and saffron (neighbouring emirate Ras Al-Khaimah is the region most famous for pumpkin growing).

Balaleet A breakfast dish with cooked rice vermicelli, sugar syrup, saffron, rosewater and sautéed onions, topped with a fried egg. Trust us – it tastes as weird as it sounds.

Chabab Sweet pancakes with various toppings.

Halwa A dessert made with saffron, flour and blanched almonds (this can be found in many supermarkets here). It's a great gift to take home as it doesn't need to be refrigerated and lasts ages.

Hareesa If you find any Emirati dish on a menu in Dubai, it is likely to be this. A mixture of ground wheat and meat with the consistency of porridge (a bit like Southeast Asian congee), it's not really to Western tastes. We have made several valiant attempts to stomach more than a mouthful and consistently failed.

Jarad You are very unlikely to find this fried desert locust dish on any menus, although one farm, near Abu Dhabi, still breeds this delicacy.

Khanfaroosh A fried yeast cake made with eggs and sugar and scented with cardamom, saffron and rosewater.

Luqaimat Resembling Indian sweets, these are fluffy fried-dough balls drenched in honey. Delicious.

Machboos Another dish you may find on a menu, it is essentially slow-cooked meat with onions and spices (each family has its own version, but it usually includes dried lime, cardamom, nutmeg and cloves), with rice cooked in the meat stock, and then topped with crispy onions, pistachios and raisins.

Mahshi A whole goat or baby lamb cooked slowly with spices, garnished with nuts, raisins and fried onions.

The RESTAURANTS

CHEAP EATS

ALMOST ALL OF DUBAI'S LICENSED EATERIES are concentrated in hotels, but a raft of fantastic budget eats are dotted around the city. The larger malls afford the best and easiest places to locate selection, boasting mammoth food courts with all the usual suspects – from international chains to independent sandwich shops and *shawarma* stands – and smaller, sit-down cafes between the stores. We haven't listed these, as they aren't worth travelling for, although most are pleasant enough for a lunchtime pit stop. For the most adventurous, though, international eating is easy – and delicious – in the following cafes. You can typically expect to pay under AED 75 per head in these for a starter, main and non-alcoholic drink. Many of the smaller cafes have no credit card facilities, so it's best to pay in cash. Even in these cheaper establishments, it is not really the custom to eat with your hands (the exceptions are obviously at burger joints and also with Lebanese meze, which you are encouraged to attack with warm pitta bread in hand). If you do eat with your hands, don't use the left – it is considered unclean.

Deli-Cafes

BAKER & SPICE *Souk Al Bahar, Old Town Island;* ☎ 04-425-2240. Organic and locally-sourced ingredients are the big draw at this smart spot in the shadow of the Burj Khalifa. At a long communal table, knowledgeable waiters serve freshly-baked breads, croissants and cakes, as well as an à la carte selection of mains, counter-service salads and freshly-squeezed juices. The afternoon tea, with its knitted tea cosies and Victoria sponge cake, is delicious.

DEAN & DELUCA *Souk Al Bahar, Old Town Island;* ☎ 04-420-0336. This Dubai outpost of the American uber-deli has a great outdoor seating area and views of the Dubai Fountain and Burj Khalifa. Fill up on create-your-own salads, pizza slices, soups and sandwiches, as well as the candy-coloured cupcakes.

BASTA ART CAFÉ *Bastakiya, Bur Dubai;* ☎ 04-353-5071. The rather drab selection of sandwiches and salads is more than made up for by the beautiful courtyard setting – a great pit stop after wandering the pedestrianised alleyways of this gallery-packed district.

CIRCLE CAFÉ *Beach Park Plaza, Jumeirah Beach Road;* ☎ 04-342-8177. Bagels, washed down with coffee and smoothies and accompanied by cakes, are the star at this chic cafe opposite the beach. Keep an eye out for the perfectly-manicured Dubai ladies who lunch here.

LE PAIN QUOTIDIEN *The Walk, Jumeirah Beach Residence;* ☎ 04-437-0141. The Jumeirah Beach Residence branch of this French chain has by far the best location. Take a seat with a view of the ocean and tuck into breakfast or soups, sandwiches and a selection of salads. Great coffee and cake too.

LIME TREE CAFÉ *Jumeirah Beach Road (opposite Dubai Marine Resort);* ☎ 04-349-8498. The weekend queues attest to this cafe's popularity. Luckily, the queue moves quickly, and while waiting you have a prime spot next to the glass-fronted fridges to choose your wraps, salads, pasta and cakes. Hot breakfasts are also served, and the carrot cake is the stuff of legend.

MORE CAFÉ *Al Murooj Rotana;* ☎ 04-343-3779. Also has branches at Dubai Mall and Gold & Diamond Park. More by name, more by nature – the portions at this cafe are aimed at hungry punters. More's menu cherry-picks from around the world and nearly always gets it right – the Thai green curry here is as good as the burger, which in turn holds its own against the Wiener Schnitzel. Locals wax lyrical about the fresh strawberry and balsamic juice.

SHAKESPEARE & CO. *The Village Mall, Jumeirah Beach Road;* ☎ 04-344-6228. This is the prettiest and most relaxed branch in the eight-strong chintzy chain, with its Souk Al Bahar stablemate coming in a close second. Sit back on a squishy floral sofa and enjoy French-influenced and Arabic light meals and pretty patisserie selections.

FASHION LOUNGE *The Walk, Jumeirah Beach Residence;* ☎ 04-427-0268; **fashionlounge.ae**. This slightly-overdressed cafe is nonetheless a nice place for a salad, sandwich or slice of cake after a day at the beach.

Burgers

BURGER HOUSE *The Walk, Jumeirah Beach Residence;* ☎ 04-437-0237. Gourmet burgers with fresh ingredients ranging from wonderful – the patties are made from humanely-raised cattle – to the slightly weird. (Pineapple on a burger? Just plain wrong.)

JOHNNY ROCKET'S *Marina Walk;* ☎ 04-434-1526. A 1950s-style diner straight out of Los Angeles. Try the Smokehouse with a side of onion rings, wash it down with a root beer and wait for the staff to break into a synchronised dance to 'Staying Alive'. Yes, really.

THE MEAT CO. *Souk Al Bahar, Downtown Burj Khalifa;* ☎ 04-420-0737. *Madinat Jumeirah;* ☎ 04-368-6040; **themeatandwineco.com.** The steaks are great at this international chain, but it's the towering burgers for which it's most famous. Best attacked with a knife and fork.

Arabic

AL MALLAH *Al Diyafah Road, Satwa;* ☎ 04-398-4723. Late-opening roadside cafe on a busy street serving fantastic and filling *shawarma* and falafel, plus a huge selection of meze. Great for people-watching – if you don't mind exhaust fumes from the souped-up Hummers.

AL REEF LEBANESE BAKERY *Al Wasl Road;* ☎ 04-394-5200. Cheap, cheerful and hot out of the oven – the freshly-baked saj, *manakish* and pastries at this Dubai stalwart have a citywide reputation.

BAIT AL WAKEEL *Near Dubai Museum, Bur Dubai;* ☎ 04-353-0530. Stick to the Arabic dishes (the noodles are downright disgusting) and spend an afternoon watching the boats bob along Dubai Creek from the outdoor wooden deck. The juices are great – try the lemon or mint.

BURJ AL HAMMAM *Beach Park Plaza, Jumeirah Beach Road;* ☎ 04-342-8034. Chandelier-bedecked upscale Lebanese restaurant with decent grilled meats and meze. It's a tad on the expensive side for what you get, though.

KABAB-JI *The Walk, Jumeirah Beach Residence;* ☎ 04-437-0122. Sensibly-sized portions, a light touch with the olive oil and fresh ingredients make this a healthier place to tuck into kebabs, meze and sandwiches.

PAR'S IRANIAN KITCHEN *Near Rydges Plaza, Al Diyafah Street, Satwa;* ☎ 04-398-4000. Set in a pretty garden dotted with low tables and banquettes scattered with plump cushions, this Iranian restaurant is a real treat. Avoid the standard-issue Arabic fare and try the Persian speciality grilled meats and seafood. Its neon sign makes it very easy to find too.

REEM AL BAWADI *Near Mercato Mall, Jumeirah Beach Road;* ☎ 04-394-7444. Over-ordering is part of the fun at this always-packed, cavernous Lebanese restaurant. Sit back and watch the table groan as it piles up with plates of fresh bread, hummus, *fattoush* and the epic mixed grill.

SHU *Jumeirah Beach Road;* ☎ 04-349-1303. The over-the-top indoor decor renders the outside space, always filled with shisha smokers, a better place to enjoy the hearty Lebanese food and juices here.

ZAATAR W ZEIT *The Walk, Jumeirah Beach Residence;* ☎ 04-423-3778. From breakfast to late-night munchies, and everything in between, this always-packed fast-food joint serves Lebanese flatbreads, wraps, pizzas and salads 24 hours a day.

Curries

RAVI RESTAURANT *Near Al Diyafah Road roundabout, Satwa;* ☎ 04-331-5353. Don't let the wipe-clean tables and the neon lighting put you off – the plentiful portions of Pakistani curries, grilled meats and breads make this a total bargain, and a very tasty one at that. It is rumoured that Sheikh Mohammed is a big fan.

SUKH SAGAR ON THE BEACH *The Walk, Jumeirah Beach Residence;* ☎ 04-437-0188. Freshly-prepared vegetarian Indian and Indian fusion food, with some Western dishes dotting the long menu.

INDIA PALACE *The Walk, Jumeirah Beach Residence;* ☎ 04-437-0279. The original, hard-to-find Garhoud branch of this mini-chain has been packing in diners for years. The beach view makes this one a better bet (and it's much easier to find) – the butter chicken and fresh breads are sublime.

Pizzas

MARZANO *Souk Al Manzil, Old Town;* ☎ 04-420-1136. Wafer-thin bases and classic, fresh toppings make these some of the best pizzas in Dubai. Decent desserts too. The mall location isn't great, but Al Manzil hotel next door has a great shisha courtyard to spend a relaxed evening in afterwards.

URBANO *Souk Al Manzil, Old Town;* ☎ 04-435-5666. Pizza, pasta and grills served with an incredible Burj Khalifa view.

Asian

WAGAMAMA *Crowne Plaza, Sheikh Zayed Road;* ☎ 04-305-6060. The international chain's biggest branch in Dubai is a great quick stop for noodles and curries.

THE NOODLE HOUSE *Souk Madinat Jumeirah;* ☎ 04-366-6345. The most popular pan-Asian chain in the U.A.E. serves up piping-hot dim sum, noodles and stir-fries in minutes. Not a place to linger, though.

LEMONGRASS *Opposite Lamcy Plaza, Oud Metha;* ☎ 04-334-2325. Constantly name-checked as the best Thai in Dubai, beating off far pricier competition with its fragrant curries, salads, noodles, juices and smoothies.

ALL-YOU-CAN-EAT
(and Drink) BRUNCHES

FORGET YOUR NORMAL WEEKEND FARE OF EGGS BENEDICT and a skinny latte – brunch in Dubai is a lot more lavish. So popular are these belt-loosening Friday food-fests that they have become something of an institution. Expats wax lyrical for hours about their favourite venue, and they sure have a fair few to choose from – there is almost no venue in town that doesn't offer some sort of five-hour daytime all-you-can-eat (and, often, drink) extravaganza. These can broadly be split into three categories – the luxury brunch, the budget brunch and the non-alcoholic brunch. Below are our top picks for each.

THE LUXURY BRUNCH

THESE ARE THE ROLLS-ROYCES OF THE BRUNCH WORLD. Most include a branded Champagne option – Moët & Chandon and Veuve Clicquot being the most popular – alongside cocktails with house spirits and wine. Usually a cheaper option will only include soft drinks. Food-wise, the meals mostly present an elegant solution to the 'what shall we eat today?' conundrum by offering everything, and then some. Many start with breakfast-style dishes, and then you can expect sushi, Chinese, Italian, seafood, grills, tapas and Arabic staples – you name it, and there will almost certainly be a live cooking station offering it. The seriously committed usually have some sort of strategy that allows them to stuff as much of the posh nosh down their necks as possible. One we've found to work well is carb avoidance – pile your plate with bread, potatoes or pasta and you won't have room for Wagyu, foie gras and lobster. Some of course forget to eat at all, such is the number of Champagne top-ups. Make sure you leave space for the dessert and cheese though – some establishments, such as the Park Hyatt's Traiteur, have entire rooms devoted to them.

AL QASR *Al Qasr Hotel;* ☎ 04-366-8888. AED 495 including sparkling wine, wine, cocktails, beer and soft drinks.

The sheer scale of this brunch is breathtaking. Only the seriously dedicated will make it round all of the food stations, where you can watch International cuisine cooked right in front of you. Spanish tapas are done better here than anywhere else in Dubai, and a pick-and-mix sweet station offers that 'shoplifting in Woolworths' experience. Brits also wax lyrical about the fish-and-chips, served in mock newspaper (a little factoid for you: they aren't allowed to serve it in real newspaper in case the text references the Prophet Mohammed). The cocktails are so good and the staff so ready to replace empties that you might want to watch that you don't fall up the grand staircase on the way out. Smugly watching other people do so can be quite good sport though. Tables on the terrace, by the Madinat's waterways, are highly sought after when it's cool enough to sit outside. Booking is essential.

ZUMA *Dubai International Financial Centre Gate Village;* ☎ 04-425-5660. AED 385 including sake, wine, Bellinis and sparkling wine.

A showcase of what the Dubai International Financial Centre's busiest restaurant does best, Zuma furnishes diners' tables with piping-hot edamame, miso soup and the house speciality crispy fried calamari, after which you can eat an unlimited amount from the sushi counter, robata grill and salad station. One of a selection of the restaurant's most popular mains can then be ordered à la carte, and desserts are sent to the table in a large bento box – some diners complain that this is a bit stingy for the price, but we can't help feel that a little of what you fancy is better than seven heaped plates full of the stuff.

SPECTRUM ON ONE *The Fairmont, Sheikh Zayed Road;* ☎ 04-332-5555. AED 550 including Moët & Chandon Champagne, soft drinks, beer, wine and house spirits.

One of Dubai's most expensive brunches has six different themed areas – Japanese, Thai, Indian, Chinese, Arabic and pan-European, with a massive dessert buffet including a crêpe station and a chocolate fountain. An impressive cheese room offers more than 30 types, as well as Port with which to wash it down. This venue is a perennial brunch favourite, but that is solely down to the quality of the food, as the restaurant is a little airport-loungey (albeit business class) for our liking.

TRAITEUR *Park Hyatt, Dubai Deira Creek;* ☎ 04-317-2222. AED 550 including Veuve Clicquot Champagne, house spirits, wine and beer.

This is a truly lovely room – huge, high ceilings, chic cream-and-brown decor and a central open kitchen that lends itself rather nicely to the brunch theme. Unlike most other large hotels, Traiteur still focuses on what it does best on Fridays – namely, classic French food. Against a backdrop of fresh produce, chefs cook up grilled and roasted meats and seafood, and plenty of potato and veggie side dishes that often get forgotten about at other brunches. There is a live jazz band, and the terrace bar, overlooking Dubai Marina, is a glorious place to have sundowners after the feast.

YALUMBA *Le Méridien Dubai;* ☎ 04-282-4040. AED 449 for Tattinger; AED 499 for Bollinger; wine, beer, spirits, juices and soft drinks.

You might as well know what you are getting into with this one – Yalumba, whilst fun and certainly well stocked with more than passable food, is a legendary booze-fest. There is a huge buffet, and as many starters and mains as you can manage can be ordered à la carte (kangaroo included – the restaurant bills itself as Australian with a twist). We recommend that you order lots if you want to soak up the alcohol and leave under your own steam. This is, in fact, the place that the tawdry 'sex on the beach' couple dined before their regrettable randy incident, and you might not be surprised from the assembled crowd, many of whom stay on after 3:30 p.m., once the all-inclusive stuff stops flowing, to take advantage of the 20% drinks discount.

THE BUDGET BRUNCH

IF YOU DON'T MIND STICKING TO WINE, beer and spirits instead of the bubbly stuff, then these offer some of the best value in Dubai. The larger hotels adhere to the same formula as the luxury brunches – cuisine culled from around the world, cooked in front of you – but scrimp slightly on the more outré ingredients, so don't go expecting oysters. Restaurants specialising in one cuisine essentially offer a 'best of' from their menu, often ordered à la carte.

MOMOTARO *Souk Al Bahar, Downtown Burj Khalifa;* ☎ 04-425-7976. AED 225 including wine, beer, sparkling wine, sake and soft drinks.

The à la carte Japanese brunch, with its selection of sushi, sashimi, noodles and grills, is a total bargain although, tucked away in the corner of Souk Al Bahar, it is a bit dark for a daytime venue.

THE CELLAR *The Aviation Club, Garhoud;* ☎ 04-282-9333. AED 205 for unlimited wine and beer; soft drinks charged as extra.

The Saturday à la carte brunch doesn't encourage gluttony in quite the same way the groaning table buffets do, but the modern fusion food is top-notch, and you can order as much of it as you like.

THAI KITCHEN *Park Hyatt, Dubai Deira Creek;* ☎ 04-317-2222. AED 245 including house wine and Tiger beer.

Outdoor tables at this outstanding Thai restaurant are hotly contested at the weekend. The buffet food, cooked in an open kitchen, is beautifully prepared and plentiful.

Eid Dining

DURING EID, MANY RESTAURANTS CLOSE ALTOGETHER in the daytime or offer a limited menu in a curtained-off atmosphere, which makes for pretty dull dining. Come evening, though, the gluttony starts. *Iftar*, served just after sundown, is the meal taken to break fast, while *Suhoor* is eaten later in the evening. Nearly all hotels and many independent restaurants will offer a special *Iftar* buffet, stocked mostly with Arabic staples, for a set price, which hovers around the AED 150 mark per person at big hotels, with cheaper cafes charging much less. *Suhoor* is essentially the second sitting in these tents but is more often an à la carte feast. Alcohol is strictly off-limits at all of these dinners, although fresh juices and teas will slake your thirst. Many larger venues erect a special tent with large tables – these meals are usually taken en famille, so if you turn up in a small group, you will be expected to sit with strangers. There is also usually a lounge area for shisha smoking. **The Ritz-Carlton**'s effort is perhaps the most chic in the city, while the **Atlantis**'s relative newcomer is distinguished by its beachside location. The tent on the lawns at the **Jumeirah Beach Hotel** is impressive for its sheer scale, and live oud players also keep diners entertained.

PALERMO *The Arabian Ranches Polo Club;* ☎ 04-361-8111. AED 225 with wine, beer and soft drinks.

The food covers all the brunch staples – the salads get a special mention – but if we're honest, it's not exactly gourmet. However, it does come with a free polo match most weekends, and the outdoor terrace is lovely.

THE NON-ALCOHOLIC BRUNCH

A LACK OF ALCOHOL LICENCE hasn't deterred Dubai's cafes from getting in on the brunch act. In fact the food is often better than wine-soaked rivals as it is the main focus of the event. The following are especially good for families.

MORE CAFÉ *Al Garhoud;* ☎ 04-283-0224. *Al Murooj Rotana;* ☎ 04-343-3779. *Gold & Diamond Park;* ☎ 04-323-4350; AED 95.

Every Friday, in all branches of this locally-operated chain, a fixed price buys you breakfast and lunch (you can eat from 11 a.m.), juices, soft drinks and unlimited tea and coffee.

SEZZAM *Mall of the Emirates;* ☎ 04-409-5999; AED 138.

Another family favourite, this giant food court has great views of the Ski Dubai slope, and on Friday and Saturday entertainers and a bouncy castle keep the kids amused. Sushi, salads, stir-fries, burgers and an impressive ice-cream counter are all on offer.

Time for Tea

DUBAI HAS, OF LATE, ADOPTED A RATHER ENGLISH TRADITION – the afternoon tea. And, by George, they do it rather well indeed. By far the best is the Burj Al Arab's offering, which is faultless from start to finish. You can while away an entire afternoon at the seven-course version in **Sahn Eddar** (**jumeirah.com;** ☎ 04-301-7600) on the first floor (a five-course affair is offered in the Skyview Bar too for AED 395). Whether you just opt for tea (AED 290) or go for the glass of Louis Roederer Champagne (AED 375), you will be bombarded with finger-size treats on towering cake stands – from vol-au-vents to cucumber sandwiches with the crusts cut off, to a slice of the roast of the day, teeny-weeny patisserie and piping-hot scones with clotted cream and raspberry jam that will send you into paroxysms of delight. You can have as many pots of tea from the long list as you can drink, while being entertained by an Arabian oud player or jazz combo. You must have a booking at one of the hotel's restaurants to get inside the Burj, and we would strongly recommend this is the thing you book.

The Ritz-Carlton in the Marina (☎ 04-399-4000) comes a close second in the tea-and-cake stakes, with its lawns providing the perfect backdrop for genteel indulgence. The tea list here is encyclopaedic, the sandwiches dainty and the scones and clotted cream spot-on, and it all comes in at a reasonable AED 110 per person. The Address Dubai Mall's **Karat Lounge** (☎ 04-438-8888) goes one better with the teas, presenting you with a case of leaves in glass jars so you can get a whiff before you order. The brioche and scones come warm; the deconstructed mini-sandwiches, which are served in little mirrored jewellery boxes, are almost too pretty to eat; and the eight tiny cakes that come after are bite-size perfection – all for AED 125 per person. Unfortunately, its location in the lobby of the hotel, stuck next to Bloomingdale's, means that it's a little soulless.

ORGANIC FOODS & CAFÉ *Al Satwa;* ☎ 04-398-9410; AED 65.
Freshly-baked breads and croissants, granola and omelettes are served from 11 a.m., and you can eat your way through to 3:30 p.m. from the selection of pizza, curries, stir-fries and sandwiches. There is a great selection for vegetarians too.

INDIA PALACE *Garhoud;* ☎ 04-286-9600; AED 70.
The buffet table here groans under the weight of some of the best Indian curries, breads and grills in the city. The setting can be a teeny bit soulless, so you may not want to linger after filling your belly.

ALMAZ BY MOMO *Harvey Nichols, Mall of the Emirates;* ☎ 04-409-8877; AED 75.
Moroccan offerings, from flaky b'steeya to toothache-inducing desserts, served with sweet mint tea and juices.

THE CHINA CLUB *Radisson Blu, Deira;* ☎ 04-205-7333; AED 95.

Tea and juices (although, confusingly, not water) are included in the price here. Waiters serve up a never-ending selection of dim sum from their trolleys – some of the best to be had in Dubai. No pork though, which true dim sum connoisseurs will find disappointing.

LEGENDS *Dubai Creek Club, Dubai Deira Creek;* ☎ 04-295-6000; AED 115.

A great setting right on Dubai Creek and plentiful food at a rock-bottom price. What the fare lacks in quality, it makes up for in quantity – from full English breakfasts to pasta, salads, dim sum and sushi.

OUR TOP RESTAURANT PICKS

CUISINE In a city that boasts more than 1.5 million expats, it is hardly surprising that almost every cuisine is represented here. What's slightly surprising is that the sort of fusion food that dots the culinary land-scape in other major cities hasn't really caught on, with a very few exceptions. Japanese tends to be just that – with perhaps a few off-the-wall flourishes; French is the sort of butter-laden cheese-fest you'd expect; and Italian is just like mamma used to make. When chefs do deviate from a world cuisine, we have noted it, although dishes are ever changing, so don't be surprised if their menus have evolved.

OVERALL RATING This is your at-a-glance guide to the entire dining experience, taking into account the quality of the food, the service, the venue and the value for money. Five stars means the best of the best, four stars is close to perfect, three is distinctly better than average and so on.

PRICE Because dining out at Dubai's better-known restaurants, mostly all based in five-star hotels, is pretty expensive across the board, we have included an exhaustive list of independent establishments, most of which are unlicensed. Of the following upmarket establishments we've covered in more detail, we have provided a rough guide of how much a complete meal – comprising a soup or salad and main course with side dish – would set you back.

Inexpensive	AED 150 (£30 or US $41) or less
Moderate	AED 150–250 (£30–50 or US $41–68)
Expensive	AED 250–500 (£50–100 or US $68–136)
Very Expensive	AED 500 (£100 or US $136) or more

QUALITY RATING If you don't glance twice at the prices on the menu, this should be the first rating at which you look. Five stars denote the use of the best and freshest ingredients, cooked with flair and presented with panache, regardless of cost.

VALUE RATING Quality and value are combined in this rating, defined as below:

★★★★★	Exceptional value; a real bargain
★★★★	Good value
★★★	Decent value
★★	Somewhat overpriced
★	Significantly overpriced

PAYMENT The type of payment accepted at each of the extensively-profiled restaurants has been listed.

WHO IS INCLUDED Although the recession has slowed the rate of shiny new hotels and their luxury dining establishments, there are still bound to be brand-new, not-yet-opened joints that are not profiled here. Please bear in mind that, in an emirate that values the new and novel, decor and chefs change more often than you might expect, so while the information here is as accurate as possible at the time of print, there may be small differences in your own experience. What we have focused on in the following pages are places with a proven track record, with as broad a range of prices as possible. The ones we have profiled extensively are those we consider to be the best. They are also all licensed for alcohol.

MORE RECOMMENDATIONS

The Best Family Dining

- **Beach Bar & Grill** (see page 233)
- **Beachcombers** Jumeirah Beach Hotel; ☎ 04-406-8999; **jumeirah.com**
- **Epicure** (see page 238)
- **Sezzam** Kempinski Mall of the Emirates, Sheikh Zayed Road; ☎ 04-409-5000; **kempinski.com**

The Best Michelin Star Chef Patrons

- **Frankie's Italian Bar & Grill** by Marco Pierre White (see page 239)
- **Indego** by Vineet Bhatia Grosvenor House Hotel, Dubai Marina; ☎ 04-399-8888; **grosvenorhouse-dubai.com**
- **Ossiano** by Santi Santamaria (see page 243)
- **Reflets par Pierre Gagnaire** (see page 247)
- **Rhodes Mezzanine** by Gary Rhodes (see page 248)

- **Ronda Locatelli** by Giorgio Locatelli   Atlantis, The Palm, Palm Jumeirah;
  ☎ 04-426-2626; **palmjumeirah.ae**
- **Verre by Gordon Ramsay** (see page 253)

Best See and Be Seen

- **Buddha Bar** (see page 235)
- **Okku** (see page 242)
- **Zuma** (see page 254)

The Best Terrace

- **The Cellar** (see page 237)
- **Margaux** (see page 241)
- **Traiteur**   The Park Hyatt, Dubai Creek, Deira; ☎ 04-317-2222;
  dubai.park.hyatt.com

The Best Views

- **Hukama**   The Address Downtown Dubai; ☎ 04-368-888; **theaddress.com**
- **Al Muntaha**   Burj Al Arab, Jumeirah; ☎ 04-301-7600; **jumeirah.com**
- **The Noble House**   Raffles, Oud Metha; ☎ 04-324-8888;
  raffles.com
- **Vu's**   Jumeirah Emirates Towers, Sheikh Zayed Road; ☎ 04-319-8088;
  jumeirah.com

The Most Romantic

- **BiCE** (see page 233)
- **Eau Zone** (see page 237)
- **Pai Thai** (see page 244)
- **Pierchic** (see page 246)
- **Reflets par Pierre Gagnaire** (see page 247)
- **Traiteur**   The Park Hyatt, Dubai Creek, Deira; ☎ 04-317-2222;
  dubai.park.hyatt.com

The following 'best of' cuisine lists are in addition to the restaurants profiled later in the chapter.

The Best Arabic and Persian

- **Al Nafoorah**   Jumeirah Emirates Towers, Sheikh Zayed Road;
  ☎ 04-319-8088; **jumeirah.com**
- **Shabestan**   Radisson Blu Hotel, Dubai Deira Creek; ☎ 04-222-7171;
  radissonblu.com
- **Shahrzad**   Hyatt Regency Deira; ☎ 04-209-1234;
  dubai.regency.hyatt.com

The Best Chinese

- **Hukama**   The Address Downtown Dubai; ☎ 04-436-8888; **theaddress.com**
- **The Noble House**   Raffles, Oud Metha; ☎ 04-324-8888; **raffles.com**

- **Shang Palace** Shangri-La, Sheikh Zayed Road; ☎ 04-343-8888; shangri-la.com

The Best Indian

- **Coconut Grove** Rydges Plaza Hotel, Al Diyafah Street, Dubai; ☎ 04-398-3800; **rydges.com**
- **Indego** Grosvenor House Hotel, Dubai Marina; ☎ 04-399-8888; **grosvenorhouse-dubai.com**
- **Iz** Grand Hyatt Dubai, Oud Metha; ☎ 04-317-2222; **dubai.grand.hyatt.com**

The Best Japanese

- **Café Sushi** The Fairmont Dubai, Sheikh Zayed Road; ☎ 04-311-8316; **fairmont.com/dubai**
- **Kisaku** Al Khaleej Palace Hotel, Deira; ☎ 04-223-1000; **alkhaleejhotels.com**
- **Miyako** Hyatt Regency Deira; ☎ 04-209-1234; **dubai.regency.hyatt.com**
- **Tokyo @ The Towers** Jumeirah Emirates Towers, Sheikh Zayed Road; ☎ 04-319-8088; **jumeirah.com**

The Best Seafood

- **BiCE Mare** Souk Al Bahar, Downtown Dubai; ☎ 04-423-0982
- **Mahi Mahi** Wafi Mall, Oud Metha; ☎ 04-324-4100
- **Peppercrab** Grand Hyatt Dubai, Oud Metha; ☎ 04-317-2222; **dubai.grand.hyatt.com**

The Best Steaks

- **Exchange Grill** The Fairmont Dubai, Sheikh Zayed Road; ☎ 04-311-8316; **fairmont.com/dubai**
- **Grand Grill** Habtoor Grand Resort & Spa; ☎ 04-399-4221; **habtoorhotels.com**
- **Rib Room** Jumeirah Emirates Towers, Sheikh Zayed Road; ☎ 04-319-8088; **jumeirah.com**

RESTAURANT PROFILES

Aangan ★★★½

INDIAN   MODERATE   QUALITY ★★★★   VALUE ★★★

Dhow Palace Hotel, Bur Dubai; ☎ 04-359-9992

Reservations Essential **When to go** Evening **Main course range** AED 50–80 **Payment** All major credit cards **Service rating** ★★★★ **Friendliness rating** ★★★★ **Parking** Valet, garage **Bar** Full service **Wine selection** Good **Dress**

continued on page 231

Dubai Restaurants by Cuisine

CUISINE AND NAME	OVERALL RATING	COST	QUALITY RATING	VALUE RATING
ARABIC/EMIRATI				
Al Hadheerah	★★★	Expensive	★★★	★★★★
ARGENTINIAN				
La Parilla	★★★★	Expensive	★★★★	★★★
Asado	★★★½	Expensive	★★★★	★★★
BRITISH				
Rhodes Mezzanine	★★★★	Expensive	★★★★	★★★
The Rivington Grill	★★★½	Moderate	★★★★	★★★★★
EUROPEAN				
Verre by Gordon Ramsay	★★★★	Expensive	★★★★★	★★★★
FRENCH				
Reflets par Pierre Gagnaire	★★★★★	Expensive	★★★★★	★★★★
Margaux	★★★★	Expensive	★★★★	★★★
Rive Gauche	★★★½	Moderate	★★★★	★★★
Bistro Madeleine	★★★	Inexpensive	★★★	★★★★½
INDIAN				
Aangan	★★★½	Moderate	★★★★	★★★
INTERNATIONAL				
Eau Zone	★★★½	Expensive	★★★	★★★
Epicure	★★★	Moderate	★★★★	★★★
Teatro	★★★	Moderate	★★★	★★★★
The Cellar	★★	Moderate	★★★	★★★
ITALIAN				
BiCE	★★★★	Expensive	★★★★★	★★★★
Armani Ristorante	★★★★	Expensive	★★★★	★★★

CUISINE AND NAME	OVERALL RATING	COST	QUALITY RATING	VALUE RATING
ITALIAN (CONTINUED)				
Segreto	★★★★	Moderate	★★★★	★★★
Bussola	★★★½	Moderate	★★★	★★★★
Frankie's Italian Bar & Grill	★★★	Moderate	★★★	★★★
Cavalli Club	★★★	Very Exp	★★★	★★
JAPANESE				
Nobu	★★★★	Expensive	★★★★★	★★★
Zuma	★★★★	Expensive	★★★★	★★★★
Okku	★★★½	Expensive	★★★★	★★★
PAN-ASIAN				
Buddha Bar	★★★	Expensive	★★★	★★★
SEAFOOD				
Ossiano	★★★★★	Expensive	★★★★★	★★★★★
Pierchic	★★★★	Expensive	★★★★	★★★★
Beach Bar & Grill	★★★	Expensive	★★★★	★★★
STEAKHOUSE				
Rare	★★★★	Expensive	★★★★½	★★★
Rhodes Twenty10	★★★★	Expensive	★★★★	★★★
Manhattan Grill	★★★½	Expensive	★★★★	★★★★
Terra Firma Steakhouse	★★★	Expensive	★★★★	★★★
Fire & Ice	★★★	Expensive	★★★	★★★
THAI				
Pai Thai	★★★	Expensive	★★★★	★★★
Spice Emporium	★★★	Inexpensive	★★★½	★★★

Restaurants in Deira & Bur Dubai

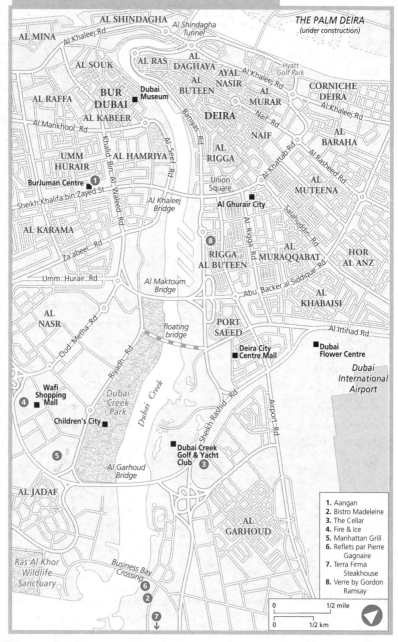

1. Aangan
2. Bistro Madeleine
3. The Cellar
4. Fire & Ice
5. Manhattan Grill
6. Reflets par Pierre Gagnaire
7. Terra Firma Steakhouse
8. Verre by Gordon Ramsay

Restaurants in Jumeirah

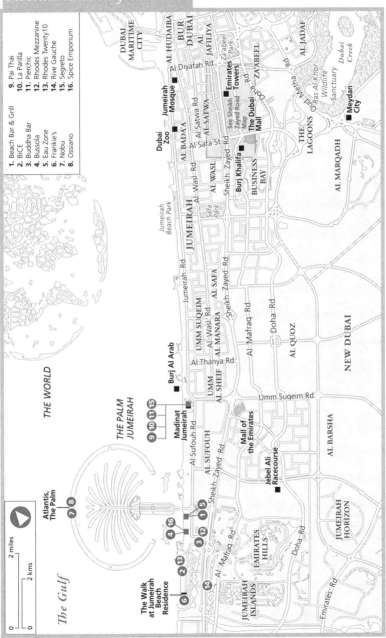

1. Beach Bar & Grill
2. BiCE
3. Buddha Bar
4. Bussola
5. Eau Zone
6. Frankie's
7. Nobu
8. Ossiano
9. Pai Thai
10. La Parilla
11. Pierchic
12. Rhodes Mezzanine
13. Rhodes Twenty10
14. Rive Gauche
15. Segreto
16. Spice Emporium

Restaurants on Sheikh Zayed Road

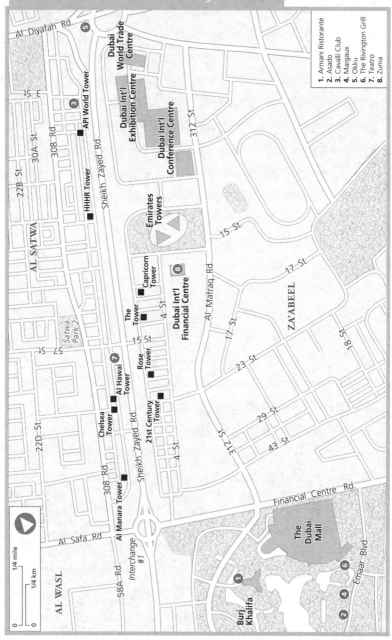

1. Armani Ristorante
2. Asado
3. Cavalli Club
4. Margaux
5. Okku
6. The Rivington Grill
7. Teatro
8. Zuma

continued from page 225

Casual **Disabled access** Yes **Customers** Expats **Hours** Daily, 12:30–3 p.m. and 7 p.m.–12:30 a.m.

SETTING AND ATMOSPHERE Indian expats flock to this unprepossessing Bur Dubai hotel for one reason only – the sublime Punjabi food at Aangan. The hotel itself is pretty weird and surprisingly pricey for the location, but you'll be able to ignore that once inside. The room is really secondary to the experience, although comfortable enough – the red velvet seating and flocked wallpaper are cosy rather than stylish and will probably put you in mind of a suburban British curry house.

HOUSE SPECIALITIES Prepare to leave very, very full. The kitchen is happy to cater to your own level of chilli kick (if you ask for something hot here, it comes with weapons-grade chilli, so bin the bravado). The lamb shank cooked with Indian spice and tomato is a star dish, as is the home-style lamb chops cooked with traditional spices. To start, try the creamy chicken kebab marinated in saffron, chilli and ginger.

OTHER RECOMMENDATIONS This is a great place for big groups – the vegetarian, meat and seafood set menus are a great value, ranging AED 130–170.

SUMMARY AND COMMENTS It may not boast a Michelin-starred chef, but if it's great Indian you're after, Aangan really can't be beaten.

Armani Ristorante ★ ★ ★ ★

ITALIAN   EXPENSIVE   QUALITY ★★★★   VALUE ★★★

Armani Hotel, Burj Khalifa, Downtown; ☎ 04-888-3888; armanihotels.com

Reservations Essential **When to go** Evening **Main course range** AED 185–195 **Payment** All major credit cards **Service rating** ★★★★★ **Friendliness rating** ★★★★★ **Parking** Valet **Bar** Full service **Wine selection** Very good **Dress** Smart **Disabled access** Yes **Customers** Locals, expats, tourists **Hours** Daily, midday–3 p.m. and 7–11 p.m.

SETTING AND ATMOSPHERE The decor is classic Armani – polished slate floors, dove-grey upholstered circular booths (ask for one by the window and you'll have a great view of the Dubai Fountain), pristine white tablecloths and sculptural arrangements of white roses. During the day, the windows let light stream in, and in the evening a back-lit marble-effect feature wall takes centre stage. There is a large open kitchen, although it's behind glass, meaning the smells and sounds are contained in a fishbowl-like effect. Staff are helpful and courteous.

HOUSE SPECIALITIES The Tuscan menu is short and sweet – the superior ingredients are left unadorned to do most of the work in the starters, which include San Daniele ham and melon, and beef carpaccio with aged Parmesan. The home-made pastas are handled well, although those with a healthy appetite should steer away from them as a main course. Desserts are disappointing, however – the tiramisu is unlike any version of the classic dessert we've ever tried, and all the worse for it – but most come with flecks of edible gold leaf, so at least you're getting your money's worth!

OTHER RECOMMENDATIONS If you intend to go for a drink at the neighbouring Armani Privé nightclub post-dinner, ask a hostess to escort you to the entrance – they have a rather draconian door policy. If you are part of a larger group, ask for one of the private rooms. Circular in design, with walls of grey slate, the private rooms rank among some of the most beautiful spaces in the hotel.

SUMMARY AND COMMENTS If you want to have a nose around the first-ever hotel by the Italian designer, you're going to need a booking. And if you're going to eat anywhere, we would recommend this signature fine-dining restaurant.

Asado ★★★½

ARGENTINIAN   EXPENSIVE   QUALITY ★★★★   VALUE ★★★

The Palace, The Old Town, Downtown; ☎ 04-428-7888; theaddress.com

Reservations Recommended **When to go** Evening **Main course range** AED 185–460 **Payment** All major credit cards **Service rating** ★★★ **Friendliness rating** ★★★ **Parking** Valet **Bar** Full service **Wine selection** Very good **Dress** Smart casual **Disabled access** Yes **Customers** Expats, tourists **Hours** Daily, 7–11:30 p.m.

SETTING AND ATMOSPHERE The bare brick walls, leather armchairs and dark wood tables make this an inviting place to spend an evening eating high-quality grills. Because of the moody lighting, it's popular with people on dates, although businessmen are also often tucking into red meat and red wine.

HOUSE SPECIALITIES The focal point of the cavernous room is a traditional *asado* grill, on which a baby goat is slowly spit-roasted for three to four hours nightly. This is the best-selling dish, but you will also be presented at your table with a selection of glistening uncooked cuts of Argentinian beef – from rib-eye and tenderloin to entrecôte – which you can choose and then watch being flame-grilled in the open kitchen. This place does divide chip fans down the middle – here, they come thick and hand-cut, so fans of thin and crispy might want to rethink.

OTHER RECOMMENDATIONS The wine list reads like a novel – Asado has one of the largest selections of Argentinian wines in the emirate.

SUMMARY AND COMMENTS A huge outdoor table is perfect for big groups and has one of the best views of the Dubai Fountain that Downtown offers. The only downside is that it's also a thoroughfare for people walking to Souk Al Bahar, so on busy nights it feels like having dinner in a fishbowl. Also, as side dishes must be ordered separately, the bill can rack up without you realising – do check the bill at the end of the evening as well, as it's not unknown here to be charged for things that never quite made it to the table.

Beach Bar & Grill ★ ★ ★

SEAFOOD   EXPENSIVE   QUALITY ★★★★   VALUE ★★★

One&Only Royal Mirage, Jumeirah, near the Marina;
☎ 04-399-9999; oneandonlyresorts.com

Reservations Recommended **When to go** Anytime **Main course range**
AED 110–240 **Payment** All major credit cards **Service rating** ★★ **Friendliness**
rating ★★★★ **Parking** Valet **Bar** Full service **Wine selection** Good **Dress** Smart
casual **Disabled access** Yes **Customers** Expats, tourists **Hours** Daily, midday–
4 p.m. and 7–11:30 p.m.

SETTING AND ATMOSPHERE   In terms of beachside dining, the Beach Bar & Grill
has no real competition in Dubai. On a sunny day, the tables outside on
the wooden decking directly overlooking the beach are always packed
with families and groups of young expats. In the evening, the twinkling
candles and sound of the lapping waves set a pretty romantic scene – if
you can ignore the construction on the Palm just behind it. Do specify
that you want an outside table when booking – it's not worth bothering
if you can't get one.

HOUSE SPECIALITIES   Predictably, fish features large on the menu here. Even
starter-size portions are huge, so share a plate of fried or grilled squid
before your freshly-grilled *hammour* or kingfish (a local speciality)
arrives. Nothing on the menu is particularly inspired, but it is all handled
very competently.

OTHER RECOMMENDATIONS   The One&Only welcomes day guests (prices vary
depending on the season), so if you make a day of it, the Beach Bar &
Grill is a great spot to spend a couple of hours out of the midday sun.

SUMMARY AND COMMENTS   The service is well-meaning but can be a little
slow, especially if there are big groups.

BiCE ★ ★ ★ ★

ITALIAN   EXPENSIVE   QUALITY ★★★★★   VALUE ★★★★

Hilton Dubai Jumeirah, Jumeirah Beach Residence Walk,
near the Marina; ☎ 04-399-1111; hilton.com

Reservations Recommended **When to go** Evening **Main course range** AED 70–
200 **Payment** All major credit cards **Service rating** ★★★★★ **Friendliness rating**
★★★★★ **Parking** Valet **Bar** Full service **Wine selection** Very good **Dress** Smart
Disabled access Yes **Customers** Locals, expats, tourists **Hours** Daily, midday–
3 p.m. and 7 p.m.–12:30 a.m.

SETTING AND ATMOSPHERE   This 100-seater restaurant is the last thing you'd
expect to find in what is, without meaning to be rude, not the chicest
hotel we've ever seen. The black-and-white pictures, rosewood floors
and slate-grey banquettes are the absolute opposite of the primary
colours and plastic plants found in the Hilton's lobby just outside. Staff
in white shirts and waistcoats are attentive and knowledgeable and
greet many of the regular guests by name. These regular guests, in turn,

greet each other with extravagant air kisses. This place is a long-time favourite of the Dubai socialite crowd, and in fact could be called the city's own version of London's A-list favourite The Ivy.

HOUSE SPECIALITIES The wine list is heavily Italian and features a great selection of Prosecco. Carpaccio is a speciality – the beef is wafer thin, and the octopus with potato, tomato tartar, olives and fresh basil is unusual and tasty. The deep-fried calamari with shrimps and courgette is feather-light and crisp. The hand-made pasta and pizza are also wonderful – try the fettuccine with Canadian lobster 'BiCE style'.

OTHER RECOMMENDATIONS The fresh fish of the day is wheeled around on an ice-packed trolley so you can meet your dinner face to face before devouring it. Waiters also come round with a trolley boasting 100-plus bottles of olive oil and balsamic vinegar for dipping and drizzling, and the large cheese board comes on wheels too.

SUMMARY AND COMMENTS The only gripe we can level at BiCE is that the piano player isn't the most skilled we've ever come across, but as the music is kept at a low enough level, it's amusing rather than annoying. Dubai's 'it' crowd use this as a starting point for an evening out on the Palm Jumeirah or at Dubai Marina – watch them pile in at 11 p.m. and order pizzas to share.

Bistro Madeleine ★ ★ ★

FRENCH   INEXPENSIVE   QUALITY ★★★   VALUE ★★★★½

InterContinental Dubai Festival City, PO Box 45777;
☎ **04-701-1111; diningdfc.com**

Reservations Recommended **When to go** Breakfast, lunch or evening **Main course range** AED 45–95 **Payment** All major credit cards **Service rating ★★★ Friendliness rating ★★★ Parking** Valet **Bar** Full service **Wine selection** Good **Dress** Smart casual **Disabled access** Yes **Customers** Expats, tourists **Hours** Daily, 8 a.m.–midnight

SETTING AND ATMOSPHERE This faux-French bistro is situated on the ground floor of a five-star hotel, so it would be difficult to describe it as authentic. But its decor certainly invokes the Gallic spirit – gingham tablecloths on simple wooden tables, adorned with a single flower in a plain vase, white napkins and salt and pepper cellars, with art nouveau–style posters on the walls. There's also some rickety outdoor seating beside the marina. But if you want a nice glass of rouge, you'll be seated behind a tall screen obstructing the view.

HOUSE SPECIALITIES Traditional French bistro fare is the order of the day, with timeless rustic dishes such as onion soup, escargot, pâté with country bread, confit duck leg and coq au vin served from midday to midnight. Bistro Madeleine is also open for breakfast, serving the standard crêpes and croissants, as well as fresh breads and a lovely dish of poached eggs on brioche with hollandaise and smoked salmon.

OTHER RECOMMENDATIONS If you're a pork lover, Bistro Madeleine serves a plethora of porcine treats (rare in Dubai) from classic cassoulet to croquet monsieurs and charcuterie. And be sure to check the daily specials displayed, naturally, on a chalkboard – if you're lucky, they'll be serving the boudin noir. There's also a kids' menu.

SUMMARY AND COMMENTS A fine French bistro serving all the classics at eminently reasonable prices.

Buddha Bar ★★★

PAN-ASIAN EXPENSIVE QUALITY ★★★ VALUE ★★★

Grosvenor House Hotel, Dubai Marina;
☎ **04-399-8888; grosvenorhouse-dubai.com**

Reservations Essential **When to go** Evenings **Main course range** AED 150–295 **Payment** All major credit cards **Service rating** ★★★ **Friendliness rating** ★★ **Parking** Valet **Bar** Full service **Wine selection** Good **Dress** Chic **Disabled access** Yes, downstairs **Customers** Expats, tourists **Hours** Saturday–Wednesday, 8 p.m.–2 a.m.; Thursday–Friday, 8 p.m.–3 a.m.

SETTING AND ATMOSPHERE This huge bar cum restaurant is quite a sight – triple-height ceilings, moody lighting, velvet drapes and squishy banquettes, presided over by a giant Buddha and populated with expensively-dressed people. At the front, a stroppy doorman will decide whether he thinks you are pretty enough to be let in (luckily, a dinner booking equals instant attractiveness). Walk into the dark space and on either side, lounging in their private rooms, you will see people who are prepared to spend more money than you. The main, warehouse-size room has a buzzing bar, and the bulk of the restaurant's tables are so badly spaced that you risk knocking over your neighbour's Champagne if you sneeze too hard. At the back are sunken tables so low that you risk a Lindsay Lohan–style knicker flash when you get up to go to the loo. Still, this place obviously trades on its name, as it is permanently packed.

HOUSE SPECIALITIES Japanese, Chinese and Thai are all done to more than competent standards here, but you will have to pay through the nose – the set menus will save you time (and a little bit of money to boot), rather than perusing the pretty epic menu.

OTHER RECOMMENDATIONS Book well ahead to avoid disappointment – or turn up after midnight and request a table for dinner – much of the clientele has moved on to admiring each other in the bustling bar area by then.

SUMMARY AND COMMENTS Somewhat inexplicably, this is still a stalwart on the Dubai scene, but bear in mind you are coming for the people-spotting, as there is definitely better Asian food to be had elsewhere.

Bussola ★★★½

ITALIAN MODERATE QUALITY ★★★ VALUE ★★★★

The Westin Mina Seyahi, Dubai Marina;
☎ **04-399-4141; westinminaseyahi.com**

Reservations Essential **When to go** Evening **Main course range** AED 60–100 **Payment** All major credit cards **Service rating** ★★★ **Friendliness rating** ★★★★

Parking Valet, garage **Bar** Full service **Wine selection** Good **Dress** Casual **Disabled access** No **Customers** Expats, tourists **Hours** Daily, midday–3 p.m. and 7–11 p.m.

SETTING AND ATMOSPHERE Bussola is a restaurant of two halves. Downstairs serves pricier, high-end Italian fare; upstairs you'll find great pizza for around half the cost. Happily, it's the al fresco pizza joint that has the better view over the beach. It isn't actually attached to the Westin hotel – it's set out on its own, right by the sea.

HOUSE SPECIALITIES Wood-fired pizzas, many including that rare Dubai commodity, pork, are the mainstay of the menu upstairs. In fact, we have heard Muslim friends complain that there is barely anything *without* pork on the menu. Downstairs, they are particularly handy with pasta and seafood – the lobster ravioli is a must-order.

OTHER RECOMMENDATIONS The wine selection is rather limited but quite well priced – grape lovers should head to the hotel's well-stocked wine bar, Oeno, for a digestif.

SUMMARY AND COMMENTS Unfortunately, this is a place best avoided in the scorching heat of summer. During winter, some people book a weekly weekend table but will often cancel it at the last minute, so if you are told there's no room at the inn, do check again on the day.

Cavalli Club ★ ★ ★

ITALIAN	VERY EXPENSIVE	QUALITY ★★★	VALUE ★★

The Fairmont Dubai, Sheikh Zayed Road, near the Marina;
☎ **04-322-9260; fairmont.com/dubai**

Reservations Recommended **When to go** Evening **Main course range** AED 150–500 **Payment** All major credit cards **Service rating** ★★★★ **Friendliness rating** ★★★★ **Parking** Valet **Bar** Full service **Wine selection** Very good **Dress** Smart **Disabled access** No **Customers** Expats, tourists **Hours** Daily, 7 p.m.–2 a.m.

SETTING AND ATMOSPHERE If you manage to make it up the pitch-black marble staircase in one piece, you'll emerge, blinking, into a ballroom bedecked in bling. Every surface has been covered with Swarovski crystals, gold-leafed or glitter-treated to within an inch of its life. Subtle, no. Impressive, definitely. Groups of girls dining together may experience unwanted (or maybe even wanted) attention from groups of male diners and drinkers – this is a bit of a pick-up joint.

HOUSE SPECIALITIES The most expensive dishes on the menu are as over the top as the decor – gold-leaf sushi, Wagyu, foie gras and lobster. It's all good, although very little is great – you are paying for the brand, as you might be able to tell from the plates, salt cellars, glasses and cutlery, which all feature the Cavalli logo.

OTHER RECOMMENDATIONS The more standard Italian fare – in homage to Roberto Cavalli's roots – is a better bet; not to mention that it's significantly cheaper.

SUMMARY AND COMMENTS Don't dine before 10 p.m. – the cavernous room is all but empty before midnight. After you've finished dining, ask your waiter to secure you a seat in one of the VIP pods or seats surrounding the bar – the bar staff can be remarkably terrierlike about their tables.

The Cellar ★★

INTERNATIONAL   MODERATE   QUALITY ★★★   VALUE ★★★

Century Village, Garhoud, near the Marina;
☎ **04-282-9333; aviationclub.ae**

Reservations Recommended **When to go** Weekends and evenings **Main course range** AED 65–175 **Payment** All major credit cards **Service rating ★★★ Friendliness rating ★★★ Parking** Valet **Bar** Full service **Wine selection** Good **Dress** No flip-flops or caps **Disabled access** Yes **Customers** Expats **Hours** Daily, midday–midnight

SETTING AND ATMOSPHERE Century Village is a bit of a surprise, tucked away behind Emirates Aviation College, predictably near the airport. The Cellar is set back by an ornamental duck pond, and during cooler months tables on the terrace are hotly contested by diners and drinkers. There is a great atmosphere, especially on Thursday nights when diners from the nearby offices pour in at 6 p.m. Inside, the lofty ceilings and stained-glass windows give it a weirdly-ecclesiastical air.

HOUSE SPECIALITIES A little bit of French, Italian, Indian and Asian dots the International menu here, but the best-sellers are always the more recognisable items, given a little twist – mint-braised shoulder of lamb in wonton pastry with garlic tzatziki; chargrilled beef fillet; or seared fillet of rainbow trout with lemon and tarragon risotto. Some of these work better than others, but as the chefs are usually mostly South African, anything meaty is usually a safe bet.

OTHER RECOMMENDATIONS The set menus and brunches are excellent value, especially when wine is included – expect to pay around AED 200 per head, all in. It's also cooked to order, so no lukewarm buffet potatoes and limp veggies here.

SUMMARY AND COMMENTS The Cellar is slightly off the beaten tourist track, so you'll be shoulder to shoulder with expats on a quiet, value-for-money night out. Even though the kitchen may slightly misfire with its 'around the world in 80 ingredients' philosophy, the atmosphere and pricing more than make up for it. Check the Web site for its regular wine-tasting dinners and wine-and-cheese tasting events, where oenophiles spill out onto the neighbouring lawns sipping rosé and Champagne.

Eau Zone ★★★½

INTERNATIONAL   EXPENSIVE   QUALITY ★★★   VALUE ★★★

One&Only Royal Mirage, Jumeirah, near the Marina;
☎ **04-399-9999; oneandonlyresorts.com**

Reservations Recommended **When to go** Evening **Main course range** AED 115–225 **Payment** All major credit cards **Service rating ★★★ Friendliness rating ★★★ Parking** Valet **Bar** Full service **Wine selection** Good **Dress** Smart

Disabled access Yes **Customers** Expats, tourists **Hours** Daily, midday–3 p.m. and 7–11 p.m.

SETTING AND ATMOSPHERE   The One&Only does romantic very well. Eau Zone, accessed via its own wooden walkway and set around atmospherically-lit pools, is a shining example of that. Unfortunately, the food gets mixed reviews – we've had some great meals and some deeply ho-hum ones. It seems to be worse when it's busier.

HOUSE SPECIALITIES   Seafood is a speciality here, often presented with an Asian twist but with a pretty fey hand with the spice. The red Thai coconut king prawn curry and the spicy crusted sea bass are menu staples, but if you like yours with real bite, ask for extra heat.

OTHER RECOMMENDATIONS   Sadly, this is probably a place best avoided in the summer months – take a seat inside rather than on the outdoor decking and the romantic effect is rather diluted. Ditto the daytime, as the swimming pools that surround it are packed with splashing children.

SUMMARY AND COMMENTS   This is one for couples, not big groups – the service can get a little confused, and the quality of the food takes a hit when large numbers ascend.

Epicure ★ ★ ★

INTERNATIONAL   MODERATE   QUALITY ★★★★   VALUE ★★★

Desert Palm Hotel, Al Awir Road; ☎ 04-323-8888; desertpalm.ae

Reservations Not necessary **When to go** Daytime or weekends **Main course range** AED 55–295 **Payment** All major credit cards **Service rating** ★★★★ **Friendliness rating** ★★★★ **Parking** Valet, garage **Bar** Full service **Wine selection** Good **Dress** Casual **Disabled access** Yes **Customers** Expats, tourists **Hours** Daily, 7 a.m.–11 p.m.

SETTING AND ATMOSPHERE   This high-class cafe is set next to the infinity pool, which overlooks a lush polo field, at the Desert Palm, Dubai's only true boutique hotel. Inside, the comfortable azure-blue banquettes are packed with families at the weekend, while younger expats spend lazy Saturdays brunching at the poolside tables.

HOUSE SPECIALITIES   Breakfast is served daily until 11 a.m. and covers everything from waffles to egg-white omelettes. The rest of the day and evening, pizzas with unusual toppings – the Thai spiced chicken and coriander is great – are a favourite. Regulars rave about the Wagyu steak sandwich and the duck leg curry.

OTHER RECOMMENDATIONS   Take your beach gear if you're planning a daytime trip. If you want a dip after lunch, the hotel charges AED 150 for a spot on a lounger, with fluffy towels thrown in for free.

SUMMARY AND COMMENTS   It's worth blocking out a few hours for your visit here, as it's a good 30 minutes outside the city's main drag. The setting is so lush and unusual that you won't regret the effort. One major complaint here is that the service can be a bit slow and confused, and at weekends they are prone to running out of key menu items.

Fire & Ice ★ ★ ★

STEAKHOUSE   EXPENSIVE   QUALITY ★ ★ ★   VALUE ★ ★ ★

Raffles, Oud Metha, Bur Dubai; ☎ 04-324-8888; raffles.com

Reservations Recommended **When to go** Evening **Main course range** AED 95–220 **Payment** All major credit cards **Service rating** ★ ★ ★ **Friendliness rating** ★ ★ ★ ★ **Parking** Valet **Bar** Full service **Wine selection** Good **Dress** Smart casual **Disabled access** Yes **Customers** Expats, tourists **Hours** Daily, 7–11:30 p.m.

SETTING AND ATMOSPHERE   Bare brick walls, lofty ceilings, high-backed chairs and dancing flames in the open kitchen give this upmarket steakhouse a gentleman's-club feel – regular live jazz adds to the ambience.

HOUSE SPECIALITIES   In its previous incarnation, Fire & Ice was all about the drama – liquid nitrogen, foams and pipettes dotted the menu. In truth, it was all pomp and purée and didn't take off as the management might have hoped – beef ice cream, anyone? Thought not. After a refurb and a rethink, they pared that right down – now it's steaks, ribs, rotisserie chicken and a rather epic burger. They also claim to have the world's best chunky chips. Not many who have tasted them would disagree.

OTHER RECOMMENDATIONS   Don't take a vegetarian date unless she's on a diet – the choice for herbivores is practically nonexistent. But do step out onto Raffles's rooftop botanical garden after your meal for a stroll and a shisha at the hotel's Crossroads bar.

SUMMARY AND COMMENTS   Raffles may be in a rather odd location – sand-wiched between Wafi Mall and a main road – but it is quite a stonking hotel once you get inside. This is the only eatery in it that won't seri-ously break the bank.

Frankie's Italian Bar & Grill ★ ★ ★

ITALIAN   MODERATE   QUALITY ★ ★ ★   VALUE ★ ★ ★

Oasis Beach Tower, The Walk, Jumeirah Beach Residence, near the Marina; ☎ 04-399-4311; rmalhospitality.com/frankies.asp

Reservations Recommended **When to go** Evening **Main course range** AED 72–295 **Payment** All major credit cards **Service rating** ★ ★ ★ **Friendliness rating** ★ ★ ★ ★ **Parking** Valet **Bar** Full service **Wine selection** Good **Dress** Smart casual **Disabled access** Yes **Customers** Expats, tourists **Hours** Daily, 12:30–4 p.m. and 5:30 p.m.–2 a.m. (last food order 11:45 p.m.)

SETTING AND ATMOSPHERE   This British-born chain is co-owned, slightly incon-gruously, by horse-racing legend Frankie Dettori and super-chef Marco Pierre White. There are no Michelin flounces here though – it's a cosy, russet-toned restaurant and bar, with parquet flooring and comfy vel-vet seats that attract a laid-back expat crowd, often in large groups.

HOUSE SPECIALITIES   All the Italian favourites are on the menu here. The pizzas are great and boast unashamedly traditional topping combinations. The pasta comes in huge portions – the lasagne and gnocchi are particularly good – and the grills gargantuan. Try the trio of tiramisu for dessert.

OTHER RECOMMENDATIONS Booking ahead is essential, as it's not a huge space and fills up quickly, but if there is no room at the inn, then take a seat at the bar – staff will happily serve you there.

SUMMARY AND COMMENTS As it's quite a dark room with no outdoor space and – despite being in the Marina – no view, an evening visit is preferable.

Al Hadheerah ★ ★ ★

ARABIC/EMIRATI   EXPENSIVE   QUALITY ★★★   VALUE ★★★★

Jumeirah Bab Al Shams Desert Resort, in the Dubai desert;
☎ **04-809-6100; jumeirah.com**

Reservations Recommended **When to go** Evening **Main course range** Buffet AED 375–395 per person **Payment** All major credit cards **Service rating** ★★ **Friendliness rating** ★★★ **Parking** Valet **Bar** Full service **Wine selection** Moderate **Dress** Casual **Disabled access** No **Customers** Tourists **Hours** Daily, 7–11:30 p.m.

SETTING AND ATMOSPHERE A 500-seater full-on *Arabian Nights* fantasy set, the vast outdoor dining area is decorated with low tables, pretty striped cushions, candles and curved wrought iron. We defy you not to gasp at the sheer size of it all – and that's before you've even seen the buffet.

HOUSE SPECIALITIES Every Arabic staple is covered at the live cooking stations. Grilled meats and seafood, *shawarma* and curries abound. Make sure to try the traditional Emirati dishes – the whole lamb cooked in a charcoal pit is especially good. Do employ SWAT-like buffet strategy here, and don't load up on carbs immediately – although this is hard when a pile of fresh-baked breads and meze land on your table before you have a chance to get your bearings.

OTHER RECOMMENDATIONS Desserts are better – and more Arabic-influenced – than standard buffet fare: piles of fresh baklava, *Umm Ali* (the Arabic version of bread and butter pudding), home-made ice cream and fresh fruit.

SUMMARY AND COMMENTS Don't even think about eating and running – at around 9 p.m., a full programme of entertainment begins, from belly dancing to a traditional Arabic horse show. Our favourites are the six sword-wielding men on horseback who stage a fight on the dunes – watch carefully and you'll see half of them get confused and change sides halfway through, perhaps a rather apt metaphor for the politics of the region. You should plan on spending an entire evening here – it's around a 45-minute drive from the centre of Dubai, in the middle of the desert. If you are planning on getting a taxi home, ask the desk to book you one on arrival – you will be asked to pay an AED 200 deposit.

Manhattan Grill ★ ★ ★ ½

STEAKHOUSE   EXPENSIVE   QUALITY ★★★★   VALUE ★★★★

Grand Hyatt, Oud Metha, Bur Dubai;
☎ **04-317-2222; dubai.grand.hyatt.com**

Reservations Recommended **When to go** Evening **Main course range** AED 130–180 **Payment** All major credit cards **Service rating** ★★★★ **Friendliness rating** ★★★★ **Parking** Valet, garage **Bar** Full service **Wine selection** Very good **Dress** Smart **Disabled access** Yes **Customers** Expats, tourists **Hours** Daily, 12:30–3 p.m. and 7–11:30 p.m.

SETTING AND ATMOSPHERE Given the preposterously-large lobby of the Grand Hyatt, this restaurant is surprisingly small and intimate, with a small terrace and a chic cream velvet and dark wood bar attached.

HOUSE SPECIALITIES Steaks every which way, from Wagyu to sirloin, with a great array of side dishes. Fish and seafood also feature, but that's not really the point now, is it?

OTHER RECOMMENDATIONS The three-course weekday lunch is a great deal at AED 100 including coffee and water, and it's a pleasant daytime space, as light streams in through the windows and the terrace overlooks the hotel's extensive gardens below.

SUMMARY AND COMMENTS Some of the best steaks and service in Dubai – but expect to pay for the privilege.

Margaux ★ ★ ★ ★

FRENCH   EXPENSIVE   QUALITY ★★★★   VALUE ★★★

Souk Al Bahar, Downtown Burj Khalifa; ☎ 04-439-7555

Reservations Recommended **When to go** Evening **Main course range** AED 139–438 **Payment** All major credit cards **Service rating** ★★★★ **Friendliness rating** ★★★★ **Parking** Valet **Bar** Full service **Wine selection** Very good **Dress** Smart **Disabled access** Yes **Customers** Expats, tourists **Hours** Daily, midday–11:30 p.m.

SETTING AND ATMOSPHERE The setting here is handsome and clubby. Floors are parquet, walls are white and the banquettes are masculine black leather. To sit inside would be a shame though (not very many do), as the terrace affords such a spectacular view of the Burj Khalifa and the Dubai Fountain. Our only gripe is that every 30 minutes your conversation will be interrupted by the incredibly loud speaker system that pipes out the opera or Arabic songs to which the fountain shakes its spray.

HOUSE SPECIALITIES The French food here is classic and the foie gras heavy, although the standout – and the best-seller – is a starter of balls of Burrata mozzarella, which oozes liquid when cut open. You need to be very hungry here to order a full complement of courses – the starters are huge (the Niçoise salad, in particular, would be generous even as a main course).

OTHER RECOMMENDATIONS The wine selection by the glass is excellent, with some very serious vintages. Ask the sommelier to pair one with each course, and he will come up with some real surprises – all of them good.

SUMMARY AND COMMENTS Leave room for dessert, as the patisserie trolley is pretty irresistible.

Nobu ★ ★ ★ ★

MODERN JAPANESE   EXPENSIVE   QUALITY ★ ★ ★ ★ ★   VALUE ★ ★ ★

Atlantis, The Palm, Palm Jumeirah; ☎ 04-426-2626; atlantisthepalm.com

Reservations Recommended **When to go** Evening **Main course range** AED 120–250 **Payment** All major credit cards **Service rating** ★ ★ ★ ★ **Friendliness rating** ★ ★ ★ ★ **Parking** Valet, garage **Bar** Full service **Wine selection** Very good **Dress** Casual **Disabled access** Yes **Customers** Tourists **Hours** Daily, midday–3 p.m. and 7–11 p.m.

SETTING AND ATMOSPHERE The food may be of the standard of other international branches set by the man himself, Nobuyuki Matsuhisa, but – predictably for a resort this size – the atmosphere isn't quite up to par. Paying upwards of £100 (or US $158) per head when you're sitting next to someone in shorts and a backwards baseball cap is a bitter pill to swallow. The design is spot-on, though, with well-spaced tables under dark bentwood canopies, and a long bar behind which sushi chefs slice and dice their wares.

HOUSE SPECIALITIES The menu is long – seriously long. All of the signature dishes are on there, including the oft-copied black cod and the chocolate bento box. The chefs do try to use local fish on the specials menu wherever possible, but ingredients – including the all-important soy sauce – are usually imported.

OTHER RECOMMENDATIONS The staff here are very knowledgeable but trained to up-sell, so keep an eye on the cost or you could end up with a shock when the bill arrives.

SUMMARY AND COMMENTS The entrance of the restaurant is located opposite the huge public viewing window of the resort's enormous aquarium, so leave time to gawp before or after your meal. It is easier to get a table here than at most of the other international branches, which either don't take bookings or have an epic waiting list, so if you've always wanted to dine chez Nobu but couldn't bear the wait, now's your chance.

Okku ★ ★ ★ ½

CONTEMPORARY JAPANESE   EXPENSIVE   QUALITY ★ ★ ★ ★   VALUE ★ ★ ★

The Monarch Hotel, Sheikh Zayed Road, Downtown; ☎ 04-501-8777; okkudubai.com

Reservations Recommended **When to go** Evening **Main course range** AED 100–300 **Payment** All major credit cards **Service rating** ★ ★ ★ ★ **Friendliness rating** ★ ★ ★ ★ ★ **Parking** Valet, garage **Bar** Full service **Wine selection** Good **Dress** Chic **Disabled access** No **Customers** Expats, tourists **Hours** Sunday–Thursday, midday–2:30 p.m.; daily, 7 p.m.–2 a.m.

SETTING AND ATMOSPHERE The killer feature of this nascent international chain is the fluorescent-lit jellyfish aquarium that illuminates the black marble bar. Unfortunately, most of the jellyfish died pretty quickly after the launch in 2008 due to overzealous cleaners, but we are happy to report that they are once again fully stocked. Slickly designed, the bar is separated from the downstairs sushi counter and dining area by a twinkling LED curtain, which provides relief from the otherwise moody lighting. Upstairs, three private dining rooms provide privacy for larger groups and have great views of the floors below.

HOUSE SPECIALITIES The modern Japanese menu offers classic sushi and sashimi alongside more outré creations – all of them spot-on in terms of quality and innovation. The menu changes frequently, but long-time favourites are 'O'-style yellowtail carpaccio, tuna tacos, spicy tuna on crispy rice, Wagyu beef and foie gras yakitori.

OTHER RECOMMENDATIONS The weekday lunchtime set menu is a steal at a price under AED 100 per head, with most of the signature dishes making an appearance, but what it makes up for in price, it lacks in daytime ambience.

SUMMARY AND COMMENTS Dubai restaurants don't come much more pouty than this moodily-lit 'beautiful people' hangout – it is co-owned by Markus Thesleff, who has a string of hip U.K. clubs to his name. If you are after a quiet, leisurely dinner à deux, avoid Thursday nights – the staff start to clear away the tables at around 10:30, the DJ cranks up the music and the black Amex brigade come out to play.

Ossiano ★ ★ ★ ★ ★

SEAFOOD   EXPENSIVE   QUALITY ★★★★★   VALUE ★★★★★

Atlantis, The Palm, Palm Jumeirah; ☎ 04-426-2626; atlantisthepalm.com

Reservations Essential **When to go** Evening **Main course range** AED 295–600 **Payment** All major credit cards **Service rating ★★★★★ Friendliness rating ★★★★★ Parking** Valet **Bar** Full service **Wine selection** Excellent **Dress** Smart **Disabled access** Yes **Customers** Locals, expats **Hours** Daily, 7 p.m.–midnight

SETTING AND ATMOSPHERE The price tag attached to an evening at this restaurant neatly solves the Atlantis's main problem when it comes to upscale dining – there are certainly no noisy, sunburned tourists here. In fact, such is the quality of the food – Santi Santamaria, the Barcelona-based holder of three Michelin stars, is chef patron – and indeed the entertainment, which comes in the form of the Ambassador Lagoon's thousands of fish, that there is an almost churchlike hush to the place. Guests descend via a vast, curved staircase and are encouraged first to sit in the bar area and sample a signature Champagne cocktail and welcome canapés before being shown to the table (insist that you are seated in one of the two rows closest to the fish tank's Perspex walls). The low-lit space is dotted with chandeliers and decorated with mosaic tiles, swirly carpet and a silver ceiling. It is perhaps a shame that this draws the eye away from the main attraction – the aquarium – but it certainly makes its point: this is as opulent as dining in Dubai gets.

HOUSE SPECIALITIES There is a very obvious Spanish slant to the handling of the ingredients here, and in fact touches of Moroccan influence are dotted throughout too – couscous, ras el hanout spice and saffron are used in many dishes. Regardless of how the dish is prepared, though, the quality of the ingredients – whether it is king crab, Brittany blue lobster or king prawn carpaccio – always shines through. Seafood haters will be quite happy – plenty of foie gras is on the menu, with duck and lamb for main courses (many of these dishes are designed to be shared between two). Vegetarians may go home hungry, however.

OTHER RECOMMENDATIONS The five- and seven-course degustation (tasting) menus are sublime (AED 650 and AED 950, respectively) – and if there is anything on which you aren't keen, the chefs will be happy to work around your tastes. The sommelier is hands-down the best in Dubai and has an encyclopaedic knowledge of Spanish wine – ask him to pair a glass with each course.

SUMMARY AND COMMENTS If you are choosing à la carte, think twice before ordering dessert – you may be then too dangerously full to enjoy the delicate petits fours that arrive unbidden (the doughnutlike, dark-chocolate-filled Catalan *bunyols* are worth the visit alone).

Pai Thai ★ ★ ★

THAI   EXPENSIVE   QUALITY ★★★★   VALUE ★★★

Al Qasr, Madinat Jumeirah; ☎ 04-366-6730; jumeirah.com

Reservations Recommended **When to go** Evening **Main course range** AED 120–300 **Payment** All major credit cards **Service rating ★★★ Friendliness rating ★★★★★ Parking** Valet **Bar** Full service **Wine selection** Good **Dress** Smart casual **Disabled access** Yes **Customers** Expats, tourists **Hours** Saturday–Thursday, 6:30–11:30 p.m.; Friday, midday–4 p.m. and 6:30–11:30 p.m.

SETTING AND ATMOSPHERE The jewel in Al Qasr's culinary crown, this has to be one of the most romantic settings in Dubai. It is set out over the water on wooden decking, overlooking the Dar Al Masyaf private villas opposite. Live Thai music and dancing, which is largely unobtrusive, entertain guests, and the waiting staff, who are mostly Thai, are very friendly and smiley, although sometimes a bit inept.

HOUSE SPECIALITIES The staples here are handled confidently – the duck red curry and the chicken green curry are very good – but cracks start to show when the dishes get more tricksy – the deep-fried *hammour* in spicy sweet-and-sour sauce, for example, doesn't taste as fresh as it should, especially given it's a local fish. If you want to try fish, stick to the barbecue station set up on the deck, where you can choose sparklingly-fresh fish, cooked to order in front of your eyes. Desserts are so-so.

OTHER RECOMMENDATIONS As with most Jumeirah hotels, the wine is on the pricey side. For something a bit different, try house cocktails, some of which come in a retro coconut. Although most of the restaurant is set outside, smokers are asked to absent themselves and sit on the benches in the neighbouring garden for their fag break. The hotel also recently started a Friday brunch, where a buffet and selected drinks cost AED 240 per head – great value.

SUMMARY AND COMMENTS Although you can walk there, it is really worth turning up 15 minutes early and reaching the restaurant via one of the Madinat Jumeirah's mini *abra* boats (they come along every five minutes from the quay outside the hotel and cost AED 50 if you're not staying at the hotel). Don't bother with a booking between June and September – the whole point here is sitting outside, and it's far too unpleasant when it's scorching.

La Parilla ★ ★ ★ ★

ARGENTINIAN   EXPENSIVE   QUALITY ★★★★   VALUE ★★★

Jumeirah Beach Hotel, Jumeirah; ☎ 04-348-0000; jumeirah.com

Reservations Recommended **When to go** Evening **Main course range** AED 120–450 **Payment** All major credit cards **Service rating** ★★★★ **Friendliness rating** ★★★★★ **Parking** Valet **Bar** Full service **Wine selection** Very good **Dress** Smart casual **Disabled access** Yes **Customers** Expats **Hours** Daily, 6:30 p.m.–midnight

SETTING AND ATMOSPHERE As this giant wave-shaped hotel is primarily a family holiday destination, Jumeirah Beach Hotel has very few restaurants and bars that are worth making a trip (especially compared to its Madinat Jumeirah neighbours). However, this Latin American gem, set on the 24th floor with a sweeping view of the coast below, is the exception. It's a low-ceilinged room, divided into lots of little nooks and crannies, although all tables have some sort of view of the dance floor in the middle, where every night (apart from Sunday) a tango dance troupe entertains the masses at a pleasingly-low volume (although there's nothing quiet about the sequin-drenched outfits). The walls are either painted deep red, are gold mosaic tiled or are bare brick; the leather chairs are comfortable, and tables are large and well-spaced.

HOUSE SPECIALITIES Breads arrive unbidden straight from the oven (the corn bread is especially good), served with a selection of olive oils and tapenade. The starters are more than competent – the gazpacho is the best of the bunch. The point of this Latin American joint, though, is the steaks. Whether it's Wagyu or Australian Angus, it will be cooked to perfection and will melt in the mouth. Accompanying sauces – whether you opt for Béarnaise, mushroom or garlic butter – come in their own copper pan, and sides are ordered separately (although go easy on them, as most mains come with their own potato and vegetable).

OTHER RECOMMENDATIONS If you are on a particularly dull date, we recommend you order the flaming *espada* (swords of grilled meat that are carved at the table) to give you a talking point. Desserts are also pure theatre – in a rather '70s style, the crêpes suzette are flambéed at the table.

SUMMARY AND COMMENTS Special mention has to go to the cowhide cushions that are brought to the table for ladies' handbags. The service here is consistently chirpy and helpful – the sommelier is particularly good, whether you're in the market for an AED 20,000 bottle of Château Latour or a glass of house white.

Pierchic ★ ★ ★ ★

SEAFOOD   EXPENSIVE   QUALITY ★★★★   VALUE ★★★★

Al Qasr, Madinat Jumeirah; ☎ 04-366-6730; jumeirah.com

Reservations Recommended **When to go** Evening **Main course range** AED 170–350 **Payment** All major credit cards **Service rating ★★★★★ Friendliness rating ★★★★ Parking** Valet **Bar** Full service **Wine selection** Very good **Dress** Smart **Disabled access** Yes **Customers** Expats, honeymooners **Hours** Daily, 1–3 p.m. and 7–11:30 p.m.

SETTING AND ATMOSPHERE During the cooler months, so many men get down on bended knee here that the waiting staff has to make sure they put them in different corners of the restaurant, lest they bang heads (the record is five in one night). The walk from Al Qasr hotel takes about 15 minutes and isn't particularly well signposted, but once you make it out onto the wooden pier from which this place takes its name, you are instantly transported (the only slight distraction comes in the shape of the resort's official photographer, who is on hand to capture your entrance). Once out over the water, it feels like you're in a Maldivian resort – or at least it would if you didn't have an amazing view of the Burj Al Arab on one side and the Palm Jumeirah on the other.

HOUSE SPECIALITIES Although it's not on the menu, ask the staff if the sea-food platter is available – with crab, tiger prawns, scallops and lobster, served with salad and rice, it's more than enough for two people. The tuna carpaccio and the king crab panna cotta are also best-sellers. The wine list, split by country, is long but expensive – the cheapest bottle comes in at AED 240.

OTHER RECOMMENDATIONS This is not a destination you'd necessarily think of for lunch, but the three-course set menu, at AED 159, is a bargain. and it's very pleasant to sit out over the crystal-blue waters. Dolphins, stingrays and barracuda have been known to swim past.

SUMMARY AND COMMENTS Getting to this restaurant can be a bit of an obstacle course for those in heels – we'd strongly advise against skinny stilettos, as the gaps in the wooden promenade do their level best to break them. If you are spending New Year's Eve in Dubai, this is an out-standing (if pricey) spot – you can see the fireworks from both the Burj Al Arab and the Atlantis hotels on either side of you.

Rare ★ ★ ★ ★

Desert Palm, Al Awir Road, PO Box 119171;
☎ **04-323-8888; desertpalm.ae**

Reservations Recommended **When to go** Evening **Main course range** AED 100–780 **Payment** All major credit cards **Service rating** ★★★★ **Friendliness rating** ★★★ **Parking/valet** Yes **Bar** Full service **Wine selection** Very good **Dress** Smart casual **Disabled access** Yes **Customers** Expats, tourists **Hours** Monday–Saturday, 7–11 p.m.

SETTING AND ATMOSPHERE A short drive from the city centre, Rare has a steady but slow flow of trade – mainly relaxed hotel guests fresh from the spa. Just the ticket if you're looking to escape the tourist hordes and enjoy a quiet dinner. The interior is warmly lit and ideal for a romantic tête-à-tête.

HOUSE SPECIALITIES At heart a steakhouse, Rare serves appetisers such as foie gras terrine and Omani lobster, followed by a long list of grilled meats with a choice of sides and sauces. But, as the name suggests, amidst the common cuts of Angus beef, you will find rare cuts of meat such as bison tartare, elk loin and bison fillet.

OTHER RECOMMENDATIONS If you're visiting during the cooler winter months, a table on the terrace overlooking the lush, green polo fields is a must. Just a ten-second amble across the terrace is the polo-themed Red Bar and Lounge, which is ideal for a pre- or post-prandial tipple, or a shisha pipe. Don't miss the daily happy hour, 6–7 p.m.

SUMMARY AND COMMENTS This restaurant is a sanctuary of calm away from the constant buzz and bustle of the city centre, serving up an exciting range of unique meats.

Reflets par Pierre Gagnaire ★ ★ ★ ★ ★

InterContinental Dubai Festival City, Deira;
☎ **04-701-1111; ichotelsgroup.com**

Reservations Recommended **When to go** Evening **Main course range** AED 290–550 **Payment** All major credit cards **Service rating** ★★★★★ **Friendliness rating** ★★★ **Parking** Valet **Bar** Full service **Wine selection** Very good **Dress** Smart **Disabled access** Yes **Customers** Expats, tourists **Hours** Wednesday–Thursday, 12:30–2 p.m.; Sunday–Friday, 7–10 p.m.

SETTING AND ATMOSPHERE The pink carpets, cut-glass chandeliers and mirrored walls won't be to everyone's taste – in fact, it looks a bit like the inside of Barbie's dream house. Around the outside of the small room are booths upholstered in grey silk. Ask for one of these if you want some privacy, as the tables in the middle of the room make you feel a little too on show, but do give you a better view of the kitchen – where Pierre Gagnaire, holder of three Michelin stars at his eponymous Paris restaurant, occasionally makes an appearance. Check the hotel's Web site for his next scheduled visit.

HOUSE SPECIALITIES The chef himself says his oeuvre is modern French cuisine – 'facing the future but respectful of the past'. In practice, this means top-notch ingredients, air freighted from France and handled with a noughties twist. The menu here changes regularly, but Gagnaire has a habit of presenting each dish in at least three parts. This means staff are not only incredibly knowledgeable about what they are serving up (the menu is short, but if you genuinely can't decide, you'd be well advised to tell them your likes and dislikes and let them concoct your order) but are also well versed in table-side culinary theatrics (they will pour, de-bone and flambé before your eyes). Amuse-bouches here are also particularly innovative – the Guinness jelly is an eye-opener, and the truffle butter bon-bons, which can be eaten on their own, have to be tasted to be believed.

OTHER RECOMMENDATIONS The business lunch is less wallet-busting than dinner, at AED 230 for three courses plus amuse-bouches and petits fours; however, the decor doesn't really lend itself to daytime dining.

SUMMARY AND COMMENTS The hushed atmosphere in this temple to gastronomy is best suited to dinner à deux – loud groups of businessmen are definitely discouraged.

Rhodes Mezzanine ★ ★ ★ ★

MODERN BRITISH   EXPENSIVE   QUALITY ★★★★   VALUE ★★★

Grosvenor House Hotel, Dubai Marina, ☎ 04-399-8888; grosvenorhouse-dubai.com

Reservations Recommended **When to go** Weekend evenings **Main course range** AED 160–240 **Payment** All major credit cards **Service rating ★★★★★ Friendliness rating ★★★ Parking** Valet **Bar** Full service **Wine selection** Very good **Dress** Smart **Disabled access** Yes **Customers** Expats **Hours** Monday–Saturday, 7–11:30 p.m.

SETTING AND ATMOSPHERE This is serious dining, although we can't help but question the reasoning behind the white padded walls, which give it a bit of an 'asylum chic' feel. At least occasional splashes of colour prevent snow blindness. Tables are widely spaced, and the busy kitchen can be seen through a Perspex screen – all the better to catch a glimpse of the often-present British celebrity chef Gary Rhodes when he travels to Dubai from his Michelin-star restaurant in London.

HOUSE SPECIALITIES The menu changes four times a year but always includes the signature white tomato soup and fluffy scones with jam. Pan-fried lobster, roast Welsh lamb and pork belly almost always make an appearance too.

OTHER RECOMMENDATIONS Two separate menus are on offer at Mezzanine. The first offers traditional hors d'oeuvres, main courses and desserts;

the second is a selection of smaller dishes that function as a create-your-own tasting menu, from AED 45–130 per dish.

SUMMARY AND COMMENTS Due to the constant construction that surrounds the hotel, no tables are on the terrace, which is a shame, as the cavernous space inside can make you conversationally self-conscious. But this is one of the must-do dining experiences in the emirate if you're serious about food. The service is exceptional too.

Rhodes Twenty10 ★ ★ ★ ★

STEAKHOUSE EXPENSIVE QUALITY ★★★★ VALUE ★★★

**Le Royal Méridien Beach Resort & Spa, PO Box 24970, Dubai Marina;
☎ 04-399-5555; leroyalmeridien-dubai.com**

Reservations Essential **When to go** Evening **Main course range** AED 95–450 **Payment** All major credit cards **Service rating** ★★★★ **Friendliness rating** ★★★★ **Parking** Valet **Bar** Full service **Wine selection** Very good **Dress** Smart **Disabled access** Yes **Customers** Expats, tourists **Hours** Daily, 7 p.m.–midnight

SETTING AND ATMOSPHERE The hype surrounding any celeb chef's restaurant in Dubai ensures an always-full reservation book. Gary Rhodes's second Dubai outpost is no exception. Dine upstairs for a quiet, romantic evening or downstairs for a brighter time seated in one of the comfortable beige booths beneath the statement chandeliers.

HOUSE SPECIALITIES Rhodes Twenty10 is a classic steakhouse. But there has been an attempt to make it stand out from Dubai's many other grills by replacing the appetisers with sharing platters and laying the emphasis heavily on customer choice. So share two or three plates between two (try the sesame duck with orange), then choose your meat or fish, sides and sauces before tucking into a dessert of warm treacle tart with marmalade ice cream.

OTHER RECOMMENDATIONS Be sure to order a predinner snifter (try the Purple Gangster), sipped in the small, mirrored bar area below an excess of Jack Vettriano prints.

SUMMARY AND COMMENTS Grills in Dubai are ten a penny, but this is one of the best in town. And now you'll be able to say that you dined at a Rhodes restaurant.

Rive Gauche ★ ★ ★ ½

FRENCH MODERATE QUALITY ★★★★ VALUE ★★★

**The Address Dubai Marina, PO Box 32923;
☎ 04-436-7777; theaddress.com**

Reservations Recommended **When to go** Evening **Main course range** AED 65–260 **Payment** All major credit cards **Service rating** ★★★ **Friendliness rating** ★★★ **Parking** Valet **Bar** Full service **Wine selection** Very good **Dress** Smart casual **Disabled access** Yes **Customers** Expats, tourists **Hours** Monday–Saturday, 7–11 p.m.

SETTING AND ATMOSPHERE This slick French brasserie – with its dark parquet flooring; muted tones; crisp, white table linens; and burgundy booths – has proved mighty popular since its 2009 opening, despite the proliferation of similar restaurants in the city. The interior is typically chic, and a terrace overlooks the marina – a lovely location for a healthy dose of mussels *marinière*, despite the rather uninspiring aspect.

HOUSE SPECIALITIES As you would expect from a brasserie kitchen, the menu offers the entire gamut of immortal French fare, from escargot to confit duck and crème brûlée with a broad selection of steaks, seafood and poultry dishes. Try the moules Asiatique – the mussels singing with ginger, chilli and lemongrass. There's also a good selection of dessert wines and digestifs.

OTHER RECOMMENDATIONS If you're a lover of that which dwells below the ocean waves (until it begins its journey to your plate), book a seat at the raw bar, take your pick from the fresh seafood on offer and watch it prepared before your eyes. Very Dubai indeed.

SUMMARY AND COMMENTS A beautiful French brasserie with a talented team in the kitchen.

The Rivington Grill ★ ★ ★ ½

MODERN BRITISH   MODERATE   QUALITY ★★★★   VALUE ★★★★★

Souk Al Bahar, Downtown Burj Khalifa; ☎ 04-423-0903; rivingtongrill.ae

Reservations Strongly recommended **When to go** Anytime **Main course range** AED 90–150 **Payment** All major credit cards **Service rating ★★★★★ Friendliness rating ★★★★★ Parking** Garage **Bar** Full service **Wine selection** Good **Dress** Smart casual **Disabled access** Yes **Customers** Expats, tourists **Hours** Saturday–Wednesday, midday–11 p.m., Thursday–Friday, midday–11:30 p.m.

SETTING AND ATMOSPHERE The white-tiled walls, wooden bar and neon modern art on the walls are reminiscent of the Rivington's London sister branch, and the food and service every bit as good. The only slight gripe is that the relatively small space isn't ideal for big groups.

HOUSE SPECIALITIES Honest British food with no fuss or unnecessary flourishes. Brunch staples – available at any time of the day – are eggs Benedict and scrambled eggs with smoked salmon. Oysters, classic prawn cocktail and steak tartare are the most popular starters, and the fish pie, fish-and-chips with mushy peas and juicy steaks are the star main courses. Leave room for the comfort-food puddings – sticky toffee pudding or Eton mess.

OTHER RECOMMENDATIONS Portions are large, so don't wolf down the loaf of freshly-baked bread that will land on your table on arrival (it smells amazing, so this will take Herculean willpower). Do try the AED 100 three-course lunch menu and peruse the wine list at length – it's great value for what's on offer.

SUMMARY AND COMMENTS All-day dining in a lovely setting – but do avoid the first-floor terrace if it's windy. It's usually a great spot to view the Dubai

Fountain when it starts up at 6 p.m., but if it's very blowy out, you – and your dinner – will get drenched. If you've had enough of The Dubai Mall by mid-afternoon, head here 4–7 p.m., when they have half-price deals on house wine and classic British snacks, including Welsh rarebit and home-made beans on toast.

Segreto ★★★★

ITALIAN   MODERATE   QUALITY ★★★★   VALUE ★★★

Souk Madinat Jumeirah, Jumeirah; ☎ 04-366-6730; jumeirah.com

Reservations Recommended **When to go** Evening **Main course range** AED 90–350 **Payment** All major credit cards **Service rating ★★★★ Friendliness rating ★★★ Parking** Valet **Bar** Full service **Wine selection** Good **Dress** Smart **Disabled access** No **Customers** Expats, tourists **Hours** Daily, 7–11:30 p.m.

SETTING AND ATMOSPHERE Set on the first floor of the Madinat, Dubai's Disney-esque fake souk, it's a surprise to find such an authentic Italian restaurant. The decor is chic and classic – white walls, tiled floors and starched linen, with latticework screens to shield amorous couples.

HOUSE SPECIALITIES Top-notch ingredients are key here. The Caprese salad, minestrone soup and antipasti selection all shine, which they really should at the price. All of the pasta is home-made – try the pappardelle with rabbit ragu, the osso buco lasagne or the divine spaghetti with Wagyu meatballs.

OTHER RECOMMENDATIONS The Madinat's waterways that Segreto overlooks can be a bit of a mosquito hot spot, so get out the repellent. In winter, the helpful staff will provide outdoor diners with pashminas to ward off chills.

SUMMARY AND COMMENTS We've been told that, strictly speaking, non-residents of the Madinat Jumeirah should pay for the *abra* ride that will take you to its doorstep. In reality, none of the drivers will ask you for the AED 50, so just jump on one outside Al Qasr hotel.

Spice Emporium ★★★

THAI   INEXPENSIVE   QUALITY ★★★½   VALUE ★★★

The Westin Mina Seyahi Beach Resort & Marina, Al Sufouh Road, Jumeirah Beach, PO Box 24883; ☎ 04-399-4141; westinminaseyahi.com

Reservations Recommended **When to go** Evening **Main course range** AED 48–92 **Payment** All major credit cards **Service rating ★★★ Friendliness rating ★★★ Parking** Valet **Bar** Full service **Wine selection** Very good **Dress** Smart casual **Disabled access** Yes **Customers** Expats, tourists **Hours** Monday–Saturday, 6–11 p.m.

SETTING AND ATMOSPHERE Quite a large restaurant that without proper lighting would be daunting, especially with only a smattering of diners. Fortunately the dim, romantic lighting and the decor – dark wood floor, light wood ceiling, numerous bits and pieces mounted on the walls and a buzzing, open kitchen in the centre – create a pleasant and inviting ambience, and the restaurant's location in the popular Westin hotel ensures a regular supply of diners.

HOUSE SPECIALITIES The menu is approachable. The kitchen, well aware of its target tourist audience, skilfully serves up the kind of dishes that anyone who's not a complete stranger to Thai food will be able to appreciate without being overwhelmed by spices. Expect beef and chicken satay, *tom yam goong,* stir-fries, green and red curries, morning glory, soy, tofu and plenty of rice, including delicious sweet, sticky rice with mango for dessert.

OTHER RECOMMENDATIONS During the cooler months, book a table outside. This is the kind of food best shared, and an al fresco setting and a couple of chilled beers would add a lot to the experience.

SUMMARY AND COMMENTS Consistently respectable Thai food in a delightful atmosphere. Always a safe option.

Teatro ★ ★ ★

INTERNATIONAL   MODERATE   QUALITY ★★★   VALUE ★★★★

Towers Rotana Hotel, Sheikh Zayed Road; ☎ 04-343-8000; rotana.com

Reservations Recommended **When to go** Evening **Main course range** AED 75–250 **Payment** All major credit cards **Service rating** ★★★ **Friendliness rating** ★★★ **Parking** Valet **Bar** Full service **Wine selection** Good **Dress** Casual **Disabled access** Yes **Customers** Expats **Hours** Daily, 6–11:30 p.m.

SETTING AND ATMOSPHERE Ignore the unprepossessing hotel entrance; this is a cosy local hangout – with heavy drapes, tiled floors and posters haphazardly dotted on the walls. It's a favourite spot for celebrations, so you'll often hear more than one rousing chorus of 'Happy Birthday' per night.

HOUSE SPECIALITIES If you are in a group and can't decide what to have for dinner, this is the ideal joint. Japanese, Indian, Thai, Italian and Chinese all jostle for space on the menu, and all competently, if not spectacularly, handled. The sushi is actually very good.

OTHER RECOMMENDATIONS Teatro fans wax lyrical about the sizzling chocolate brownie.

SUMMARY AND COMMENTS Ask for a table by the window so you can see the whizzing traffic on the Sheikh Zayed Road.

Terra Firma Steakhouse ★ ★ ★

STEAKHOUSE   EXPENSIVE   QUALITY ★★★★   VALUE ★★★

Al Badia Golf Club, PO Box 79126, Dubai Festival City; ☎ 04-701-1128; albadiagolfclub.ae

Reservations Recommended **When to go** Evening **Main course range** AED 95–360 **Payment** All major credit cards **Service rating** ★★★ **Friendliness rating**

★★★ **Parking** Valet **Bar** Full service **Wine selection** Very good **Dress** Smart casual **Disabled access** Yes **Customers** Expats, tourists **Hours** Tuesday–Sunday, 7 p.m.–midnight

SETTING AND ATMOSPHERE Restaurants at golf clubs are not famed for high-quality cooking, which is perhaps why Terra Firma remains largely undiscovered by the local dining populace. They're missing out. The plush interior boasts a beautiful arched ceiling, soft lighting, booth seating and a star-studded feature wall, but the best tables are on the terrace overlooking the golf course.

HOUSE SPECIALITIES The archetypal steakhouse buffed up to the highest levels of luxury is common in Dubai, but few are as polished as Terra Firma. The starters are consummately prepared and presented (try the superb lobster bisque), but it's the various cuts of Angus steak and, even more so, the Wagyu reared by Australian producer David Blackmore, that is the pride of Terra Firma's menu.

OTHER RECOMMENDATIONS If you're not in the mood for beef, try the venison loin with bitter chocolate jus, or if you're of the vegetarian persuasion, order the tofu bon-bon and celeriac truffle reduction.

SUMMARY AND COMMENTS A steakhouse of this quality begs to be sought out, but the fact that it's tucked away at the golf club means that you can enjoy some extremely fine cooking in peace and quiet.

Verre by Gordon Ramsay ★ ★ ★ ★

MODERN EUROPEAN EXPENSIVE QUALITY ★★★★★ VALUE ★★★★

Hilton Dubai Creek, Sheikh Zayed Road, Deira; ☎ 04-212-7551; hilton.com

Reservations Recommended **When to go** Evening **Main course range** AED 180–225 **Payment** All major credit cards **Service rating** ★★★★★ **Friendliness rating** ★★★★ **Parking** Valet **Bar** Full service **Wine selection** Very good **Dress** Smart **Disabled access** Yes **Customers** Locals, expats, tourists **Hours** Daily, 7 p.m.–midnight

SETTING AND ATMOSPHERE This was Dubai's first-ever celebrity chef restaurant, which goes some way to explaining the location, which is now really on the wrong side of Dubai Creek for the prices they charge. Still, the Ramsay name, and the quality of the food, do still tempt punters across the bridge. Opened in 2001, it was closed for refurbishment in 2010 so has ceased to show its age – decor is black, white and chrome, with an illuminated glass wall dominating the entrance.

HOUSE SPECIALITIES The menu changes seasonally but is what you'd expect from the stroppy Scot – modern updates of traditional Euro dishes, often given a Brit twist. So a starter of seared foie gras comes with a Granny Smith apple salad, and the pressed terrine of smoked duck is accompanied by a rhubarb and almond crumble. It also serves the best pork belly in Dubai.

OTHER RECOMMENDATIONS Go for the seven-course tasting menu, at a price of AED 615, for a blow-out treat, and take a walk along Dubai Creek to work it off after – the twinkling lights and bustle of the docks are pretty at night. There is also a chef's table offering a special degustation menu if you want to be right in on the action.

SUMMARY AND COMMENTS   The original, and arguably still the best. As long as you're not bothered about hitting the hippest joint in town, this is very accomplished cooking.

Zuma ★ ★ ★ ★

MODERN JAPANESE   EXPENSIVE   QUALITY ★ ★ ★ ★   VALUE ★ ★ ★ ★

Gate Village 06, Dubai International Financial Centre, Sheikh Zayed Road; ☎ 04-425-5660; zumarestaurant.com

Reservations Recommended **When to go** Evening **Main course range** AED 40–250 **Payment** All major credit cards **Service rating** ★ ★ ★ ★ ★ **Friendliness rating** ★ ★ ★ ★ ★ **Parking** Valet, garage **Bar** Full service **Wine selection** Very good **Dress** Smart chic **Disabled access** Yes **Customers** Expats, businesspeople **Hours** Saturday–Wednesday, 12:30–3 p.m. and 7 p.m.–midnight; Thursday, 12:30–3 p.m. and 7 p.m.–1 a.m.; Friday, 12:30–4 p.m. and 7 p.m.–1 a.m.

SETTING AND ATMOSPHERE   This perennially-popular after-work hangout of Dubai's movers and shakers more than deserves its always-full reservations book. The slickly-designed two-floor space holds its own against the other branches in this international chain. Upstairs, large groups lounge on sofas or perch by the glass bar; downstairs, diners have a full view of the skilled sushi chefs and the robata grill, or out of the floor-to-ceiling windows.

HOUSE SPECIALITIES   Crispy fried squid, green chilli and lime; fried soft shell crab with mizuna wasabi mayonnaise; jumbo tiger prawns with yuzu pepper from the robata grill; and miso-marinated black cod wrapped in a *hoba* leaf.

OTHER RECOMMENDATIONS   You'll be surrounded by men in suits, but to taste the best of Zuma at an incredibly low price, try the Ebisu lunch Sunday–Thursday. If three courses isn't enough, Friday's Champagne brunch sees the counters groaning with an all-you-can-eat main course buffet, with à la carte main courses, dessert selection and free-flowing Champagne and sake, for under AED 500 a head.

SUMMARY AND COMMENTS   At the weekend, book a table late in the evening, and afterwards spend the small hours people-watching in the upstairs bar – it's Dubai's 'beautiful people' hangout.

PART EIGHT

SPAS *and* SALONS

PAMPERING *and* PAPER PANTS

IN THE U.A.E., GROOMING IS NOT CONSIDERED A LUXURY – it's an absolute necessity. Walk past a man in local dress, and you will almost certainly get a waft of heady-smelling *oud* (a musky, oil-based perfume); look sandalwards and you'll see a set of perfectly-manicured toenails. And you may not be able to see the glossy manes or the perfectly-painted toenails of Emirati women, but believe us, they are there. Even the expats here are blow-dried to within an inch of their lives. Dubai's own breed of New York's Park Avenue Princess or London's Sloane Ranger is the Jumeirah Jane, and when she's not sipping soy lattes at the Lime Tree Café, her most regular daytime haunts are the nail bars and hair salons that line, you guessed it, Jumeirah Beach Road.

This means that there is an almost unbelievable number of places to get groomed all over the city, and these can be broadly split into three categories. First, there are those in hotels, which, especially during the summer months, are great places to while away the time when it gets too hot outside. As an added bonus, when the mercury rises – usually from mid-June to the end of September – many give serious discounts or two-for-one offers on treatments, or a range of whole-day packages. Unfortunately, many of these won't be advertised online, so it's best to enquire about these over the phone when making your booking.

At the larger, more luxurious hotels, the price of a treatment (or at least those that cost over a certain amount – cheaper grooming treatments such as an eyebrow shape or leg wax sometimes don't count) may also include a stint in a relaxation area afterwards, with tea, juices, fresh fruit or dates, and use of the steam room, sauna and whirlpool bath, which are usually attached to the single-sex changing rooms to preserve modesty. Some, such as the Park Hyatt's **Amara** Spa and the **Satori Spa** at Bab Al Shams, will also let you claim a lounger by the pool. It's worth checking what is included before your visit, so you can come fully prepared with a bikini or gym kit to take full advantage. Use of towels, robes and slippers or flip-flops – and your own pair of disposable paper knickers – is included in the price, and these are usually found in the self-service lockers. These spas will almost certainly have both male and female therapists.

One rung down the ladder sit the smaller, independent spas that are usually housed in either malls or private villas, which tend to be 20%–30% cheaper. These include the burgeoning **SensAsia** chain, the **Dragonfly** in BurJuman Centre and the local favourites **Sisters** and the **Lily Pond.** These are usually a little cheaper than the large hotels and offer a broader range of branded products, although there is often a little more sales pressure to actually buy them at the end of the treatment. This tends towards the inept rather than the annoying – many have been the times we've heard the plaintive cry of 'Oh, madam, very spotty! Buy this; after you look pretty!' or, our personal favourite, the utterly incomprehensible, 'Madam! Very small skin! Need more cream!' Even if you do manage to resist purchasing the unguents, you'll almost certainly leave clutching a list of recommended lotions and potions. On the downside, most of these don't have the swimming pools, saunas or steam rooms in which to while away the day, and many are exclusively for women. Broadly under the same category, a selection of slickly-designed, dedicated nail bars often have one or two treatment rooms offering waxing, basic massage and maybe the odd facial. You will find these laughably cheap compared to back home – a mani-pedi in a dedicated nail bar will cost around AED 120. You are better off just sticking to standard mani-pedis in these places, as massage tables can be wobbly and treatments perfunctory.

Lastly, you have the small backstreet salons you'll see if you take to the pavements of Satwa or Bur Dubai. Their blacked-out windows might suggest that they offer more than the standard blow-dry, if you know what we mean, but most aren't as dodgy as they look. Actually, the interiors of these single-sex 'ladies' saloons' (we have no idea how or why the extra 'o' slipped in there, but it has been almost universally adopted) are obscured by legal necessity and probably the only place that you may see an Emirati lady without her head covered (that is, if you too are in possession of XX chromosomes). Treatments here come in at less than half the price of hotel spas.

If you are a man, do not even consider walking into these places to keep your other half company – you will be summarily ejected, and it's possible the police may even be called. There are actually versions of these for guys, where a shave with a cutthroat razor can cost from as little as AED 10 and a 'fancy haircut' AED 20. Unless you are either determined to have a cultural experience or are willing to sport either a mullet or a buzz cut for the foreseeable future, it's best not to bother. For women, you are also advised to steer clear of anything drastic – haircuts or the oft-advertised permanent (that is, tattooed) makeup can be a bit of a horror show, unless you especially like lipliner that looks like black permanent marker – but they are brilliant places for budget manicures, pedicures, threading and waxing. Some will even have small hammams or offer traditional Ayurvedic treatments. As these salons open, shut and move around so often, it is difficult to recommend specific locations, although a concentration of them are on Al Diyafah Street, opposite the BurJuman Centre in Bur Dubai, and in the area surrounding the Dubai Museum.

unofficial **TIP**
If you plan to have more than one spa experience, pick up a copy of the *Entertainer Body*, available from all good bookshops and most large supermarkets. This AED 250 book is stuffed with two-for-one spa vouchers valid for one year from the publication date. Also useful is the monthly health and beauty magazine *Aquarius*, available free in most hotels, as it lists current offers in spas and salons.

HOW *to* SPOT *a* SUBPAR SPA

YOU SHOULD FEEL RELAXED from the minute you walk into a spa – especially if it is at the pricier end of the scale. The receptionist should begin by asking you to fill out a form detailing any existing conditions (pregnancy, high blood pressure, allergies), what you want to achieve from the treatment (detoxification, relaxation, rejuvenation) and the sort of pressure you want during the massage, if you're having one.

Once on the table, your therapist should check if the room temperature is OK with you and whether you are happy with the music (you are well within your right to ask them to change it or switch it off if you're not into whale song or Tibetan chanting). If your therapist is chatting more than you would like – this is most likely during a facial, where they will let you know what is going on – then let them know. They should not leave the room at any point – in fact, the best trained will barely take their hands off you – and all materials should be within easy reach so they don't need to go clattering around by the sink. When the treatment is finished, the lights should be kept low for several minutes while you gather yourself and have a glass of water or tea, before you are led to a relaxation area.

For your part, the spa will expect you to arrive at least 15 minutes early for your treatment (if you are late, expect your massage time to be shortened accordingly), and do try to cancel at least 24 hours in advance if you cannot make it. Factor in at least another 15 minutes after the treatment as well, so you can ease yourself back into the light.

UNISEX *or* JUST SEX

FOR THE RECORD, IT IS COMPLETELY and punishably illegal to be pummelled by a member of the opposite sex here, no matter what the masseur or spa manager tells you. This doesn't, however, mean that you won't be offered the option. All we can advise is that it is best not to acquiesce. Of course much of the time, it will just be because a same-sex therapist is unavailable, but it is not unheard of for 'extras' to be offered – or indeed thrown in free of charge without prior consent. A good rule of thumb: if the charge seems unreasonably high (it would be unusual for a smaller salon to quote more than AED 250 for a 60-minute massage), it may not be on the level. There have also been cases of same-sex therapists offering similar extras at big-name, five-star hotels. The bottom line: it's up to you whether it's worth breaking the law for a few seconds of pleasure, if you know what we mean (nudge, nudge, wink, wink).

Of course, getting nearly naked is pretty much a given if you have booked in for a full-body massage, and a good therapist will make you feel as comfortable as possible about this. Paper knickers will be provided, and it is recommended that you use them. In the more upmarket spas you will also have a fluffy white robe and slippers to pad around in (in spas with only two or three treatment rooms, you will be required to disrobe next to the massage bed, while the therapist waits outside to give you some privacy). As many local women prefer to get changed out of the way of prying eyes, there will usually be at least one private cubicle – out of cultural sensitivity, it is a good idea to be quite discreet about being naked even if you are more European about the whole thing. Once you are in the treatment room, a towel or sheet should be held up while you disrobe and climb onto the bed, and again when you turn to lie on your front. If there are any areas that you would prefer they didn't massage, let them know in advance – ideally at the same time as you fill out the form you will be handed on entry.

DUBAI'S SIGNATURE TREATMENTS

ALTHOUGH NOT, STRICTLY SPEAKING, from Dubai, the hammam – or Middle Eastern steam bath – is the closest the country has to a 'traditional' treatment, and it is offered in a few of the larger hotels, as well as some small salons. The **One&Only Royal Mirage** and **The Palace** hotels both boast luxurious dedicated steam rooms, with heated marble slabs upon which you will be covered with black soap, scrubbed and then massaged. Some independent spas, such as the Sisters salon in the Dubai Mall, offer essentially the same treatment for around 30% less, although it's more of a 'sweaty cupboard' than

PART NINE

SHOPPING

A BROWSER'S PARADISE

SHOPPING IN DUBAI IS ALMOST A NATIONAL SPORT. The rest of the year, it might be all about sun, sea and sand, but one of the reasons that the city has managed to pitch itself as a year-round holiday destination is the proliferation of village-size malls that offer air-conditioned respite, retail and recreation during the scorching summer months. There are few big international brands you won't find here, from affordable high street names to luxury designer labels. So seriously do Dubai dwellers take their spending, that instead of the usual post-Christmas and summer sales, slashed prices here are cause for a carnival. During Dubai Summer Surprises and winter's Dubai Shopping Festival, in addition to serious in-store discounts, there are concerts, shows and cultural tours that take place citywide.

Although goods in the U.A.E. are tax-free, in truth, you probably won't be saving much on prices at home unless you are visiting during sales time. The only exceptions are electronics (but of course, anything larger than suitcase-size and you will likely have to ship it home) and gold. The other thing to note is that consumer rights here are a little shaky, to say the least. If you have purchased something faulty and notice while you are still in the country, most larger stores should offer you a refund or exchange. If you just happen to change your mind, you'll probably be offered a credit note at best.

Not all of the shopping here takes place in the sterile environment of the malls, although obviously the summer makes scouring local souks more than a little sweaty and unpleasant. Whether you're in the market for fake handbags and sunglasses (which we don't condone, but each to his or her own), Arabic perfume and spices or Indian textiles, there is a bustling market in Dubai for you, where prices are often rock-bottom. Dubai has always been a big importer of goods, so don't expect to find local, handmade treasures – but you will come across goods from India, Afghanistan, Pakistan, Sri Lanka and China. Although credit cards are accepted in all malls, carry cash if you are going to the souks, as your plastic will be met with blank stares.

The REVENGE of the MEGA-MALLS

AS FAR AS DUBAI IS CONCERNED, big is beautiful when it comes to shopping experiences, so the malls here are predictably super-size. There is also a bit of an arms race going on when it comes to added value. Whether it's an indoor snow ski slope à la **Mall of the Emirates** or an aquarium filled with sharks as at **The Dubai Mall,** the malls are each pretty canny at thinking up new ways to attract your dirhams. One thing you should bear in mind is that malls provide a social hub for Emirati families, especially in the summer when the air-conditioned environs and breakfast-to-bedtime activities mean that one can spend a whole day. For visitors, this means two things: first, the malls are at their busiest when you would least expect, namely weekend evenings. So if you want to get a cab out of there at these times (especially on Thursday, Friday and Saturday around 6–11 p.m.), you may have a bit of a wait. If you are sneaky, the best places to get a cab during these times are the hotels that are often attached to the malls. Second, you should dress modestly – mall police will issue warnings or ask you to leave if too much leg or cleavage is on show.

*un*official **TIP**
If you are driving to The Dubai Mall, make sure that you collect a free ticket at the entrance telling you on which level you've parked. Don't panic if you lose the car though – cameras are above each parking space, so attendants will be able to help you locate your car in seconds.

As these malls are widely used by the whole family, there's always lots to keep children entertained, from ice-skating lessons to cookery schools and supervised playgroups. In terms of shops, you will find the 'best of' the world's favourite brands – American, British, French and Spanish are all represented here. Opening hours are also very long – in most cases, shops are open at 10 a.m. and remain so until at least 10 p.m., and this extends until midnight at weekends and during the month of Ramadan. Here's our pick of the most impressive monoliths.

THE DUBAI MALL

THERE WAS SOME CONCERN when this mega-mall (Downtown; ☎ 800-382-246-255; **thedubaimall.com**) opened its doors in 2008 that it was simply too big – there was nowhere near the full complement of shops, and it had a bit of a nuclear winter vibe for the first six months. Not so now – it is permanently packed with shoppers, diners and cinema-goers and is, for our money, the best retail destination

Where to Shop in Jumeirah

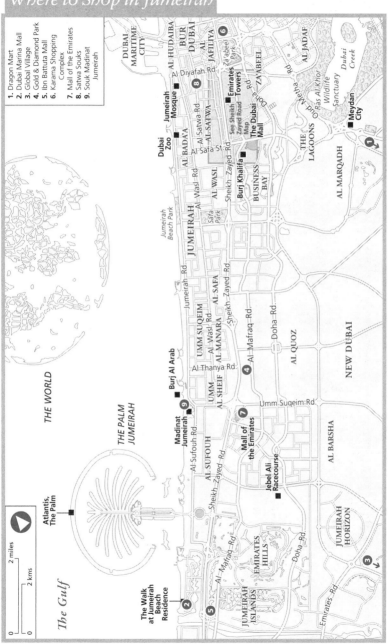

1. Dragon Mart
2. Dubai Marina Mall
3. Global Village
4. Gold & Diamond Park
5. Ibn Battuta Mall
6. Karama Shopping Complex
7. Mall of the Emirates
8. Satwa Souks
9. Souk Madinat Jumeirah

DUBAI MARITIME CITY

AL HUDAIBA

BUR DUBAI

AL JADAF

Dubai Creek

Al Diyafah Rd.   Emirates Za'abeel   6
Za'abeel Park
Towers

AL JAFILIYA

Ras Al Khor Wildlife Sanctuary

Jumeirah Mosque   8   See Sheikh Zayed Road Map   ZA'ABEEL   Al Metha Rd.

Dubai Zoo   Al Satwa Rd.   Emirates Towers   The Dubai Mall

AL BADAA   AL SATWA

Al Safa St.   Al Safa Rd.   Sheikh Zayed Rd.   Burj Khalifa   BUSINESS BAY   THE LAGOONS   Meydan City   1

AL WASL   AL WASL Rd.

AL MARQADH

Jumeirah Beach Park   Safa Park

JUMEIRAH   Sheikh Zayed Rd.

Jumeirah Rd.   UMM SUQEIM   AL WASL Rd.   AL SAFA   Al Mafraq Rd.   Doha Rd.

AL MANARA

Burj Al Arab

AL SAFA   Sheikh Zayed Rd.   AL QUOZ   NEW DUBAI

Al Thanya Rd.   4

UMM AL SHEIF   Umm Suqeim Rd.

Madinat Jumeirah   9   Mall of the Emirates   7

Al Sufouh Rd.   AL SUFOUH   AL BARSHA

Jebel Ali Racecourse

Sheikh Zayed Rd.

THE PALM JUMEIRAH

JUMEIRAH HORIZON

Atlantis, The Palm

THE WORLD

EMIRATES HILLS   Doha Rd.

The Walk at Jumeirah Beach Residence   2

JUMEIRAH ISLANDS   5   Al Mafraq Rd.   Emirates Rd.   3

The Gulf

0   2 miles
0   2 kms

Where to Shop on Sheikh Zayed Road

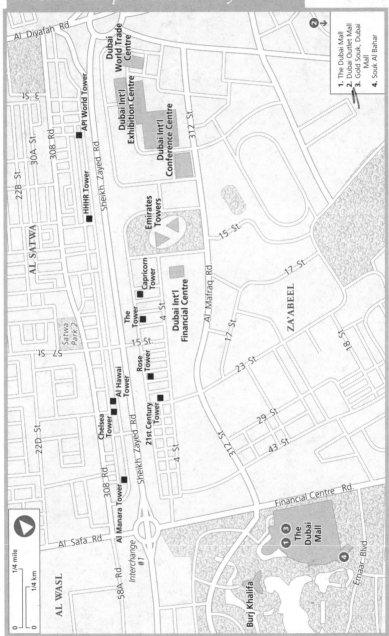

1. The Dubai Mall
2. Dubai Outlet Mall
3. Gold Souk, Dubai Mall
4. Souk Al Bahar

continued from page 271

(☎ 04-434-0626). The basement floor is packed with independent stores, as well as a large **Waitrose** (☎ 04-434-0700) and the **Organic Foods & Café** supermarkets (☎ 04-434-0577). **Hamleys** (☎ 04-339-8889) toyshop on the third floor usually has some slightly demented-looking mall worker in an animal suit hovering outside to entertain little ones. **Candylicious** (☎ 04-330-8700), the world's biggest candy store, makes Willy Wonka's chocolate factory look like Woolworths. If you've overindulged on the purchasing front, there is a bag-carrying service – just enquire at one of the 14 guest services desks dotted around the mall. The mall can be accessed from the Burj Khalifa Dubai Metro stop, but it is a good 25-minute walk to the entrance, although it is also served by a feeder bus.

MALL OF THE EMIRATES

SKI DUBAI MAY BE THE BIG TOURIST DRAW here (see page 202), but there's some serious shopping to be done and some brilliant dining spots too (see Part Seven, Dining and Restaurants). Unfortunately, the layout is rather confusing, as it hasn't been master-planned. It looks a bit like someone has picked up The Dubai Mall, shaken it around and seen where the stores fall. So a bookshop is next to a toyshop is next to a perfume shop. Our advice is to pick up a map from the guest services kiosk and decide where you want to shop, or risk getting lost and frustrated. The stores at Mall of the Emirates (Sheikh Zayed Road; ☎ 04-409-9000; **malloftheemirates.com**) are too many and varied to list, but there is a raft of international high street favourites including Swedish **H&M** (☎ 04-341-4921), the Spanish **Zara** (☎ 04-341-3171), French **Promod** (☎ 04-341-4944) and American **CK Jeans** (☎ 04-341-1044). MoE (as it's known to locals) is also home to the city's only **Harvey Nichols** (☎ 04-409-8888), with high-end fashion for women and children and a huge shoe department – a personal shopper service is available if you are overwhelmed by choice. There is also a large **Debenhams** (☎ 04-262-9100), a **Carrefour hypermarket** (☎ 04-409-4899) and a **Virgin Megastore** (☎ 04-341-4353). You'll find a particularly high concentration of jewellery stores, including Middle Eastern chain **Damas** (☎ 04-341-0633); independent boutique **Boom & Mellow** (☎ 04-341-3993; **boomandmellow.com**), which stocks a range of costume pieces from international and local designers; **Bvlgari** (☎ 04-341-0662); and **Chopard** (☎ 04-341-4545). Near **Ski Dubai** (ask your taxi to drop you off at the Kempinski Hotel entrance) is **Magic Planet,** a noisy, flashing selection of kids' arcade games, and a food court with a selection of unhealthy offerings (a trip here is not to be recommended if you have a nervous disposition or a hangover). If you have younger children who are unhappy about being dragged around the shops, **Peekaboo** nursery (☎ 04-347-0622; **peekaboo.ae**) offers supervised creative play for tots under the age of 7 daily, 10 a.m.–9 p.m., although **Cuddle Carts** (baby cars) can be hired on the ground-floor level at parking entrances A–F and G–L. There is ample parking here, although take it from someone who has spent two hours finding the car: it is imperative that you take a note of the entrance at which you came in. The Mall of the Emirates Dubai Metro stop will also lead you directly into the shops.

DUBAI OUTLET MALL

DUBAI RESIDENTS' DIRTY LITTLE SECRET is that, for all the conspicuous consumption, they like a bargain as much as the next person. So they love this spendthrifts' paradise (Al Ain Road; ☎ 04-423-4666; **dubaioutletmall.com**), just 20 minutes' drive from Downtown. Although it is large, it doesn't offer much apart from shops (a small children's play area is in the foyer, some cafes are dotted around and a fast-food court is at the back), although there is a **Chuck E. Cheese's** (**chuckecheesesdubai.com**), which, as well as serving up artery-hardening food, has a large soft play area and arcade games. But back to the bargains. The best of a wonderful bunch is **Priceless** (☎ 04-425-9818), where Al Tayer Group, which owns the U.A.E. licences for Harvey Nichols, Jimmy Choo, Yves Saint Laurent and Bottega Veneta among others, offers previous seasons of all the above plus much more, for men, women and children, at drastically-reduced prices (on average, 80% off). The really canny phone ahead to see when the next big delivery is coming in, usually once or twice a week. Boutique 1, the multi-brand store with outposts in Jumeirah Beach Residence's The Walk and Mirdif City Centre Mall, also has a store called **The Outlet** (☎ 04-426-4900), which sells everything from ballgowns to bras, from international names. Don't ignore the uninspiringly-named **Allied Factory Outlet** (☎ 04-426-4981) – you have to sift through, but you can find clothing, bags and shoes from Marc Jacobs, Tod's and Paul & Joe, as well as discontinued perfume and cosmetics from brands such as Clinique and Nars. Statement stilettos from Christian Dior, Alaia and Marc Jacobs are on offer at **Opera** (☎ 04-425-5918), and more-reasonably priced heels can be found at **Aldo** (☎ 04-425-5901). **Bauhaus** (☎ 04-425-9828) is great for casual wear and denim and, as it is owned by the same company as Manolo Blahnik, does occasional one-day sales of the shoe king's wares. **Kraze** (☎ 04-425-9822) is less of a discount store, more of a standard boutique, but it does have a hard-to-find selection of clothing and accessories from Emirati designers. Sports fans are well catered for, with **Adidas** (☎ 04-426-4927), **Nike** (☎ 04-426-4952), **Reebok** (☎ 04-425-5822) and **Puma** (☎ 04-426-4965) outlets.

unofficial **TIP**
The end of February and the beginning of September, just after the sales finish, are the best times to hit the Outlet Mall, as stock that hasn't sold in other stores is shifted here and further discounted.

IBN BATTUTA MALL

THIS IS WHAT HAPPENS WHEN MALLS are forced to differentiate themselves with deeply-weird quirks. The 'world's largest themed shopping mall' (Sheikh Zayed Road; ☎ 04-362-1900; **ibnbattutamall. com**), named after the 14th-century Moroccan explorer, is kitsch in the extreme. The six Vegas-like courts are Andalucian, North African, Egyptian, Persian, Indian and Chinese inspired, although only the polystyrene architecture, fake pyramids and large sailing ships point to the global bent – the shops are your standard high street staples. The not-very-authentic China Court boasts a 21-screen cinema, a **Pizza Express** (☎ 04-368-5134) and the electrical giant **Sharaf DG** (☎ 04-368-5115), while Persia hosts the not-entirely-indigenous **H&M** (☎ 04-364-9819), **Forever 21** (☎ 04-368-5232) and **Debenhams** (☎ 04-368-5282). The standout smaller stores are **Ginger & Lace** (☎ 04-368-5109), which stocks pretty women's clothing from niche designers, and the **Betsey Johnson** store (☎ 04-368-5109), stocking the American designer's signature retro womenswear styles. **Modhesh World** (**modheshworld.com;** ☎ 600-545-555) has arts, crafts, singing and dancing for tots under age 6; a hairstyling salon for those under age 12; and a Play Zone with arcade games. During the winter months, a static hot-air balloon takes shoppers up for a ten-minute look at Dubai from the air. If we're being honest, there isn't much reason to come here apart from the balloon, as there are almost no stores that you wouldn't find at home. It does benefit from its own Dubai Metro stop, though, so it's a fairly easy 15-minute journey towards Jebel Ali from Dubai Marina if you fancy a couple of hours window-shopping.

MIRDIF CITY CENTRE

SENSIBLY, THE POWERS THAT BE here have decided to differentiate themselves by the quality of the stores, many of which are unique to the mall (Mirdif; ☎ 800-6422; **mirdifcitycentremall.com**), instead of showing off with extraneous bells and whistles. Apart from **Playnation,** the children's play area that features, among other things, an indoor sky-diving experience (see page 189), the whole point of this place is spending money, so there are more designer boutiques than you could shake a Prada bag at. **Boutique 1** (☎ 04-284-3777) opened a gleaming white-and-silver mens- and womenswear store here in 2010, selling brands including Manoush, Issa and Diane von Furstenberg. Other exclusives are the **See by Chloe** shop (☎ 04-284-0409), preppy U.S.-based chain **American Eagle Outfitters** (☎ 04-231-6631) and king of 12-ply cashmere **Michael Kors** (☎ 04-284-3462). The home wares score highly too – the only U.A.E. outpost of American brand **Crate & Barrel** (☎ 04-284-3151) is here, and there's a large **Pottery Barn** (☎ 04-606-2610). **Cinestar** (☎ 04-284-0001; **cinestarcinemas.com**) operates a cinema here with one Gold Class screen, where you will be served drinks and dinner at your reclining chair. If you don't fancy dinner *at* the movie, there are some great sit-down eateries, including British chain **Tiffinbites** which opened its first Dubai diner here (☎ 04-284-0305), **YO! Sushi** (☎ 04-284-3995) and **Mango Tree Bistro** (☎ 04-284-3635) for a fantastic Thai feast. Having said that, it's only really worth the trip if you are staying in Garhoud, Festival City or Bur Dubai – it's way too much of a trek otherwise and doesn't have its own Metro station.

DUBAI MARINA MALL

RESIDENTS USE THIS AS THEIR LOCAL SUPERMARKET stop as it houses a large **Waitrose** (☎ 04-434-2624), or alternatively come to grab a bite to eat at **Carluccio's** Italian restaurant (☎ 04-399-7844) or **Gourmet Burger Kitchen** (☎ 04-399-7705). Dubai Marina Mall (Dubai Marina; ☎ 04-436-1000; dubaimarinamall.com) is not a super-exciting retail experience, but if you are staying at this end of town, it is certainly worth an hour's stroll around. There is a **Mothercare** (☎ 04-434-2713) and a branch of **Boots** (☎ 04-434-2720) for health and beauty essentials, and a **Pace e Luce** hair and nail salon for preening and pampering (☎ 04-399-7770). A smattering of luxury fashion boutiques includes **Balmain** (☎ 04-399-7725), which stocks straight-off-the-runway womenswear, and **Juicy Couture** (☎ 04-434-2638), with the ubiquitous velour leisure suits and also a range of charm bracelets. The proximity to the beach, though, probably means that you'll be keener to check out the swimwear and surf brands **Quicksilver** (☎ 04-434-2567), **Roxy** (☎ 04-399-7075) and **Billabong** (☎ 04-434-2577), or the bikinis at lingerie brand **Yamamay** (☎ 04-399-7566). There is also a small cinema (reelcinemas.ae). The Dubai Marina Metro stop is a 15-minute walk down a straight road but shouldn't be attempted in the height of summer, as there is no shade.

BURJUMAN CENTRE

THE BIGGEST DRAW AT THIS BUR DUBAI MALL (Khalid Bin Al Waleed Street, Bur Dubai; ☎ 04-352-0222; burjuman.com) is the **Saks Fifth Avenue** department store (☎ 04-351-5551), housed in the newest extension of one of the oldest malls in the city. A large beauty hall features hard-to-find brands including Serge Lutens and By Terry, and mens-, womens- and childrenswear from international brands. There is a particularly good swimwear section, and an eveningwear department that is excellent for browsing (maybe less so for buying, unless you have room in your wardrobe for an AED 30,000 crystal-encrusted stunner). There is, in fact, no shortage of the extremely expensive here. **Dolce & Gabanna** (☎ 04-351-5551) offers the sort of high-octane glamour that you'll see a lot of in Dubai's bars and clubs, and a large **DKNY** (☎ 04-351-3788)

unofficial **TIP**
In the weeks running up to the Dubai World Cup in March, milliners from all over the world set up stalls in the public spaces of BurJuman Centre – check burjuman.com for more details nearer the time.

offers a more understated look. Men will appreciate **Paul Smith** (☎ 04-359-0099), which has a large selection of great suits and T-shirts, and the classic American **Polo Ralph Lauren** (☎ 04-352-531). High street brands are also well represented, with a **Mango** (☎ 04-355-5770), **Ted Baker** (☎ 04-355-3842), a large **Zara** (☎ 04-351-3332) and a **New Look** (☎ 04-355-6578). **Paul Café** (☎ 04-351-7009) on the ground floor is always packed, as is the **Noodle House** (☎ 04-352-6615) on the third level. As the directors of the mall refused to pay to have a Dubai Metro stop named after them, you have to alight at Khalid Bin Al Waleed station, but it is literally outside the front door. Unless you intend to buy, don't drive because you will be charged for the privilege if you do not spend more than AED 100.

FESTIVAL CENTRE

THIS HUGE COMPLEX (☎ 800-33232; **festivalcentre.com**) near the airport is home to Dubai's only **Ikea** (☎ 04-203-7505), which ensures it is packed at all hours with newbie expats clutching starter packs of plates. There is also a massive **Hyperpanda** supermarket (☎ 04-232-5997) that has a good selection of cheap music, DVDs and electronics as well as great Middle Eastern take-away food (worth a stop en route to Al Mamzar Beach Park for a picnic of *fattoush*, olives, hummus and fresh-baked bread). Of course there are more upmarket places to drop your dirhams, including the **Paris Gallery** (☎ 04-375-0550), packed with almost every cosmetics name under the sun, as well as a selection of Arabic scents. There is also a large **Marks & Spencer** (☎ 04-206-6466) with a food section, in case you can't live without their own-brand treats (don't expect to find Percy Pigs sweets, though, for obvious reasons), and a big **Magrudy's** bookshop (☎ 04-344-4009). Princess of pink **Paris Hilton** also has her own shop here (☎ 04-232-6616). An outdoor promenade, next to the *abra*-filled waterways, is packed with unlicensed restaurants and cafes – the best are **Steam Dim Sum** (☎ 04-232-9190) and Lebanese **Wafi Gourmet** (☎ 04-232-9244). A trolley-sitting service costs AED 15 per day if you'd rather not dine with your purchases – enquire at the concierge desk. There is also a 12-screen **Grand Cinema** (☎ 04-232-8328; **grandcinemas.com**) and **Bowling City,** which has karaoke cabins, billiards, arcade games and, you guessed it, a bowling alley.

DEIRA CITY CENTRE

IT MIGHT NOT BE IN THE SEXIEST SPOT in town, but this mall (Deira; ☎ 04-295-1010; **deiracitycentre.com**) has remained a favourite with Emiratis and so is always busy in the evenings with groups of young guys and girls eyeing each other up surreptitiously while sipping on milkshakes. There's not much excitement in terms of shopping, but Brits may like the fact that a lot of unisex American fashion brands that are unavailable or difficult to find in the U.K. are represented, including **Club Monaco** (☎ 04-295-5832), **Banana Republic** (☎ 04-294-1163),

Forever 21 (☎ 04-295-2031) and **Lucky Brand Jeans** (☎ 04-294-0503). If you want to bring your own traditional Emirati dress back home, many shops here can help, including **Ameerat** (☎ 04-295-6173), **Habayeb** (☎ 04-295-1778) and **L'Artisan** (☎ 04-295-9754), and a **Smoker's Centre** (☎ 04-295-1275) sells shisha pipes. This mall is also the place to go for pashminas, with several specialist shops including **Regional Trading** (☎ 04-295-1723) and **Pride of Kashmir** (☎ 04-295-0655). At **Magic Planet** for kids, noise reaches eardrum-bursting levels. A Dubai Metro stop is just three minutes' walk away.

WAFI MALL

THIS MALL'S TAG LINE, 'a rare collection of wonderful things', may not be quite true, but it is certainly a singular place (Oud Metha; **wafi.com**). This ancient Egyptian–themed mall (yes, really) is housed in a giant pyramid, flanked by a Nefertiti or two. Luckily, this theme stops at the front door – once inside, you are bombarded by luxury boutiques. For scores of labels under one roof, check out **Desert Rose** (☎ 04-324-9936) and **Etoile La Boutique** (☎ 04-327-9151), which stocks labels including Dolce & Gabbana and John Galliano and has gold fixtures and fittings, as well as deep-pile carpets. The quirky **Ginger & Lace** (☎ 04-324-5699) has sweet and froufrou womenswear, evil-eye accessories from Middle Eastern label By Sophie and bags by Dubai export Zufi Alexander. **Oasis Fashions** (☎ 04-324-9074) sells well-priced race-worthy dresses, hats and fascinators – worth a trip if you decide to hit the Dubai World Cup at Meydan in March – and **Valleydez** (short for 'valley of the designers', apparently) is a sweetie shop of brightly-coloured dresses from up-and-coming designers (☎ 04-324-2883). If you want a glass of wine to celebrate your purchases, an annexe of restaurants and bars is next door, and also five-star bolt-hole Raffles is attached via an air-conditioned walkway.

GOLD & DIAMOND PARK

SUCH IS THIS CITY'S OBSESSION with all things sparkling that an entire mall (Sheikh Zayed Road; ☎ 04-347-7788; **www.goldand diamondpark.com**) is devoted to the stuff. Because it's not really the sort of place you idly browse (spend too long looking in the windows and a head will pop out of the doorway, beckoning you inside for 'very good price'), it's totally lacking in atmosphere, but if you're a fan of diamonds, your eyes will be on stalks. You might question when anyone would get a chance to wear these gems, but we can tell you – attend any big Emirati wedding (where the men and women are separated), and the family's gems come out. If you're not quite in the market for mega-carats, it's still worth a trip, as it's less stressful than Deira's hectic Gold Souk if you just want a small trinket as a souvenir, or if you are looking for an engagement or wedding ring. Designs here are also available in platinum and silver, and if you are staying in the city for a week or more, many of the stores will be able to work from your own design or copy something from a magazine. Traders will still expect you to haggle here, but you'll probably only achieve a maximum 30% discount on the first-quoted price. By far the most popular shop in the whole place is **Cara** (☎ 04-347-8089; **carajewellers.com**), probably as it has the broadest selection of price ranges – they are particularly good for birthstone pendants and over-the-top cocktail rings.

DRAGON MART

YOU'RE PROBABLY NOT GOING TO BELIEVE this place until you see it. A 20-minute drive on Emirates Road from the centre of Dubai, this dragon-shaped mall (☎ 04-368-7070; **dragonmart.ae**) is 1.2 kilometres (0.75 miles) long and boasts more than 4,000 shops selling goods imported from China. There really is very little that you can't buy here. No, really – want a pair of sauna pants? No, neither do we, but we have to admit that we were intrigued. Plastic toys, cotton dresses, garden gnomes, quad bikes – take your pick, and all at rock-bottom prices. Kitsch lovers will especially appreciate the framed oil paintings of past and present U.A.E. sheikhs. Stores here are meant to be grouped according to their wares, but that isn't really the case, so it's best just to wander around, soak up the atmosphere and wait for potential purchases to catch your eye.

SHOPPING AREAS *and* FAVOURITE STREETS

SITTING SOMEWHERE IN BETWEEN THE MEGA-MALLS and the hectic souks are a few shopping streets and districts dotted around the city. You will see a lot of smaller malls in residential areas – these will usually only have one or two shops that would be of interest to tourists, with the rest of the space taken up with nail bars, coffee shops and services such as dry cleaning. We have included the best of these here, although new ones are always popping up, so if you pass somewhere you think looks interesting, it's always worth sticking your head round the door. In the older parts of the city, such as Satwa and Karama, there's an approximation of what you will recognise as a typical high street, with clusters of shops selling cheap suits and shirts, costume jewellery, cosmetics and perfumes (be wary of these, though – many are copies with questionable ingredients) and tourist tat.

THE WALK, DUBAI MARINA

AT THE BOTTOM OF THE JUMEIRAH BEACH RESIDENCE towers sits the only luxury outdoor shopping experience in the city. Starting just opposite The Ritz-Carlton hotel and extending down to the Sheraton at the other end, this buzzing row of shops and restaurants has popped up in the last couple of years and is great for mall-avoiders. In the temperate months, there is always something going on to distract you from the stores – musicians, stilt walkers, funfairs and even the ever-present super-cars being driven up and down the road by racers (don't worry – the traffic is so slow that they never go over 16 kilometres, or 10 miles, an hour). The flagship store here is **Boutique 1** (☎ 04-425-7888; **boutique1.com**), where high fashion for men and women – think Missoni, Diane von Furstenberg and Elie Saab – is on sale in the three-floor space, alongside sunglasses, jewellery, cosmetics and home wares. The personal shopping service, which has an entire floor devoted to itself, is second to none, although it may make your bank manager weep. Fans of French design should take a look at **Tara Jarmon** (☎ 04-438-0339) and the fabulous boho-inspired clothing at **Antik Batik** (☎ 04-434-3080). There are also numerous sunglasses shops and a small branch of **Boots** (☎ 04-437-0215), which is useful for suncream and other beachy supplies, as The Walk is just opposite the beach. Parking can be a pain here, so we suggest taking a taxi, but if you must drive, park behind Jumeirah Beach Residence or in the designated car parks in the Murjan section, as traffic moves at a snail's pace on The Walk itself.

GATE VILLAGE, DUBAI INTERNATIONAL FINANCIAL CENTRE

THIS IS WHERE THE SERIOUS MONEY in Dubai gets made, so logically it's where quite a lot of it gets spent too – much of it at the serious art galleries dotting the slate courtyards. The two-floor **Opera Gallery** (☎ 04-323-0909; **operagallery.com**) is the biggest, and although the exhibitions are ever changing, there are usually at least a couple of museum-quality pieces by artists you may have heard of in the basement Black Room (Claude Monet, Paul Cézanne, Pablo Picasso). Unusually, the gallery specialises in bringing in artists from outside the Middle East to a new audience here. The **Empty Quarter Gallery** (☎ 04-323-1010; **theemptyquarter.com**) is one of the only places in the city that focuses its efforts on the photography of the region and even has its own publishing arm. **Cuadro** (☎ 04-425-0400; **cuadroart.com**) and **Artspace** (☎ 04-323-0820; **artspace-dubai.com**) show artists from the Gulf and Middle East. Once a month, all of these galleries put on an Art Night, with food, drink, live entertainment and artist talks – check **difc.ae** for dates.

THE BOULEVARD, EMIRATES TOWERS

ATTACHED TO EMIRATES TOWERS by a covered walkway, this area is only worth a visit if you are staying in the hotel or have serious money to spend (or both). It is home to stand-alone stores from the world's biggest designer labels – including **Yves Saint Laurent** (☎ 04-330-0445), **Bottega Veneta** (☎ 04-330-0449), **Chloe** (☎ 04-330-0700),

Buying Bespoke

DUBAI IS FULL OF SKILFUL TAILORS, but getting things made as a tourist can be a touch tricky. Here are some tips though. First, work out exactly what it is you want. Then you have a few options. You could look through magazines or your favourite online stores and print out shots of your favourite pieces – we'd suggest you do this before you arrive in the city. Second, you could visit the malls with a camera-wielding friend in tow to capture a few shots of you wearing items you like. Lastly, and perhaps most easily, select a piece from your own wardrobe. Then it's time to head to the tailors. It's a bit of a chicken-and-egg situation, but if you visit a good one (we have listed our top choices on the next page) before sourcing fabric (unfortunately, there are no one-stop shops here), they will be able to advise you on what and how much you need.

Balenciaga (☎ 04-330-0564), **Emilio Pucci** (☎ 04-330-0660) and **Gucci** (☎ 04-330-3313).

BUR DUBAI

THE AREA OF OLD DUBAI CONCENTRATED around the Dubai Museum is as close as you'll get to what the city looked like before the skyscrapers and super-malls, and it actually does a pretty good impression of the bustling streets of Delhi or Mumbai. There are bargains galore here, but be prepared to browse long and bargain hard. Shops selling one specific thing, many of which have been here for decades, are helpfully grouped together, so **Cosmos Lane** (also known as **Meena Bazaar**) is packed with fabric stores and Indian clothing shops (embroidered, floaty kaftans are great bargains here from around AED 50); neon-lit **Al Fahidi Street** near the Astoria Hotel is packed with electronics shops; and the area immediately surrounding the Dubai Museum and Arabian Court hotel sells Indian jewellery. If you want your shopping a bit more sanitised but are still keen to spend small change, visit the **Centrepoint** mini-mall in between the BurJuman Centre and the large Spinney's supermarket on Khalid Bin Al Waleed Street (known locally as Bank Street), easily reached by Dubai Metro. This mall houses local budget clothing, accessories and home ware chains Babyshop, Splash and Shoe Mart.

The wealth of fabric choice can be confusing for a novice, so there are a few things to keep in mind. Natural fibres are usually better – the merchant should be able to tell you exactly the composition. If you are buying embroidered fabric – especially saris you plan to have made into Western clothing – consider where on the garment you want the detail to fall. Once you have brought your *unofficial* **TIP**

There is a wealth of choice when it comes to Indian saris here. If you want to wear traditional dress without the headache, ask the sales assistant if they have a selection of pre-stitched saris so you can avoid the fuss of tucking and pleating yourself.

spoils to a tailor, there are two ways for him to work. If you have spent big on the fabric, insist he makes a toile – a version of your item in much cheaper cotton, so that he can get the cut just so before he slices and dices your silk. This will take longer, and usually involves three or four fittings, so unless you have an extended stay, this won't be an option. As a rule of thumb, allow at least one week for a more complicated piece to be made from scratch, especially if it's a suit, and three days for a direct copy. Don't pay more than 50% upfront, and don't hand over the balance until you are completely satisfied.

Best for Fabric

Regal's Meena Bazaar, Bur Dubai; ☎ 04-359-6123

Ratti Textiles Meena Bazaar, Bur Dubai; ☎ 04-353-8142

Jashn Opposite Karama Fire Station; ☎ 04-334-3128

Deepak's Al Hudaiba Street, Satwa ☎ 04-344-8836

Best for Tailoring

Dream Girls Meena Bazaar, Bur Dubai; ☎ 04-352-6463

Hollywood Tailors Meena Bazaar, Bur Dubai; ☎ 04-352-4243

Grace Tailors Meena Bazaar, Bur Dubai; ☎ 04-352-0295

Parmar Tailors Opposite Astoria Hotel, Bur Dubai; ☎ 04-353-8313

Ishmar Opposite Emirates Post Office, Satwa; ☎ 04-349-2434

JUMEIRAH BEACH ROAD

THIS LONG STRETCH OF ROAD from the Iranian Hospital up to Jumeirah Beach Park is packed with mini-malls frequented by well-heeled families living in the surrounding millionaire villas. Starting at the Iranian Hospital end is one of the biggest outlets of **THEOne** (☎ 04-345-6687; **theoneplanet.com**), a U.A.E.-based chic interiors chain that sells a small range of suitcase-friendly accessories, including photo frames and tableware. It also has a great cafe. Just opposite is the whitewashed **Palm Strip Mall,** which has a selection of small fashion and cosmetic boutiques. (Not one for summer, sadly, as all of the shops are outside.) A little farther up is **The Village Mall** (☎ 04-349-4444; **thevillagedubai.com**), home to locally-based, Indian-born designer **Ayesha Depala**'s boutique (☎ 04-344-5378; **ayeshadepala. com**) and hip fashion store **S*uce** (pronounced 'sauce'), which sells local and international niche designers (☎ 04-344-7270; **shopatsauce.com**).

SHOPPING *in the* SOUKS

SOUKS ARE THE TRADITIONAL TRADING AREAS, and they are found in several areas in Dubai. Bargaining is expected and cash is required. Start by halving the price you've been offered, and expect to pay about three-quarters of what you were originally asked. For a slice of real life, buckets of atmosphere and the best bargains, a visit to the souks is an absolute must.

This city has two distinct types of souks. First, there's the noisy, bustling, bargain-filled Old Dubai sort, selling everything from slippers to saffron. It's best to treat these as tourist attractions rather than places to actually do your holiday shopping, and don't even think about visiting if you have a limited amount of time. The fun here is to be had in wandering about the labyrinthine alleys, bargaining with traders from all around the region. The second sort are attached to malls and hotels and have been designed for those who want the experience of Old Arabia without having to put up with the hawking, hassle and heat.

Dubai has souks that sell pretty much everything. They are for the most part small open-fronted shops, in narrow streets, where you are expected to haggle over the price or risk disappointing the vendor. During the summer it can be hot walking around outside, even though the little stores do have erratic air conditioning, so we recommend you go early morning or in the evening. The souks are in the older districts, and if you want to be treated with the respect you deserve, we recommend that women, especially, dress with a little decorum. Have plenty of cash – lots of souks don't accept cards. Enjoy the chaos, the bustle of the market areas, the banter with the shopkeepers, the smells and the noises. The Spice Souk is exactly how you imagine a Middle Eastern market to be; the Gold Souk is awe-inspiring; the Textile Souk is awash with colour; and the Perfume Souk is rich with heady aromas. When you've run out of energy and money, try an Arabic coffee and some tasty snacks in the small, unassuming restaurants that punctuate the side streets. You won't be disappointed.

FISH MARKET, DEIRA

IT'S UNLIKELY THAT YOU'LL BE BUYING FISH here to cook, but this huge covered market, in front of the Hyatt Regency in Deira, is worth a look around if you can bear the olfactory assault. There is also an attached Fruit and Vegetable Market. The weather gets hot, so the smell can be overwhelming. Go early, when the fish is freshest and the weather's cooler. All the hotels buy their seafood from here. It doesn't matter if you love eating fish or not; this is a fascinating market to visit. It will make the fish counter in your local supermarket seem utterly mundane in comparison.

This is the largest and busiest fish market in Dubai and is a fascinating place to visit. Go at dawn or late at night, when it is bustling with vendors and fishermen with their catch just in. It is smelly, and you need to wear waterproof shoes and old clothes, but the opportunity to see blue lobster from Fujairah, baby sharks, metre-long (3.3-foot-long) kingfish, *hammour*, red snapper, lobster and the rest is a treat. This is a really exciting, unusual trip, and well worth getting up early for. If you go later in the day – which we don't recommend, especially in the summer – be prepared to cope with strong fishy odours and lots of heat – not the best combination. You can haggle over prices, and whilst it is primarily a wholesale market, vendors will sell you smaller domestic quantities. It is fascinating watching the traders – they turn the intricate cleaning and cutting process into a fine art. Once you've visited the market, visit Bait Al Wakeel Fishing Museum.

FRUIT AND VEGETABLE MARKET, DEIRA

HERE YOU WILL FIND THE LARGEST ARRAY of fresh fruit and vegetables for sale in Dubai. The minimum quantity you can buy is a kilo (about 2.2 pounds), so be prepared to come back with a lot of produce. It's a good place to try the many varieties of local dates. This market is worth a visit to see the sheer volume of beautiful produce for sale and to get a real feel for the trading atmosphere of the past. Again, it's worth going really early, when the produce is freshest and the heat is not so oppressive. This is primarily a wholesale market, so the vendors are used to selling large quantities, though they are happy to sell a kilo rather than an entire box. Be prepared to haggle over the price.

GOLD SOUK, DEIRA

THIS ATMOSPHERIC MARKET NEAR the Hyatt Regency in Deira is the one must-visit on our list, even if you aren't in the market to buy. Literally hundreds of shops sell gold, silver and precious stones, and customers range from tourists to traders hoping to offload bullion and uncut stones. This also means that the stores here are heavily regulated, so you can be pretty sure that you are buying what they say you are. If you're nervous about purchasing from an independent trader, many large chains also have a presence here, including **Damas** (☎ 04-210-5555) and **Joy Alukkas** (☎ 04-235-2860). You're not going to find incredible bargains here, but the jewellery is marginally cheaper than in the U.K. (depending on the exchange rate), and there is a vast choice. Credit cards are widely accepted, but you're likely to negotiate a bigger discount for cash. In the past few years, the stores have wised up to the fact that Western tastes differ from Arabic and Indian preferences, which tend towards the ostentatious, with a heavy emphasis on yellow gold. If you don't see anything to your taste, many outlets will be happy to custom-make something to your own design, or set or re-set a stone that you already own. Try to avoid the hours between 1 p.m. and 4 p.m., as firstly, it's usually too hot, and secondly, many of the shops will be closed (although they do stay open until 10 p.m.). Bargaining here is a bit of an exception to the rule – you may get a 10–30% discount, but as the price of gold is set daily, there isn't the sort of leeway you'll find with other products. The vendor will weigh the piece and quote you a price based on this – there is also a charge for workmanship, obviously rising the more intricate the piece is.

Widely considered to be the largest gold market in Arabia, it is not difficult to see why Dubai has earned itself the title 'City of Gold', with more than 300 jewellery shops, so be prepared to be overwhelmed by the magnificent range of gold and precious stones on display here. Your biggest challenge will be trying to work out where to start. It gets busiest late afternoon and evening, so if you want to avoid the crowds, go in the morning. There are many different shades of gold available – white, pink, yellow and even purple. There are also a few shops selling silver jewellery, semiprecious stones, diamonds and platinum. You will find astonishing bargains here; everything is worked out by weight and whether a piece is made by a craftsman or a machine. Most jewellery is 24 carat, and none is less than 18 carat. Be prepared to do some serious haggling, and if the price is not what you want, you can walk away and be safe in the knowledge that a neighbouring shop is more than likely to offer a similar product. If you're very serious about gold, check the daily gold price in the newspapers.

GOLD SOUK, DUBAI MALL

THIS IS AS CONSUMER-FRIENDLY AS SOUKS GET. It is lacking in atmosphere and doesn't have nearly as high a footfall as the rest of the mall, but there are still more than 200 retailers vying for your dirhams. It is especially popular with couples shopping for an engagement ring who may be intimidated by its Deira counterpart.

SPICE SOUK, DEIRA

CERTAINLY MORE FRAGRANT THAN the nearby Fish Market, this souk, just opposite the Gold Souk, will transport you right to the heart of Arabia. Stalls sell Middle Eastern spices by weight, and there are also shops selling perfumes. One of the best buys here is saffron, which is far cheaper here than in Europe. This is our favourite souk. Not only do the pyramids of spices look stunning, but the range is also unimaginable. You'll see powdered aromatic spices, baskets full of dried herbs and petals for tisanes, as well as every natural remedy and sacks overflowing with dried rose heads, preserved lemons, hibiscus and so on. Giant cinnamon sticks, large roots of turmeric, huge vanilla pods, cloves, cardamom seeds, nuts and large rocks of salt, as well as frankincense and different grades of saffron – the gold of the spice world – can be had for a fraction of the price you buy it back home. Try some of the dates – natural or stuffed with all types of delicious fillings. Sacks of prawns dried and preserved in salt sit randomly on the floor. The aromas are unique and delicious, the little shops are like historical apothecary's stores and the shopkeepers are happy to explain what everything is for and let you try samples of nuts and seeds. Ask to see the chocolate pebbles. If you're lucky, they'll let you try some. Delicious. This souk is a fabulous adventure for the senses.

TEXTILE SOUK, BUR DUBAI

THIS COVERED SOUK, WHICH RUNS ALONG DUBAI CREEK just next to the Dubai Museum, is our favourite for souvenirs and well-priced gifts. As the name suggests, plenty of shops sell all sorts of imported fabric by the metre, but even if you're not interested in these, there's plenty to buy. There are shops literally packed to the rafters with 'antiques' of dubious origin, from Iraqi banknotes to Afghani carpets. There are stores selling every possible shade of pashminas; others sell Indian slippers, kaftans and jewellery. Here you will find a stunning array of beautifully-coloured fabrics, imported from all over the world. Silks, satins, cottons and brocades – you can find everything here. Be prepared to bargain for your lengths of material, and then take them to the tailor with a picture of the dress or suit you would like to have skilfully replicated at a fraction of its retail price. We have suggested tailors in our Satwa section, but the one we like closest to this souk is **Lobo** (☎ 04-352-3760/3345) in Meena Bazaar, near Bastakiya.

The parking is a nightmare, so do get a cab and think about combining it with a trip to the Deira souks, just an AED 1 *abra* ride across Dubai Creek.

COVERED SOUK, BUR DUBAI

IN THE PAST, RESIDENTS OF BUR DUBAI and Bastakiya had to take an *abra* to Deira to do their shopping. Now Bur Dubai has its own renovated souk, which is colourful and bustling with energy. Covered by an arched wooden pergola, it is a riot of colour. This souk is at its busiest on a Friday evening. You'll find cheap clothes, saris and textiles. Tailors are busy at work, and the backstreets are intriguing to explore. You can find all manner of souvenirs and knickknacks here.

SOUK AL KABEER, OR MEENA BAZAAR, BUR DUBAI

A SLICE OF INDIA, THIS AREA IS populated primarily by the Indian population, and Meena Bazaar (as it is familiarly known) has become popular with tourists from all over the world because of the excellent bargains that can be found there. You will be spoilt for choice with fashion, jewellery and good, inexpensive food; and for every type of electronic goods, head for Al Fahidi Street.

I Give You Good Price!

THE NOT-SO-GENTLE ART OF BARGAINING is as essential in Dubai's souks as it is anywhere in the Middle East. Although the very idea can put visitors off, Dubai is a good place to cut your teeth, as the traders aren't aggressive as in some other Arabic countries. Not bothering is not an option, unless you want to get ripped off at every turn. As a general rule of thumb, you should hope to pay around 50% of the first-quoted price, so go low with your first offer (say a third of the first price) and work your way up by degrees. Stay vaguely disinterested; if the vendor isn't budging, walk away – he will often follow you out of the store with a better offer. Do shop around too – it's unlikely that the item you've spotted is a one-off, and a shop down the road may well be cheaper. Try to enjoy it as a cultural experience, and don't get frustrated. At the end of the day, the piece you buy will be worth what you are willing to pay for it and will almost certainly be cheaper than you'd find it back home.

OLD SOUK, DEIRA

THE SIMPLEST WAY TO LOCATE DUBAI'S largest and oldest souk is to head for the wind towers on the Deira side of the Creek, walk beneath their arches and find yourself in the busiest, most crammed-to-the-gills range of little shops imaginable. It actually feels more Indian than Arabic here, with an enormous variety of merchandise for sale. Everything – from plastic toys to textiles, spices, kitchenware, clothing, watches and henna – can be found here. You very much feel as if you have slipped through a time warp to another era.

PERFUME SOUK, DEIRA

A PROFUSION OF SHOPS SELLS HEADY, exotically-perfumed oils. Find frankincense and *oud*, the traditional fragrances sprinkled over glowing coals and used in homes and offices to scent the air. Incense in the form of compressed powder, crystal, rock or wood is also sold. There are hundreds of perfumes from which to choose, and if you can't find one you like, the shopkeepers will blend one specifically for you. Arabic perfumes are stronger and spicier than Western perfumes and are oil-based, so a little goes a long way. Traditionally perfume was a luxury for the rich and was stored in beautiful bottles with tops made of semiprecious stones. You will find jewel-coloured bottles of all shapes and sizes, creating rainbow reflections, wherever you go in this souk.

GLOBAL VILLAGE

OPINION IS SPLIT ON THIS HALF SOUK, half theme park (☎ 04-362-4114; **globalvillage.ae**) that is open November–February.

Nobody loves it because of the rides, which are, well, a bit rubbish, but some swear by it for great souvenirs and assorted international odds and ends. There are themed pavilions from around the world, and while many of the wares available at these stalls appear to have been made in China (even if they purport to have come from Canada or Peru), there are some gems. You can find Yemeni honey, Pakistani embroidery and paintings by Iraqi artists at knock-down prices, if you are prepared to search. The carnival atmosphere makes it a fun way to spend a mild evening.

KHAN MURJAN, WAFI MALL

WHAT DO YOU BUILD TO ADD THE FINISHING touches to an ancient Egyptian mall? A replica of a 14th-century Baghdad market, obviously. Attached to Wafi shopping centre (**wafi.com**) in Oud Metha, this is the most impressive of all the nouveau souks. Full of carved wood, stained glass and mosaic tiles, it's way prettier than the real things and – set over two levels and split into four sections – is nearly as big. The stores here predictably focus on products from the region – *oud* and perfume; Arabic calligraphy; bath salts from the Dead Sea; and carpets and pashminas from Iran, Turkey and Pakistan. This all comes at a price, however, and bargaining isn't encouraged.

SOUK MADINAT JUMEIRAH

PART OF THE ENORMOUS COMPLEX THAT HOUSES two hotels and numerous bars, restaurants and cafes, this souk (**jumeirah.com**) is home to quite a mixed bag of stores and stand-alone stalls, but it is a nice place to while away an afternoon. The lofty interiors are decorated in traditional Emirati style, and the touristy shops sell less-traditional stuffed camels and pairs of plastic Crocs. The stalls sell costume jewellery, trinkets and, unfortunately, quite a lot of tat.

SOUK AL BAHAR, DOWNTOWN

WHEN IT FIRST OPENED, this souk had high hopes of being the boutique retail destination for The huge Dubai Mall just across Dubai Lake. Unfortunately, it didn't quite pan out like that, and it has become far more famous for its restaurants and bars. There are still some nice niche retailers, though, but don't make the trip if all you intend to do is shop, as you'll be able to zip around in ten minutes. **Gallery 1** (☎ 04-420-3619) offers pictures and postcards featuring Dubai past and present, and there's a small **Marina Home** (☎ 04-340-1112; **marinagulf.com**).

A **SELECTION** *of* **SPECIAL SHOPS**

ASIDE FROM THE SOUKS AND AWAY FROM THE MALLS, there are a few very special retail experiences. By far the best of these is **The Antiques Museum** (Al Quoz 1; ☎ 04-347-9935; **fakihcollections. com**) in Al Quoz. This unique place neither sells antiques nor is a museum, but it resembles a rather more ramshackle, chaotic version of Mr Magorium's Wonder Emporium for grown-ups and is the most eccentric place to visit. It is piled high and crammed full to the bursting point with everything you would ever find in any tourist shop or souk, and at even better prices. It's worth a visit if only to see how fire, health and safety regulations have been bypassed in the most spectacular of ways. It is closed on Fridays. Al Quoz is also home to the largest and cheapest **Marina Home** (☎ 04-340-1112; **marinagulf.com**) in the city. The warehouse-size space sells the brand's signature hardwood furniture as well as soft furnishings and smaller design flourishes. Stepping into **Burlesque Interiors** (☎ 04-346-1616) on Jumeirah Beach Road is like falling down the rabbit hole. Chequered floors, baroque furniture, moss-covered stairs and velvet walls make it a feast for the eyes even if you walk out empty-handed. The bohemian, feminine **O'de Rose** (☎ 04-348-7990), housed in a villa on Al Wasl Road, is the place to find modern Morroccan- and Middle Eastern–inspired gifts and clothing. We especially like the Marhaba ('welcome') place mats, the evil-eye ashtrays and keffiyeh-wearing smiley-face T-shirts.

Check out **Ohm Records** (Al Kifaf Building, Trade Centre Road; ☎ 04-397-3728). The collective is responsible for the coolest club nights in town and has its own store, with rare vinyl as well as CDs, kits for would-be DJs and decks on which you are free to mess around. **IF Boutique** (Umm Al Sheif Street, Umm Suqeim; ☎ 04-394-7260) stocks the sort of conceptual clothes that architects wear – Comme des Garçons, Yohji Yamamoto, Junya Watanabe and Ann Demeulemeester. Basically, if it's black and you can't work out where the armholes are, you can probably buy it here.

If you like clothing less austere, Pakistani boutique **Soiree** (Villa No. 11, between interchange 1 and 2, Al Wasl Road; ☎ 04-349-4995) stocks some deliciously over-the-top threads. Some of the country's most prominent designers are stocked here in all their embroidered finery. During Ramadan, the store holds fashion *Suhoor* evenings, where ladies who haven't lunched (Muslims can't eat during daylight hours during Ramadan) have their second meal of the evening. **Studio 8** (opposite Dubai Zoo, Jumeirah Beach Road; ☎ 04-344-3934; **studio8.ae**), owned by local socialite Sara Belhasa, is a concept store that stocks a rotating roster of eight designers from the U.A.E.,

Pakistan, India and Saudi Arabia. The clothes won't be to everyone's taste, but the bright colours and excessive use of sparkle are *very* Dubai indeed.

OPEN-AIR MARKETS

ASIDE FROM THE TRADITIONAL SOUKS, outdoor markets take place around the city from time to time. Unfortunately, we can't give you a definitive list as they pop up and disappear again regularly, but check *Time Out* (**timeoutdubai.com**) for listings when you arrive. During the cooler months, the **Bastakiya** area runs monthly art markets, where you can find pieces from local artists as well as jewellery, shawls and cushions. Down in Dubai Marina, Jumeirah Beach Residence's The Walk is home to **Covent Garden** Market (**coventgardenmarket.ae**), with stalls lining the road at weekends and some evenings. This is where young local designers come to cut their teeth, and stalls sell vintage clothing and accessories, ethnic jewellery and hand-painted T-shirts. At the very hit-and-miss monthly **Dubai Flea Market** in Safa Park (**www.dubai-fleamarket.com**), people come to sell their own second-hand wares (the emirate's expat population is forever kissing goodbye to Dubai, so there's always someone willing to sell off their worldly possessions). It's not worth the journey on its own, but combined with a walk around the park, it's a pleasant way to spend an afternoon. Mirdif's **Second Hand Bazaar** (**2ndhand-bazaar. com**) is similar – once a month on a Friday, Uptown Mirdif's La Piazza is full of the spoils of expat spring cleans. Of course, quite a lot of the residents in this area are wealthy, so the cast-offs are often never-worn and the stalls designer label–laden.

SHOPPING FESTIVALS

THERE'S NOTHING ESPECIALLY SURPRISING about **Dubai Summer Surprises** (**mydsf.ae**), which runs from the middle of June to the first week of August, but you may well be amazed at the effort put into what is essentially the summer sales. Around the end of May, Modhesh, a strange-looking, sunshine-yellow cartoon character that looks a bit like a tadpole with eyes and a demented grin, pops up all around the city to herald the season of discounts. He actually has his own theme park, Modhesh World, at the Dubai Airport Expo Centre (**modheshworld.com**), which changes every year but has in the past offered an indoor beach, horse riding and a heritage centre. Although during the rest of the year prices aren't that far removed from back home, the sales here slash them big-time. Pretty much everything gets discounted by 50%, but towards the end of the period, 80% or even 90% is not uncommon. More effort is put into the summer sales than in the winter period – they are used to entice tourists from around the world when the beach is no longer a viable draw. Every large mall hosts a super-raffle, where making a purchase of a couple of hundred dirhams will make you eligible to win a car, a stack of cash or even a Dubai apartment. Stilt walkers and storytellers roam stores, the shops stay open until midnight and many host special evenings with food, drink and entertainment. The **Dubai Shopping Festival** (**mydsf.ae**), which runs from late December to the end of February, doesn't feature the little yellow fella but again has a full programme of events, concerts and raffles, as well as the obvious marked-down prices.

unofficial **TIP**
Although strictly speaking it's not allowed, many shops will hang onto their sale stock once the shopping festivals are officially over. So swallow your pride and ask the sales girl – she may point you in the direction of an 80%-off rail.

GREAT DUBAI GIFTS *and* WHERE *to* FIND THEM

AS YOU MIGHT HAVE ALREADY REALISED, Dubai is not a place where you're going to magically happen upon a wonderful local antique or artisan-made gem. Most of the classic souvenirs here are mass-made in India or China and tend towards high kitsch. That's not to say that there aren't any cute gifts, but you kind of have to like camels, Persian carpet coasters and singing alarm clocks. Our favourite versions of the latter come in the not entirely politically-correct shape of small plastic mosques that will wake you up with a call to prayer. **Royal Dirham** (opposite Musalla Road, Bur Dubai; ☎ 04-355-4331) does the best and cheapest of these, alongside a lot of other tat, including Burj Al Arab picture frames, cuddly camels and Sheikh Mohammed mugs. Fans of snow globes (there must be some of you, surely?) should head to **Saks Fifth Avenue** (Bur-Juman Centre; ☎ 04-352-0222), where they sell beautiful glass and ceramic versions encasing all the Dubai sights. Branches of **The Camel Company** are all over the city, including at Mall of the Emirates (☎ 04-340-2670) and Souk Madinat Jumeirah (☎ 04-368-6084), selling all things dromedary-related, from fridge magnets to pens, teddies to T-shirts. Supermarkets including **Carrefour** (Mall of the Emirates; ☎ 04-409-4899) usually have a selection of U.A.E. flags in various guises, from 4x4 wheel covers to headrests and notebooks. They are also wonderful sources of foodie gifts – dates and nuts are a staple of the diet here, some being locally produced but many originating from Saudi Arabia. They are sold either loose by weight or in gift packs. For more upmarket and expensive versions, Saudi Arabian chain **Bateel** (Dubai Mall; ☎ 04-399-9819; **bateel.ae**) is very popular, with its wares enticingly laid out like chi-chi chocolate shops. It also sells sparkling date juice, date preserves and date balsamic vinegar. For a really special treat, epicureans should make the effort to visit the wonderful – and completely unexpected – **Bee Kingdom** (Al Rolla Street, Bur Dubai; ☎ 04-352-245), where Egyptian owner Assad bottles honey that he receives in honeycomb form from the U.A.E., Jordan, Pakistan and Oman. The most expensive Emirati stuff sells for more than AED 500 per kilo (about 2.2 pounds). One of the most unusual gifts you'll find is camel-milk chocolate from Al Nassma, sold in stores at Jumeirah hotels.

The hipster trend for the traditional red-and-white or black-and-white keffiyeh may have slightly abated, but they are still great gifts to buy for friends. The cheapest, at around AED 25, come from the cobbled shopping streets near the Dubai Museum. But probably the nicest are the flower- and butterfly-embroidered versions made by local design duo **Dinz** – these are sold at **Harvey Nichols** (☎ 04-409-8888) and accessories boutique **Marami** (The Dubai Mall; ☎ 04-434-3536). Fashionistas might also appreciate the special-edition T-shirts produced by **Marc by Marc Jacobs,** sold in his boutique (Festival Centre; ☎ 04-232-6118). Evil eyes have also recently been adopted by the stylish, and they can be found everywhere here (they are usually round and blue, with a white iris and black pupil in the middle). Said to ward off bad spirits, they come in all shapes and sizes – from giant glass ones to hang by your door to necklaces, and even printed on T-shirts. You will see these everywhere, from Bur Dubai's souks to the Gold & Diamond Park to the stalls that dot Souk Al Bahar in Downtown. Be warned though – you have to buy these as gifts, because if you buy one for yourself, it attracts bad luck instead of repelling it. If you would like to treat yourself, many jewellers here are happy to make a pendant out of your name in Arabic (they will translate, and they do it accurately on the whole). This does take three to five days, so you'll have to forward plan. The expat's favourite jeweller is **Cara** (Dubai Gold & Diamond Park; ☎ 04-347-8089), but you should haggle. Prices for gold and silver go up and down, but around AED 400 for a pendant made in gold is fair, and around AED 150 for silver, not including chain.

Sadly, the sort of gifts that abound in cities with more museums and galleries aren't really on offer here. Even the Burj Khalifa's **At the Top** shop, next to the ticket office in The Dubai Mall, is unreliable, selling picture frames, tissue boxes and chocolates with no discernible branding. Only the primary-coloured, pop art–inspired posters are worth a look. If it's artwork you're after, **Gallery One** (Dubai Mall, ☎ 04-434-1252; Mall of the Emirates,☎ 04-341-4488; Souk Al Bahar, ☎ 04-420-3619; **g-1.com**) has a huge selection of photos from past and present. The Dubai International Financial Centre's **Empty Quarter Gallery** (☎ 04-323-1210) has great art books depicting the region, but if you want literature specifically on Dubai, **Book World by Kinokuniya** in The Dubai Mall (☎ 04-434-0111) has the biggest selection, from glossy coffee table photography books to tomes of poetry by Sheikh Mohammed.

For truly local items, men might want to invest in a tailored *dishdasha* and keffiyeh covering, and women could think about buying an *abaya* (the black, flowing gown) and *sheyla* (headscarf). Do think of these as souvenirs, though, as you will get some very funny looks if you decide to sport them while you are still in Dubai. Deira City Centre has the largest selection, and The Dubai Mall's basement floor is filled with stores selling them. Allow five days if you want one fully tailored. Men can expect to pay AED 150–200 for a *dishdasha*, and the sky's the limit for a woman's *abaya* – the most basic will set you back AED 200.

A strong oil-based scent, or *ittar,* is something that few Emirati dressing tables are without. (We asked one local why the men always smell so nice – the slightly unexpected answer was, 'It's hot! We need something to cover up the other smells!') For some, the heady, musky aroma will cause an instant headache; for others it is the very essence of Arabia. If you want your hand held through the buying process, both the **Paris Gallery** (☎ 04-330-8289) and **Sephora** (☎ 04-339-9828) in The Dubai Mall have large sections devoted to Arabic perfumers, but for a really authentic experience, visit **Arabian Oud** (Souk Madinat Jumeirah, ☎ 04-368-6586; Wafi Mall, ☎ 04-324-4117; The Dubai Mall, ☎ 04-433-8981; Ibn Battuta Mall, ☎ 04-368-5683; **arabianoud. com**). Traditionalists don't actually wear scent on their body as a heavy oil would stain the pristine white local dress. Instead, small pieces of *oud* wood are burned, and the smoke is allowed to scent clothing. This can be incredibly expensive – up to AED 50,000 for a small pot. *Bukhoor* is similar but comes in coal form, is most commonly used to scent homes and costs far less. Both are burned in a *medhan*, which can be very basic or quite ornate. **Arabian Oud** also sells these, as do many of the small shops in Deira City Centre and The Dubai Mall. If you're feeling adventurous, there is also the Deira Perfume Souk (Sikkat Al Khali Street). If you prefer your smoking more interactive, shisha pipes are on sale almost everywhere and range from modernist-looking silver and glass to elaborate enamel affairs. They can cost anything upwards of AED 80 and many have their own carrying cases, making them easy to transport.

PART TEN

EXERCISE *and* RECREATION

STAYING FIT *in a* DRIVING CITY

IF THERE'S ONE THING THAT DUBAI DWELLERS COMPLAIN about more than anything else (apart from the summer weather, at least), it's the effect that the emirate has on their waistlines. In fact, the expat weight gain even has its own name – the Dubai stone, which settles on the stomach and thighs within months of arriving. It's true that the lack of incidental exercise can be an enemy to the scales – you certainly won't be pounding the pavement sightseeing like you might in any given European country, and food portions here veer towards supersize – but there are plenty of opportunities for exercise if you are prepared to seek them out. With a growing obesity problem – a staggering 60% of U.A.E. nationals are classified as overweight, with the second-highest rate of type-2 diabetes in the world – promotion of sport has actually become a serious focus for the Dubai government in the past few years. There was even some talk in 2007 of a possible bid for the 2016 Olympics, although it was never submitted – but there is every chance, with the ongoing construction of the epic Dubai Sports City and new facilities popping up everywhere, that officials might once again sharpen their pencils in the future. So should you wish to get moving, the emirate is indeed your oyster.

With an embarrassment of coastline, the most obvious place to offset the rich Arabic diet is the beach, but a plethora of other options is available, from running to skiing, swimming to volleyball. A few lush parks with running tracks also allow you to get some fresh air while pounding the asphalt. If you are really determined to keep up a strenuous routine, many hotels have personal trainers attached to their gyms, and there are also several independent gymnasiums and fitness studios.

SOME FAIRLY SINGULAR SPORTS ATTIRE

A DUBAI SIGHT THAT TENDS TO FELL FOREIGNERS out for a jog is the local ladies' version of sportswear. Hit the park after dark and you will almost certainly see women – in no small number – jogging in long, flowing national dress, with enormous white Nikes poking out from underneath. We've previously spotted a lady complete an hour-long outdoor boot camp class, doing sit-ups, press-ups and, astonishingly, skipping, covered from head to toe in a black *abaya*. Well, at least that's one way to hide the sweat patches. You, luckily, will not be required to practise such extreme modesty.

For a tourist, dress laws are much more lax, so leggings, jogging bottoms and longer-length shorts are all fine, as are T-shirts and sleeveless vests. In hotels or independent gyms, you can go even skimpier if you wish, but if you are exercising in public areas, then ditch the Britney-style belly-baring tops and Kylie-size shorts, so as not to offend local sensibilities and also to eliminate the ogle factor, which can be considerable. We can tell you from extensive personal experience that groups of silent, leering men standing by the park gates might make you run faster – in the other direction – but aren't especially conducive to an invigorating workout. Our advice? Err on the side of overdressed or be prepared for the perving.

Although it is culturally fascinating to see female swimmers in sharia-compliant costumes – that is, loose suits that cover the legs and arms and include a head cover of some sort – you will never be required to don one. If you are keen to see probably the loosest definition of swimwear we have ever come across, the ladies' nights, held every Thursday May–September at **Wild Wadi** waterpark (**jumeirah. com**), boast probably the finest selection – we have seen with our very own eyes women hit the flumes in ankle-length evening dresses and business suits (it's a well-known enough phenomena that there is actually a sign at the door discouraging it).

As a tourist, the sort of swimwear that you would wear at home (that is, a two-piece or a swimsuit) is also perfectly acceptable here by the pool or on the beach, although do cover up when you step off the sand, as bra-bearing in residential areas – especially in Jumeirah and Umm Suqeim, which have largely Emirati populations – will be considered offensive. Slinging a see-through sarong over your bikini bottoms simply won't be enough. In absolutely no circumstances, ever, should you sunbathe topless. So ingrained is it as a no-no here that even expat sunbathers from countries where it's perfectly acceptable to get 'em out to

unofficial **TIP**
Combine calorie burning with consumerism every Saturday at the Mall of the Emirates. The Mall Walkers Club meets every Saturday, Monday and Wednesday at 8:30 a.m. on the first level at parking entrance A–F.

avoid unsightly tan lines will tap you on the shoulder and tell you to get dressed. Similarly, bare chests are not acceptable for guys.

SPF *and the* CITY

WHATEVER YOUR PERSONAL FEELINGS ABOUT Muslim women being required to cover up head to toe in public, there is actually a very good practical reason here to adopt the local dress. (As an aside, the best explanation we've ever received as to why *abayas* are predominantly black was at a Q&A session at a Jumeirah mosque; we don't know about you, but 'because they make lady slimmer' doesn't ring quite true to us.) We're not actually recommending that you rush out and buy an *abaya*, but it would be sensible to incorporate the same idea into your daytime dress with a combination of sunscreen and, ideally, a hat with a wide brim. The sun, at its peak, can be searing, and although we hate to stereotype, it's easy to spot a European in the first three days of their holiday as their skin often adopts the angry hue of raw meat. Take it from us – we've been there, done that and then bought the aloe vera.

In the summer, you would actually be hard pushed to bear being outside for long enough to burn, but we don't recommend that you test our theory. If you are intending to spend the whole day on the beach, reapply suncream every two hours, as saltwater, sand and towel-drying will conspire to rob you of protection. Do remember that you are also vulnerable to burning when you are in the water – almost as much UV rays reach you on the rebound, bouncing off reflective surfaces, as they do directly from the sun. The light here can be very deceptive in winter, as even when it is hazy, it is entirely possible to burn to a crisp through the clouds. A high SPF is also important if you are fishing or diving from a boat. We have previously suffered comedy sunburn (well, everyone else thought it was funny) when a lack of shade and a shortie wetsuit conspired to give us puce knee-high socks and elbow-length gloves for the best part of a week.

All hotel beaches and the two large beach parks have a large stock of umbrellas for shade, and it would be sensible to use them – at least when the sun is at its strongest, 11 a.m.–3 p.m. A baby's skin is much thinner than an adult's, so don't expose a child under 12 months old to any direct sunlight. A lightweight UV buggy cover is also advisable for when you are on the move. For the most part, baby pools here are shaded, so tots can safely enjoy a splash in the water to cool down. For children over 1 year old, UV sunsuits and a sun hat are essential investments.

You're not completely safe from the sun's harmful rays in your car either. Although the front windscreen of a car can block up to 93% of UV rays, the back windows usually let more through, so if you are intending on driving long distances in a hire car and you have young children, try to use a shade visor labelled with SPF 15 or higher or hang a blanket over the side windows.

To shield your eyes, make sure your lenses carry the CE mark, denoting they conform to the BS EN 1836:2005 standard, offering a safe level of UV protection. They should also be marked with a filter category number 0–4, with 4 being the darkest lens, offering more comfort in bright sunlight as it prevents straining the eyes. These are, however, unsuitable for driving (they should have a warning symbol and the words 'not suitable for driving and road use'). The majority of all-purpose sunglasses are Category 3, while many specifically designed for driving are Category 2. Categories 0 and 1 do not reduce bright sun glare, although they will still give protection against UV rays.

UV OR NOT UV – THAT IS THE QUESTION

MANY THINGS THAT YOU MIGHT EXPECT TO BE CHEAPER or at least on a price par with home are actually surprisingly expensive in the U.A.E., and sun protection comes under that category. Our advice is to stock up on the SPF at home and bring it out with you – although of course, do make sure you don't pack it in your hand luggage. Don't just harvest a few bottles from the back of your bathroom cabinet either – most have a shelf life of 2–3 years, so if they have been knocking around for longer than that, bin them and buy more. And make sure you bring enough. Most people don't get the protection factor that the bottle promises, as they apply far too thin a layer, so be generous. To get the best out of your cream, the average-size person should apply two tablespoons of suncream to cover the entire body at least 15 minutes before sun exposure. Even suncream that is marked as 'water resistant' or 'waterproof' should be reapplied after a long stint in the drink.

Experts recommend always using a broad-spectrum suncream (meaning it offers protection against UVA and UVB rays) of SPF 30 or higher – this will filter out 97% of UVB radiation. It is important to protect yourself from both, as UVA causes up to 85% of the skin's aging, while UVB is responsible for most sunburn and can cause cancer. In the U.K. skin cancer is diagnosed in around 75,000 people each year. No suncream will protect you from 100% of the sun's rays, so don't use an SPF 100 as carte blanche to deep-fry yourself in the Dubai sun.

BEACHES

WITH DUBAI PERCHED ON THE GULF, its beaches are the reason that, because of a dwindling supply of oil, the emirate has been able to refocus its energies on tourism in the past decade. So now the wives and girlfriends of Brit footballers flock to the city to show off their surgically-enhanced silhouettes and bikinis on the soft yellow sand and in seawater that remains a pleasant temperature year-round

(20–22°C, or 68–76.1°F, in winter and 25–30°C, or 77–86°F, at the height of summer). Although there aren't any stones on the beach to shred your soles, from May onwards the sand can be scorching, so remember: flip-flops are your friends. The beaches are wide – even on a busy day at the height of peak season, you won't be fighting for space – and the average wave height is a placid 0.67 metres, or 2.2 feet (when there is a strong current, a red flag will be raised to alert swimmers, and lifeguards are militant about clearing the water). The sea does get quite deep quite quickly, so non-swimmers should beware. Unfortunately, the summers do sometimes bring a plague of jellyfish which, while not life-threatening, can give you a painful sting. If the problem is serious, lifeguards will raise a red flag to alert swimmers to stay out of the water.

Not including the World Islands, the two finished Palm islands and the semi-dredged Palm in Deira, Dubai boasts 72 kilometres (44.7 miles) of coastline, but unfortunately there is no way you can get from one end to the other with your feet in the sand. Realistically, there are three choices if you are keen to get beach-bound. First, there are the hotels. Aside from the sandy stretches reserved for the royal palaces, most of which sit between the Madinat Jumeirah and the One&Only Royal Mirage, most hotels along the coastline have sole lounger rights to their own beachfronts. (Sadly, the beaches on the Palm are solely for the use of residents and hotel guests.) Second, you have facility-free 'open beaches', on which anyone is allowed to sit (or stand around looking shifty and staring, as is sometimes unfortunately the case), and third, you have the beach parks, which charge a nominal entrance fee in return for toilets, shade, lifeguards and snack bars.

In terms of open beaches, there are a multitude of options from Dubai Marina up to Jumeirah. (Although the beach does stretch beyond Dubai Marina, realistically you wouldn't want to sit on it, as, until you reach the Jebel Ali Hotel that has its own private beach, the coast largely backs onto industrial areas and stinky iron smelting plants.) The expat-heavy area in front of the **Jumeirah Beach Residence,** from the Sheraton Hotel at one end to The Ritz-Carlton at the other, is open to the public, although the Hilton in the middle does sometimes try to claim otherwise. There is plenty of public parking just by the sand, and taxis are easy to find, but there is very heavy traffic at the weekend as Emirati youths ride up and down The Walk in their pimped-up Hummers.

The next public beach you'll find as you head into Dubai from the marina is a scrubby stretch in between the entrance to the Palm and the Madinat Jumeirah, which is actually sandwiched in between two royal palaces. At the time of writing, you can easily drive your 4x4 onto the sand from Jumeirah Beach Road, so it is a great place for a barbecue, although this is one to avoid otherwise as it's actually quite a trek from the entrance to the sea. Don't drive too close to the water either – as the sand gets softer and less scrubby, your chances of getting your wheels stuck increase, and nothing ruins a good barbecue like a five-hour wait for a tow truck in the dark.

The next public access beach is just past the Jumeirah Beach Hotel. On-street parking is easy: just take a left towards the coast after Jumeirah Beach Hotel and you'll be able to stop right by the sea wall. If you are arriving by taxi, ask them to take you to the main gate of **Umm Suqeim Park,** and you'll see the sea just opposite. As this is an open beach, this is also where you will find the closest public conveniences. The next public beach along, locally called **Kite Beach,** sits between the Dubai Offshore Sailing Club and Jumeirah Beach Park and is where Dubai's hottest new sport is literally taking off. Kite-surfing lessons start at AED 300 including equipment (visit **ad-kitesurfing.net** for details). It is easier to park at the Jumeirah Beach Park end, as private villas, many of which seem to be modelled on Bond villains' lairs, line the sand the closer you get to the Dubai Offshore Sailing Club. Again, just turn off Jumeirah Beach Road and head for the coast. It is perhaps not ideal for families on a full day out as no facilities are directly on the beach, although some great snack bars and restaurants are just a minute's drive away. It is, however, a nice place to go for a sunset stroll for an idea of local life. Emirati parents often spend hours here with their children, and it is busy well into the evening.

After Jumeirah Beach Park is **Jumeirah Open Beach** (affectionately known as 'Russian Beach' due to its clientele), situated behind the Village Mall and next to the Dubai Marine Resort. Parking is more than ample, whether you do it on the residential streets next to the beach or in the surrounding malls. Unlike other open beaches, there are actually toilets, showers, cycling and running tracks and life-guards on duty. The only problem you might have is with men openly and aggressively staring. Unfortunately, returning their gaze in an attempt to embarrass them into stopping doesn't work as well as you might think. Just ignore as best you can, and if you are approached in a manner that makes you feel uncomfortable, do alert the lifeguard.

Sitting somewhere between the five-star service of the hotel beaches and those free to the public are Dubai's beach parks, which charge a nominal entrance fee, giving you access to lockers, shade, showers, toilets, a few snack bars (of admittedly dubious quality) and children's play areas. **Jumeirah Beach Park** (☎ 04-349-2555), halfway down Jumeirah Beach Road, is the most popular and can get very busy at weekends – not ideal for running or walking, unless you want to pick your way over prostrate sunbathers. However, swimmers are kept safe by a lifeguard, on duty 8 a.m.–sunset, and there are volleyball nets, all for the entrance fee of AED 5 (or AED 20 per vehicle). If you are hor-rified by the junk food on offer, just cross the road and grab a snack at the Beach Park Plaza, which has some more appealing dining options. In the evening, the 12-hectare (29.7-acre) park becomes a focal point for the Filipino community, who make good use of the tables, chairs and barbecue pits on the grassy area behind the sand. If you too decide to get your grill on, do remember that alcohol is forbidden, although we have seen some rather suspicious-looking liquid in fizzy drinks bottles before now. The park also benefits from being so well known that even the most directionally-challenged taxi driver could find his way there. Monday is for ladies and children only.

Not usually frequented by tourists because of the often-heavy Deira traffic, **Al Mamzar Beach Park** (☎ 04-296-6201) near Alexandria Street is a rather well-kept secret, especially now that dredging for the Palm Deira has been put on hold. It has five beaches (so you'll never be jostling for towel space with your fellow sunbathers); an embarrassment of umbrellas; lots of open, grassy spaces; and two swimming pools, one 25 metres (82 feet) long, for which entrance is an extra AED 10. It is open 8 a.m.–11 p.m. and entrance costs AED 5 per person on foot, AED 30 per car. This is as popular with Indian and Pakistani families as Jumeirah Beach Park is with Filipinos, and there is a huge amount of parking, so if you drive, you'll never be stuck waiting for a spot. For more privacy, chalets can also be rented for AED 150 or AED 210.

PARKS

THERE IS A SURPRISING NUMBER OF GREEN, leafy spaces in Dubai. Most charge a very small entrance fee (AED 3–5), and while this is ostensibly to pay for upkeep, one rather suspects that it is actually designed to keep out low-income workers, who can often be seen spending their short leisure time sitting in groups on any available grass verge or in the middle of roundabouts.

An oasis of green sandwiched in between the beach and the desert, **Safa Park** on Al Wasl Road is one of the biggest oases in the city. While there are other parks in Dubai, this is one of the easiest to locate and teems with activity at all hours (or at least until its closing time of 11 p.m.), but especially first thing in the morning and after dark, when lone joggers and panting groups of boot-campers pack the open spaces and 3.4 kilometres (2.1 miles) of specially-sprung track just outside the park's railings. There are also basketball and tennis courts and volleyball nets, although use of these is not included in the AED 3 entry fee. **Dubai Creek Park** (☎ 04-336-7633), which, predictably, runs along Dubai Creek in Bur Dubai, is a great place to spend an afternoon with children – there is a dolphin show, children's fun land and a cable car – but only if it's a gentle stroll you're after, as there is no running track or really any other sports facilities of which to speak. However, in-line skating is allowed, and you can rent bicycles by the hour (although you aren't allowed to take in your own). **Za'abeel Park,** near the Trade Centre roundabout, covers 51 hectares (126 acres) and has a 4.3-kilometre (2.7-mile) jogging track and a cricket pitch. If you want to join an organised run in one of these parks, the **Dubai Road**

Runners have comprehensive listings (**dubai-road-runners.com**) of start times and schedules.

DUBAI *for* DIVERS

ALTHOUGH PERHAPS NOT AS FAMOUS for its underwater action as Oman or the neighbouring emirate Fujairah, Dubai still offers ample opportunities for diving. Experienced divers will appreciate the wreck diving, with sites ranging in depth 25–35 metres. Some of these wrecks were deliberately sunk to form artificial reefs; others went down due to bad weather or marine accidents. Due to the nature of the sandy seabed in the Gulf, these dive sites are gathering spots for marine life, including barracudas, large rays, dolphins, turtles, sea snakes, batfish and Arabian angelfish. Dolphins can be sighted out at sea, and whale sharks have been spotted on both the Dubai and Fujairah coasts in the spring and summer. Sea temperatures vary from 22°C (71.6°F) in the winter (December–March) to 32°C (89.6°F) in the summer months (June–September).

If you're new to diving, give the shallow reefs near Jebel Ali a go first. Even at under 10 metres (32.8 feet) depth, you'll still see a rainbow of colours, tropical reef fish and, if you're very lucky, sea turtles. If you're a bit bolder, a sunken cement barge is also at 10 metres depth, not far from the Burj Al Arab hotel. To attract fans of the underwater sport, Sheikh Mohammed has created an artificial reef, 17.7 kilometres (11 miles) off Dubai, at around 20 metres (65.6 feet), by deliberately sinking a barge – home to some impressive large marine life. Iraqi oil tanker *Zainab,* which originally carried illegal oil, sits in 30 metres (98.4 feet) deep, just over 3 kilometres (1.9 miles) off Dubai – it sank fairly recently and is still pretty intact, with barracudas swimming around the hull.

For Advanced Open Water divers there are three wrecks, named *Ludwig, Lion City* and *Jassim,* positioned quite far from shore almost halfway between Dubai and Abu Dhabi. Regular divers cite these as the most exciting in the emirate, but you really need good weather conditions to go. **Al Boom Diving Centre** (☎ 04-342-2993; **alboomdiving.com**) is perhaps the best known in Dubai and also offers longer dhow diving trips to Mussandam and speedboat trips to Fujairah. The Jumeirah Beach Hotel has its own centre, **The Pavilion** (☎ 04-406-8828), also offering PADI (Professional Association of Diving Instructors) accredited courses, day trips, Dubai dives and excursions farther afield. Launched in 2010 the **Atlantis** also has its own diving centre (☎ 04-426-3000; **atlantisdivecentre.com**) situated in the resort. Newbies are trained in the hotel's own saltwater pools, and the more experienced can do night dives and underwater photography courses. **Emirates Diving Association** (**emiratesdiving.com**) has more detailed information on dive sites.

For exhibitionist novice divers the **Dubai Aquarium** (**thedubai aquarium.com**) at The Dubai Mall offers a unique experience. At 3 p.m., 5 p.m. and 7 p.m. daily, you can swim with the sharks – dive gear rental, the training presentation, DAN (Divers Alert Network) diver insurance and a certificate of participation are included in the price. Those brand-new to the sport will need to complete a pool training session beforehand, or you can just snorkel within the shark cage instead – this can be done every 30 minutes. Just bring your swimsuit and sign up at the ticket desk on the ground floor.

YOGA, PILATES *and* DANCE

THE BENDY OF BODY ARE WELL CATERED FOR, with an abundance of teachers and shiny new studios. **Zen Yoga** (**yoga.ae**) is the largest of the studio chains, with spaces in Dubai Media City, Emirates Hills and the Village Mall, offering a variety of yoga disciplines from ashtanga and vinyasa to hatha. **Club Stretch** (☎ 04-345-3121; **clubstretch.ae**), next to the Capitol Hotel on Al Mina Road in Bur Dubai, has a studio dedicated to Pilates and one for Bikram yoga, which is practised in an intensely-heated room (maybe not exactly what you want in the height of summer). **Exhale Studio** (☎ 04-424-3777; **exhaledubai.com**) on the Plaza Level of Murjan 1, Jumeirah Beach Residence, also offers yoga and Pilates, as well as a huge range of dance classes from hip-hop to belly dancing. The **Talise Spa** at the Madinat Jumeirah (**jumeirah.com**) holds once-a-month full-moon evening yoga sessions on Al Qasr hotel's beachfront for AED 200 – check its Web site for upcoming dates.

IN *or* ON *the* WATER

SAILING IN DUBAI IS NOT ONLY GREAT FUN but will also give you a unique perspective on the coastline – especially if you are able to pass the Burj Al Arab, the Palm or the World Islands. **Dubai Offshore Sailing Club** (**dosc.ae**) is the oldest in the emirate – it's as hard to get into as Studio 54, as long-time expats rarely relinquish their membership – but it does offer a range of both adult and child courses for those serious about learning to sail. They are usually very oversubscribed, so it is worth contacting the facility well in advance if you are thinking of hitting the waves. About an hour's drive from Dubai, **Club Joumana** at the Jebel Ali Golf Resort & Spa (☎ 04-814-5555; **jebelali-international.com**) has a fleet of boats and offers windsurfing, kayaking and sailing. The **Dubai International Marine Club** (☎ 04-399-5777; **dimc.ae**), next to the Mina Seyahi hotel in Dubai Marina, plans to offer adult sailing courses in the future. Jet skis are unfortunately banned from Dubai's beaches.

If you're keen to get even wetter, it is possible to ride the waves in the emirate. Don't expect towering rip curls, but with an average wave height of 0.6 metres (about 2 feet), it is a fun place to learn the slacker's art, and the warm water makes it a pleasant experience. **Surf Dubai (surfingdubai.com)**, based near the Burj Al Arab, offers private and group lessons, as well as surfboard rental.

FOUR-LEGGED FUN

THERE IS ALMOST NO ORGANISED DESERT ACTIVITY in Dubai that won't offer some sort of short sit on a camel, and really that is all you need, as they are not the most comfortable form of transport ever invented. If you want to do the dunes on a far more graceful beast, **Al Maha Desert Resort & Spa** (☎ 04-832-9900; **emirateshotelsresorts. com**) offers guests with equine experience the chance to ride former racehorses from the stables of Sheikh Mohammed on the surrounding sand. Riding hats are provided, but sturdy, closed-toed shoes are required. If you want to master the art before arriving, the **Dubai Polo & Equestrian Club** (☎ 04-361-8111; **poloclubdubai.com**), next to the Arabian Ranches, offers regular 45-minute group 'desert hack' lessons on their Arabian horses for AED 130. Held early morning and evening, the two-hour desert hacks cost AED 300.

Polo is one of the most popular sports among the well heeled in the Emirates, and lessons are widely available. The **Dubai Polo Academy,** also based at the Dubai Polo & Equestrian Club (**dubai poloacademy.com**), offers lessons in the sport of sheikhs, with no prior knowledge of polo or even riding experience necessary. Group lessons start at AED 550.

WILDLIFE WATCHING
(and Catching)

THE U.A.E.'S GEOGRAPHICAL POSITION MAKES it a major stop-off on the migration route between Asia and Africa, and large numbers of birds make Dubai their home year-round. There are around 400 species to be spotted here, many rare and unusual, dotted in many different habitats, from mangrove swamps to arid desert, so it is quite the ornithologist's delight.

Even for non–bird lovers, the **Ras Al Khor Wildlife Sanctuary** – with its mangroves, mudflats and lagoons, as well as Western reef herons, spotted eagles, broad-billed and Terek sandpipers and more than 1,000 greater flamingos – is breathtaking, especially given its proximity to the centre of town. There are three hides there, but unfortunately, the authorities don't make it easy to visit them. An application form can be downloaded from the Web site **wildlife. ae** and submitted to the Marine Environment and Sanctuaries Unit (☎ 04-606-6822; FAX 04-227-0160) at least three days prior to visit. If that feels too much like hard work, even a walk in the park should throw up some interesting species – anything can turn up in **Safa Park** during migration or winter, and the same goes for **Al Mamzar Beach Park.** For more information, **U.A.E. Birding** (**uaebirding.com**) has lists with photographs of birds and reptiles recently spotted in the U.A.E. The amateur organisation also has a roster of guides who offer half- and full-day 4x4 tours of the most densely-populated spots, from AED 600 per car. It also lists where you are most likely to see the species that visitors are most interested in spotting.

If you prefer your wildlife cooked in a nice garlic butter and served with French fries, then crab hunting is a popular day out. **Flamingo Beach Resort** (☎ 06-765-0000; **flamingoresort.ae**) runs trips every night at 6 p.m. to the nearby mangrove islands of Umm Al Quwain, the neighbouring coastal emirate. The AED 170 price includes a spear to spike your dinner and a post-trip buffet that includes your self-caught dish of the day. The squeamish need not apply.

As a slightly more sedate way of catching an evening meal, many companies offer organised boat trips into the Gulf to fish for mackerels, queenfish, bonitos, groupers and barracudas. **Ocean Active** (☎ 050-459-2259; **oceanactive.com**) is one of the largest operators, with boats that can accommodate up to ten anglers. Prices start at AED 2,500 for four hours on a 12.2-metre (40-foot) console boat for a maximum of six people, including crew and equipment. The boats will travel around 48.3 kilometres (30 miles) off the coast (the farther out you travel, the greater chance you have of catching larger fish), and they have the added bonus of giving you a great view of Dubai's skyline from the water. The **Dubai Creek Golf & Yacht Club** (☎ 04-205-4646; **dubaigolf.com**) also has crewed sport-fishing vessels that do four-, six- and eight-hour trips, from AED 3,500 for up to six people. More economical for smaller groups, if you don't mind sharing your boat with strangers, **Arabia Horizons** (☎ 04-294-6060; **arabiahorizons. com**) runs four-hour morning fishing trips, suitable for those with no experience, from AED 375 per person.

WINTER SPORTS

YES, YOU READ RIGHT – Dubai does have a rather surprising line in skiing and ice skating. One of the more ridiculous recreation destinations in the emirate is **Ski Dubai** (☎ 04-409-4000; **skidxb.com**), the 22,500-square-metre (242,188-square-foot) real-snow indoor ski slope and snow park with an Alpine theme attached to the Mall of the Emirates. There are five runs (including the world's first indoor black run), reached by a quad chairlift or tow lift. The longest of the runs is 400 metres (or 1,312.3 feet), with a fall of 60 metres (196.9 feet). There are also beginner slopes and a Freestyle Zone reserved for snowboarders. It is kept at a constant -1°C to -2°C (or 30.2°F to 28.4°F), is 85 metres (278.9 feet) high and 80 metres (262.2 feet) wide and even boasts a fake blue sky to complement the Swiss chalet stylings. Small-group and private ski and snowboard lessons are available for beginners (☎ 04-409-4129), and more experienced skiers can buy a day pass for AED 300 (AED 240 for children), which includes all equipment – even a rather natty standard-issue blue-and-red ski suit. If you have no skiing experience, the stern man at the counter will likely tell you that you have to either book a lesson or endure the embarrassment of only being allowed access to the snow park, where you can hang out with the 5-year-olds and throw snowballs, while being laughed at by drinkers in the bar upstairs. Aside from the Burj Al Arab, it's probably Dubai's best-known attraction, so don't expect it to be quiet, ever. But if you are a serious skier and would rather avoid the hordes of children, then a weekday evening is the best time to go.

Not to be outdone, **The Dubai Mall** (☎ 04-448-5111; **thedubaimall. com**) has an Olympic-size ice rink that holds daily open sessions, private and group classes and weekend disco sessions. There are also occasional hockey matches – check the Web site for updates. A much smaller rink is in the **Galleria Mall** (☎ 04-209-6000; **thegalleria. hyatt.com**), which is attached to the Hyatt Regency Hotel in Deira. Due to its diminutive size, it does become packed with children after school, although the morning sessions are usually quite quiet. **Al Nasr Leisureland** (☎ 04-337-1234; **alnasrll.com**) also has a down-at-heel rink that we can't really recommend unless you are fond of local 'yoof' spraying ice in your face to a soundtrack of mid-90s techno.

OTHER RECREATIONAL SPORTS

WITH THEIR ASTONISHING PROLIFERATION of Ferraris and Porsches, Dubai's roads can sometimes feel like a racetrack. (Just for your information, if you ever see the number plate Dubai 1 at the traffic lights, you should probably refrain from revving up – it's likely to be head honcho Sheikh Mohammed at the wheel.) But if you really want to cut your track teeth with the proper petrol heads, the **Dubai Autodrome** (☎ 04-367-6700; **dubaiautodrome.com**) offers a range of experiences in its own fleet of cars on the 3.6-kilometre (2.2-mile) track (you will need an international driving licence). Even youngsters are catered for with the First Drive programme (as long as they are taller than 125 centimetres, or 49.2 inches, and aged 12–18), from AED 400 for three hours. Indoor and outdoor go-karting tracks also run daily Arrive & Drive sessions, AED 100 for 15 minutes for adults and children from age 7 upwards.

If you prefer your sport more lofty, the emirate has two climbing walls. Located outdoors, on the side of the World Trade Centre on Sheikh Zayed Road, **The Wall at Climbing Dubai** (☎ 04-306-5061; **climbingdubai.com**) is open every day to walk-ins. They also offer regular one-day beginners' outdoor climbing expeditions. The **Pharaoh's Club** (☎ 04-324-0000) is home to the U.A.E.'s first climbing wall, which rises into the pyramid interior of the Wafi shopping centre. Beginners are welcome, but advance booking is essential – AED 62 including instructor.

Serious golfers are very well catered for in Dubai (see pages 315–323 for more information), but if you prefer your putting less po-faced, the **Hyatt Regency** in Deira (☎ 04-209-6475; **dubai.regency. hyatt.com**) has a very sweet park out the back with an ornamental pond, a cute cafe, 9-hole pitch-and-putt (AED 30 per round) and an 18-hole crazy golf (AED 15 per round). Golf balls can be bought for AED 15, and clubs are for hire from Frosty's in the Galleria Mall, attached to the hotel.

You have to be made of pretty stern stuff to want to hit Dubai's roads on two wheels, but people do, and some, in fact, swear it's the only way to travel. While we really couldn't recommend you take to the big roads under pedal power (some delivery drivers do – often the wrong way down dual carriageways, in fact), there are other options. In 2009 the government promised to build more than 900 kilometres (559.2 miles) of designated track by 2020, taking cyclists past souks, dhow harbours and museums, although after a lot of fanfare, none of this has yet materialised. Currently, the only designated cycle lanes are on Jumeirah Open Beach and Jumeirah Beach Road, although we have it on good authority that the latter is a) quite boring and b) quite dangerous. **Wolfi's Bike Shop** (☎ 04-339-4492; **wbs.ae**) serves as the hub for the city's cycling scene, and you can hire a racing or mountain bicycle from here, from AED 100 per day. They also offer helmets that, while not a legal requirement, are absolutely essential. If you want to get outside the emirate, the **Dubai Roadsters** (**dubairoadsters. com**) run weekly Friday rides, departing at 5:30 a.m. from outside the Lime Tree Café on Jumeirah Beach Road. Monthly 100-kilometre (62.1-mile) rides to Hatta are supplemented with a support car in case riders get into trouble.

An old Dubai stalwart, **Al Nasr Leisureland** (☎ 04-337-1234; **alnasrll.com**) might have the air of a post-apocalyptic theme park, but there is one thing to recommend it. As home to the only alley in Dubai where you can have a drop of the hard stuff, the bar-and-bowling combo is predictably popular with groups of young expats celebrating birthdays or, indeed, just the fact that it's the weekend. With just eight lanes, it is small and the decor is dated, but there's plenty of parking and it has a Filipino nightclub next door called The Odd Spot, for a post-bowl boogie. Emiratis take their bowling quite seriously – as evidenced by the fact that no less than an Abu Dhabi sheikh serves as the president of the Emirates Bowling Federation – so they flock to the **Dubai Bowling Centre** (☎ 04-339-1010; **bowlingdubai. com**), housed in a mock castle in Al Quoz. Come the weekend, the 24 lanes are packed with locals showing off their mega-expensive kit and shaming hapless amateurs with consecutive strikes running into double figures. There is also a juice bar, a coffee shop and an Action Zone with spotty teenagers playing on ear-splitting arcade games. Remember to bring a scarf or cardigan, as it can be quite aggressively air conditioned. **Dubai International Bowling Centre** (☎ 04-296-9222; **dubaibowlingcentre.com**) is the mother ship, though, with 36 lanes and a devoted clientele. Located in Al Mamzar, opposite the Century Mall, it's so big that you could pretty much live in it. It has its own spa, shisha lounge, Lebanese restaurant and pool hall. An average of 700 customers visit a day, so do book in advance if you can.

Even the lowliest apartment block here has a gym, so the chances are, unless you're planning on pitching a tent in the desert, your tourist lodgings will have at least basic workout facilities. If you are planning to combine a gym trip with a spa treatment, turn to page 255, as many large hotels offer free day membership of their health clubs when you book a treatment. A few independent fitness centres also offer day rates. While **Hayya! Health Clubs** (**www.hayya.com**) won't allow non-members use of gym equipment, you are welcome to pay non-member fees for their assorted classes. The four locations (The Lakes, ☎ 04-362-7790; The Meadows, ☎ 04-362-7770; Town Centre, ☎ 04-362-7784; Old Town, ☎ 04-367-3282) offer yoga, karate and circuits among other activities – a timetable is available on the Web site. The **Aviation Club** in Garhoud (☎ 04-282-4122; **aviationclub.ae**) allows non-members to buy day passes for AED 250, providing access to the tennis courts, gym, swimming pool and classes. Hour-long group classes in the large air-conditioned studio or the spinning room cost AED 50. **Pharaoh's Club** at Wafi (☎ 04-324-0000) is also open to non-members who want to use the pool, for AED 100 per day during the week and AED 130 at weekends, or attend studio classes at AED 50 per session.

With such a large expat population from the Indian subcontinent, Dubai is quite the hub for cricket. From the Pakistan international cricket team to kids with sandy knees setting up makeshift pitches on building sites, the sport has a huge base of spectators and players here. Unfortunately, asking to join in an impromptu game will likely just make you look like a bit of a weirdo, so if you fancy playing a few wickets, you would do better to head to the **Chevrolet Insportz Club** (☎ 04-347-5833; **insportzclub.com**), a fully air-conditioned indoor sports centre in Al Quoz industrial district that offers cricket, football, basketball, hockey and table tennis for adults and children.

SPECTATOR SPORTS

WITH NO INTERNATIONALLY-FAMOUS TEAMS of which to speak, it is interesting that Dubai is nevertheless a great place to watch world-class sport, with visiting sportspeople and a host of newly-opened venues. A word of warning, though – very few of Dubai's largest venues are served by sensible, functioning public transport systems. Parking is often miles from the venue and involves a shuttle bus, long taxi queues can become fraught after an event and walking is simply not an option. It is definitely worth planning your exit strategy at the same time as buying your tickets.

The best-loved sporting event of the year is the **Dubai Rugby Sevens** (**dubairugby7s.com**), held at a specially-built stadium, The Sevens, which opened in 2008 on Al Ain Road. Every December, 16 of the best international sevens teams compete on the main pitch during the three-day event, while youth and local teams play on neighbouring pitches. Unsurprisingly for such an expat haven, there is huge support for each of the international teams, and the event has a carnival-like atmosphere, with beer tents, bands and children's rides and games. The food and drink stands work on a ticketing system, so you have to buy a book of tokens that you can redeem at various stands. However, it is all reasonably priced, even if the queues can be a bit epic between games. It is possible to stay in the shade all day if you are prepared to move around in the stands (it is unreserved seating), but it would be sensible to bring a hat. The parking is more than ample, but this is a boozy event, and there is a zero-tolerance policy for drink driving, so think seriously before putting your key in the ignition. Courtesy buses are on hand to take you to various drop-off points in the city, including Dubai super-club Chi, where the party goes on well into the wee hours. **The Dubai Football Sevens** (**dubaifootball7s.com**), held in March at the same venue, is a much newer but similar event.

The **Dubai World Cup** (**dubaiworldcup.com**), the world's richest horse race, is another event ringed in red on the emirate's calendar, held every March. It would be disingenuous to call this merely a sporting event – seemingly the whole city (or at least 50,000 of its inhabitants) dust off their hats and suits to sit trackside and watch as international thoroughbreds run for their share of the AED 36,734,880 (approximately £6.28 million or US $10 million) prize money at the spectacular Meydan Racecourse. A variety of tickets and packages are available, and despite its popularity, they rarely sell out, due to the Meydan's epic size. This is no Ascot, however, so we need to let you in on a few things if you fancy putting on a posh frock and having a flutter. First, actually betting on races is fiendishly tricky, what with gambling being illegal and all. There is a complicated lottery system – sort of like gambling but without any of the skill. However, very few racegoers bother getting their head round it. In truth most people ignore the horses completely and

No Tickets? No Problem!

EDWARD BAGNALL, FROM THE DUBAI OFFICE of luxury private concierge service Quintessentially, gives his advice on securing sold-out tickets for Dubai's biggest sporting events.

'When looking to buy tickets for major events, the number-one rule here is to plan ahead', he says. 'Dubai is a small city and news travels fast, so things often sell out quickly. If you are planning a visit to the city, keep an eye on *Time Out* tickets (**timeouttickets.com**) and *7 Days* (**7days.ae**), as they have all the up-to-date news on what's going on and when'.

He also advises, 'For events such as the Barclays Dubai Tennis Championship, you will need to head down to the stadium the day they go on sale if you really want a chance of getting the best seats for the final. Historically, these are gone within the first hour, with the remainder usually sold out within the day'.

But, he reveals, 'Don't give up hope, though, as some events hold back a portion of tickets to sell a month later to re-ignite interest. This new release is usually announced in the press. If you miss the boat with tickets from the official vendors, then your other options are going to be pricier. There is a secondary market for tickets, but the prices get hiked up in relation to demand. **Dubizzle.com** and **souq.com** are the sites to use for these, but do be aware that tickets on these sites usually sell out the day they become available, for up to four times face value'.

Lastly, Bagnall says, 'If you can bear to, hold off until the day before or even the day of the event, as the prices come back down when the vendor wants to get rid of tickets. Packages are another way to get access to events and are ideal if you plan to go with a group of friends. The high-end packages for events such as the Dubai World Cup usually don't sell out, due to the price, but if you're willing to spend the money, you will have a fantastic meal, drinks included'.

focus on drinking, which can lead to some astonishingly bad behaviour. By the end of the night it resembles nothing so much as a town at pub chucking-out time. This also makes getting home a trial – when the party ends, there is an immediate rush for transport, and it can get ugly. There are buses back and forth to the car park, so if you aren't planning to drink, then driving would be your best course of action. Don't be too disheartened by the taxi queue, though, as it moves quickly, but under no circumstances try to jump it – we have seen people come to serious blows over this.

Horse fans may also be interested in visiting the **Dubai Polo & Equestrian Club** (**poloclubdubai.com**) during the polo season (October–April), where Monday, Wednesday, Friday and Saturday from 3:30 p.m. onwards you can watch chukkas being played while enjoying your own picnic basket (parking costs AED 50 per car) or eating on the terrace of the club's Palermo restaurant. The **Desert Palm Hotel** on Al Awir Road (**desertpalm.peraquum.com**) has a similar pitch-side location. The hotel's wrap-around terrace, complete with infinity pool, has a great vantage point for the chukkas, and you can even watch the horses from their pitch-facing spa suites. It costs nothing to attend the matches, but you are expected to spend on lunch or a drink.

In 2008 Pakistan signed an agreement to play its home one-day internationals and Twenty20 matches at **Dubai Sports City** (**dubai sportscity.ae**) because of the reluctance of international teams to tour its own country due to the terrorist threat. Inaugurated in April 2009, the state-of-the-art stadium is the first of four to be completed in the gargantuan complex. Although it is a bit of a trial to get to, it has been receiving rave reviews from spectators for its great views of the action across the board.

Every February, the **Dubai Tennis Championships** (**barclaysdubai tennischampionships.com**) sees the world's best male and female players congregate at the Aviation Club Tennis Centre to slog it out over two weeks on the centre court, which can hold 5,000 spectators. Tickets start at AED 30 for the qualifying rounds or can be bought for the whole week. As the numbers aren't overwhelming, the atmosphere is quite sedate, but the parking is still a bit of a disaster, so we would recommend taking a taxi. The **Dubai Desert Classic** PGA European Tour golf tournament (**dubaidesertclassic.com**), held at the Majlis Course at Emirates Golf Club in March, attracts similarly high-profile players – past winners include Colin Montgomerie and Tiger Woods.

DUBAI GOLF

ALL DUBAI GOLF COURSES ARE OASES OF GREEN reclaimed from desert sand and a harsh, hot climate at huge expense. The key element is massive irrigation, supplied by recycling waste, desalination or both. The winter high season, which runs October–May, is ideal for golf, with guaranteed sunshine and sustainable temperatures. In the four summer months, the thermometer regularly rises higher than 38°C (100.4°F), often with 90% humidity. At such times, play is not recommended except in the early mornings or on floodlit courses in the evening – if at all.

Because of the cost, golf is a high-end leisure pursuit, available only to those who can buy into Dubai's expansionist dream. The facilities reflect the market: mainly businessmen, both local and foreign, supplemented by tourists. The courses are all pay-and-play, but with none of the everyman connotations that this might suggest in other parts of the world. In Dubai, the green-keeping is immaculate, and the clubhouses offer state-of-the-art luxury. Greens fees include range balls and golf buggies, usually with GPS, a course guide, iced water and towels. Although all the clubs have members, a schedule of competitions and roll of honour boards on the walls, the major priority is providing chic venues for corporate clients who put networking above a fun day out.

This doesn't affect tourist golf, which is pleasantly easy-going. The no-expense-spared approach includes hiring top course designers and showcasing their work in the best possible condition. The dress code is relaxed, though not to the point of allowing jeans and T-shirts. Soft spikes or trainers are mandatory. In reasonable traffic, the existing courses are within a 30- to 40-minute drive of the city centre and Jumeirah's beachfront hotels. With the exception of the courses at Jumeirah Golf Estates, the courses profiled here are public. The local weekend is Friday and Saturday, and some greens fees are higher on those days, but the prices ensure that there are no crowds.

Design rules every aspect of contemporary life in Dubai, and golf is no exception. The pioneering 18-hole sand layout, which opened at the Dubai Country Club in 1971, was followed in 1988 by the Majlis, the first grass course in the Middle East, located at the new Emirates Club. When Sheikh Mohammed Al Maktoum green-lighted the project, he stipulated that it should reflect Dubai's culture. The architects followed his instructions with flair and ingenuity, creating the striking Majlis Clubhouse, with its seven linked white concrete domes. *Majlis* translates from Arabic as 'a place of sitting', and the domes conjure up vivid images of men smoking shisha pipes in a tented Bedouin encampment in the desert.

Five years later, the Dubai Creek Golf & Yacht Club upped the ante with an even more imaginative cultural interpretation, this one composed of three interlinked white sails that invoke an Arab dhow (traditional trading boat). Located on the banks of Dubai Creek in the city centre, the clubhouse is an iconic and inspirational building, the perfect complement to a golf course that puts a high premium on negotiating water hazards.

The architects that followed put the ever-increasing need for conference rooms and gourmet restaurants ahead of the sheikh's wishes, sacrificing exterior innovation to interior splendour. To date, Al Badia has the most grandiose building, though two works in progress may outpoint it when it comes to conspicuous expenditure.

One challenger is the projected Tiger Woods Dubai clubhouse, which shows a fantasy Arabian Nights complex of towers, domes, arches and walkways set among lush gardens with waterfalls and bright tropical flowers that will easily overshadow it – if it ever gets built. It is said that six of the holes on Al Ruwaya course, Tiger Woods's first golf design, have already been grassed, but the project has been haunted by stoppages from the outset. Given the economic slowdown and the golfer's diminished reputation, the pressing question, 'When will it be ready?', is not easy to answer, but it likely won't be in 2011.

Al Badia Golf Club

ESTABLISHED: 2005   DESIGNER Robert Trent Jones II

☎ 04-601-0101; albadiagolfclub.ae; PO Box 79126, Dubai Festival City, Al Badia Community, Al Rebat Street, Ras Al Korn, Deira (4 miles inland from Dubai City Centre)

TEES **Black** 7303 yards, par 72, slope 138 **Blue** 6726 yards, par 72, slope 135 **White** 6200 yards, par 72, slope 131 **Red** 5398 yards, par 72, slope 124

FEES *October–April:* Friday, Saturday and public holidays, AED 795; Sunday–Thursday, AED 595. *May–September:* AED 395. Rates include shared buggy and range balls; 30% discount for guests at the InterContinental Dubai Festival City (☎ 04-701-1110).

FACILITIES Pro shop, locker rooms, floodlit driving range, short-game practice area, practice green, TaylorMade clubs for hire and Golf Academy with TaylorMade Performance Laboratory.

REFRESHMENTS Spike Bar (6:30 a.m.–10 p.m.) serves breakfast, lunch and snacks on an elevated terrace overlooking the course; Tee Lounge (10 a.m.–1 a.m) offers snacks, cocktails and Friday brunch (midday–3 p.m.); Blades (5:30 p.m.–1 a.m.) cooks up Middle Eastern and Asian cuisine; Terra Firma Steakhouse (7 a.m.–midnight) has a menu with more than just Angus and Wagyu.

COMMENTS This well-designed, handsome and perfectly-manicured course features white flamingos on the fairways and elaborate focal points involving man-made cascades and waterfalls. Those who avoid the 11 lakes, smaller ponds and streams can benefit from the generous fairways to score well. It is easier to escape from the 'rivers of sand' down the sides of the fairways than it is to keep the ball dry, and the greens are large and true. Robert Trent Jones II picked out two par 5s, the 5th (index one) and the 18th, as particularly worthy of respect. Even low handicappers are advised to plan three shots to reach the 5th green, cutting across the fairway with water on both sides, while the 18th, a dogleg left, requires a dangerous shot across water to set up the birdie. Al Badia is run by the InterContinental Hotel Group, taking over from Four Seasons, who handled it when it first opened. Although there are no on-site accommodations, the opulent clubhouse fulfils all the functions of a high-end corporate hotel chain, with conference suites, private dining rooms and hot tubs in the locker rooms. The circular building, with its exterior dark glass wall on top of a hill, suggests the headquarters of a progressive software company rather than a golf club, but the interior decor is the ultimate in contemporary elegance and the service is impeccable.

Dubai Creek Golf & Yacht Club

ESTABLISHED 1993   DESIGNER Karl Litten   REDESIGNED BY Thomas Bjorn

☎ 04-295-6000; dubaigolf.com; PO Box 6302, Bur Dubai

TEES **Blue** 6857 yards, par 71, slope 135 **White** 6333 yards, par 71, slope 125 **Red** 5325 yards, par 71, slope 128

FEES *October–May:* Friday, Saturday and public holidays, AED 800; Sunday–Thursday, AED 700. *June–September:* Friday, Saturday and public holidays, AED 400; Sunday–Thursday, AED 300. Rates include shared buggy and range balls.

FACILITIES Pro shop, locker rooms, floodlit driving range, short-game practice area, putting greens, floodlit 9-hole par 3 course (open until 10 p.m.) and Ping clubs for hire. All-day use of swimming pool included in the greens fee. There is a large yacht marina, and sport fishing for kingfish and sailfish can be arranged.

REFRESHMENTS Lake View (6:30 a.m.–midnight) terrace bar restaurant features a spectacular panorama over Dubai Creek and the Dubai skyline; Legends Restaurant offers a Friday brunch (11:30 a.m.–3 p.m.); Aquarium restaurant at the Yacht Club has tables laid out around a central glass pillar filled with tropical fish.

COMMENTS The original 1993 course was comprehensively redesigned in the early 21st century to free up land for villas and the low-rise waterfront Park Hyatt Hotel (225 rooms). The back nine holes were largely unchanged, but the front nine were devised from scratch by Thomas Bjorn in 2005, with money no object. The lakes are ringed by costly stone walls, and humped bridges link greens to tees. The new holes loop behind the marina, with its yacht-shaped clubhouse, returning to join the original 10th. The course puts down its marker on the 1st, a long par 4 that requires a straight drive to set up a clear approach to the green with the second shot. With out-of-bounds to the right and water to the left, the 8th, the longest of the par 3s, is a strategy hole where shot selection depends on the location of the pin. The best comes last, with two celebrated creek challenges. At the narrow 17th, hitting the tee shot towards the right-hand bunkers – and hoping to miss them – may be the least dangerous way of setting up a mid-iron shot to the elevated green. The 18th, its green framed by the magnificent clubhouse sails, demands a risky shot over saltwater to get home in regulation.

The Els Club

ESTABLISHED 2008   DESIGNER Ernie Els

☎ 04-425-1010; elsclubdubai.com; PO Box 111123, Dubai Sports City, Emirates Road

TEES **Black** 7538 yards, par 72, slope 138 **Blue** 6828 yards, par 72, slope 132 **White** 6242 yards, par 72, slope 125 **Red** 5343 yards, par 72, slope 123

FEES *October–April:* AED 830. *May–September:* AED 450. Rates include shared buggy and range balls.

FACILITIES Pro shop, locker rooms, floodlit range (members and those with booked tee times only), short-game practice area, putting greens, Callaway clubs for hire and carts with GPS. The Butch Harmon School of Golf is the only one outside the U.S. The Els Club is part of Dubai Sports City, a hedonistic £1.9 billion (US $3 billion) complex that also includes a 60,000-seat multipurpose stadium, a 25,000-seat cricket ground, a 10,000-seat indoor arena, a David Lloyd Tennis Academy and a Next Generation health club.

REFRESHMENTS The Mediterranean-style clubhouse, opened early 2011, has an Ernie Els Spike Bar and a Big Easy restaurant (similar to his flagship in Stellenbosch), specialising in fine South African wines as a complement to gourmet food.

COMMENTS A three-times major winner, Ernie Els used two decades of experience on the world's best courses to inspire signature links, with Royal Melbourne cited as a major influence. Unlike most of its Dubai rivals, the course has just two holes with water hazards: the 7th and the 15th run up and down the twin reservoir lakes that occupy the centre of the layout. With wide fairways on rolling terrain and deep bunkers guarding undulating greens, the level of the challenge varies as the desert winds shift. Low handicappers can test their skill on the par 4 9th, which was inspired by Muirfield, and the drivable short par 4 16th before pulling out all the stops off the tee on the monster par 5 18th.

EMIRATES GOLF CLUB

☎ 04-380-2222; dubaigolf.com; PO Box 24040, off Sheikh Zayed Road, Emirates Hills

SHARED FACILITIES Pro shop, locker rooms, two floodlit driving ranges, short-game practice area, putting greens, Emirates Golf Academy, 9-hole par 3 Academy course and Callaway clubs for hire. Also offers floodlit tennis, squash, gymnasium and exercise studio.

REFRESHMENTS Spike Bar (6 a.m.–midnight) serves an à la carte breakfast and buffet lunch; Conservatory Bar offers refreshments; enjoy games on TV at the Sports Bar; La Classique is a gourmet restaurant.

COMMENTS The Emirates Golf Club has two complementary courses: the flagship Majlis and the Wadi by Nick Faldo.

Majlis Course

ESTABLISHED 1988   DESIGNER Karl Litten

TEES Black 7211 yards, par 72, slope 143 Blue 6846 yards, par 72, slope 139 White 6529 yards, par 72, slope 135 Red 5563 yards, par 72, slope 131

FEES October–April: AED 1,000. May–September: AED 400. Rates include shared buggy and range balls.

COMMENTS This, the first grass course in the Middle East, hosted the Dubai Desert Classic in February 1989 within a year of opening and is now the Classic's established home. Past winners include Ernie Els,

Seve Ballesteros, Tiger Woods, Rory McIlroy and, in 2010, Miguel Angel Jimenez. It is a desert layout set among dunes, its natural character preserved by indigenous plants and swathes of sand scrub alongside the fairways. The greens are large and quick. The dogleg opener is deceptively encouraging, but only low handicappers should attempt the risk/reward options on the tougher par 4s farther around the course. A long straight drive at the 5th (index one) may promise a par, but a green sloping down to water at the back can drown the excessively long approach. At the uphill 8th, a wayward drive on either side ends in natural bush, making it almost impossible to reach a small undulating green guarded by five bunkers in regulation. As is fitting for a championship course, the 18th is a spectator special, a dramatic par 5 dogleg left that invites big hitters to go for the green in two. This game plan frequently ends in the lake beside the double green, as Tiger Woods discovered in 2002 when victory over Thomas Bjorn seemed certain.

Wadi by Faldo

ESTABLISHED 1995   DESIGNER Karl Litten   REDESIGNED BY Nick Faldo in 2006

TEES **Black** 7328 yards, par 72, slope 139 **Blue** 6900 yards, par 72, slope 135 **White** 6139 yards, par 72, slope 129 **Red** 5407 yards, par 72, slope 127

FEES *October–April:* Friday, Saturday and public holidays, AED 700; Sunday–Thursday, AED 610. *May–September:* AED 300. Rates include shared buggy and range balls.

COMMENTS Overlooked by 90 high-rise buildings constructed in the past decade, the Wadi is the most urban of Dubai's golf courses. The skyline is striking but distracting, and the apartments are close enough to spy on people watching TV and loading dishwashers. The course is named for the wadi – 'valley' in Arabic – that winds through it, not a marked hazard but a distinctive feature throughout. As a champion with six majors to his credit, Nick Faldo was a master of tactics, and his course rewards a thinking golfer rather than one with a 'grip it and rip it' approach. Intelligent bunkering, strategically-placed trees and water hazards on 16 of the holes demand accuracy and concentration, qualities that marked Sir Nick's outstanding career but come less readily to amateur players.

JUMEIRAH GOLF ESTATES

☎ 04-390-3333/9999; jumeirahgolfestates.com;
PO Box 262080, off Emirates Road

SHARED FACILITIES Temporary clubhouse with pro shop and locker rooms, driving range, short-game practice area and putting green. Golf instruction is available, but the Tour Performance Institute will not be open until 2011. The Tennis Academy opened in late 2010.

REFRESHMENTS Available in the temporary clubhouse.

COMMENTS The Jumeirah Golf Estates project comprises four golf courses within easy reach of the Palm development and the top tourist beaches. Jumeirah Golf Estates hit the headlines in November 2009 when it staged the inaugural Dubai World Championship on the Earth Course designed by Greg Norman. The title is misleading because the event, previously held at Valderrama but now rechristened the Race to Dubai, is for the leading money-winners over the year on the European Tour. They compete primarily for the cumulative European number-one position but also for victory in the championship, which carries its own £800,000 (about US $1.3 million) first prize. In 2009 England's Lee Westwood won the tournament and overhauled Northern Ireland's Rory McIlroy to become European champion with a final round of 64, a double that earned him £1.8 million (US $2.8 million). In January 2010 he returned to open Fire, the second Greg Norman course in the complex. The concept is back to nature, with two future courses to be named Water and Wind. As yet, there are no projected completion dates for Water, designed by V. J. Singh, and Wind, billed as Sergio Garcia's architectural debut, though with assistance from Pete Dye and Norman.

Earth Course

ESTABLISHED 2009   DESIGNER Greg Norman

TEES **Championship** 7706 yards, par 72, slope 140 **Tournament** 7045 yards, par 72, slope 134 **Signature** 6473 yards, par 72, slope 131 **Forward** 5435 yards, par 72, slope 128

FEES AED 32,000 for peak annual membership.

COMMENTS As the name suggests, Earth has a rustic appearance, with 4,000 trees, thick rough and orange bunker sand. It is a work in progress, with the stretch from the 10th to the 13th showing the most maturity at the moment. The three final holes provide an appropriate climax to a championship layout. When the wind is behind, as it often is, it's easy to reach the green at the downhill par 4 16th in regulation, but not so easy to stay dry, with water to the right and behind. The island green at the par 3 17th can wreck a card and, with water on both sides, it's easy to add to the damage on the par 5 18th.

Fire Course

ESTABLISHED 2010   DESIGNER Greg Norman

TEES **Championship** 7480 yards, par 72, slope 136 **Tournament** 7062 yards, par 72, slope 130 **Signature** 6507 yards, par 72, slope 125 **Forward** 5619 yards, par 72, slope 121

FEES AED 32,000 for peak annual membership.

COMMENTS Fire is designed to reflect the beauty of the desert, with informal bunkering running alongside narrow fairways and a variety of grasses. The undulating terrain allows for elevated greens that are further defended by intelligent bunkering. There are an estimated 3,000 trees, with more to be planted as required.

The Montgomerie Dubai

ESTABLISHED 2002   DESIGNER Colin Montgomerie

☎ 04-390-5600; themontgomerie.com; PO Box 36700, Emirates Hills

TEES **Black Pearl** 7266 yards, par 72, slope 135 **Sapphire** 6720 yards, par 72, slope 132 **Emerald** 6145 yards, par 72, slope 128 **Ruby** 5394 yards, par 72, slope 126

FEES *October–May:* AED 795. *June–September:* AED 395. Rates include shared buggy and range balls.

FACILITIES Pro shop, locker rooms, driving range, short-game practice area, putting greens, Troon Golf Institute Academy, floodlit Academy 9-hole par 3 course and Callaway clubs for hire. Luxurious 21-room boutique hotel (☎ 04-390-5600) with Angsana Spa, whose staff trained at the Banyan Tree Academy in Thailand (☎ 04-360-9322; **angsanaspa. com**).

REFRESHMENTS Bunkers Spike Bar and Terrace (6 a.m.–10:30 p.m.) serves traditional British fare (for example, fish-and-chips and shepherd's pie); Nineteen restaurant features Pacific Rim cuisine (lunch and dinner); Cigar Bar offers cocktails, cigars and malt whiskies in a clubby atmosphere with billiard and pool tables.

COMMENTS Located in Emirates Hills, 32 kilometres, or 20 miles, down the coast from Dubai City Centre, this is an immaculate layout. When the course opened in 2002, it was an oasis of green isolated in desert sand. Nowadays, it is a real estate development entirely surrounded by villas that have quadrupled in value since they were completed in 2004. Look out for the Montgomerie house near the 7th tee – it's the one with diaphanously-clad statues and old-world carriage lamps. Scottish course designer Colin Montgomerie, the European number one for a record seven times, welcomed the chance to incorporate elements from the links courses in his native land into a desert layout. The result caters for mixed-standard groups, with challenges for low handicappers and easy options for less skilled or experienced players. With 14 lakes and 79 bunkers, nothing should be taken for granted, but a sensible approach will yield a good score, provided the fierce desert wind doesn't interfere. The gimmicky par 3 13th, a circular lake with a green in the middle and a range of tee boxes on the perimeter, is unforgettable for all the wrong reasons, but plans to change it haven't been implemented as yet.

The Tiger Woods Dubai

ESTABLISHED Coming Soon   DESIGNER Tiger Woods

☎ 04-360-0131; tigerwoodsdubai.com; PO Box 66133, Dubailand

IN 2005 TIGER WOODS ANNOUNCED that his first golf course design would be Al Ruwaya – it means 'serenity' in Arabic – but the overview of the course plan, dominated by many intrusive lakes, doesn't suggest that it will be relaxing to play.

FACILITIES When it opens, it will have a pro shop, locker rooms, driving range, short-game practice area and putting greens. In addition, an academy will offer PGA-qualified instruction. A boutique hotel will feature interiors by Lebanon's Elie Saab, and a signature restaurant will be led by three-star Michelin chef Guy Savoy. A grill, lounge and workout facilities are planned for the clubhouse.

PART ELEVEN

NIGHTLIFE

DUBAI IS A CITY THAT LOVES TO PARTY. Apart from the holy month of Ramadan, where no live music or entertainment is allowed (apart from the Arabic musicians who play the traditional oud at a very low level in restaurants), you will never struggle to find something to do in the evening. In terms of clubs and bars, there is a bit of a fuzzy line as to what exactly the difference is – some people are happy to shake their stuff in the latter, while others want to just sit and have a chat in the former. The only way really to tell what the venue considers itself to be is by ascertaining the closing time. In general, nightclubs will shut up shop at 3 a.m., while bars are required to do so at around midnight or 1 a.m. (the licensing laws are quite capricious, so do check this when you arrive as it is subject to change). Alongside these more upmarket venues, in this chapter we have included a special subcategory of covers-band bars. These are not flashy or upmarket (in fact, your feet will stick to the carpet in some) and tend to be in down-at-heel hotels in the older end of town, but, boy, are they a good time. If you want to visit a concert where you have actually heard of the artist, big-name bands or singers do occasionally visit. Touring theatres or musical companies also sometimes hit town. If you prefer your entertainment to be a little more low-key, smoking shisha and watching the world go by in one of the city's many dedicated shisha cafes is a wonderful way to mingle with the locals.

DRINKING *and* DANCING

PROBABLY THE BIGGEST MISCONCEPTION about Dubai for first-time visitors is that the emirate is dry. That, we can assure you, is most definitely not the case – although neighbouring Sharjah is, and laws do vary from emirate to emirate. Apart from the occasional dry day (mourning the passing of an important sheikh and the day before Ramadan begins), licensed venues in Dubai are allowed to serve alcohol to those over the age of 21, and nightclubs in theory are open to those over the age of 25, although in practice you will rarely be asked for ID. Almost without exception, these venues are located in hotels, which means a slightly unfortunate homogeneity in the nightlife scene, although Dubai is still indisputably the 'going out' capital of the Gulf Cooperation Council.

Dubai's five-star hotels are the places to go for a well-made cocktail or a decent glass of wine – we have included a listing of the very best in this chapter – but obviously this is at the pricier end of the scale. On the whole, most lobby bars don't serve alcohol so as not to offend local sensibilities, but there are usually three or four other watering holes elsewhere in the hotel. These are also, on the whole, where to go if you want a romantic, low-key evening without blaring music. Where this is not the case – at Barasti or Sho Cho, for example, we have indicated it. Many have happy hours or drinks deals, or even completely free drinks for ladies at least one night of the week, which can help to soften the financial blow. Most shut at midnight or 1 a.m. during the week and 1 a.m. or 2 a.m. at the weekends. Dress codes aren't superstrict for the most part, but doormen do have a pathological aversion to flip-flops, especially on men, and have been known to look down their noses at flat shoes on ladies, even if they have cost as much as a small family car. Do be prepared for your designer threads to smell of cigarettes, though – at the time of writing, smoking is still permitted inside all bars and restaurants. However, as most have decent ventilation systems, non-smokers shouldn't struggle too much.

If you want to bar-hop, the best places for this are **Souk Al Bahar** in Downtown, the **Madinat Jumeirah** and **Dubai Marine Resort** on Jumeirah Beach Road and **Century Village** in Garhoud. All of these pedestrianised areas are licensed and are home to at least three or four restaurants and bars. We've said it before, but it's worth reiterating: if you plan to drive to your night out, do not drink. There is zero tolerance here, and almost without exception it's easy enough to dump your ride with the valet or in a free parking spot overnight. In general, parking is very easy to find, but we would suggest using the valet service, as it's almost always free and means you can jump out of your car right up at the front door. Really, though, taxis are so readily available at any time of the day or night, it is way easier just to use these. If you are planning to go from bar to club in a taxi and have managed to get a little merry, try to keep your behaviour in check. Your driver may well be horrified if you start singing along to the radio, bellowing to your friends on the back seat or getting a little amorous with your other half. In short: save it for the club, people.

If you want to booze on a budget, you can do it in Bur Dubai, Satwa and Deira, although you need to be prepared for some pretty spit-and-sawdust venues. This is where most of the city's sports bars are too, but these are pretty unpleasant. If there is a big sporting match you just can't miss, ask at your hotel, as they may well be showing it. As you may have realised by now, Dubai is home to a great number of nationalities, many of which mix like oil and water. So in the old part of town, many establishments are exclusively frequented by lower-income Indian, Pakistani, Filipino, African and Russian immigrants. Although you won't be refused entry to many of these establishments, if you are not of the same nationality, you may get a few funny looks. The beer is cheap though (sometimes as little as AED 10 a pint), and the atmosphere can be fun and lively.

Dubai has its fair share of nightclubs too, where you can dance and drink until the wee hours – or at least 3 a.m., when they are legally required to unplug the decks. Big-name international DJs visit regularly, when you can watch the entire party-going city converge in one place. There are, of course, clipboard-wielding tyrants at the best known of these. Dubai is a dressy city, so you'll fare better if you don designer threads and even better than that if you can pull up at the valet with a canary-yellow Porsche. The worst offenders for tough door policies are **400 Club** and the **Cavalli Club** at The Fairmont hotel, **Armani Privé** at the Armani Hotel and **Sanctuary** at the Atlantis. If you want to secure entry to these places, you will need a table reservation, or you are looking at a lot of wrangling from the wrong side of the velvet rope on arrival. Do check when you are booking what you are expected to spend, as most will have a minimum of a bottle of spirits or Champagne. Couples or groups of women will always find it easier to get into the better-known clubs than groups of men. It is entirely dependent on the venue as to whether an entry fee is levied, although as a rule of thumb, ladies get free or discounted entry, and the earlier you arrive, the cheaper it is likely to be. Of course, once a club is full, doormen citywide operate a one-out, one-in policy – generally, no amount of pleading will help your cause then.

During Ramadan, most bars remain open, although only in the evening, as it is still legal to serve alcohol after sundown. Venues that offer live music and dancing usually close for the whole period, as any sort of live music is illegal, and even background music must be kept to a minimum.

NUDGE, NUDGE, WINK, WINK

WHILE WE ARE ALL FOR ADVENTUROUS READERS going off-guide and trying out small and niche establishments in the older end of town (such as Bur Dubai and Deira), this comes with a slight caveat. Without wanting to put too fine a point on it, a fair number of these establishments are frequented by single men who leave a little bit less single and wake up the next morning a couple of hundred dirhams lighter. Although you won't necessarily be approached in these bars and clubs by ladies of the night, it may make you feel uncomfortable, so honestly, our advice is to avoid them. Some doormen will even save you the embarrassment by refusing you entry for being 'the wrong sort of customer'. That's not to suggest that all of these bars and clubs are pick-up joints, but if they look seedy, they probably are. Even the city's most expensive hotel bars have professional types on hand to service clients, but they tend only to approach single men who have taken a seat at the bar – or rowdy groups of guys in suits. Money will usually come up quite quickly in the conversation. If it does, and you're not interested, be polite but firm and they will move on to the next black Amex.

An **EVENING** at a **SHISHA CAFE**

IT IS ACTUALLY AGAINST THE LAW for a man or woman in national dress to enter a nightclub in Dubai (although of course they can always don jeans and a shirt to hit the dance floor), so if you want to mix with locals in *dishdashas* during the wee hours, by far the best place to do it is at one of the city's many shisha cafes. It's a very social scene, with groups of young men (and, very occasionally, women) chewing the fat together. It's rare to see a solo smoker, as shishas are meant to be shared. But this has been taken into account, and hygienic plastic tips are usually handed out to all at the table, so the tip can be replaced when it's your turn to inhale. You may not be able to drink alcohol in many of these places, but the freshly-squeezed juices; thick, bitter local coffee; and fruit-flavoured tobacco inhaled through bubbling water pipes will almost certainly give you enough of a buzz. Said pipes usually last for hours and are prepared by specialists who will ask you which flavour you'd like (grape, apple, mint and rose are the most popular – flavours can also be combined) and then bring it to your table, replacing the hot coals as they eventually burn out. A shisha should cost you anywhere between AED 30 and AED 100 depending on the establishment.

The **Shakespeare & Co.** chain of cafes has a large selection of shishas – the best places to sample them are the terrace at the Village Mall branch (near Dubai Marine Resort; ☎ 04-344-6228) or in Souk Al Bahar (☎ 04-422-4558), looking out over the twinkling lights of the Burj Khalifa. **Zahr El-Laymoun** (☎ 04-448-6060) in Souk Al Bahar is also popular with Lebanese and local shisha smokers – even if the bright floral cushions and weird watering-can decor is a bit over the top. The Jumeirah Beach Road is a hub of Emirati racers in Hummers burning rubber and eyeing those sitting behind the blacked-out windows of the cars next to them at the traffic lights. This provides an excellent night-time procession for smokers in the cafes that line the road. The ringside seat for this is the outside terrace at **Shu** (☎ 04-349-1303) near Jumeirah Beach Park. It may seem anathema to British smokers, who are forced to puff away outside bars and restaurants, but not all shisha cafes are outdoors. The best place to smoke inside is the Lebanese joint **Reem Al Bawadi** (☎ 04-394-7444), again on Jumeirah Beach Road, with its foliage-draped ceiling and speciality of shishas served in hollowed-out pineapples. You won't see many locals at **Bait Al Wakeel** because of the touristy location (it's set out on a terrace over Dubai Creek, next to the Textile Souk in Bur Dubai), but it's a very atmospheric night out and is a pretty place to puff away.

unofficial **TIP**
We should probably play mum for a minute and warn you that, even though the fragrant water pipes do not come with an official warning, they are every bit as bad for you as cigarettes – some say that just an hour smoking is as bad for you as a 20-pack. Others argue that the water filtration process removes much of the tar and nicotine. Regardless, you'll almost certainly wake up with a bit of a tickle in your throat at the least.

There are of course shisha bars in hotels too, where you can enjoy a glass of wine or beer with your smoke. The best of these are the **Rooftop** at the One&Only Royal Mirage on Al Sufouh Road (☎ 04-399-9999), the small *Majlis* tents set by the pool at **The Palace** hotel in Downtown Dubai (☎ 04-428-7888), the **Tamanya Terrace** at the Radisson Blu Media City (☎ 04-366-9111) and the pretty – and extremely popular – **Courtyard** bar (☎ 04-428-5888) at the Al Manzil hotel Downtown. If you want a view of the water, **QD's** at Dubai Creek Golf & Yacht Club (☎ 04-295-6000) is set on an enormous wooden deck overlooking Dubai Creek, and it serves more than passable food and great shisha until 3 a.m.

COVERS BANDS

COVERS BANDS ARE SO MANY AND VARIOUS in Dubai that they do in fact warrant their own special section. They range from brilliant to toe-curlingly awful but are always enjoyable in a high-camp kind of way. They are mostly Filipino, although some are Russian, African or Indian too, and they are the main draw of most of the clubs and bars that host them. Many will do requests – scrawl almost any pop or rock song on a napkin and send it to the front and they will dedicate it to you – and some also have a troupe of backing dancers in questionable '80s threads. As most of these venues are serious dive bars, we haven't profiled them individually in this chapter as they aren't the sort of places for which you'd don a little black dress and prop up the bar with a cold glass of Pinot Grigio. But if you are up for a quintessentially Dubai experience and don't mind roughing it a little bit, below are those we consider to be the best nights out. Just be warned – the clientele wouldn't look out of place in that bar in *Star Wars*.

Blue Bar

Novotel World Trade Centre, Za'abeel Road; ☎ 04-332-0000

Hours Daily, 4 p.m.–2 a.m.

IT'S A BIT UNFAIR TO LUMP THIS IN with the covers bands section, but we can't in good conscience recommend that you go to the bar for its ambience otherwise (although the selection of Belgian beer is very good). Its odd location means that Dubai's jazz fans and businessmen having a quick beer after their computer conferences are the only customers. That's a shame, as it does showcase some genuinely good local talent.

Blues & Cues

Ramada Continental Hotel, Abu Hail, Deira;
☎ 04-266-2666

Hours Daily, 4 p.m.–3 a.m.

UNTIL 9:30 P.M., THIS IS PRIMARILY A POOL BAR, but when the Sri Lankan covers band and their full set of Eastern European dancers hit the stage, all heck breaks loose. The clientele is a mix of Arabs, Filipinos and curious expats – you'll almost certainly be the only tourist in there.

Club Africana

Rush Inn Hotel, Bank Street, Bur Dubai;
☎ 04-352-2235

Hours Daily, 7 p.m.–2:45 a.m.

THIS IS A COMPLETELY UNIQUE EXPERIENCE for Dubai. Every night at 9 p.m., the predominantly African clientele show their appreciation for a rather exceptional, and very large, covers band (of course, they actually know the songs that are being covered – you may not, but you'd have to have cloth ears not to get into the groove yourself). Just ignore the plastic palm trees, dodgy wallpaper and apathetic service.

Garage Club

Ramee International Hotel, Nasser Square, Deira;
☎ 04-224-0222

Hours Daily, 9:30 p.m.–3 a.m.

ONE OF THE WEIRDEST JOINTS IN TOWN, this neon-lit nightclub in a down-at-heel two-star hotel is furnished entirely with knackered old cars and buses. These have been repainted and the insides have been hollowed out, to be transformed into cosy booths for four or eight, from where you can watch the decent African band and knock back ludicrously cheap beer.

Maharlika Café Filipino
President Hotel, Trade Centre Road, Karama; ☎ 04-334-6565

Hours Daily, 6 p.m.–3 a.m.

THE CLIENTELE IN THIS FOURTH-FLOOR NIGHTCLUB in the decidedly dodgy President Hotel is solely Filipino. In fact, on our last visit we asked for our table in English, only to be directed to the 'white people over there'. It is also, without exception, up for a fun night out – when the band is on a break, the patrons storm the dance floor to cheesy chart tunes, although when the headline acts come on, they respectfully vacate to give the scantily-clad dancers room to do the splits. They will play anything – anything – you request, and play it surprisingly well. Drinks are cheap, food is disgusting and it's probably best not to even mention the toilets.

The Music Room
The Majestic Hotel, Mankhool Road, Bur Dubai; ☎ 04-359-8888

Hours Daily, 6 p.m.–3 a.m.

THE MAJESTIC HOTEL MAY NOT LIVE UP TO ITS NAME, but don't hold that against it, as it is home to arguably the best Filipino covers band this side of Manila. The club itself is pretty sparse, with blacked-out windows and a couple of pool tables, but the hard rock stylings of the Rock Spiders, clad in black leather and fishnets, will keep your toes tapping and your head banging. There are also regular open-mic nights for new talent.

Rock Bottom Café
Regent Palace Hotel, Trade Centre Road, Bur Dubai; ☎ 04-396-3888

Hours Daily, 7 p.m.–3 a.m.

THIS BASEMENT BAR PULLS AN IMPRESSIVELY-LARGE CROWD every night after the classier joints kick out. Said impressive crowd is usually pretty intent on pulling each other while shaking their drunken stuff to a very good covers band, who hail from South Africa. A cut above the average, they tackle everything from Radiohead to Rihanna with equal aplomb. There is a kebab stall *inside* the club – which probably tells you everything else you need to know.

Troyka
Ascot Hotel, Khalid Bin Al Waleed Road, Bur Dubai; ☎ 04-352-0900

Hours Daily, 8 p.m.–2 a.m.

STRICTLY SPEAKING THIS IS MORE OF A RESTAURANT than a bar, although the management will have no gripes if you settle yourself in the

continued on page 335

Bars and Nightclubs in Deira & Bur Dubai

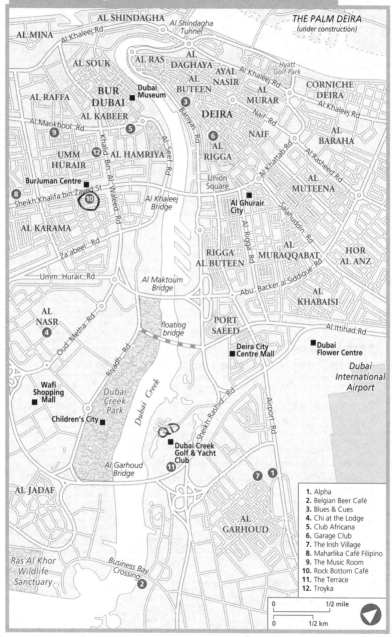

1. Alpha
2. Belgian Beer Café
3. Blues & Cues
4. Chi at the Lodge
5. Club Africana
6. Garage Club
7. The Irish Village
8. Maharlika Café Filipino
9. The Music Room
10. Rock Bottom Café
11. The Terrace
12. Troyka

Bars and Nightclubs in Jumeirah

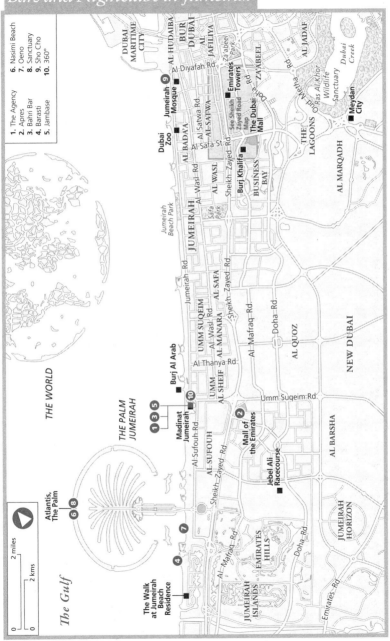

1. The Agency
2. Apres
3. Bahri Bar
4. Jambase
5.

6. Nasimi Beach
7. Oeno
8. Sanctuary
9. Sho Cho
10. 360°

Bars and Nightclubs on Sheikh Zayed Road

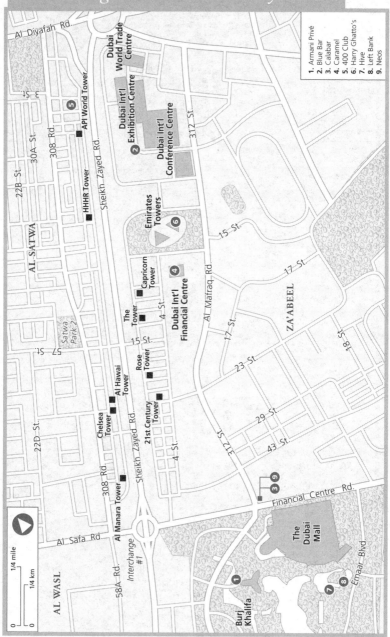

1. Armani Privé
2. Blue Bar
3. Calabar
4. Caramel
5. 400 Club
6. Harry Ghatto's
7. Hive
8. Left Bank
9. Neos

continued from page 331

conference-style seating to enjoy the weird and wonderful Russian band and cabaret.

BAR PROFILES

The Agency

WINE BAR WITH BETTER-THAN-AVERAGE SNACKS

Souk Madinat Jumeirah, Al Sufouh Road; ☎ 04-366-8888; jumeirah.com

Mixed drinks AED 50+ **Wine** AED 36+ **Beer** AED 35+ **Dress** Smart casual **Specials** Five drinks for AED 100 on Wednesday and Sunday evenings **Food available** Snacks and full menu **Hours** Daily, 6 p.m.–2 a.m.

WHO GOES THERE Well-heeled tourists and expats aged 30+

WHAT GOES ON A lot of wine drinking. The first branch of this Dubai long-timer is attached to Emirates Towers in the financial centre. This outlet is much bigger and more relaxed – although similarly impossible to get a table on most nights of the week. It fills up after 6 p.m. with the post-work set, attracted by the fact that noise levels never reach the unbearable (that is, you can actually have a conversation without shouting over thumping music), and the crowd never gets rowdy – quite unusual for bars in the Madinat Jumeirah. The food is particularly good too – the cheese fondue pairs well with many of the lengthy list of wines served by the glass.

SETTING AND ATMOSPHERE Dark and inviting, with black-and-white tiled floors and walls, dark wood furniture and lots of mirrors. The last tables to go are always the tall ones with bar stools – because they are incredibly uncomfortable. For the cooler months a 70-seater terrace overlooks the Madinat's waterways.

Après

AFTER-SKI BAR WITH BRILLIANT SLOPE VIEWS

Mall of the Emirates, Sheikh Zayed Road; ☎ 04-341-2575; elr.ae

Mixed drinks AED 39+ **Wine** AED 32+ **Beer** AED 28+ **Dress** Casual **Specials** Deals on drinks and 20% off food daily, 5–7 p.m. **Food available** Snacks and full menu **Hours** Daily, 10 a.m.–1 a.m.

WHO GOES THERE A young, pre-party crowd aged 20–30, shoppers, skiers (from Ski Dubai)

WHAT GOES ON This kitschy bar, which overlooks the real-snow slopes of Ski Dubai in the Mall of the Emirates, has always packed them in. It's not just the view of the skiers below (which can be hysterically funny – the best way to watch a total wipe-out is from a bar stool, we've found), but also because the atmosphere is unfailingly fun and friendly. Luckily, the drinks aren't themed – they serve draught lager, have a decent selection of well-priced wine and offer a very long list of cocktails, all of which are competently made, if not great. An epic cheese fondue for four is a pretty good way to soak up some of the booze, and there are also stone-baked pizzas, salads and burgers.

SETTING AND ATMOSPHERE OK, so the furniture does look a bit like it's been bought in a job lot from the Hollyoaks set, with black bar stools and red-tiled walls, but the button-backed white leather banquettes are cosy, and the exposed brick wall gives a nod to the Alpine theme.

Bahri Bar

GREAT TERRACE WITH STUNNING VISTAS OF BURJ AL ARAB

Mina A'Salam, Madinat Jumeirah; ☎ 04-366-8888; jumeirah.com

Mixed drinks AED 50+ **Wine** AED 36+ **Beer** AED 35+ **Dress** Smart casual **Specials** None **Food available** Snacks **Hours** Saturday–Wednesday, 4 p.m.–2 a.m.; Thursday–Friday, 4 p.m.–3 a.m.

WHO GOES THERE Grown-up drinkers, camera-happy tourists, businessmen

WHAT GOES ON Lots of pointing at the Burj Al Arab, which can be seen from the expansive terrace at this hotel bar. Apart from Fridays, when it inherits the rowdy post-brunch crowd of the Mina A'Salam's eateries, and those of neighbouring Al Qasr too, it is remarkably quiet – a few businessmen here, a honeymooning couple there. Drinking in any of Jumeirah's properties is expensive, and this is no exception – you do get what you pay for with the well-mixed cocktails and great service, but the wine is a tad overpriced.

SETTING AND ATMOSPHERE Although the Art Deco–themed bar inside is pretty enough, the terrace is the real draw. It is strewn with Persian carpets; has plenty of comfy, cushioned seating; and provides moodily-romantic lighting. Giant fans keep things cool for summer.

Barasti

BEACH BAR WITH LIVE MUSIC AND A PARTY CROWD

Le Méridien Mina Seyahi, Al Sufouh Road; ☎ 04-399-3333; lemeridien-minaseyahi.com

Mixed drinks AED 40+ **Wine** AED 31+ **Beer** AED 32+ **Dress** Casual **Specials** Deals on drinks and 20% off food daily, 5–7 p.m. **Food available** Snacks, full menu for lunch and dinner, and *shawarma* **Hours** Saturday–Wednesday, 11 a.m.–1:30 a.m.; Thursday–Friday, 11 a.m.–3 a.m.

WHO GOES THERE Everybody, all the time – this is Dubai's most popular, and most famous, watering hole.

WHAT GOES ON If it didn't leave you, our dear reader, none the wiser, we'd say 'what happens in Barasti stays in Barasti'. This is probably where some of the most raucous behaviour in the emirate takes place, and at the weekend it can get pretty full-on. It doesn't quite deserve its local moniker – Bar Nasty – but expect shouting, terrible dancing and more Lycra than a mid-size Topshop. It's set over two levels, and downstairs tends to be a little quieter – bands and DJs ensure it's nigh-on impossible to talk on the upper level, but nobody seems to mind. Do not, under any circumstances, order a cocktail – this is a pint or spirit-and-a-mixer sort of a place. If you visit during the week or during the day, there is a much more laid-back, beachy vibe, and they serve a perfectly-decent selection of pub grub.

SETTING AND ATMOSPHERE This place launched more than 15 years ago and was initially just a beach shack. It's still one of the few places you can sip a beverage with the sand between your toes in Dubai. Downstairs, shaded white sofas and loungers sit out by the sea, and a small air-conditioned indoor space features a dance floor. Upstairs, an ornamental swimming pool provides a bit of a hazard for those who've had one too many Jaegerbombs (the house speciality – if you have to ask what it is, you probably shouldn't order one), and a large wooden decking area has tables that look out over the waves.

Belgian Beer Café

A THEMED BAR FOR BEER DRINKERS

Crowne Plaza Hotel, Festival City; ☎ 04-701-1111; ichotelsgroup.com

Mixed drinks AED 42+ **Wine** AED 28+ **Beer** AED 35+ **Dress** Casual **Specials** None **Food available** Snacks and full menu **Hours** Saturday–Wednesday, midday–4 p.m. and 6 p.m.–1:15 a.m.; Thursday–Friday, midday–4 p.m. and 6 p.m.–2 a.m.

WHO GOES THERE Beer drinkers aged 30+

WHAT GOES ON Dubai is dotted with joints that Brits will recognise as classic pubs, but there really aren't any that we could hand-on-heart recommend as a nice night out – most are at the seedier hotels with cigarette-stained carpets and a fairly insalubrious clientele. This place is very different indeed. It has a very large draught beer selection for the sophisticated hops fans, affable service from polite and knowledgeable waiters, superior bar snacks (the deep-fried cheese balls are a guilty pleasure) and some serious dining too – much of it pork-based.

SETTING AND ATMOSPHERE Seats on the small terrace overlooking Dubai Creek are hotly contested in summer, and tables are always packed with groups of expats enjoying after-work drinks that almost always turn into dinner. The decor is beautifully done and manages to give the impression of a historical Belgian boozer without screaming 'theme pub'. There is a long mahogany bar with gleaming draught pumps and a row of high stools, with lots of dark wood tables and school chairs dotted around the place. Walls are rag-rolled and plastered with old tin signs and Art Deco movie posters. The mezzanine level is a bit lacking in atmosphere.

Calabar

CHIC COCKTAIL BAR WITH BURJ KHALIFA VIEWS

The Address Downtown Dubai; ☎ 04-436-8888; theaddress.com

Mixed drinks AED 50+ **Wine** AED 40+ **Beer** AED 45+ **Dress** Smart **Specials** None **Food available** Snacks **Hours** Daily, 6 p.m.–2:30 a.m.

WHO GOES THERE Poseurs and Downtown-dwellers over age 30

WHAT GOES ON You can get up-close and personal with the world's tallest building while sipping on a cocktail at this very chic nightspot. Set next to The Address hotel's three infinity pools, at the weekends the bar packs in the crowds, attracted by the pretty view – of each other and the Burj Khalifa. Unfortunately, there are a few things that let down what has the potential to be a wonderful nightspot. The service can veer between reluctant and downright rude – we have been moved off tables that then sat empty all night in the past because 'one of our VIPs might come' – and the drinks are far from reasonable. Food is available but not really the point of an evening here.

SETTING AND ATMOSPHERE The outdoor space, set over multiple levels, is strewn with cushions, beanbags and dark wicker tables. To be honest, this is the whole point of the bar, which means during summer months it can be a bit dead – however, indoors is a high-ceilinged space with low-slung velvet sofas and plenty of tall stools at the bar.

Caramel

INDOOR AND OUTDOOR AMERICAN-STYLE COCKTAIL BAR

Building 3, Dubai International Financial Centre;
☎ 800-227-2635; carameldubai.com

Mixed drinks AED 55+ **Wine** AED 38+ **Beer** AED 32+ **Dress** Smart casual **Specials** Ladies' night on Tuesday, 6–9 p.m., half-price Cosmopolitans **Food available** Snacks **Hours** Sunday–Thursday, 11 a.m.–2 a.m.; Friday, 5 p.m.–2 a.m. (last order midnight); closed Saturday

WHO GOES THERE City boys in suits and girls in very, very short skirts hoping to snare one

WHAT GOES ON This is actually a restaurant and a bar, but it's used primarily as the latter by high-rolling bankers who work in the vicinity. It's owned by the Light Group, which operates a number of venues in Las Vegas, but the vibe here is distinctly New York. Thus, cocktails are innovative and well mixed, bar snacks superior (mini lobster tacos, truffle-infused mac 'n' cheese and mini Wagyu burgers) and the supermodel-like hostesses are dressed in short, tight little black dresses. Music cranks up as the night goes on, and although strictly speaking it's not allowed, the clientele shake their pert posteriors on the makeshift dance floor to the DJ's tunes once the party gets going.

SETTING AND ATMOSPHERE The best seats in the house during the winter months are on the leafy terrace, which is packed with comfy sofas and dark corners. Inside is dark and slick-looking, with a few tables for diners and a long, tall illuminated table for drinkers to lean on while chatting up members of the opposite sex.

Harry Ghatto's

LIVELY KARAOKE JOINT FOR POST-OFFICE DRINKERS

**Tokyo @ The Towers, Jumeirah Emirates Towers, Sheikh Zayed Road;
☎ 04-319-8796; jumeirah.com**

Mixed drinks AED 55+ **Wine** AED 32+ **Beer** AED 34+ **Dress** Smart casual
Specials Two-for-one on selected drinks 8 p.m.–10 p.m. **Food available** Japanese
Hours Daily, 8 p.m.–2:30 a.m. (karaoke starts at 10 p.m.)

WHO GOES THERE Karaoke fans and the criminally out of tune
WHAT GOES ON Dubai is a city of show-offs, so no surprises that the private room karaoke thing never really took off here. Harry Ghatto's is the most popular singalong joint in town (in fact, one of the only) where you can bawl your little lungs out. Most definitely not the place to come for a quiet pint, as the assembled crew of city boys who work in the neighbouring Dubai International Financial Centre take turns to wrestle the mic off each other and stand swaying along to soft-rock hits in front of the two giant screens. The sound is terrible, and it takes a good hour for your chosen song to come up, but the atmosphere here is always buzzing.
SETTING AND ATMOSPHERE The decor of this bar attached to a Japanese restaurant is vaguely oriental, although it won't be winning any design awards. Think predominantly black and red, with a bit of bamboo thrown in for good measure, and some token paper lanterns. There aren't too many places to sit either – just a few bar stools, a couple of long benches and some armchairs pushed up against the walls – although that doesn't seem to be a problem, as most people spend the night craning to see who's doing that uncanny Freddie Mercury impression.

Hive

DJ BAR WITH A LIVELY EXPAT CLIENTELE

Souk Al Bahar, Downtown; ☎ 04-425-2296; hive.ae

Mixed drinks AED 55+ **Wine** AED 28+ **Beer** AED 33+ **Dress** Smart casual
Specials Daily happy hour, 6–7 p.m., with 25% off drinks; Tuesday is ladies' night with three free glasses of sparkling wine for women **Food available** Snacks
Hours Daily, 4 p.m.–2 a.m. (alcohol served 6 p.m.–midnight)

WHO GOES THERE Girls in short skirts, guys with shirts undone to the waist (well, nearly)
WHAT GOES ON For about six months in 2010, absolutely nothing went on, as this Downtown nightspot was so popular that it was shut down due to complaints from residents about noise. Luckily, it was allowed to reopen with slightly curtailed opening hours and is once again drawing in a lively

crowd. It becomes very much standing room only at the weekends and on the popular ladies' night, and the party spills out onto a large terrace with its own satellite bar (open October–May). There are resident DJs at the weekends and, once a week, a live acoustic night. The rest of the time, it's a nice place to kick back and order a burger or a pizza, washed down with one of the signature cocktails.

SETTING AND ATMOSPHERE Leather sofas, bare brick walls and dark wood beams on the ceilings make this cosy rather than ultramodern. It is set over multiple levels, so there are plenty of nooks and crannies and big tables for larger groups (just watch the steps after you've had a few – they are lethal). Outside is a mix of sofas and armchairs and tall bar stools, from which you get a great view of the Dubai Fountain below.

The Irish Village

IRISH BAR WITH PINTS OF BEER AND PUB FOOD

Century Village, Garhoud; ☎ 04-282-4750; theirishvillage.ae

Mixed drinks AED 30+ **Wine** AED 30+ **Beer** AED 30+ **Dress** Smart casual **Specials** Occasionally – check the Web site **Food available** Snacks **Hours** Saturday–Wednesday, 11 a.m.–2 a.m.; Thursday–Friday, 11 a.m.–3 a.m.

WHO GOES THERE Homesick Brits, sports fans and after-work drinkers from nearby offices

WHAT GOES ON Exactly what you'd expect of a British pub garden airlifted into the Dubai sunshine. One of the best-loved watering holes in the city, it's a totally laid-back place to knock back a few pints, chat with friends (old or new – it often gets so busy that you'll have to share tables) and listen to the live bands that play most nights. Service is surly across the board, although it's enough of a novelty for most Brits to have their pints brought right to the table that they'll put up with it. Food is fair-to-middling standard pub grub as long as you don't get adventurous with ordering – if it doesn't come with chips or in a bun, best to steer clear.

SETTING AND ATMOSPHERE The Irish Village does slightly give the impression that it's been designed by someone who gleaned their knowledge of British pubs entirely from soap operas. So inside, it's sticky carpets, cigarette-branded ashtrays and chairs that look as if they were bought second-hand from a suburban Harvester. Outside is far more pleasant (not to mention less of a smoke-filled fug), with lots of wooden benches set next to a patch of grass and an ornamental duck pond. Hardy drinkers insist on sitting outside even in summer, as super-charged fans spray mist at every table.

Left Bank

BOUDOIR-STYLE COCKTAIL BAR

Souk Al Bahar, Downtown; ☎ 04-368-4501; elr.ae

Mixed drinks AED 39+ **Wine** AED 32+ **Beer** AED 28+ **Dress** Smart casual **Specials**

None **Food available** Snacks and full meals **Hours** Saturday–Wednesday, 6 p.m.–midnight; Thursday, 3 p.m.–midnight; Friday, midday–midnight

WHO GOES THERE Cocktail lovers, couples, regulars, birthday parties

WHAT GOES ON This large Souk Al Bahar branch of the burgeoning Emirates-based chain is usually full of couples on first dates, sunk low in the velvet banquettes and surrounded by gauzy black curtains. Most of them probably met there in the first place – at the weekends, young singles pack out the place, sitting at the bar or hovering around the long communal table near the entrance (all the better to bag the best totty on arrival). Staff are super friendly, which is just as well – when it gets busy, they are massively overstretched, so it can take a while to get served one of their remarkably good cocktails. You're still best to stick with the mixed drinks, though – the house wine is like paint stripper, and it comes in thimble-size glasses. Bar food is above average – and there are often deals including drinks and a selection of sampler platters.

SETTING AND ATMOSPHERE A little bit 'tart's boudoir by way of Ikea' – black flock wallpaper, opulent red velvet sofas and low chandeliers. There is a 16-seater raised booth for big groups, and high tables with white leather seating are towards the back of the bar. The only gripe is that it can get a bit smoky – there is only a very small terrace for lovers of the evil weed, so everyone just puffs away at their table.

Nasimi Beach

BEACH BAR WITH SHISHA AND INTERNATIONAL DJS

Atlantis, The Palm, Palm Jumeirah; ☎ 04-426-2626; atlantisthepalm.com

Mixed drinks AED 40+ **Wine** AED 30+ **Beer** AED 40+ **Dress** Casual **Specials** Daily happy hour, 4–6 p.m., half-price selected drinks **Food available** Snacks outside, full menu inside **Hours** Sunday–Wednesday, midday–midnight; Thursday, midday–2 a.m.; Friday, midday–3 a.m.

WHO GOES THERE Dubai expat kids who can't afford a flight to Thailand

WHAT GOES ON It was a good year after the Atlantis hotel opened that the management wised up to the fact that this restaurant and beach bar could be nightlife gold. During the day, it's a lovely spot too – and the restaurant serves great burgers, grills and sandwiches – but the real draw is the regular Friday Full Moon Parties, where you can dance to big-name international DJs with the sand between your toes (entry is AED 100 after 9 p.m.). During the week, it's also a great place to enjoy a shisha and a glass of wine, but be prepared to be patient – staff get overstretched, and it's a big distance they have to cover to get from the bar to your table. A paltry few bar snacks are available, but if you want to eat properly (or are a vegetarian), you'll have to take a proper seat in the restaurant just behind.

SETTING AND ATMOSPHERE Apart from the Full Moon Parties, where clubbers are shoulder to shoulder, it's a very low-key spot. The beach is lit by flame torches and strewn with squishy beanbags, and there are several private *Majlis* tents for bigger groups. There is also, of course, the sound of the lapping ocean in the background, but you aren't encouraged to jump in post-party.

Neos

SEE BURJ KHALIFA FROM THE 63RD-FLOOR CHAMPAGNE BAR

The Address Downtown Dubai; ☎ 04-436-8888; theaddress.com

Mixed drinks AED 60+ **Wine** AED 40+ **Beer** AED 42+ **Dress** Smart **Specials** None **Food available** Snacks **Hours** Daily, 6 p.m.–2 a.m.

WHO GOES THERE High rollers, hotel guests and, erm, hookers

WHAT GOES ON It's not the hotel's fault that this place has become a bit of a magnet for high-class ladies of the night. It is a beautiful space, set on the 63rd floor of The Address hotel, and the picky door policy and eye-watering drinks prices attract those with money to spare (or, in fact, burn). Unless you're looking for it, or you are a single guy sitting at the bar waving your wallet around, it's unlikely that you'll even clock the ladies, as the view is distracting enough to keep you enthralled all night. From the tables by the floor-to-ceiling windows (it's best to book these in advance, as they are hotly contested), you have a bird's-eye vantage point of the Dubai Fountain, and you can also peer into the Burj Khalifa opposite. There really isn't a better seat in the city.

SETTING AND ATMOSPHERE Accessed via its own lift, Neos has deliberately culti-vated an exclusive air, which does occasionally mean that the door staff can be a bit snotty (we've seen 'it' girls on the door plead to be let in, explain-ing that their shoes may be flat, but they cost £500, or about US $800, thank you very much). Set over several tiered levels, its decor is dark and sumptuous, done in an Art Deco style – purple and grey velvet, geometric-patterned carpets, leather chairs and walnut wood. They have cleverly optimised window table space by having curving banquettes snake around the edge of the bar, and there is a small private room off to the right of the space.

Oeno

GROWN-UP WINE AND CHEESE BAR

**The Westin Mina Seyahi, Al Sufouh Road;
☎ 04-399-4141; westinminaseyahi.com**

Mixed drinks AED 45+ **Wine** AED 35+ **Beer** AED 35+ **Dress** Smart casual **Specials** Ladies receive three complimentary glasses of bubbles on Tuesday, 6–9 p.m. **Food available** Cheese and snacks **Hours** Monday–Wednesday, 6 p.m.–1 a.m.; Thursday–Friday, 6 p.m.–2 a.m.; closed Sunday

WHO GOES THERE Serious oenophiles and cheese freaks

WHAT GOES ON A jazz band provides the nightly soundtrack for this small white-and-chrome bar tucked away in a corner of the Westin hotel. A lot of thought has been put into the wine list, and an impressive number of these are available by the glass. Even more unusual for Dubai, the staff are willing and able to suggest a fabulous cheese to go with the drinks (they have a very large selection of unusual ones – probably the best in the emirate). Even more surprisingly, many of the wines won't break the bank – they offer wine flights of three or five complimentary glasses for AED 69 or AED 100. Apart from Tuesday night, when the free bubbly for ladies brings in a slightly screechy clientele, Oeno attracts a sophisticated, grown-up crowd.

SETTING AND ATMOSPHERE It often gets forgotten by drinkers (and, unfortunately, the waiting staff), but the mezzanine-level space is actually the nicest place to park yourself – the James Bond–style two-metre-high (6.6-foot-high) chairs are quite something. The colour palette is inoffensive cream and white, with a two-storey wall of wine and a Roman mural providing the visual centerpiece to the room. Two small, glass-fronted rooms, where small groups can book private wine and cheese tastings, are near the bar.

Sho Cho

BEACHSIDE HANGOUT OF BEAUTIFUL PEOPLE

**Dubai Marine Resort, Jumeirah Beach Road;
☎ 04-346-1111; sho-cho.com**

Mixed drinks AED 40+ **Wine** AED 35+ **Beer** AED 34+ **Dress** Smart casual **Specials** None **Food available** Snacks **Hours** Daily, 7 p.m.–3 a.m.

WHO GOES THERE A body-beautiful selection of Beirut transplants aged 25+

WHAT GOES ON This little slice of Lebanon in Dubai Marine Resort is perennially popular with expats dressed to the nines. Weekends are predictably the busiest nights, although the '80s shindig every Sunday also packs them in. Decent sushi is served in the indoor space, but everyone ignores it in favour of the decking, which juts out over the lapping waves. The bar is split into three sections – the pheromone-fuelled free-for-all in the middle, the VIP area to the left (only high rollers who book tables and order bottles sit here, surveying the paupers) and the restaurant section to the right, where ladies-who-avoid-lunch push sashimi round their plates. The music is good but loud, the men's shirts louder and the designer-label count off the hook.

SETTING AND ATMOSPHERE The colour scheme is all-white, so as not to distract from the real decoration – the clientele. It's a shame that there aren't more venues like this in the city. The pretty setting makes it feel like a cross between a Greek island and an Ibiza nightclub.

The Terrace

LOUCHE CREEKSIDE OYSTER AND CHAMPAGNE BAR

Park Hyatt, Dubai Creek, Deira; ☎ 04-602-1234; dubai.park.hyatt.com

Mixed drinks AED 45+ **Wine** AED 45+ **Beer** AED 35+ **Dress** Casual **Specials** Sunday happy hour, 6–9 p.m., half-price drinks; Sunday ladies' night, 6–11 p.m., half-price drinks for ladies **Food available** Snacks and full menu **Hours** Daily, midday–2 a.m. (from 4 p.m. in the summer)

WHO GOES THERE Hotel guests, businessmen, golfers

WHAT GOES ON This bar is a well-kept secret in Dubai. The best place to sit is on the outdoor terrace, overlooking Dubai Marina and Dubai Creek Park opposite, but actually the indoor space, with its ice-packed, seafood-focused Raw Bar, is rather lovely too, with a long, white communal table and high stools. It's a pretty place to spend a whole day, as there are many sofas on which to lounge. During the winter season, DJs play chilled-out lounge music Wednesday–Friday, and there are daily deals on cocktails.

SETTING AND ATMOSPHERE Very relaxed indeed. The tables on the expansive wooden deck are well spaced for privacy, and everything is decked out in very Riviera-chic creams and browns.

NIGHTCLUB PROFILES

Alpha

A RESTAURANT, BAR AND CLUB WITH INTERNATIONAL DJS

**Le Méridien Village, Airport Road, Garhoud;
☎ 04-702-2640; alphaclub.ae**

Entrance Free–AED 100 depending on the night and act **Mixed drinks** AED 30+ **Wine** AED 30+ **Beer** AED 25+ **Dress** Casual **Specials** AED 149 for the unlimited house drinks, 4–7 p.m. **Food available** None **Hours** Friday, 3 p.m.–3 a.m.; Tuesday and Thursday, 6 p.m.–3 a.m.; closed Sunday, Monday and Wednesday

WHO GOES THERE Indie kids and post-brunchers

WHAT GOES ON For what is quite a small club, Alpha packs a pretty big punch on the Dubai nightlife scene. Set in Le Méridien Village, it soaks up the post-brunch crowd from neighbour Warehouse on Fridays with its cheap drinks deals, and then keeps them entertained until late with big-name live music and DJs flown in from the U.K. During the week, there are various theme nights, from funk to R&B, but one thing is a constant – the friendly, up-for-it attitude of the punters.

SETTING AND ATMOSPHERE This high-ceilinged venue was a Greek restaurant in a former life, hence the incongruous Doric columns, strange statuary and wrought-iron flourishes. Not that you'll see them, given how dark it is. The main space is circular, topped with a high dome, and there is seating around the outside. A series of private rooms and a terrace are upstairs, but these barely get used.

Armani Privé

THE GLAMMEST DESIGNER NIGHTCLUB IN TOWN

**Armani Hotel, Burj Khalifa, Downtown; ☎ 04-888-3308;
armanihotels.com**

Entrance Free, but must be mixed groups or couples **Mixed drinks** AED 70+ **Wine** AED 65+ **Beer** AED 60+ **Dress** Formal for men and elegant for ladies **Specials** None **Food available** Snacks **Hours** Monday–Saturday,10 p.m.–3 a.m.; closed Sunday

WHO GOES THERE Armani fans and high spenders aged 30+

WHAT GOES ON For a place that bills itself as a nightclub, there isn't really a whole lot of dancing that goes on here. There is, though, a lot of gawping. The central focus of the windowless space, which has its own separate entrance, is the two-storey LED screen that plays moving images of Mr Armani's catwalk creations on a loop. If that's not enough pretty for you, the people decorating the large booths – which will cost you a minimum spend of AED 3,000 if you want your own – are also fairly easy on the eye. Some patrons make a half-hearted attempt to dance to the mainly house music, but most just pout. Cocktails are predictably expensive but well mixed, and the Arabic- and Italian-influenced bar snacks delicious – try the Lebanese seafood kibbeh.

SETTING AND ATMOSPHERE This feels like a venue determined to make you break an extremity – everything is Armani black, from the walls to the banisters, banquettes to bar stools, which can make negotiating the multi-level space perilous to say the least. Still, it has been beautifully done.

Chi at the Lodge

INDOOR-OUTDOOR MEGA-CLUB PACKED WITH EXPATS

Al Nasr Leisureland, Oud Metha; ☎ 04-337-9470; chinightclubdubai.com

Entrance Free–AED 100, depending on the night **Mixed drinks** AED 40+ **Wine** AED 35+ **Beer** AED 35+ **Dress** Smart casual **Specials** Free Champagne on Tuesdays and free regular drinks on Saturdays for ladies; AED 100 for four drinks on Fridays **Food available** None **Hours** Daily, 9 p.m.–3 a.m.

WHO GOES THERE Absolutely everyone

WHAT GOES ON Long-term Dubai transplants will tell you that this was *the* nightclub when they first arrived. Literally, the only nightclub. It has managed the impossible and remained resolutely popular, and it's easy to see why – with its multiple rooms, both indoor and outdoor, big-name bands and DJs, as well as cheap drinks deals, it really does have something for everyone on any given night. The most popular and long-running night is the monthly Cheese event, where pop-tastic tunes are played (with little regard for cool or credibility) in the open-air garden. Nobody is shy about hitting the dance floor here, in the indie-focused Red room or in the Lounge, where the dancing to R&B tunes gets a bit more raunchy. Such is the capacity of the place, and so few are the barmen, that there is always a long queue for drinks. Regulars know to buy two at once – then if you spot a fellow dancer you fancy, you can always pretend you bought it for them.

SETTING AND ATMOSPHERE As the name suggests, the club has gone for a vaguely oriental theme, but you'll barely notice it. The Red room has a plethora of sofas and booths; the Garden outside is leafy and boasts impressive laser shows; the Lounge is blue-lit and a bit pokey. The point of Chi is the dancing, though, and there is more than ample space for this.

400 Club

AN OPULENT CLUB FULL OF THE CITY'S SEXIEST SINGLES

The Fairmont Hotel, Sheikh Zayed Road;
☎ **04-332-4900; the400nightclub.com**

Entrance Free, but couples and mixed groups only **Mixed drinks** AED 59+ **Wine** AED 49+ **Beer** AED 44+ **Dress** Smart casual; no sportswear **Specials** None **Food available** None **Hours** Tuesday–Friday, 11 p.m.–3 a.m.; closed Saturday and Monday

WHO GOES THERE People who don't mind buying vodka and Champagne by the bottle

WHAT GOES ON A lot of cheering – every time a magnum of Champagne or spirits is ordered, it comes to the table held aloft on a velvet cushion, illuminated by sparklers (depending on how much you are spending, it may also prompt the DJ to play 'Eye of the Tiger'). This largely Lebanese crew go through a lot of sparklers. The doormen are very strict about the couples and mixed groups policy, so there is always a queue behind the velvet rope, but such is its reputation that people are prepared to wait it out on the red carpet. The music is loud and dancing mainly gets done on chairs and tables, partly because the dance floor is tiny and the club shoulder to shoulder, and partly to show off the short, tight Lycra favoured by the clientele. It is worth booking a table if you are a group, as staff will keep moving you on if you dare to park your bottom on a chair that doesn't have your name on it.

SETTING AND ATMOSPHERE Opulence-by-numbers – gold, red velvet and chandeliers offset by black walls and lots and lots of mirrors. It is very much see and be seen, so be prepared to be looked up and down continually – just give as good as you get.

Jambase

A SUPPER CLUB WITH A BRILLIANT COVERS BAND AND PACKED DANCE FLOOR

Souk Madinat Jumeirah, Al Sufouh Road; ☎ **04-366-8888; jumeirah.com**

Entrance Free on Wednesday, Thursday and Saturday; AED 60 including one drink Thursday and Friday **Mixed drinks** AED 50+ **Wine** AED 36+ **Beer** AED 38+ **Dress** Smart casual; no shorts and open-toed shoes for men **Specials** Wednesday, buy two Cosmopolitans, get one free; Saturday, AED 100 for four house drinks **Food available** Full menu **Hours** Tuesday–Saturday, 7 p.m.–2 a.m.; Thursday–Friday, 7 p.m.–3 a.m.; closed Sunday and Monday

WHO GOES THERE A sophisticated dinner crowd who magically morph into party animals once the music gets loud and the tables get cleared away

WHAT GOES ON This is a supper club in the traditional sense of the word. Grown-up clubbers turn up at 10-ish to have a proper sit-down dinner (the food is remarkably good) and listen to the excellent live band. The music gets louder and the beat more insistent (although the tunes remain unchallenging pop and rock) as the night goes on, so by the time the clock strikes midnight, everyone is up and throwing some shapes on the dance floor. If you just want to come for drinks, it is still best to arrive early, as it gets packed at the weekends and there are always queues – it is possible to book a late table at the edge of the dance floor, but you must spend a minimum of AED 1,500.

SETTING AND ATMOSPHERE The club is accessed down a large circular staircase, so it feels like a subterranean venue although it's actually right next to the Madinat's waterways. It is dark and inviting, with low chandeliers and leather chairs. A stage is at the front of a large dance floor, which itself is flanked by booths. Diners sit just off this, although they still have a view of the entertainment.

Sanctuary

THE PALM'S MOST EXCLUSIVE NIGHTSPOT

Atlantis, The Palm, Palm Jumeirah; ☎ 04-426-2626; atlantisthepalm.com

Entrance Free–AED 100–150; couples or mixed groups only **Mixed drinks** AED 50+ **Wine** AED 59+ **Beer** AED 40+ **Dress** Smart and elegant clubwear **Specials** None **Food available** None **Hours** Daily, 9 p.m.–3 a.m.

WHO GOES THERE Hotel guests, Russians, Indians, Emiratis in mufti

WHAT GOES ON A lot of wrangling to get into the VIP areas. The hierarchy for tables here is worse than the wrestle for any New York Fashion Week front-row seat, and the pricing policy is Mensa-level hard. At weekends, if you want access to the terrace or the far side of the dance floor, you have to pay AED 50 extra for a different-coloured wristband. For a table in the VIP area, you must spend a minimum of AED 3,000 or AED 4,000, and there are drinks deals, but they are only available to hotel guests. Got it? No, neither do we really. But clearly a lot of people do, as queues reach past the Atlantis's giant fish tanks come Friday and Saturday, attracted by the four different rooms of music and the beautiful (and rich) people. And judging by the packed dance floor and the smiling crowd, they are always pleased they did.

SETTING AND ATMOSPHERE It's nice enough inside – lots of banquettes, cushions and drapes, and two womblike private rooms. The terrace is probably the biggest draw, with its huge daybeds and views of the beach – although sadly it closes June–October.

360°

CIRCULAR OVER-WATER BAR WITH NIGHTLY DJS

Jumeirah Beach Hotel, Al Sufouh Road; ☎ 04-348-0000; jumeirah.com

Entrance Free **Mixed drinks** AED 60+ **Wine** AED 40+ **Beer** AED 40+ **Dress** Smart **Specials** None **Food available** Snacks **Hours** Friday–Saturday, 4 p.m.–2 a.m.; Sunday–Thursday, 5 p.m.–2 a.m.

WHO GOES THERE Tourists, moneyed expats and anyone else who can get past the grumpy doormen (make sure you bring an ID even if you are pushing 40)

WHAT GOES ON Going to 360° combines all the elements of a classic Dubai night out. First, there is the walk through a random hotel lobby; second, the ride on a golf buggy (do not attempt to walk to 360° – it is a good 15-minute trot out to the venue, which is on its own promontory out to sea); third, the obstreperous doormen; and then the payoff – one heck of a view and a pretty decent cocktail to boot. This circular bar cum club that looks a bit like a helipad is one of the oldest and best loved in Dubai and, despite being a bit of a tourist trap for the photo it affords of the blue-lit Burj Al Arab, is a real must-drink.

SETTING AND ATMOSPHERE It really depends on the evening. During the week, the huge white sofas and beanbags on the two levels of the bar are filled with people having a quiet, late drink and a shisha, often after dinner at Marina Seafood just below. At weekends, the volume gets cranked up and the queues often snake around the pier – it's essential to register for the guest list on Friday and Saturday at **platinumlist.ae.**

MUSIC, THEATRE *and* COMEDY *in* DUBAI

ALTHOUGH NOT KNOWN AS A HUB OF MUSICAL EXCELLENCE, the city does sometimes host big international pop and rock artists, although Emirates Palace in Abu Dhabi has rather stolen Dubai's thunder on that front – the outdoor venue there is more adept at coping with the huge numbers that usually descend. Having said that, **Meydan Racecourse (meydan.ae)**, which opened in 2010, has already featured Sting and Elton John, who entertained the crowds once the thoroughbreds were led away for the day. The **Dubai Media City amphitheatre** also holds concerts during the cooler months, most notably the annual **Dubai International Jazz Festival** in February (**dubaijazzfest. com**). From time to time, the Madinat Jumeirah also holds one-off concerts at the **Madinat Arena,** although unless it's a sell-out, it is wont to feel a bit like an empty aircraft hangar, and the acoustics aren't great. **The Dubai Palladium (thepalladiumdubai.com)**, a relative newcomer to the scene, has far better sound and often holds big tribute shows – whether it's the songs of ABBA or Duke Ellington. It's also known for its Laughter Factory comedy nights, which bring in names from the U.S., U.K. and Australia, and kids' shows run during the summer. Very occasionally, the **World Trade Centre** hosts big-name DJs or live acts – check local listings for details. Tickets for all of the above can be bought at *Time Out* tickets (**timeouttickets.com**).

The larger bars and nightclubs, including **The Irish Village, Chi at the Lodge** and **Barasti,** often also have international live acts playing (although do double-check the small print, as often they will just be DJ sets from the stars rather than a live performance). These aren't stadium rockers – rather inexplicably, Bob Geldof and the Proclaimers are repeat visitors – but the gigs have a nice, intimate feel. Again, check *Time Out* for listings (**timeoutdubai.com**) or log on to *DJ Magazine*'s platinum list (**platinumlist.ae**), which also has full listings of bands visiting Dubai.

Theatre buffs are sadly not very well served here. Very occasionally, touring theatre companies will bring a play here (more often than not, one of Shakespeare's better-known plays), and musicals are popular too, although most of the performers are amateur, which can make occasionally painful viewing. The best venue for this is the **Madinat Theatre** (**madinattheatre.com**) – check its Web site for current and future shows. It also stages occasional comedy nights. The **Dubai Community and Arts Centre** (or DUCTAC, as it's known) holds regular shows, many of which err on the side of amateur. There are occasional professional poetry readings, chamber music evenings or comedy nights too – check its Web site for full listings (**ductac.org**). There is also the odd one-off night around town fusing art, poetry and writing – the best of these are the **Pecha Kucha** events that happen two or three times a year (**pecha-kucha.org**). **Wafi Rooftop** (**wafi.com**) holds open-mic music nights at Peanut Butter Jam on Fridays throughout the temperate season (usually October–May) – they are a great place to mingle with expats, chill outdoors on squashy beanbags and soak up the atmosphere. Another unique experience where you are encouraged to get involved is the monthly desert drumming hosted by **Dubai Drums** (**dubaidrums.com**), where beginners and professionals all join in to create beats under the stars – and enjoy a barbecue buffet – all for AED 190. They'll even provide you with drums.

ACCOMMODATIONS INDEX

Note: Page numbers of hotel profiles are in **bold face** type.

RESTAURANTS INDEX

SUBJECT INDEX

Note: Page numbers of spa profiles are in **bold face** type.

Unofficial Guide Readers Survey

If you'd like to express your opinion about travelling in Dubai or this guidebook, complete the following survey and mail it to:

> Unofficial Guide Reader Survey
> PO Box 43673
> Birmingham, AL 35243
> USA

Inclusive dates of your visit:_____

Members of your party:

	Person 1	Person 2	Person 3	Person 4	Person 5
Gender:	M F	M F	M F	M F	M F
Age:					

How many times have you been to Dubai? _____
On your most recent trip, where did you stay? _____

Concerning your accommodations, on a scale of 100 as best and 0 as worst, how would you rate:

The quality of your room? _____   The value of your room? _____
The quietness of your room? _____   Check-in/checkout efficiency? ___
Shuttle service to the airport? _____   Swimming pool facilities? _____

Did you hire a car?_____   From whom?_____

Concerning your hired car, on a scale of 100 as best and 0 as worst, how would you rate:
Pickup-processing efficiency?_____   Return processing efficiency?____
Condition of the car?_____   Cleanliness of the car?_____
Airport shuttle efficiency?_____

Concerning your dining experiences:
Estimate your meals in restaurants per day? _____
Approximately how much did your party spend on meals per day? _____
_____

Favorite restaurants in Dubai: _____
_____

Did you buy this guide before leaving? _____ While on your trip?_____

How did you hear about this guide? (check all that apply)

Loaned or recommended by a friend ❑   Radio or TV ❑
Newspaper or magazine ❑   Bookshop salesperson ❑
Just picked it out on my own ❑   Library ❑
Internet ❑

What other guidebooks did you use on this trip? _____
_____
_____
_____

On a scale of 100 as best and 0 as worst, how would you rate them?
_____
_____
_____

Using the same scale, how would you rate the *Unofficial Guide*(s)?
_____

Are *Unofficial Guides* readily available at bookshops in your area? _____

Have you used other *Unofficial Guides*? _____

Which one(s)? _____
_____
_____

Comments about your Dubai trip or the *Unofficial Guide*(s):
_____
_____
_____
_____
_____
_____
_____
_____
_____
_____
_____
_____
_____
_____
_____
_____
_____
_____
_____
_____